Paul Cassel, C

**SAMS**
**Teach Yourself**

# Access® 97

# in 21 Days

**SAMS**

*A Division of Macmillan Computer Publishing*
*201 West 103rd St., Indianapolis, Indiana, 46290 USA*

## Sams Teach Yourself Access 97 in 21 Days

## Copyright © 1998 by Sams Publishing

International Standard Book Number: 0-672-31298-0

Library of Congress Catalog Card Number: 97-81456

*Printed in the United States of America*

First Printing: May 1998

00                    8   7

## Trademarks

**EXECUTIVE EDITOR**
Rosemarie Graham

**ACQUISITIONS EDITOR**
Corrine Wire

**DEVELOPMENT EDITOR**
Marla Reece-Hall

**MANAGING EDITOR**
Patrick Kanouse

**PROJECT EDITOR**
Andrew Cupp

**COPY EDITOR**
Pat Kinyon

**INDEXER**
John Sleeva

**TECHNICAL EDITOR**
Dallas Releford

**SOFTWARE DEVELOPMENT SPECIALIST**
Andrea Duvall

**PRODUCTION**
Marcia Deboy
Michael Dietsch
Jennifer Earhart
Cynthia Fields
Susan Geiselman

# Overview

# Contents

*This book is dedicated to my wife and kids. Their undying devotion to my many causes, even when it means putting up with lost "together" time, is the source of my strength.—Craig Eddy*

# Acknowledgments

While this book bears my name as author, it couldn't have come about without a collaborative effort from many people. Whatever mention I can make of them here cannot match their true contribution.

First of all, I'd like to thank Corrine Wire, an acquisitions editor who pushed this project to an astonishingly fast conclusion. All of the development, technical, project and copy editors at Sams are truly outstanding. They make the job of authoring such a work as this practically painless by allowing the author to concentrate on what he does best: write.

Nothing is perfect. No doubt this book contains some omissions or inaccuracies. Any of these are wholly my fault. The degree to which this book is complete and accurate is due to the efforts of the above-mentioned people.

# About the Authors

**Craig Eddy** has been fascinated by and, according to his wife, addicted to computers since the days of the TRS-80. This fascination lead him to pursue a degree in Electrical Engineering at Virginia Tech, which he received in 1988. After moving to Richmond, VA, and working for several years as a Hardware Design Engineer, Craig returned to his true love: computer programming.

He is currently a Senior Developer/Program Manager at Pipestream Technologies, Inc. Pipestream is a leading developer of sales-force automation and customer information management software. Craig's current projects at Pipestream include database synchronization and the development of Web Continuum, the Web-based version of Sales Continuum 98.

Craig can be reached via email at `craig.eddy@cyberdude.com`.

**Paul Cassel** has been designing and programming database systems on a wide range of computers for more than 20 years. His clients have included Intel Corp., Los Alamos National Laboratory, Sandia National Laboratories, Pacific Gas and Electric, the Attorney General of New Mexico, federal and state agencies, the Navajo nation, and many small to medium-sized companies. He currently travels nationally giving lectures, teaching seminars, and consulting about numerous small computer topics, including Microsoft Access. He is cohost of the weekly Egghead Software Hour radio show and publishes between 20 and 30 magazine articles a year.

Since 1981 Paul has done PC database development in dBASE, FoxPro, R:Base, Paradox, and, most recently, Access, which is his favorite Windows database package. He lives in the high desert of New Mexico with his three-year-old daughter, who regu-larly outthinks him.

**Joel Goodling** designs client/server and Internet/intranet applications for clients of ETI. Currently, Joel is designing a multi-tier e-commerce application that is designed to be used over the Internet and an intranet. The application is designed to be able to use any ODBC compliant database as a backend, including Access 97. Joel has built several commercial applications using Access 97, often tying Access as a front-end to a Microsoft SQL Server back-end.

**Robert Stewart** is an Access 2.0 certified professional and assisted with the development of the Access 95 certification test. He lives outside of Houston, Texas in a small, rural community. Robert has been a SIG leader at the Houston Area League of PC Users, one of the largest user groups in the U.S., as well as a leader for Access SIG's. He is currently starting a new SIG for Microsoft Solution Developer Certification.

# About This Book

This book starts where you are likely to start—at the point when you first start Microsoft Access and a whole new world opens up before your eyes. You might be in a state of panic, shock, or total excitement.

This book provides hands-on tutorials, useful tips, and technical information to get you started and keep you going with Access. It takes you from the most basic and elementary database tasks, such as setting up tables and printing quick reports, to advanced techniques such as sophisticated queries and linked-table databases.

In *Sams Teach Yourself Access 97 in 21 Days*, you'll find the following valuable insights to help you learn this exciting Microsoft Office Application:

- Designing an Access database. In Day 3, "Designing an Access Database," you'll learn all about relational database design, how it applies to Access 97, and how to create a relational database using Access 97.
- Along with relational design goes the concept of table relationships. Day 5, "Linking Tables with Relationships," describes how to create relationships, modify their properties, and use the Relationships window.
- Expanded coverage of form controls, the items on a form with which users interact.
- In addition to coverage of programming with ActiveX controls, this book also covers how to use the Data Access Objects (the native objects around which Access 97 is built) to programmatically control your database and the data it contains. Don't miss this coverage in Day 18, "Advanced Programming with Data Access Objects and ActiveX Controls."
- You'll spend a whole day on database maintenance issues. Although not necessarily for the faint of heart, this material is a must-read if you're designing database applications that will be used by more than just yourself.
- If you purchased the entire Office 97 suite, you'll appreciate the coverage of Office Links in Day 20, "Integrating Access with the Rest of Microsoft Office." Here you'll learn how to leverage your Access investment with the other applications in the Office 97 family.
- There's expanded coverage of integrating Access databases with the Internet or intranet. Day 21, "Integrating Access with the Web," describes how to create not only static Web pages, but also dynamic pages that change as the data in your database changes.

## Who Should Read This Book?

Whether you just need help with a specific database task or want a step-by-step tutorial on every aspect of the program, you will find what you need in this book. While geared to the more technically advanced reader, there's plenty of information for beginners as well. Beginners will find coverage of the basic concepts of database management and the basic techniques of using Access. For people who just need to "dip into" the book and learn about a specific topic, the clear organization of the sections and lessons makes it fast and easy for them to find what they need.

# Special Features of This Book

Throughout the book, the emphasis has been on providing useful information in a way that is fast, easy, and fun.

**Note**
Notes present supplemental information to the text. Sometimes these can be real world experiences with Access 97.

**Tip**
Tips are suggestions to help you in real world situations. These can often be shortcuts or information to make a task easier or faster.

**Caution**
Cautions provide information about detrimental performance issues or dangerous errors that can occur. Pay careful attention to Cautions.

You'll also see the following specific features throughout the book:

| **Do** | **DON'T** |
|---|---|

**Do/Don't boxes:** These give you guidance on what to do and what to avoid doing in specific Access database tasks.

**NEW TERM** *New Terms* explain database jargon in plain English, so you can impress your friends at parties when the conversation turns to database management.

## Conventions

The most notable conventions in the book are

- Access commands, which are in code listings or embedded in regular text, appear in a monospace font. For example, "Enter the expression =DatePart("d",[Date of Record]) on the first row of the Sorting and Grouping box contains a command in monospace.
- Access menu choices are indicated by the name of the menu, followed by a vertical slash character (I), and then the name of the menu choice.

Sometimes a line of code will not fit within the margins of this book. When that happens, the line will be broken and this code continuation character will be placed on the second line. This icon indicates that you should type the code as a single line:

➡

In the case of VB code for some chapters, you might see the VB-specific code continuation character at the end of a broken line. VB uses the underscore character (_) to show that the code continues on the next line.

# Introduction

## Why I Wrote This Book

I wrote *Sams Teach Yourself Access 97 in 21 Days* because Microsoft Access is one of the simplest to use, most powerful desktop databases available today. Simply put, I think it's a terrific program.

Access 97 can, in a few hours time, automate any data tracking system you currently have in place. That includes replicating the data store (the information), the data forms (how you record that information), and the data reporting (how you use that information to produce results). Given a few more days, you can crank out a workable Windows-based application that most users of Windows 95/98 or Windows NT will find immediately familiar and easy to use. Of course, there's nothing to prevent you from doing just the opposite of this, but it's my opinion that Microsoft Access will make your job of creating a user-friendly database much easier than you could possibly imagine at this point.

## What This Book Will Do For You

Any database package that gives great results without a lot of work is my kind of program. And that's what Access and this book can do for you. After you've completed this 21-day course, you should be able to create your own database applications. This book covers quite a lot for a three-week course, but it doesn't cover every single aspect of Access in-depth. One thing that all computer experts agree on is that their education never ends. Consider this book to be your foundation in Access, not everything you will ever need to know.

## What This Book Won't Do For You

This book teaches you much of what you need to know to create solid, powerful database applications. But no book can be a substitute for your own creativity, imagination, and practical experience. As you work with Access, you'll constantly find new ways to do old things. As you do, you can refer to this book for the essential foundations that show you how to turn your new ideas into productive database systems.

*Sams Teach Yourself Access 97 in 21 Days* uses specific examples to demonstrate general principles. This book shows you "how to." It doesn't attempt to be a reference work. You can find full reference documentation in the online help system that comes with Access.

# How This Book Works

None of the exercises in this book require you to do much data entry. You'll be working as a database manager for a fictional bookstore. The focus is always on learning database concepts and techniques—you didn't buy this book to get some practice typing in data.

## The Sample Data and Your Sanity

This is important for your sanity! The sample database used with each chapter is included on the CD-ROM that came with this book. As you study a chapter, you should open that chapter's version of the database. Although for the most part each day's accompanying database builds directly on top of the previous day's version, I cannot guarantee this happens in every chapter. They'll all be pretty close, though, so don't panic!

Also included on the CD-ROM are some real-world databases you can use as the basis for projects you may encounter. Many of these are enhancements of the template databases available with the New Database Wizard, but a few are completely original creations.

# How This Book Is Structured

This book's lessons are presented in 21 chapters. Each chapter consists of several examples or exercises. To get the most out of the book, you should complete each lesson before going on to the next. Once you've finished the lessons, of course, you can go back and dip into the book any time you need a quick refresher course on specific points.

At the end of each chapter you'll find a daily summary, a question and answer (Q&A) section, and a workshop section. The workshop section consists of a quiz (the answers are be found in Appendix A, "Quiz Answers") and a small "do-it-yourself" section entitled "Exercises."

# But Most of All—HAVE FUN!

I've spent many hours working with Access and enjoyed each hour—well, almost every hour. After going through this book, you'll have the level of expertise needed to create database applications easily with Access—and have fun doing it!

So, enough talk! Let's get started. I hope that you enjoy Access as much as I do and find many productive uses for your newfound database skills. But remember: If you're not having fun, you're missing half the point of doing it!

# WEEK 1

## At a Glance

This first week starts you off with the familiar features of Windows and Office that are also carried over into Access 97. You'll work your way around the Access user interface, and see how the Office Assistant, wizards, and online help work in Access in a similar manner as these features do in other applications, but you'll also see how to customize them for use in Access.

Throughout the week you'll learn the "easy way" first, by creating various parts of a database from a template or wizard and then learn how to navigate through each part, viewing important features and learning how the database works together as a whole.

Some of the things you'll learn this first week are the following:

- How to create databases—from wizards and from scratch.
- How to define primary keys, foreign keys, and relationships as you realize the end result: a relational database.
- How to add a new table, modify that table, and learn all about fields.
- How to use input masks and change field widths and row heights.
- How and when to use combo and list boxes in tables.
- The implications of field properties and how to set a default value for a field, and then get into data validation.
- How to create some queries and examine criteria in queries.

1

2

3

4

5

6

7

Before this week is over, you'll have a good feel for not only the theory behind how an
Access database works, but you'll also start to see some of the many ways you can use
Access to build applications that effectively manage data.

# DAY 1

# A Short Tour, Including a Stop at Northwind Traders

On the first day of Access you learn the following:

- The parts of the Access user interface
- How to change the shape and location of toolbars and menus
- How to customize toolbars
- What the Office Assistant is
- What wizards are
- How to use the Office Assistant
- How to use wizards
- How to use other online help facilities

If you haven't installed Access yet, Appendix B, "Installing Access 97," describes how to install the application. Make sure you install all of the suggested components, especially the Advanced Wizards, because you'll need them throughout the course of this book.

## Launching Access from Windows

To start Access from the Start menu, choose Programs and find Microsoft Access. By default, the shortcut to run Access is installed on the Programs menu.

> **Tip**
>
> If you're using Internet Explorer 4.0 or Windows 98, you can copy the Start menu shortcut to your desktop by clicking the menu item, holding down the Ctrl key, and dragging the menu item to the desktop. To simply move the shortcut to your desktop, don't hold down the Ctrl key while you're dragging.

Once you've started Access, you'll see the opening dialog, shown in Figure 1.1. From here, you can open an existing database either from the list at the bottom or from a File Open dialog (if you leave More Files selected), manually create a new database, or use a wizard to create a new database. If you're following along, click the Cancel button to move to the Access interface. If you've just set up Access, your list box won't yet contain any databases like those shown in Figure 1.1.

**FIGURE 1.1.**

*Access's opening dialog.*

## The Parts of the Access 97 User Interface

**NEW TERM** If you're following along with the text, you'll notice that the title bar reads Microsoft Access and the rest of the window seems to be pretty sparsely populated (if you're not following along, you'll just have to trust me on this one). That's because you haven't loaded a database. All of the menu items and toolbars found in

1

Access are *context sensitive*, meaning that what's available on the toolbars and menus changes with the current context. If you had loaded a database (or created a new one), the toolbar would look much different.

Like most Windows applications, you'll find a menu bar directly under the title bar. Again, the menu options available at any given moment depends on what mode Access is in and whether your Access application has a custom menu system. At this point, Access has nothing loaded so, of course, there will be few available menu items. (You'll have to open a menu, such as the Edit menu, to discover this fact, though.)

Below the menu bar is the toolbar. There are many different toolbars in Access. Toolbars enable you to quickly and easily perform common tasks while using the Access program. You're not stuck with the default toolbars. You can customize the standard ones, adding your favorite buttons or removing the ones you really despise. In addition to the standard ones, you can also make your own custom toolbars.

Toolbars also sport what are known in Microsoft Office as ScreenTips. These are little windows that pop up when you let the cursor rest over a button for a few seconds. The window contains text describing the function of the toolbar button.

 **Note**

> Many people, myself included, refer to ScreenTips as *ToolTips*. I'll probably use the terms interchangeably throughout the book, but the terms refer to the same little helper.

**New Term** You can disable the ScreenTips by right-clicking over the toolbar area, clicking Customize, and moving to the Options tab. There you'll find that the dialog resembles Figure 1.2. If you want ToolTips, make sure the Show ScreenTips on Toolbars box is checked. If you don't want them, make sure the box is not checked.

**FIGURE 1.2.**

*The Customize dialog's Options tab.*

You can also display a button's shortcut key in the ScreenTip by checking the Show shortcut keys in ScreenTip's box. Shortcut keys are keystrokes you can use in place of toolbar buttons and menu items. The Cut button, for example, has a shortcut key of Ctrl+X. Highlighting text and pressing Ctrl+X has the same effect as highlighting text and clicking the scissors toolbar button or using the Edit|Cut menu item.

The toolbars in Access 97 are more plentiful and easier to use than in previous Access versions. By default, Access will show only a few related toolbars with each active window in your database. You can modify Access's toolbar behavior from the default. You'll see how to do this later in this chapter.

## Arranging Toolbars

**NEW TERM**  When Access starts, the toolbar is in a single row right below the menu bar. This works all right for many tasks, but you might prefer a different arrangement. Access is happy to comply with your wishes. Move your cursor to the place on the toolbar with two parallel lines, to the left of the New Database button. This is called the toolbar's *move handle*.

As with most Windows applications you've used, you can move the toolbars in Access to a number of locations: horizontal, vertical, and floating. You can dock the menu bar and any floating toolbars by dragging them to their hotspots. These spots aren't only at the top of the screen, although that's their traditional place. There are other hotspots on the Access desktop. How you arrange your Access screen is a matter of how you like to work and your aesthetic sense. This book uses the Microsoft default locations for all bars.

## Customizing Access Toolbars

This is a fairly simple topic with many permutations. Once you get the hang of customizing, you will know how to do it all.

Customizing toolbars within Access is the same as within other Office 97 applications. You can do this either by choosing View|Toolbars|Customize from the menus, or by right-clicking any bar and choosing Customize from the shortcut menu. After you get to the Customize menu, you'll see a dialog offering several toolbars. Figure 1.3 shows the Web toolbar.

**FIGURE 1.3.**

*The Web toolbar made visible.*

1

## Adding Buttons to the Toolbar

To add buttons to a toolbar, first make sure the toolbar is displayed as explained earlier. Then move to the Commands tab of the Customize dialog and find the command in question. The commands are sorted by category in the list box on the left side of the dialog. Click an entry in the list box and the available commands list box (on the right side) will reload with the commands for that category. Drag the command you want into position on the toolbar. Voilà! You've just added a button to the toolbar.

Removing a button from the toolbar is even easier. With the toolbar visible, simply drag the button off of it and release the mouse button. That button won't bother you ever again (unless, of course, you add it again!).

## Creating a New Toolbar

If you're working in a database, you can even create your own toolbar, containing just the buttons to which you're partial. Toolbars that you add are stored with the database, so if you're particularly fond of a toolbar, you'll have to add it to each database with which you work. To add a toolbar, return to the Customize dialog's Toolbars tab and click the New button. Enter a name for the toolbar and click OK. An empty toolbar appears on the screen, awaiting population with buttons, as described earlier.

If you want to a delete a toolbar that has been added in this manner, select it in the list box on the Toolbars tab and click the Delete button. The toolbar is removed from the database.

There are so many things you can customize about toolbars that you create in this manner that I can't possibly enumerate them all here. But in Day 14, "Putting the Finishing Touches on Forms," you'll learn everything there is to know about adding toolbars and even menu bars, as well as how to add them to a form.

## Modifying a Toolbar's Properties

In addition to changing what commands are available on a toolbar, you can also modify some of the properties of a toolbar. For either the standard toolbars or for toolbars that you add, select the toolbar in the list box on the Toolbars tab and click the Properties button. The Toolbar Properties dialog, shown in Figure 1.4, appears.

**FIGURE 1.4.**

*The Toolbar Properties
dialog.*

For the standard toolbars, you can modify the valid places to dock the toolbar (Allow
Any, Can't Change, No Vertical, and No Horizontal are the items available in the drop-
down list), and you can specify whether the toolbar can be customized, resized, moved,
and shown or hidden. For toolbars you've added, you have access to all of these properties plus the ability to change the toolbar's name, the type of toolbar (toolbar, menu bar,
or pop-up), and specify whether the toolbar should appear on the Toolbars menu. The
Toolbars menu is the shortcut menu you get when you right-click over a toolbar and the
menu accessed from the View|Toolbars menu.

# Office Assistant

As part of the eternal quest to satisfy the need for easy-to-use software, Microsoft has
begun introducing software agents to assist users in their work. One such agent is the
Office Assistant. The Office Assistant is also part of Microsoft's attempt to incorporate
artificial intelligence into its help systems. This artificial intelligence was first seen in
Office 95 as the Answer Wizard. Some people, while they enjoy and admire how the
Office Assistant works, dislike its cute animations. Others enjoy the Assistant's sound
effects and animations. You can also get to the information in Access's online help sys-
tem by using the Help|Contents and Index menu, bypassing the Office Assistant.

In addition to providing a gateway to the Access Help system, the Office Assistant is also
responsible for displaying any message boxes that appear when it's active. These message boxes appear whenever an error occurs, or when the system needs to question you
about a course of action.

Like so many things in a visual apparatus like Access, you can best learn how to use the
Office Assistant by trying it out. The following task serves as an introduction.

## Task: Introduction to the Office Assistant

1. Launch Access if you have not already done so. Click Cancel in the opening dialog to go to the Access interface without opening a database.

2. By default, the Setup routine uses the Office Assistant that looks like a paper clip, and the Office Assistant is active when you start Access. If not, you can activate it by clicking the Office Assistant icon, the right-most icon on the toolbar just below the menu bar. (It looks like a cartoon's dialog balloon with a question mark in the center.) Alternatively, you can press the F1 key.

   You've just activated the Office Assistant. Here, you can ask the Help system questions in natural language. Microsoft's language parser tries to match your question to a topic in the Help system.

3. As shown in Figure 1.5, enter How do I make a table in the box where the Office Assistant has the instructions Type your question here, and then click Search. Click the Search button. You don't need a question mark.

FIGURE 1.5.

*The Office Assistant.*

4. Access offers you a quick overview of several topics that relate to your question. Click the button next to Create a Table (it should be the first topic on your list). The Office Assistant, its job done for the moment, will do a fade and you'll enter into the Help system's files at the Create a Table page.

5. To see any of these topics, click the >> button just to the left of the topic. Click the first >> button—the one next to the Create a New Blank Table entry.

6. Access moves on to the next page of instructions, which describes in summary the four ways you can use Access to create a blank or empty table.

▼ If you want to see what any of these choices are, click the topic with the >> button at the bottom of the Help screen. Note, you might have to scroll down to see the jump or >> buttons. Figure 1.6 shows the Help screen brought up by clicking the >> button for Create a New Blank Table. Note that some of these instructions assume you have a database open, which you do not. Pressing the F11 key at this point won't, for example, switch you to the database window. With no database

▲ open, no such window exists.

**FIGURE 1.6.**

*A typical Help screen.*

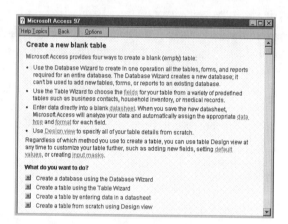

## Positioning the Assistant and Help Windows

The Office Assistant floats on top of any other Windows object, so you can refer to it as you work. The Office Assistant exercise you just went through only offers an overview of certain database concepts; the Assistant can step you through actual Access operations. You can also set the Help system itself to float on top of Access while you work so you can easily refer to it as you go along. Most other help systems go behind the application when you're in the main program, forcing you to call them back up at each step.

To get the help system itself to float on top of Access (or any other application), click the Options button shown in Figure 1.6. A drop-down menu appears. Select the Keep Help on Top menu and then choose the On Top option. After you set Help to be on top, the Help windows will float above any windows. If they get in your way, you can always set the On Top property back to the default, or you can minimize the Help system so that it appears as an entry on the taskbar.

| Do | Don't |
|---|---|
| **DO** use the Office Assistant and on-top Help screens as memory joggers or to lead you through operations with which you don't feel completely familiar. | **DON'T** forget you can minimize the on-top Help screens to get them out of the way. |

**1**

# Opening the Northwind Traders Database

Now that you've seen some of the user-interface features available in Microsoft Access, let's get down to some work. For the next section, "Wizards," you'll need an opened database with which to work. Use the sample provided with Access. If you followed the instructions in Appendix B, you've installed the sample database. This database, for the now-mythical company Northwind Traders, has been the sample database for Microsoft Access for as long as I can remember.

To open the Northwind Traders database follow these steps:

1. If Access is not running, launch the program. In the initial dialog, make sure the Open an Existing Database option is selected and that More Files is selected in the list box at the bottom of the dialog. Click the OK button. If Access is already running, use the File|Open menu. In either case, the Open dialog is displayed.

2. Navigate to the Office Samples folder, typically located at `c:\Program Files\Microsoft Office\Office\Samples`. If you've installed Access to a directory different than the `default`, navigate to that directory instead.

3. Select `Northwind.MDB` in the file list and click Open. If a splash screen is displayed, click the OK button to make it go away.

4. If the Database window is not the current window, use the Window|1 Northwind: Database menu item to make it the current window. Your screen should now look like Figure 1.7.

**NEW TERM**   A *database window* is Access's term for a tabbed screen like the one in Figure 1.7, where you can see a database's object collection.

**NEW TERM**   A *splash screen* is a form that displays when a database is opened or as an application loads.

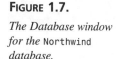

**FIGURE 1.7.**

*The Database window for the* Northwind *database.*

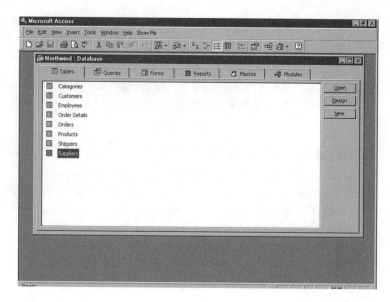

You've just opened the Northwind database ready for a wizard to work its magic!

# Wizards

The Office Assistant can give you natural language guides to Help topics, and the Help topics tell you how to do what you want to do, but you need to perform the steps themselves to get results. Wizards take the next logical step in an active Help system. They ask you a few questions, and after you and the wizard agree what needs to be done, the wizard goes out and does it.

Most people use wizards when they are using Access. Even the most highly paid senior-level developers rely on wizards to do some of the grunt work in form and report design. In some areas, such as programming buttons on forms or reports, wizards make the chore so easy that even a fairly naive Access user can make applications that work just like the ones that are done by experts. True, there's nothing you can do with a wizard that you can't do manually, but ignoring wizards only makes for more work.

The following task uses a wizard to add a ShipTo table to the Northwind database. In the Orders table, there are fields for the shipping address to be stored with each order. If a customer has multiple ship-to addresses, it can get tedious to have to change the address each time an order is taken for that customer. You're going to create a ShipTo table that allows the user to easily select the ship-to address for each customer from the known ship-to addresses for that customer. You're going to do a couple of tricky things as you go, and I'll try to explain each step as well as I can. However, you won't learn about some of the reasons you'll do certain steps until later chapters, so just hang in there.

Let's get started...

## Task: Using the Analyze Table Wizard

1. On the Database window, make sure the Tables tab is active. If it's not, click the Tables tab to display the list of existing tables in the database.

2. Click the New button to display the New Table dialog, shown in Figure 1.8.

**FIGURE 1.8.**

*The New Table dialog.*

3. Select Table Wizard in the list box and click OK. You can also double-click Table Wizard instead. The Table Wizard, shown in Figure 1.9, appears.

**FIGURE 1.9.**

*The initial dialog of the Table Wizard.*

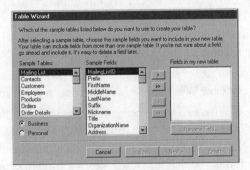

4. The list box on the left, Sample Tables, contains a list of sample tables that the Table Wizard feels are commonly used. Select Orders in this list box. The Sample Fields list box will change to reflect the sample fields for this type of table.

5. Select the field CustomerID in the Sample Fields list box and click the > button (or double-click each of the items). This adds a CustomerID field to the Fields in My New Table list box. This will be used to identify the customer that belongs to a ship-to address record.

▼   6.  Next, add a `ShipToID` field to uniquely identify each row in the table. Since there's no way to add a field and specify its name without selecting it from the Sample Fields list box, just double-click the `OrderID` field.

7.  Click the button labeled Rename Field, change the name to `ShipToID`, and click OK. Don't make the mistake of double-clicking the field in the Fields in My New Table list box because this will remove the field from the list.

8.  Select `ShipName`, click the button labeled Rename Field, and remove the leading `Ship` from the field name and click OK.

9.  Repeat step 8 for `ShipAddress`, `ShipCity`, `ShipState`, `ShipPostalCode`, `ShipCountry`, and `ShipPhoneNumber`.

10. Click the Next button to move to the next dialog.

11. In the text box, enter `ShipTo`. Click the option button labeled No, I'll Set the Primary Key. Click Next. For more information on primary key fields, see Day 3, "Designing an Access Database."

12. The next dialog is where you specify which field should be used as the primary key. In the drop-down list box at the top of the dialog, select the `ShipToID` field. Leave the Default option button (consecutive numbers Microsoft Access assigns automatically to new records) selected. Click Next.

13. The dialog that appears is where you can specify any relationships the table you're creating has to existing tables. The `ShipTo` table is related to the `Customers` table (each customer can have one or more records in the `ShipTo` table) and to the `Orders` table (each order points to one record in the `ShipTo` table). For more information on relationships, see Day 5, "Linking Tables with Relationships." Click the Not Related to Customers Row in the list box and click the Relationships button.

14. A Relationships dialog appears. In this dialog, click the option labeled One Record in the Customers Table Will Match Many Records in the ShipTo Table. Click OK.

15. Next, click the Not Related to Orders item in the list box. Click the Relationships button. Click One record in the ShipTo Table Will Match Many Records in the Orders Table. Notice that the panel at the bottom of the Relationships dialog changes and informs you that the New Table Wizard will create a new field in the `Orders` table to use as the link to the `ShipTo` table. Click OK.

16. Click Next to move to the final dialog of the wizard. Here you can specify what to do after the new table is created. If you would like the Help system to display information on working with new tables, check the box labeled Display Help on Working with the Table. Leave the Default option button (Enter Data Directly into
▼   the Table) selected and click Finish.

▼  17. The datasheet window for the new table is opened, as shown in Figure 1.10. Here
        you can enter the ShipTo data for the customers, if you want. For now, simply
▲       close the window to complete this exercise.

**FIGURE 1.10.**

*The datasheet window
for your new* ShipTo
*table.*

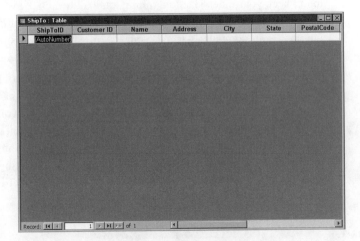

You just used the wizard to add a new table to the Northwind database. Although it
seemed to take a lot of steps to get the job done, the wizard really does a lot of grunt
work for you, as you'll see in Day 4, "Creating a New Database From Scratch." This is
particularly true in the case when the wizard created some relationships and modified an
existing table for you (steps 13 through 15). Of course, you can modify any of the work
the wizard has done if the output doesn't quite fit your needs, but typically what the wizard produces is right on target.

# Using Help

Sometimes you'll need help beyond what the Office Assistant or wizards can do. In those
cases (such as clarifying the use of a particular function), you'll likely go directly to
Access's Online Help system. The following task steps you through some parts of
Access's Online Help.

### Task: Help with Help

1. Launch Access if you have not already done so, or just leave it open from the second task. The figures for this section were shot with the Northwind database from
   the last task. If you don't have a database open, your screens will differ at the
   menu bar.

▼   2.  Click the Help|Contents and Index menu items. Access displays its Help Topics
        window.

    3.  Click the Find tab at the top of the Help Topics window. Click the top option but-
        ton to keep your index size to a minimum, and then click the Next> button. Click
        Finish to create an indexed list of all help topics. This might take a while depend-
        ing upon your computer's speed, your RAM, whether this is the first index you cre-
        ated, and how many other tasks you have going on at the same time.

    4.  What you've done is to create an indexed, or ordered, list of all Access Help topics.
        There are roughly 5,300 topics to choose from (the total number of topics will
        depend on which help files were installed). You'd surely become an Access expert
        by just going through this list, but, in most cases, you'll want to locate a specific
        topic rather than just browse through thousands of topics. Enter the word date at
        the top of the dialog to narrow the topics to only those relating to dates. Your
        screen will resemble Figure 1.11. Note that the topic number is now cut down to
        300—a much more manageable size.

**FIGURE 1.11.**

*Narrowing help topics.*

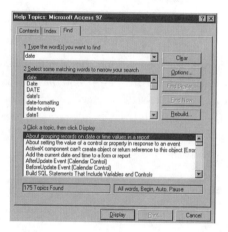

    5.  Click the DATE entry in the list box labeled Select Some Matching Words to
        Narrow Your Search. Click the Display button to bring up the specific Help topic
        matching the highlighted key word.

    6.  This brings up a help system. If appropriate, the help page you bring up might con-
        tain links to other help. In the case of the Comparison of Data Types topic, Access
        Help brought up a page discussing the various data types available in Microsoft
        Access. To see the detail information on any of these data types, simply click the
▼       underlined entry.

1

▼ 7. If the topic you brought up was the one you wanted, you're in luck. If not, you can repeat the search as many times as you want until you hit on the exact topic and angle you seek.

8. You can also use Access's supplied Help index by clicking the Index tab and entering your choice as shown in Figure 1.12. Access's supplied index has the most frequently sought topics, but won't be as complete as the generated Find index. The

▲ downside of using the Find index is that it takes time and eats disk space.

**FIGURE 1.12.**

*Access has a default index of most Help topics.*

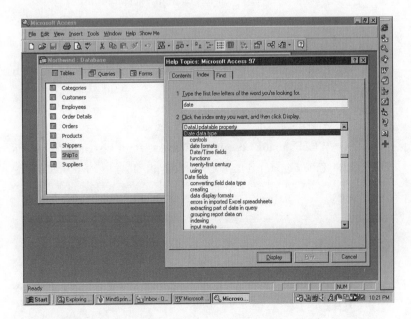

You've just taken the five-cent tour of Access's Help system and finished today's lesson. Close Access by either double-clicking its control menu icon or by choosing File|Exit from the menu bar.

# Summary

You launch Access by double-clicking its icon. The top three layers of the Access interface are the title bar, the menu bar, and the toolbar. The bottom-most strip of the Access interface is the status bar.

You can adjust the shape and location of any Access toolbar by using the mouse to drag it to where you want it and adjust its outline. You can also add buttons to existing toolbars, and even add your own custom toolbars to a database.

Access has three systems in addition to the printed documentation to help you use the program: the Office Assistant, wizards, and Online Help. The Office Assistant is a special Help system with step-by-step instructions for certain operations, wizards to interact with you to perform certain functions, and Online Help is (for the most part) a reference system similar to the printed manuals that come with Access. Even the most experienced Access developer makes liberal use of wizards and the Help system. Wizards especially do wonders in decreasing development time, and since they can't make many human-type errors, they assure you of clean implementations.

## Q&A

**Q  Can I adjust the size and location of the menu or status bars the same way I can the toolbars?**

**A**  Yes and no. Access only enables custom location of toolbars, of which the menu bar is one. The status bar isn't movable.

**Q  When should I use the Office Assistant instead of wizards?**

**A**  If the output from your wizard isn't close to what you want, you'll have to manually design your database object. If you're unclear about how to do this, the Office Assistant will often help step you through it.

## Workshop

Here's where you can test and apply what you have learned today.

### Quiz

1. What shape does the cursor assume when it's capable of reshaping a toolbar?

2. How do you launch Access from the Start menu in the Windows interface?

3. What are the two clues (aside from the picture) hinting at or telling you what a button on a toolbar does?

4. Can you move or resize the menu bar?

## Exercises

1. Launch Access.

2. Launch the Help system.

3. Click the Find tab.

4. After Access brings up the Find dialog, enter average as a word to limit the length of the list. Click any topic that interests you. Read through the topic. Return to the Find dialog box by clicking the Help Topics button in the Help topic. When you're satisfied, close the Help system.

5. Exit Access.

1

# DAY 2

# Creating Your First Database

On the first day of your journey to learn Access 97 you studied the basics of starting Access, working with toolbars, interacting with the Office Assistant, and how to launch a wizard. Today you'll learn the following:

- Another use of Access's opening dialog
- How to use an Access database template
- The basics of navigating a database
- Simple filtering and reporting

If you're fairly comfortable creating new databases and getting around in an existing database, you might just want to skim through this day.

# Starting Access, a Different Approach

On Day 1, you learned how to open an existing Access database and use the New Table Wizard to add a table. While that's all well and good, chances are you're reading this book because you want to create your own Access databases. For those of you in this boat, take heart, because the remainder of the book discusses creating a new database.

If Access is currently running and you want to follow along with the text, go ahead and exit and restart the application. When Access finishes loading, you'll see a screen similar to Figure 2.1. You've seen this screen before, but now you're going to use it in a different way.

**FIGURE 2.1.**

*The initial Access 97 dialog.*

On Day 1, you used the bottom portion of this dialog to indicate that you wanted to open an existing database. On Day 4, "Creating a New Database from Scratch," you'll use the top-most option in this dialog, Blank Database, to create a new empty database. For today, though, you'll use the second option, Database Wizard, and create a database with the help of the New Database Wizard.

# Creating a Database Using a Template

Now you're ready to roll with the Database Wizard. Select this option from the initial dialog and click OK. The New Database dialog, shown in Figure 2.2, appears. The Databases tab is enabled and is populated with a list of the Wizard's template databases.

**Note**

> If the Database Wizard option does not activate, or if you receive an error message when you select the Database Wizard option and click OK, it's likely you haven't installed the Database Wizard. To review the instructions on installing Access 97, see Appendix B, "Installing Access 97."

**FIGURE 2.2.**

*The Databases tab of
the Access 97 New
Database dialog.*

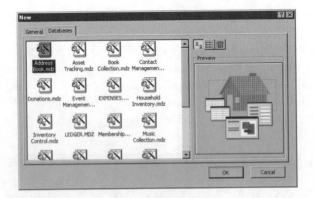

2

The New Database dialog has a window that will show you a preview of the selected template. This preview is really just a picture that indicates whether the selected database template is a business, home, or personal database. The Address Book template shown in Figure 2.2 is a home database. The Asset Tracking template is a business database. Click this database and notice that the preview changes to match its type (business).

In the following task, you'll follow the steps for creating a database using the Household Inventory template. All of the templates will take you through the same set of steps, but with different field and table names.

## Task: Creating a Household Inventory by using the Database Wizard

1. If you've been following along in Access, you're currently in the New Database dialog. If the New Database dialog is not visible, either start Access or click the New Database button on the toolbar.

2. Select the Household Inventory entry in the Databases list. Click the OK button.

3. The File New dialog appears. In this dialog you'll specify a file name and folder to be used to store the Household Inventory database you're about to create. Select an appropriate folder on your system and change the suggested name to Household Inventory. You don't need to append the .mdb to the file name because Access will do this for you. Click the Create button.

4. The first dialog of the Database Wizard appears. This dialog describes what's going to be contained in the database you're about to create. Click Next.

▼

**Note**

You can press the Finish button at any time while using the Database Wizard. The Wizard will create the database by using the default selections for the dialogs that you haven't visited.

▼    5. The second dialog of the wizard, shown in Figure 2.3, lists the tables and fields
        that will be created in the database. The wizard is telling you that it will create
        three tables: one for the inventory items, one for rooms, and one for categories.
        There may also be additional fields you can select to be included in the database.
        These fields will be in *italics* in the list box on the right pane of the dialog. The
        fields that are not in italics are mandatory and cannot be deselected. Select the
        Manufacturer entry by checking its box in the list.

**FIGURE 2.3.**

*The field selection dia-
log of the Database
Wizard.*

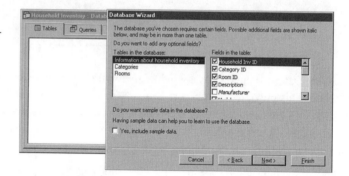

6. The wizard can also create a set of sample data in the new database. This is very
   useful in the initial stages of a database's design because without data you'll have a
   hard time testing any queries or reports you create. Check the box labeled Yes,
   Include Sample Data. Click Next.

7. In the next dialog, shown in Figure 2.4, you specify how you want the screens to
   appear. A list of available styles is on the right side. A preview window on the left
   side of the dialog shows you how the screens will appear. Select different styles to
   find one that suits your mood. When you've settled on a style, click Next.

**FIGURE 2.4.**

*The screen style selec-
tion dialog.*

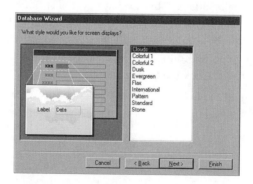

▼

8. The next dialog that appears is where you'll specify the style for printed reports. Again, a list of available styles appears on the right and a preview window appears on the left. Select a style and click Next.

9. The next dialog allows you to change the title that will appear on the Switchboard window. Leave the suggested name in place. You can also specify a picture to be displayed in reports by clicking Yes, I'd Like to Include a Picture. Once you select this option, you can click the Picture button to locate the picture you'd like to include. After you've decided what to do about a picture, click Next.

10. This is the final dialog of the Database Wizard. Leave the Yes, Start the Database box checked. Click Finish.

Access will grind away, displaying a progress dialog informing you of what's happening as it goes. When finished, the Main Switchboard window, shown in Figure 2.5, appears. You've just created the Household Inventory database, complete with sample data! Throughout the remainder of the day you'll be using this database, so keep it open and proceed to the next section.

**FIGURE 2.5.**

*The Main Switchboard for the Household Inventory database.*

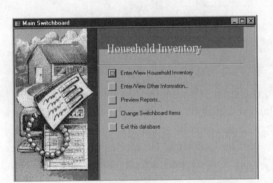

# Navigating the Household Inventory Database

Now that the Household Inventory has been created, it's time to put it through its paces. The remainder of today will be spent exploring the various tables, forms, and reports. You'll look at them in both run-time and design modes. The run-time mode is when the item in question is really doing the work it's intended to do: displaying data in a datasheet, accepting input into a form, or printing a report. You can do this right away because you instructed the Wizard to create sample data when it created the database. The design mode is used to determine exactly what will happen (or will be allowed to happen) in run-time mode.

## Using the Switchboard

For now, return to the Main Switchboard (shown in Figure 2.5). This form was created by the wizard for navigational purposes. You can't enter any data anywhere on this form. Instead, you use it as a navigational aide to help you jump between forms and reports.

Not surprisingly, the Main Switchboard is easy to use. To enter information into the main inventory, for example, simply click the button to the left of Enter/View Household Inventory. The Household Inventory form, shown in Figure 2.6, launches and displays the first item in the inventory.

**FIGURE 2.6.**

*The Household Inventory data entry form.*

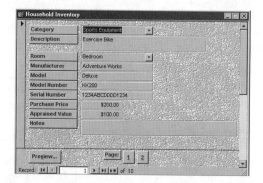

For now, close this form by clicking the X button in the upper-right corner of the window. This will take you back to the Switchboard. Once there, click the Enter/View Other Information button. This will take you to a different Switchboard from which you can launch the forms for the Rooms and Categories tables that were created by the wizard. To return to the Main Switchboard from this one, click the Return to Main Switchboard button.

The third button on the Main Switchboard, Preview Reports, will take you to the Reports Switchboard shown in Figure 2.7. From here you can launch various reports that will give you a summary of your household inventory. Click a couple of them to see what the reports look like. Notice that they resemble the style you chose in step 8 of the previous task. Close the reports and return to the Main Switchboard, again using the bottom button on the Reports Switchboard.

**FIGURE 2.7.**

*The Reports
Switchboard form.*

## Entering Information

You should be at the Main Switchboard. If not, navigate back to it.

**Note**

If you accidentally close the Switchboard form, it's easy to get it back. Use the Window|1 Household Inventory: Database Menu item to restore the Database window. Select the Forms tab. You'll see an entry in the list box named Switchboard. Click this entry and click the Open button. The Main Switchboard will be restored.

The wizard provided you with some sample data, but left out a crucial room and, of course, didn't add any of your stuff to the database. In the following task you'll create this additional room and enter some of your "stuff" into the inventory. After you've completed the task, the next task will show you how to invoke a filter that will narrow the data to a specific subset.

### Task: Enter new data into the Household Inventory

1. First, you'll add a new room to the database. Most people, especially those with computers, have a room they call their office. However, the Wizard didn't include this one so you'll have to add it. From the Main Switchboard, click Enter/View Other Information to move to the Forms Switchboard.

2. Click the Enter/View Rooms button. The Rooms form (shown in Figure 2.8) opens, displaying the first record in the Rooms table.

**FIGURE 2.8.**

*The Rooms data entry form.*

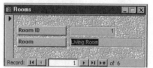

3. You can view all of the rooms currently in the database by clicking the button at the bottom of the window that has a right-facing arrow. It's the little button just to the right of the text box with the number 1. This is the current record counter. To the far right are the words of 6. This is the total number of rooms in the database. Click this repeatedly to scroll through all the rooms. You'll know you've gone past the last room when the button becomes disabled. Return to the first room by clicking the left-most button at the bottom of the form.

4. To add the new room, click the button at the far right that has the right-facing arrow and asterisk. This is the New Record button. The form changes to allow for entry of a new record. Note that the RoomID text box is disabled and labeled (AutoNumber). This indicates that Access will provide your new room with a value for this field. In the Room text box, enter Office.

5. Notice that after you started typing, the little arrow at the top-left side of the window changed to a pencil. This indicates that the current record has been modified. After you've entered Office in the text box, click this pencil button to save the new record. The button returns to its arrow state (and it's no longer a button). Close this window.

6. You should now be back at the Forms Switchboard. Return to the Main Switchboard and click the Enter/View Household Inventory button. The Household Inventory form, shown in Figure 2.9, appears and displays the first item in the inventory.

**FIGURE 2.9.**

*The Household Inventory data entry form.*

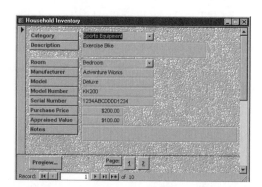

▼    7.  You navigate through the items in the inventory in exactly the same manner as you navigated through the list of available rooms. The Household Inventory form also has a few other navigational buttons. The Preview button will launch a report for the current item. Because all of the fields wouldn't fit in the window, the Wizard added the page buttons. These will scroll the window up or down for you to display additional fields. After you've examined some of the other items from the sample database and experimented with the navigational buttons, click the New Record button.

**2**

8.  Enter some new inventory items using the same process by which you entered the new room. Use the drop-down list boxes to select a Category and a Room for each item. Notice that Office appears in the Room drop-down list. You didn't have to change the design of this form to make that happen because the form reads the data directly from the Rooms table. If you're entering multiple items, you don't have to click the pencil and then the New Record button each time. Instead, you can simply click the New Record button. This will save the current changes and clean the slate so you can enter a new item.

9.  Enter about five more items into the inventory, enough to make the remainder of this day interesting. After you've saved the last item, leave the Household
▲       Inventory window opened.

Now that you've seen how to enter information into the Household Inventory, see how you can get directly to the information you're interested in at any particular moment. You'll do this using what's known as a *filter*. Just as the name implies, a filter will sift through your data and return only the parts you want. The unwanted (at this moment) data will still be there—you just won't be able to view it as long as the filter is active.

There are two different ways to activate a filter. One way is called Filter by Selection. The other is called Filter by Form. You'll best understand the difference between these methods by using each of them. The following task steps you through using each type of filter.

## Task: Using a filter to find that favorite chair

1.  You should have the Household Inventory window opened. If not, return to the Main Switchboard and open it. Alternatively, you can go to the Forms tab on the Database window and double-click the Household Inventory form name.

2.  Navigate through the records until you come across an item whose Room value is set to Living Room.

▼  3.  Click anywhere in the drop-down list box for the Room field to set focus to that field.

▼ 4. First you'll use Filter by Selection. Click the Filter by Selection button. In Figure 2.10 the mouse is pointing to this toolbar button.

**FIGURE 2.10.**

*The Filter by Selection toolbar button.*

5. The screen changes slightly and should look similar to Figure 2.11. Now as you navigate through the records, you'll notice that the only ones available are the items that have Living Room for their Room value. You'll notice that the Remove Filter button is depressed, and that the bottom of the Household Inventory window has the word (Filtered) displayed. Both of these are indicators that you're viewing a filtered set of the data.

**FIGURE 2.11.**

*The Household Inventory window with a filter applied.*

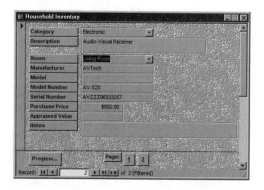

6. You can further refine the filter by applying another filter on top of the current one. Navigate to a record with Electronic in the Category field. Click the Category drop-down list box and click the Filter by Selection button once again. Now the only items available are the electronics items in the living room.

7. Once you've played around with this filter for a while, remove it by clicking the Remove Filter toolbar button. The available items are now the entire inventory. If you click this same button again (it's now the Apply Filter button if you look at the tooltip for it), you'll re-apply the original filter from step 5. Try this once and return to the non-filtered state to continue.

8. Now you'll do the same thing using the Filter by Form method. The Filter by Form toolbar button is immediately to the right of the Filter by Selection button. Click it.

9. The Household Inventory window changes to the Household Inventory: Filter by Form window shown in Figure 2.12. Notice that your original filter condition, Room is Living Room, is still intact and that the toolbar has changed slightly.

▼

**FIGURE 2.12.**

*The Household Inventory: Filter by Form window.*

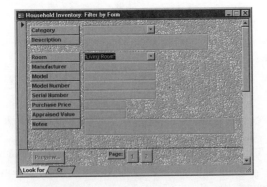

10. Click the Apply Filter button. It's the same Apply Filter/Remove Filter button as before. The filter is applied and you'll see the same items as in your previous filter example.

11. Click the Filter by Form button again. This time click in the Category drop-down list box and select Electronic in the drop-down list. Click the Apply Filter button and the available items will be the same as the ones from step 6.

12. And now for something completely different. Click the Filter by Form button again. Then click the Clear Grid button. It's the one immediately to the right of the button labeled Close in Figure 2.12. This will remove all of the current filter conditions.

13. Click in the Manufacturer field's text box. Notice that it changes to a drop-down list box. This box contains a distinct list of all of the values entered in the Manufacturer field. Select Adventure Works from the drop-down list. Click the Apply Filter button. The only items that appear now are the ones manufactured by Adventure Works.

14. Close the Household Inventory window and open it again. Notice that the filter seems to have been lost. However, if you click the Apply Filter button, you'll have the same items available as you did in step 13. Close the window again to return to the Main Switchboard.

## Printing a Report

Now that you've seen how to enter and view the data contained within the Household Inventory, examine how you can print a listing of your inventory. The following task steps you through previewing and printing one of the reports produced by the Database Wizard. This report would probably be suitable for insurance purposes.

## Task: Printing a simple report

1. You should be back on the Main Switchboard. If not, return to it at this time. Click the Preview Reports button.

2. The Reports Switchboard appears. Click the Preview the Inventory by Room Report button.

3. The Inventory by Room report appears in Print Preview mode, as shown in Figure 2.13. Notice that the cursor has changed to a magnifying glass with a minus sign in the middle. This is the zoom out cursor and signifies that if you click in the report, the preview window will zoom out to show more of the report. Click anywhere within the report.

**FIGURE 2.13.**

*The Inventory by Room report in Print Preview mode.*

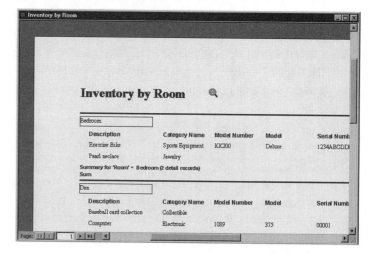

4. The report becomes hardly readable. The cursor has now changed to a zoom-in cursor. Click again to return the preview window to a more reasonable magnification level.

5. You can also change the magnification level by using the drop-down list box that has the value 100% in it in Figure 2.13. Open the list box and select 10%. The report becomes really small. Click in the text area of the drop-down list and type 80. The report returns to a more reasonable size.

6. To print the report to a printer, you must have a printer attached to your computer (either locally or over your network) and available to the operating system. If you meet these conditions, click the Print toolbar button. It's the one with the picture of the printer on it. This will immediately print the report without any further intervention on your part.

▼    7.  Next, use the File|Print menu item to bring up the Print dialog. In this dialog you can set some options that affect your printout, such as Number of Copies and the range of pages to print. You can also view your printer's settings by clicking the Properties button, or even change to a different printer by selecting it in the Name drop-down list box. If you printed the report in the previous step, click Cancel now, unless you want to print the report again.

     8.  Close the Inventory by Room print preview window to return to the Reports Switchboard.

▲    9.  Click the Return to Main Switchboard button.

# Exploring the Design Views

Now that you've experimented with navigating the Household Inventory database using the Switchboard form the Wizard created, it's time to embark on an unguided journey through the objects in the database. In this section you'll examine each type of object created in the database in its corresponding Design View window.

If you've closed the database, open it again. Close the Switchboard form and restore the Database window by using the Window|1 Database: Household Inventory menu item.

## Table Design View

The Table Design View is used to change the fields contained in a table, as well as to modify their properties. Starting on Day 4, "Creating a New Database from Scratch," you'll spend more time using the Table Design View. For now, you'll just glance at the window.

To open a table in Design View, move to the Tables tab of the Database window. Select the table you want to view (such as Household Inventory) and click the Design button. The table is opened in the Table Design View, shown in Figure 2.14.

The Table Design View window displays each field's name, data type, and description in a grid at the top of the window. At the bottom of the window is a tabbed section which displays the properties for the currently selected field. Click some of the fields in the top grid to get a feel for some of the different properties that are available for each data type.

When you've finished looking around, close the window. If you are prompted to save changes to the design of the table, click No unless you actually intended to make these changes. You should now be back at the Database window.

FIGURE 2.14.

**FIGURE 2.14.**

*The Household
Inventory Table in
Table Design View.*

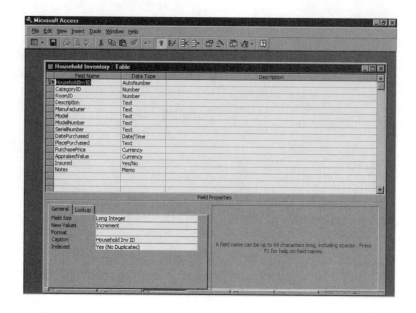

## Form Design View

The Form Design View is where you create and modify the design and layout of a form.
Click the Forms tab of the Database window, select the Household Inventory form, and
click the Design button. The Form Design View for the Household Inventory opens.
Forms design is a slightly complicated beast. You'll get your first taste of it on Day 8,
"Designing Forms for Data Manipulation." For now, simply close the window to return
to the Database window.

## Report Design View

The Report Design View is very similar to the Form Design View. Click the Reports tab
of the Database window, select the Inventory by Value report, and click the Design button. The selected report is opened in design view. Report design is first introduced on
Day 9, "Creating Functional Reports." Close the Report Design window.

# Summary

It's been a busy day. You created your first database using Access 97's Database Wizard.
Then you added some meaningful data to that new database and did some filtering to
locate the data that was of interest to you.

You even printed a report that was generated by the Database Wizard and took a peek
under the covers to see how the tables, forms, and reports appear in Design mode.

Tomorrow, "Designing an Access Database," you'll learn the ins and outs of database design and relational database theory. While it doesn't sound like a particularly interesting topic (and, to most people, it isn't), it's necessary information if you are ever going to create any real-world Access databases.

# Q&A

**Q  Can I modify the output of the Database Wizard?**

**A**  Of course. Once a database is created, even by the Database Wizard, you can modify it to your heart's content using the various design windows. Throughout most of the remainder of this book you'll be modifying the objects in a database.

**Q  I don't seem to have any printers specified in Windows. How do I add a printer?**

**A**  Click the Windows 95/NT Start button, click Settings and then Printers. This will open the Printers folder. Double-click the Add Printer icon in this folder. The Add Printer Wizard appears to guide you through the process of adding a printer to your system.

# Workshop

Here's where you can test and apply what you have learned today.

## Quiz

1. Can I remove any of the suggested fields from the Database Wizard's list of fields?

2. What is the term used for the navigational form in the Database Wizard generated databases?

3. What are the two types of filters you can apply on a form?

4. Can you view the output of a report even if you do not have a printer attached to your computer?

## Exercise

1. Open the Household Inventory database.

2. Activate the Database window and select the Reports tab.

3. Select the Inventory by Category report and click the Preview button.

4. Print the report to your printer.

5. Exit Access.

# DAY **3**

# Designing an Access Database

Today's chapter serves as a primer on designing databases. The title of the chapter leads you to believe you'll learn about designing databases for Microsoft Access. That is, indeed, the focus of this chapter, but the concepts you learn here can easily be transferred to other database platforms as well.

Today you learn all about

- Database terms
- Design issues
- Indexes and keys
- Relationships
- Normalization

# Relational Databases

RDBMS, relational database management system, is one of the acronyms feared by beginners. We are going to try to remove some of the mystery from behind this. A database is simply a collection of data. A DBMS is a system designed for two main purposes; to add, delete, and change the information stored in the database, and to provide different ways of viewing the data. An RDBMS is a system that helps with the data-specific rules that have to be enforced when you want a relational database.

Why use a relational database system? Most databases that are worth maintaining for a business or for personal use are complicated. Business databases can contain millions of records of information. This information can and generally is very intricately connected. In the small example of an online book sales company, you are limited to a small number of books compared to the Library of Congress, which contains over 16 million books. A single table cannot contain all of the information.

## Database Terms

NEW TERM    Listed here are some of the terms that will be used throughout this book and their meanings. This will help you understand the concepts this book is going to present.

A *database* is a collection of related tables.

A *table* is a set of rows or records of a specific type. A `Customers` table would contain information about customers.

A *row* or *record* contains columns of data about a single subject. A row in a `Customers` table would contain information about a specific customer. It would not have the name of one customer and the address of a different customer.

A *column* is a single piece of information about the subject. The name column would contain the name of the customer. The mailing address column would contain the mailing address of the customer.

A column can have *constraints* or limitations on it. The `Customer ID` column cannot be left blank and has to be a unique value. The fact that it cannot be blank and must be unique are its constraints. The notes column may not have any constraints placed on it.

*VBA*, Visual Basic for Applications, is the programming language used to create functions and procedures.

*SQL*, structured query language, is the language that the JET database engine uses to access data. It is what is refered to as *declarative* language. Declarative means that you tell the computer what you want to end up with, and then let the machine determine how to give the correct result. You never see the details like you would when writing a data access procedure in something like C++.

*Relationships* are predefined links between tables. The Orders table has a Customer ID field and so does the Customers table. You can define a link between the two tables using the Customer ID field as the linking point.

*Joins* are the different ways of defining the links between tables.

A *key* is a column or set of columns in a table that identifies each row within that table. There are different types of keys; primary, foreign, and composite. Keys are important for normalization, indexing, sorting, and searching for data.

*Database integrity* is where a lot of peoples' eyes start to glaze over. A database has to have integrity before you can trust the information contained in it. Access contains tools to enforce *referential integrity* and help keep incorrect data from being entered through constraints.

## Relationships and Joins

Relationships are the way to relate information in one table to another table. Figure 3.1 shows the window used to define relationships.

**FIGURE 3.1.**

*A view of the Relationships window.*

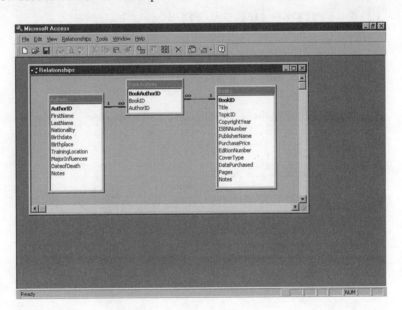

The lines between the tables shown in Figure 3.1 are called *join lines*. These join lines define how the tables are related.

A join takes two or more tables and builds a new table from them by combining the rows from one table with the rows of the other table(s). Figure 3.2 shows the dialog boxes used to define the relationship and join properties.

**FIGURE 3.2.**

*A view of the Relationships and Join Properties dialogs.*

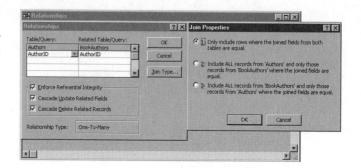

> **Note**
>
> Chapter 5, "Linking Tables with Relationships," covers relationships, how they're created, and how to maintain them.

# The Three Types of Keys

There are, in general terms, three types of keys for tables: primary, foreign, and composite.

## Primary Keys

Table 3.1 shows the table structure for three tables. We will use these tables to discuss keys.

**TABLE 3.1.** SAMPLE TABLES FOR KEYS.

| Customers | Orders | Order Detail |
| --- | --- | --- |
| Customer ID | Order Number | Order Number |
| Name | Order Date | Quantity |
| Address Line 1 | Customer ID | Book ID |
| Address Line 2 | Shipping Method | Price |
| City | | Shipping Cost |
| State | | Ship Date |
| Zip Code | | Order Total |

Looking at the `Customers` table, you need to determine the best and most unique way of storing and retrieving customer information. If you make the name the primary key, no one can have the same name. This is not acceptable; all you have to do is look under Smith in the phone book and see how many there are with the same first, middle, and last names. The same thing is true of all the other fields except `Customer ID`. This can be made unique. Access has a data type of `AutoNumber` that will uniquely identify a record using a sequential number.

**NEW TERM** A key that uniquely identifies a record is called the *primary key*. There can be other fields that are unique with the table but were not defined as the primary key. These keys are called *candidate keys* because they are candidates for the primary key.

## Composite Keys

Doing the same analysis on the `Orders` table, you see that the `Order Number` has to be the field that is unique. But the `Order Detail` table does not have a single field that can be identified through a unique key. You have to identify the unique key using a combination of fields. This is called a *composite key*, because it is made up of more than one field. You would use the `Order Number` and the `Book ID` as a composite. You would adjust the quantity ordered rather than enter the same book twice on the order.

## Foreign Keys

The third type of key is a *foreign key*. A foreign key in the sample tables in Table 3.1 would be the `Customer ID` in the `Orders` table. It is the key or link into the foreign table `Customers`.

A table can contain many foreign keys. The number is based on the number of tables that are related to it.

**Tip**

First off, foreign keys in a table map to primary keys in the foreign (or linked) table. Secondly, if the linked table has a composite primary key, you'll have one foreign key field for each primary key field in the linked table. Finally, it's best for documentation purposes (though neither a requirement nor always possible) to name your foreign key fields the same as the primary key fields.

## Task: Identifying the keys in the online book sales database

Using the information provided about keys, identify the primary, foreign, and composite keys in the following example tables.

**TABLE 3.2.** TASK SAMPLE TABLES.

| Publications | Authors |
| --- | --- |
| Publication ID | Author ID |
| Publisher ID | First Name |
| Title | Last Name |
| Year Published | Nationality |
| Web Page | Birth Date |
| Category ID | Birth Place |
| ISBN Number | Training Location |
| Edition Number | Major Influences |
| Pages | Date of Death |
| Author ID | Photograph |
| Catalog Card Number | Notes |
| List Price | |

# Referential Integrity

Here is another one of those scary phrases database programmers use *referential integrity*. If you look back at your Orders and Order Detail tables, it simply means that you cannot add order details for an order that does not exist already.

This feature allows users to design databases that maintain their data properly. After selecting that you want to maintain referential integrity, you have the choice to cascade and update the foreign key in the child tables if you change the primary key in the parent table. You can also cascade deletions, but be careful when applying this feature. If you delete an order, you will want to delete the order details for that order, but you do not want to delete the books from the Publications table as a result of deleting an order. Figure 3.3 shows the screen used to define these properties.

**FIGURE 3.3.**

*The Relationships dialog.*

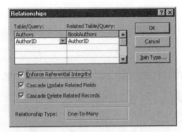

These properties will be covered in depth in Day 5.

# The Three Types of Relationships

There are different kinds of relationships between tables: one-to-one, one-to-many, and many-to-many.

## One-to-One Relationships

A one-to-one relationship is established when the two tables can have only one record in each that are related to each other. An example of a one-to-one relationship would be a contributors-authors relationship. A contributor would be someone who writes a small portion or contributes to a book and does not receive the full rights as an author. Since he or she is considered an author, he or she would be related on a one-to-one basis to his or her entry in the Authors table. Also, when establishing a one-to-one relationship, the primary key must be the same for each table.

## One-to-Many Relationships

A one-to-many relationship is established when one record in a table can be related to many records in another table. An example of a one-to-many relationship would be the publishers-books relationship. A publisher can publish many books. We will assume that only one publisher can publish an individual book.

## Many-to-Many Relationships

A many-to-many relationship is established when one record in a table can be related to many records in another table, and a record in the second table can have many related records in the first table. An example of a many-to-many relationship would be the books-authors relationship. Many authors can write a book, and an author can write many books.

NEW TERM    Access cannot establish a many-to-many relationship without the creation of a *resolver* or *intersection table*. The BookAuthors table shown in Figure 3.1 is an example of such a table.

## Task: Identifying the relationships in the online sales database

In this exercise, you will use Tables 3.3, 3.4, and 3.5 to do the following:

- Identify which tables are related
- Identify the type of relationship

**TABLE 3.3.** TASK SAMPLE TABLES.

| Publications | Authors | Publishers |
| --- | --- | --- |
| Publication ID | Author ID | Publisher ID |
| Publisher ID | First Name | Name |
| Title | Last Name | Contact Name |
| Year Published | Nationality | Contact Email |
| Web Page | Birth Date | Address |
| Category ID | Birth Place | City |
| ISBN Number | Training Location | State |
| Edition Number | Major Influences | Zip |
| Pages | Date of Death | Phone |
| Author ID | Photograph | Fax |
| Catalog Card Number | Notes | Active |
| List Price | | Comments |

**TABLE 3.4.** TASK SAMPLE TABLES.

| Categories | Reviews |
| --- | --- |
| Category ID | Publication ID |
| Category | Author Name |
| | Author Email |
| | Review Date |

**TABLE 3.5.** TASK SAMPLE TABLES.

| Customers | Orders | Order Detail |
|---|---|---|
| Customer ID | Order Number | Order Number |
| Name, Order Date, Quantity | | |
| Address Line 1 | Customer ID | Book ID |
| Address Line 2 | Shipping Method | Price |
| City | Shipping Cost | |
| State | Ship Date | |
| Zip Code | Order Total | |

# Steps to Creating a Relational Database

In this section we will identify the steps you need to go through when you decide to create a database. These steps are the same regardless of the size of the system you want to create. The difference is the amount of analysis that is required at each step and the sheer volume of possibilities you have to contend with.

## Identifying Required Data

The best method for determining the data required by your database is to write it out using paper, a word processor, or a spreadsheet. Just create a list of data and describe what it is. By doing this electronically, you can move elements of data around and copy them when you start separating them out to create tables. Figure 3.4 is an example of how you can lay out the information by using Excel.

Look at the requirements for the orders and list the things you need to record information for. Table 3.6 shows the information and a description of it.

**TABLE 3.6.** DATABASE DESIGN REQUIREMENTS.

| Information | Description |
|---|---|
| Order Number | No duplicates; identifies the order |
| Order Date | Date the order was taken |
| Customer | Name of the customer |
| Shipping Address | Address to ship the order to |
| Shipping Method | How the order is being shipped |
| Quantity | How many of the book was ordered |

*continues*

**TABLE 3.6.** CONTINUED

| Information | Description |
| --- | --- |
| Shipping Cost | How much is the shipping |
| Book ID | What book(s) were sold |
| Ship Date | Date the order was shipped |
| Order Total | Total amount of the order |

**FIGURE 3.4.**

*Using Excel for identifying required data.*

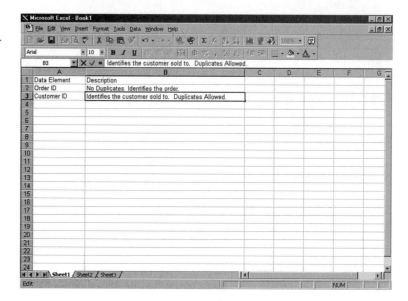

The address information can be broken down further as demonstrated in Table 3.7.

**TABLE 3.7.** MORE DATABASE DESIGN REQUIREMENTS.

| Information | Description |
| --- | --- |
| Address Line 1 | First line of shipping address |
| Address Line 2 | Second line of the shipping address |
| City | City for the shipping address |
| State | State for the shipping address |
| Zip code | Zip code for the shipping address |
| Phone | Phone number for customer |
| Fax | Fax number for customer |

## Collecting the Identified Fields into Tables

NEW TERM | Once you have identified the information, you need to decide what tables to store the information in. Here you look at the data you want to store and determine what subject, orders or customers, it is related to. This process is called *decomposition*. You then place that data element under the appropriate subject heading. You would also want to determine the kind of data that would be stored (field type) and how much data to allow in each field (field size). Figure 3.5 shows how to do this using Excel.

**FIGURE 3.5.**

*Using Excel for collecting data elements into tables.*

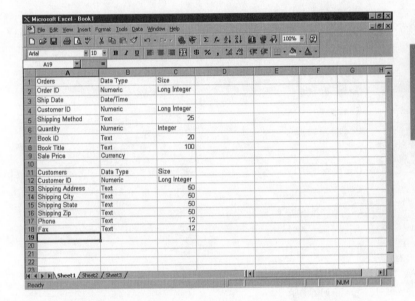

## Identifying the Primary Keys

Once you have the table structure layout, you can look for how you are going to identify each record uniquely. You do this through the use of a *primary key*. It is called a primary key because it is the primary field or fields used to uniquely identify a record or row of information.

Table 3.8 is a summary of the table layouts you have established so far.

**TABLE 3.8.** INITIAL TABLE LAYOUT.

| Table/Field | Data Type | Field Size |
| --- | --- | --- |
| Orders | | |
| Order ID | Numeric | Long Integer |
| Ship Date | Date/Time | |
| Order Date | Date/Time | |
| Customer ID | Numeric | Long Integer |
| Shipping Method | Text | 25 |
| Quantity | Numeric | Integer |
| Book ID | Text | 20 |
| Book Title | Text | 100 |
| Sale Price | Currency | |
| Shipping Cost | Currency | |
| Order Total | Currency | |
| Customers | | |
| Customer ID | Numeric | Long Integer |
| Name | Text | 50 |
| Shipping Address 1 | Text | 50 |
| Shipping Address 2 | Text | 50 |
| Shipping City | Text | 50 |
| Shipping State | Text | 2 |
| Shipping Zip | Text | 10 |
| Phone | Text | 12 |
| Fax | Text | 12 |

## Drawing a Simple Data Diagram

Sometimes a picture is worth a thousand words. You can draw out how the information looks with a simple entity-relationship diagram. Figure 3.6 shows one created in Visio.

You do not have to use complex drawing tools to do this; a blank sheet of paper and a ruler will work.

## Normalizing the Data

 As part of any database design, you have to analyze the information you are going to store. You do not just start designing tables and writing code. Part of the analysis process is the normalization of the tables. Don't panic just because you don't know how to do this. *Normalization* is just the process of moving your database to the best possible design. We are going to expose you to the five normal forms and go into depth on the first three.

**FIGURE 3.6.**

*Entity-relationship diagram.*

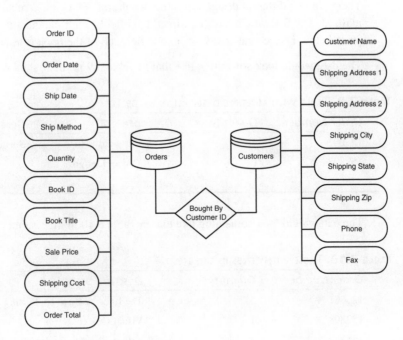

The five commonly recognized normal forms are:

- First Normal Form
- Second Normal Form
- Third Normal Form
- Fourth Normal Form
- Fifth Normal Form

As you can see, a lot of imagination went into naming them. Each level of normalization is more powerful than the one before it, but the last two are rarely used except in very complex databases. Using the tables you are going to establish in the book, Orders and Order Detail, you will analyze the requirements and run them through the three normal forms.

3

## First Normal Form

The first normal form is the simplest, eliminates repeating groups, and doesn't combine information in a single field.

There are two different design types that would reflect a table structure that was not normalized. The first would have multiple ISBN fields, multiple quantity fields, and multiple price fields. The second could list, in one field, all of the book titles.

The data would look something like that in Table 3.9 in the first case.

**TABLE 3.9.** TABLE WITH MULTIPLE DESCRIPTION FIELDS.

| Order Number | Quantity | Description 1 | Description 2 |
|---|---|---|---|
| 123001 | 3 | The Encarta How-To | Surfing the Web |
| 152898 | 1 | Visual Object Design | |
| 156889 | 3 | Arthur | Gaelic Made Easy |

The data would look something like that in Table 3.10 in the second case.

**TABLE 3.10.** TABLE WITH TITLES IN ONE FIELD.

| Order Number | Quantity | Description |
|---|---|---|
| 123001 | 3 | The Encarta How-To, Surfing the Web |
| 152898 | 1 | Visual Object Design |
| 156889 | 3 | Arthur, Talisen, Gaelic Made Easy |

As you can see from the data, it will be difficult to get reports on what and how many books were sold.

The normalized version of the data shown previously would look something like Table 3.11.

**TABLE 3.11.** FIRST NORMAL FORM.

| Order Number | Quantity | Description | Price |
|---|---|---|---|
| 123001 | 2 | The Encarta How-To | $29.95 |
| 123001 | 1 | Surfing the Web | 39.95 |
| 152898 | 1 | Visual Object Design | 59.95 |
| 156889 | 1 | Gaelic Made Easy | 49.95 |
| 156889 | 1 | Arthur | 5.95 |
| 156889 | 1 | Talisen | 12.95 |

Looking at this data, it is much easier to determine how many books were sold, the price, and which books they were.

## Second Normal Form

The second normal form is the next level of normalization. It requires that the tables are in the first normal form and that the information you are storing describe the thing you are tracking.

In the last table, you had the order number, quantity, description, and price. The description is not a description of the order; it is a description of the book being sold. You should be using a book identification number instead of the book title or description. The table would then look like Table 3.12.

**TABLE 3.12.** SECOND NORMAL FORM.

| Order Number | Quantity | Book ID | Price |
|---|---|---|---|
| 123001 | 2 | 0-15226-989-0 | $29.95 |
| 123001 | 1 | 1-15524-557-2 | 39.95 |
| 152898 | 1 | 4-45589-246-0 | 59.95 |
| 156889 | 1 | 7-89958-841-0 | 49.95 |
| 156889 | 1 | 1-56592-297-2 | 5.95 |
| 156889 | 1 | 0-98676-010-0 | 12.95 |

## Third Normal Form

The third normal form assumes that the information is in the second normal form. In addition, there should be no information that is derived from other information. In other words, if it is calculated, do not store it.

If you go back to the first table that describes the information you are going to store, your order header would look like Table 3.13.

**TABLE 3.13.** THIRD NORMAL FORM.

| Information | Description |
|---|---|
| Order Number | No duplicates; identifies the order |
| Order Date | Date the order was taken |
| Customer | Name of the customer |
| Address Line 1 | First line of the street address |

*continues*

**TABLE 3.13.** CONTINUED

| Information | Description |
| --- | --- |
| Address Line 2 | Second line of the street address |
| City | City |
| State | State |
| Zip code | Zip code |
| Shipping Method | How the order is to be shipped |
| Shipping Cost | How much the shipping is |
| Ship Date | Date the order was shipped |
| Order Total | Total amount of the order |

Normalizing this to the second normal form it would look like Table 3.14. The customer information would be removed to its own table.

**TABLE 3.14.** SECOND NORMAL FORM OF THE Orders TABLE.

| Information | Description |
| --- | --- |
| Order Number | No duplicates; identifies the order |
| Order Date | Date the order was taken |
| Customer ID | Customer ID |
| Shipping Method | How the order is to be shipped |
| Shipping Cost | How much is the shipping |
| Ship Date | Date the order was shipped |
| Order Total | Total amount of the order |

Looking at the last bit of information, Order Total, you can calculate this through various methods and should not be storing it as part of the table. On the other hand, shipping cost is not derived from other stored data and would be left in the table structure. This would make the table fully third normal form-compliant.

**Note**

For most practical purposes, the third normal form is about as far as you need to go to have a workable relational database. The fourth and fifth normal forms, while academically required to produce a truly "relational" database, are generally overkill for most business applications.

## Fourth Normal Form

The fourth normal form requires all tables be at the third normal form. Its object is to isolate independent multiple relationships. No table can contain two or more one-to-many (1:n) or many-to-many (n:m) relationships that are not directly related. This step applies only when the design includes 1:n or n:m relationships. An example of a one-to-many relationship in your tables would be that a customer could have many orders. An example of the many-to-many relationship would be that a customer can order many books, and a book can be shipped to many customers.

## Fifth Normal Form

The fifth normal form's object is to isolate semantically related multiple relationships. Looking back at your tables again, if you want to record the information about the types of books each publisher deals with; western, computer, romance, and so on. You would not want to store that information with the publisher, and you would not want to store the publisher directly with the book type. You would create a resolution table to link the information between the two tables together. The resolution table would contain the publisher ID and the book type ID.

## Identifying Field-Specific Information

NEW TERM   Just before you create the actual tables, you need to identify information that is going to be specific to the individual fields. This is called the *field properties*. The following is a list of the field properties with a brief description of each. In some cases, I will give you examples of how you can use the property. Figure 3.7 shows a view of the window used to define a table.

**FIGURE 3.7.**

*Table design window for the* Orders *table.*

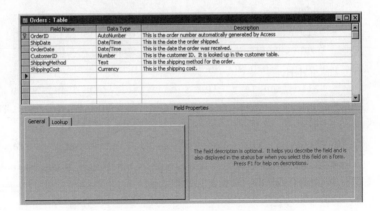

- `Data Type`  This is the type of information that the field can contain. Some of the data types are `Text`, `Date/Time`, `Numeric`, and `Memo`. Each data type has its limitations. For example, the `Text` data type is limited to 255 characters at a maximum, but the `Memo` data type can contain up to 65,535 characters. It is important to use the correct data type when storing information. You can get complete information about the data types by pressing F1 when in this field.

- `Description`  This is a description of the information contained in the field. This also shows on the status line when you enter information into the field on a form.

- `Field Size`  This is the maximum number of characters the field can hold. This is used only for text data types when specifying a size of 50, for example. When a `Numeric` data type was defined, you define a range of numbers the field can hold: `byte`, `integer`, `long integer`, `single`, and `double`.

- `Format`  This property allows you to define the way the data is displayed on the screen. For example, you can enter a date as 03/12/98 and display it as Thursday, March 12, 1998.

- `Decimal Places`  This is only valid for `Numeric` data types.

- `Input Mask`  This is valid for all data types except Boolean and memo types. This gives the user a mask for entering data. For example, for (409) 555-1313, the user would not have to enter the parentheses or the hyphen because they are part of the mask.

- `Caption`  The caption is used in the column headings for queries and when designing forms and reports. If it is not defined, the field name is automatically used.

- `Default Value`  This is the value the field starts off at when a new record is being added.

- `Validation Rule`  This is the rule you design to help keep invalid information from being entered into a field. For example, `= "M" Or = "F"` could be the validation rule when entering the sex of a person.

- `Validation Text`  This is the text you would display when a validation rule is violated. Using the same example, you could put `You have to enter an M for Male or an F for Female`.

- `Required`  This property allows you to make entries into this field required.

- `Allow Zero Length`  This property determines if you can enter zero-length strings into the field.

- Indexed    You have three options here: No, Yes Duplicates Allowed, and Yes No Duplicates Allowed. Indexing the fields you think you are going to search for information in will generally speed the searches. Indexing will also slow up the process of appending data into your tables. Generally the benefits will far outweigh the issues.

## Creating the Actual Tables

In this section, you will create the actual tables you have been analyzing and generally tearing apart.

Click the Table tab of the database window, and then click New. Select Design View and click OK. Figure 3.8 shows the empty table design window.

**FIGURE 3.8.**

*Empty table design window.*

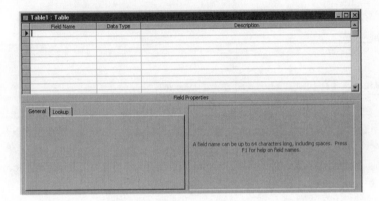

Enter the information from Table 3.15 into the appropriate places. Fill in the description and caption where you feel you need to. Save the table as Orders after completing all of the entries.

**TABLE 3.15.** Orders TABLE DESIGN.

| Field | Data Type | Field Size |
|-------|-----------|------------|
| Order ID | AutoNumber | Long Integer |
| Ship Date | Date/Time | |
| Order Date | Date/Time | |
| Customer ID | Numeric | Long Integer |
| Shipping Method | Text | 25 |
| Shipping Cost | Currency | |

Do the same thing for the information in Tables 3.16 and 3.17.

**TABLE 3.16.** Customers TABLE DESIGN.

| Field | Data Type | Field Size |
|---|---|---|
| Customer ID | Numeric | Long Integer |
| Name | Text | 50 |
| Shipping Address 1 | Text | 50 |
| Shipping Address 2 | Text | 50 |
| Shipping City | Text | 50 |
| Shipping State | Text | 2 |
| Shipping Zip | Text | 10 |
| Phone | Text | 12 |
| Fax | Text | 12 |

**TABLE 3.17.** Order Detail TABLE DESIGN.

| Table/Field | Data Type | Field Size |
|---|---|---|
| Order Detail ID | AutoNumber | Long Integer |
| Order ID | Numeric | Long Integer |
| Publication ID | Numeric | Long Integer |
| Quantity | Numeric | Integer |
| Sale Price | Numeric | Double |

# Summary

Today you learned about designing Access databases. The day started with a review of the more common database terms. You then learned about some of the issues surrounding database design. This was followed by a discussion of the various kinds of key fields and the relationships they create. Finally, the chapter concluded with a section that showed you, step-by-step, how to design a database, including the process of normalizing the database to make it truly a relational database.

# Q&A

**Q** **Where can I go to learn more about database design techniques?**

**A** I'd recommend two sources. The first is a magazine titled *DBMS*, which is published by Miller Freeman and widely distributed in most bookstores. The second is the group of Internet newsgroups that are named `comp.databases.*`.

**Q** **If the third normal form is sufficient for most purposes, why are there five normal forms?**

**A** Actually, there are more than five normal forms. The others, though, are not widely preached. And as to why there are five when three typically suffice, this is strictly my opinion but it's kind of like vector calculus; most people (99.9 percent probably) will never use it, but it's indispensable to those who do. Those extra normal forms are the same way; for some really high-powered databases, they're a necessity. For most of what you'll use Access for, they're overkill.

**Q** **Are there other tools that can be used to design databases?**

**A** Yes. There are many data modeling tools on the market. There are also tools that will help you maintain entity-relationship (E-R) diagrams. These are diagrams of your tables and how they relate to one another. One such tool I've used is called ERwin. It's produced by Logic Works, Inc. (`http://www.logicworks.com`).

3

# DAY 4

# Creating a New Database from Scratch

Today you'll learn the following:

- What database project this book uses for its examples
- How to use a wizard to create your first working table
- The various field data types
- How to modify an existing table
- How to manually create a table

# The Database Project

As with almost all computer programs, the right way to learn Access 97 is to use it. Rather than go through a series of boring tasks that are unrelated to each other, as you work your way through this book you will devise a solution to a hypothetical problem. Although this particular situation—a bookstore which, by the time you finish the book will be an online bookstore—is fictional, you can directly apply the principles you learn to your own particular situation.

Note that the tasks covered in this section have some overlap with what was covered in Day 1, "A Short Tour, Including a Stop at Northwind Traders." This is by design. The focus of this chapter is table and database creation; Day 1 covered wizards, Office Assistant type help, and help in general. If you find yourself on familiar ground at certain places in this chapter, more power to you.

The fictional database you'll create throughout the course of this book must track information regarding published books, the authors who wrote them, the publishers who published them, and even some reviews of the books. By changing the labels and making a few modifications, this system can also be used for the following:

- Tracking customer orders and account balances
- Maintaining a medical or dental practice
- Tracking retail sales and inventory
- Keeping a personal inventory
- Creating a simple accounting system
- Maintaining a personnel management system

The principles you learn while building this system can be applied to almost any Access application. Actually, the online bookstore system you'll create as you work through this book is more complex than most Access applications. The real problems you'll use Access to solve will probably be much simpler than this sample application.

The previous lesson, "Designing an Access Database," discussed planning databases and what the relational model is. Remember, in a relational database system like Access, you distribute or divide your data into logical groupings of tables. For those needing near perfection, there's a complex model for performing this process; most people, however, don't need to worry that they've completely optimized their data. As in many other fields, close is good enough for most database work.

**CLOSE IS GOOD ENOUGH?**

Most Access database projects, even large ones, don't require a laborious design process. Database purists will cringe at that statement, but it's true. Access has the power and the flexibility to let you get away with a rather loose design.

However, the theory behind the relational model is valid for most business-type database projects. The closer you adhere to the relational model, the more efficient your database will be. How much efficiency you require depends on your database size, your desired response time, and your general business goals.

# Starting Access, Still Another Approach

The most obvious place to start when creating an online bookstore is with the actual books themselves, so the first table you'll add to your database will be named Publications (a fancy name for books—computer geeks like myself just love fancy names!). Before you go further, though, you need a new database in which to store the database objects. The following task shows you how to create the new database.

## Task: Creating the new database

▼ TASK

1. If Access is not started, launch it. The opening dialog appears with options for creating a new blank database, creating a database using the Database Wizard, and opening a new database. Select the top option button to create a blank database.

2. If Access is already running, use the File|New Database menu item, or you can click the New database toolbar button, the left-most one on the standard toolbar. The New database dialog, shown in Figure 4.1, appears. Leave the Blank Database item selected and move on to step 3.

**FIGURE 4.1.**

*The New database dialog.*

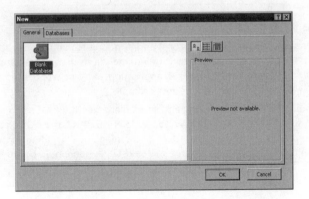

▼

4

▼     3. Click OK to move to the next dialog.

4. Access displays the File New Database dialog, shown in Figure 4.2. As you can see, this dialog is similar to the Open Database dialog. By using the drop-down list box and buttons located at the top of the dialog, you can navigate the folders on your computer and on your network to create the new database in its proper location. If the default folder (usually the My Documents folder on Windows 95 or the Personal folder on Windows NT) isn't where you'd like to create this database, navigate to the folder you want to use.

**FIGURE 4.2.**

*The File New Database dialog.*

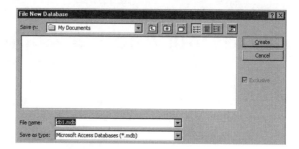

5. Once you're in the proper folder, it's time to name the database. Access has suggested the rather drab db1.mdb as a name. Override this suggestion and enter BookStore in the dialog for the new database's name. You can either include the extension .mdb, or leave it out and let Access attach the file extension automatically. Access uses the file extension .mdb to identify its native format databases.

6. Access will grind away for a while and after verifying that all's okay with its
▲     world, it will create a new database.

---

**ACCESS 97 AND LONG FILENAMES**

With Windows 95 (and later versions) and Windows NT, you can use long filenames (beyond the standard eight-character filename, three-character extension). Access 97, being a fully compliant Windows 95 application, can also work with long filenames (the filename BookStore.mdb is a perfect example).

This book uses a mixture of long and short filenames. If you're using a system that doesn't support long filenames, Windows 95/NT always has a DOS-equivalent filename, which is usually the first six characters of the filename (excluding spaces and other punctuation) followed by ~1. For example, BookStore.mdb would be truncated to bookst~1.mdb.

# The First Table

Right now the BookStore database is empty of any objects. Remember that the first order of business is to make a table to store all of the books. Consider what information describes a publication and, therefore, belongs in this table. Here's where the particular needs of your database must be considered. While you'll design a table to store information about books, you'll design tables to meet your data and application needs.

This application initially stores the following information in the Publications table:

PublicationID

Title

CategoryID

AuthorID

PublisherName

YearPublished

EditionNumber

ISBNNumber

Pages

Now that you've decided some of the fields you need for the first table, it's time to go ahead and create it.

### Task: Creating the Publications table

1. Make sure the Tables tab, the left-most one on the Database window, is selected.

2. Click the New button—it's the only button that's enabled at this time.

3. Access responds by giving you a few choices for your new table. The first two, Datasheet View and Design View, are manual options for creating a table that you'll investigate later today. The last two, Import Table Wizard and Link Table Wizard, are wizards to help you copy existing external tables into your database or link to those tables, respectively. You need the middle choice for this task, so click the Table Wizard selection, and then click OK. The Table Wizard, shown in Figure 4.3, launches.

4

**Figure 4.3.**

*The Table Wizard,*
*again in action.*

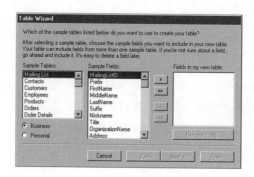

4. Click the Personal option button in the lower-left corner. Although an online book-store is obviously a business application, the sample table you're going to use is actually in the Table Wizard's Personal category.

5. Select the Books entry in the list. (You'll have to scroll through the Sample Tables list to find it.)

6. Access is making it easy for you. Notice that the Sample Fields list box contains a lot of the fields you want to include in this table.

| **Do** | **Don't** |
|---|---|
| **DO** check to see whether Access comes up with a sample or solution that closely fits your needs. It's not necessary to reinvent the wheel. | **DON'T** force a fit. If you can't find a sample or solution that's close to your needs, don't be afraid to create your own from scratch. Later in this day, you'll learn how easy it is to create your own tables without help from the wizard. |

7. Select the BookID field and click the > button just to the right of the Sample Fields list box to add it to your new table. Do the same for Title, TopicID, PublisherName, CopyrightYear, ISBNNumber, EditionNumber, and Pages.

8. Now, select the BookID field in the right-most list box. Change the field name to read PublicationID by clicking the Rename Field button and entering the new name in the dialog, as shown in Figure 4.4. Click OK to accept this name. Use this same procedure to change the TopicID field to CategoryID and the CopyrightYear field to YearPublished.

**FIGURE 4.4.**

*Altering field names within the wizard.*

---

**JUST HOW SMART IS THE WIZARD?**

You chose the BookID field because you needed an ID (short for identifier) type of field to serve as the primary key for the table. Along with the names of the sample fields, Access, behind the scenes, also sets the data type and length of the sample fields in the tables created by the Table Wizard.

---

9. In the Sample Tables list box, click Authors. Then double-click the AuthorID field in the Sample Fields list to add it to the list of fields for your new table. Notice that this is a great way to combine fields from different sample tables into your own hybrid table.

10. Click the Next> button. You enter a name for the new table in the dialog that appears. Access suggests "Books." Override Access's suggestion and name your table Publications.

11. Move to the middle of the wizard dialog and change the choice from having Access set the primary key for you to No, I'll Set The Primary Key. In this case, Access's choice for a primary key would do nicely, but it's a good exercise to learn how to set keys manually. Click Next> to move to the next dialog.

12. The PublicationID will be the unique identifier for each record. You could have assumed that the ISBNNumber for each publication would be unique, but for safety's sake, create a separate field for this purpose. Leave the first option button selected to inform Access that PublicationIDs should be automatically assigned consecutive numbers as records are created. Your screen should now look like Figure 4.5.

**4**

**FIGURE 4.5.**

*Specifying the unique identifier field for the Table Wizard.*

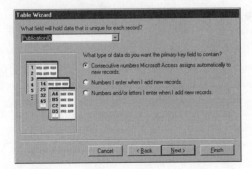

▼    13. Click the Next> button. Access gives you three choices for what to do after the table is created. If the top option button isn't selected, click it to tell Access that at the end of the wizard you want to modify the table's design (you'll need to be at the table design window for the section that follows), and then click Finish. Remember that at any time prior to finishing you can review and alter the options for a wizard by clicking the <Back buttons. Access will trundle around a bit, create the new table, and take you to the Table Design View. Your screen should look like

▲         Figure 4.6.

**FIGURE 4.6.**

*The finished Publications table shown in Table Design View.*

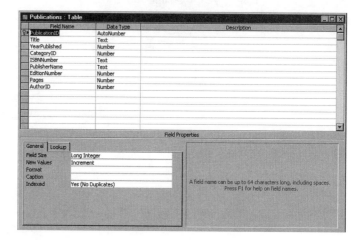

## A Look at Field Type and Properties

Refer to Figure 4.6 or to your screen. The top part of this window shows a list of the field names and their data types. The bottom part of the window has a section labeled Field Properties with two tabs, General and Lookup. Each field in an Access table has three elements: the field name, such as PublicationID; a field type, such as Number; and a set of properties.

It's important that you set each field in your database to an appropriate field type. It's generally less important, but still a matter of concern, that your table fields have their properties set correctly. In fact, you could create your entire database using the set of default properties that Access provides for each field type. Doing so, of course, could greatly limit the effectiveness of your database and any applications built around the database.

# Data Types

The data type for a field tells Access what type of data you plan on storing in that field. Access allows the following data types:

Text   Also known as Alphanumeric. This data type accepts any normal characters and is limited to a maximum field length of 255 characters. You can set an individual Text field's length to be less than 255 but doing so in Access will not conserve disk space as it will in some other database systems. Access will only store the number of bytes required to store the actual data, not the number of bytes required if the field were filled to the brim with data. Still, it's good database design practice to limit the field's length to a practical value that matches the data to be stored in the field.

Number   This data type accepts numbers. You can specify the level of precision for a Number data type. Although you could store numeric values in a field whose data type is Text, it would be neither wise nor good database design practice. Use the Number data type when you plan on applying arithmetical operations to the field.

Date/Time   A specialized form of Number data type, for entering date or time data. Like the standard Number data type, the Date/Time data type enables you to perform arithmetical operations on dates and times. For example, you can find the number of days between two dates if they're entered as Date/Time data types. (If you entered date or time information in a Text data type field, Access would accept the entry, but you couldn't perform arithmetical operations on the entries without first converting the contents of the field to a variable whose data type was a Date/Time data type—which gets into the programming topics covered in Day 17, "Introduction to Programming in Access.")

Currency   This is another specialized Number data type, which fixes a certain number of decimal places. It's useful for entering monetary information.

AutoNumber   When you make a field an AutoNumber data type, Access automatically assigns values to the field as you enter new records. If you have the New Values field property set to Increment, Access will assign sequential numbers to the field. If you have it set to Random, Access automatically generates random numbers for each new record.

When set to Increment, Access starts the numbering at 1. Incrementing or random fields work for primary keys because Access never reuses a number after it has been assigned to a record in a table.

When using AutoNumber for a primary key, most people use Increment. The Random New Number property is a special case, used when the Increment property might result in creating a duplicate primary key as data is entered at two or more locations.

4

Yes/No   Accepts only two values—Yes or No, True or False, On or Off—depending on the setting of the Format Field property. Yes/No fields are typically used for flag fields.

Lookup Wizard   Links the field to values contained in another database object (typically another table, although it could be linked to the results of a query). For example, if you want to allow entry only of data that's been previously entered in another table, you'd set this field to look up data in that table. You'll see examples of this further along in the book.

Hyperlink   A table entry that has either a Universal Naming Convention (UNC) entry, which has the form \\servername\directory\file, or a Universal Resource Location (URL), such as http://www.microsoft.com/sitebuilder/.

OLE Object   Enables you to either link or embed an object created in another program that can acts as an OLE Automation server. Access 97 is both an automation client (meaning it can act upon automation servers) and an automation server (meaning other applications can request objects from Access). OLE Object fields can also store any type of binary data you care to put into them, whether or not the data comes from an Automation server. The fields can store data up to 1GB in size, but (from a more practical standpoint) are limited by available disk space.

Memo   A field for adding notes or memoranda to a record. Can be up to 65,535 characters in length but if you manipulate the fields using the Data Access Objects (programmable ActiveX objects which you'll learn about on Day 18, "Advanced Programming with Data Access Objects and ActiveX Controls") and the fields contain only alphanumeric data, the field size is only limited by available disk space.

Keep in mind that you can't index on either the Memo, Hyperlink, or OLE fields. Generally speaking, use the Text data type unless you're sure either that all your data will conform to one of the less flexible data types or that you'll need to perform math on a field's data. You can't do math on a Text field, even if that field contains only numbers, without doing some programming to assign the field values to variables of a numeric data type.

| Do | Don't |
|---|---|
| DO try to get your data types correct the first time. | DON'T despair if you defined a data type incorrectly. In most cases, you can change data types even after you've entered data into the table. In some cases, you might lose some entered data, but Access will warn you if this could happen. |

# Modifying a Table

Access enables you to modify almost any aspect of an existing table, whether it's made manually or by using a wizard. In almost every case, a wizard-based table needs some sort of customizing. You saw this in the preceding task when you renamed three fields supplied in the sample table.

Many times you'll design a table and then realize that a particular field's data type is wrong, or you included a field you shouldn't have, or you left one out that you need. In all these cases, you would need to modify an existing table design.

The Publications table was fairly close to what you needed when it came out of the wizard. It needs a few modifications: adding a hyperlink field to link a publication to the Web page describing it, removing the PublisherName field and replacing it with a PublisherID field, and adding some Caption properties to fields which the wizard didn't assign captions to.

The PublisherName field was a good idea when you first designed the Publications table. But upon further design, it was obvious you needed a separate table to hold information about the various publishers whose books will be featured in the online bookstore. This table will have a primary key field named PublisherID. As you learned on Day 3, "Designing an Access Database," whenever you want to link two tables you should create a foreign key field in one table with the same field name as the primary key field in the other table. In this case, you'll have a one-to-many relationship between the Publishers and Publications table (one publisher can have many publications). So, you need to remove the PublisherName field from the Publications table and replace it with a PublisherID field. On Day 5, "Linking Tables with Relationships," you'll learn how to actually establish the one-to-many relationship because Access can't just assume that two identically named fields constitute a relationship.

You change a table's design by clicking in the appropriate area of the table design grid, and then making whatever changes you want. Sound simple? It is.

## Task: Modifying a table

1. If you've closed Access, the BookStore database, or the Publications table, you'll need to reopen them. If necessary, launch Access and open the BookStore database by using either the opening dialog or the File|Open menu item. Make sure the Tables tab is selected on the Database window. With the Publications table highlighted (it should be the only table in the database unless you've taken the initiative to create some additional tables), click the Design button.

▼    2. Locate the field named PublisherName. Move your cursor to the row header imme-
         diately left of the field name. The cursor will change to a right-facing arrow. Click
         your left mouse button to highlight the entire field (row). This portion of your
         screen should look like Figure 4.7.

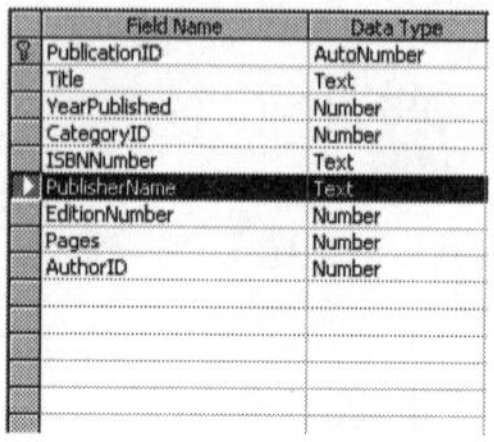

**FIGURE 4.7.**

*Highlighting a field
before deleting it.*

| Field Name | Data Type |
|---|---|
| PublicationID | AutoNumber |
| Title | Text |
| YearPublished | Number |
| CategoryID | Number |
| ISBNNumber | Text |
| PublisherName | Text |
| EditionNumber | Number |
| Pages | Number |
| AuthorID | Number |

3. Press the Delete or Del key, and Access gets rid of the field. Access may prompt
   you to confirm the deletion of the field. If it does so, instruct Access to go ahead
   and delete the field. Your screen should now look like Figure 4.8. In the following
   task you'll see how to add the PublisherID and hyperlink field to the table.

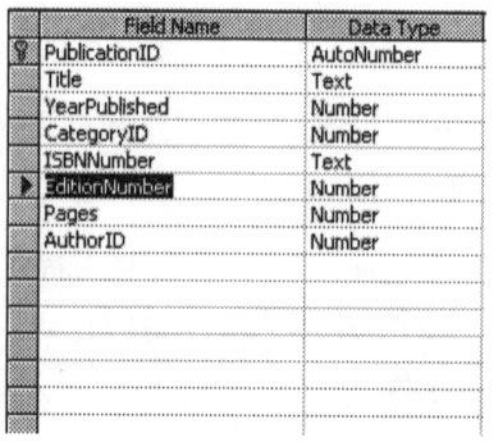

**FIGURE 4.8.**

*The Publications table
after field deletion.*

| Field Name | Data Type |
|---|---|
| PublicationID | AutoNumber |
| Title | Text |
| YearPublished | Number |
| CategoryID | Number |
| ISBNNumber | Text |
| EditionNumber | Number |
| Pages | Number |
| AuthorID | Number |

4. Now you'll add some missing captions. Captions aren't an absolute must for fields,
   but having them makes form and report creation in Access much easier. The first
   field needing a Caption property is the Title field. Click anywhere on its row in
   the grid.

5. Next, click in the Caption property text box at the bottom of the window. Enter
   Title.

6. Repeat this process for YearPublished (Year Published) and Pages (Page
   Count).

7. Save the table's design to this point by clicking the Save button on the toolbar or
▲    by using the File|Save menu item.

> **Tip**
>
> Because of a long-standing database convention, Access wizards use field names lacking white space. This stems from a time when database programs limited their field names to eight characters and couldn't handle white space within those names. Those days are, for the most part, long gone, but many database veterans still get nervous seeing a field name such as First Name, so the designers of Access concede the point and concatenate First Name to FirstName.
>
> There's a practical side to this as well. Field names without white space export to these older database programs much better. They also work properly with Structured Query Language (SQL), which Access uses. However, feel free to add white space to your field names if you're fairly sure you won't have to contend with older technologies and will use the Access query grid exclusively to create queries. At this point, you probably can't answer these questions, but keep them in mind for later.

# Adding Fields

You can easily add a field to an existing Access database. Here's how to add the `PublisherID` and hyperlink fields to the `Publications` table.

**4**

> **WHY THE WASTED EFFORT?**
>
> If you're thinking it would have been easier to just not include the `PublisherName` field when in the wizard than including it only to eliminate it later, you're right.
>
> The point of these two tasks isn't to be highly efficient, but to demonstrate how to do different things from within Access. After seeing how to do these operations, you should become not only proficient, but efficient using the program.

## Task: Adding a field to an existing table

▼ TASK ▼

1. This task, like the previous one, requires that you be on the Table Design View window for the `Publications` table. If you're not there, get there.

2. Although field position in the Design View window is mostly irrelevant, you'll add the `PublisherID` field immediately following the `PublicationID` field in an attempt to group the ID fields together. Move your cursor to the left border of the `Field Name` column in the row for the `Title` field. Your cursor will change to a right-facing arrow to highlight the row. Click your left mouse button.

▼  3. With the entire row containing the field name `Title` highlighted, press the Insert
      key on your keyboard. Access will insert a new empty row and push the field
      `Major` down one row. Your screen should now look like Figure 4.9.

**FIGURE 4.9.**

*Getting ready to add a new field name to an existing table.*

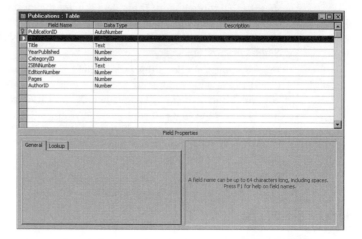

You don't need to highlight an entire row to insert a new field. Just clicking
in the `Title` field and then on the toolbar button Insert Field will do it.
Similarly, you could have deleted a field (row) by clicking in it and then clicking the Delete Row button in the toolbar.

   4. Click in the `Field Name` column of the highlighted row. The row will lose the
      highlight and your cursor will be at the extreme left of the `Field Name` column.
      Type the word `PublisherID`.

   5. Press the Tab key or click in the `Data Type` column. From the drop-down list box,
      select `Number`. Notice in Figure 4.10 that the field properties at the bottom of the
      Table Design window have changed to match a numeric type field. The defaults
      Access uses for this type of field are perfect for the `PublisherID` field.

**FIGURE 4.10.**

*The* Publications
*table after adding the*
PublisherID *field.*

| Field Name | Data Type |
|------------|-----------|
| PublicationID | AutoNumber |
| PublisherID | Number |
| Title | Text |
| YearPublished | Number |
| CategoryID | Number |
| ISBNNumber | Text |
| EditionNumber | Number |
| Pages | Number |
| AuthorID | Number |

▼

▼

**AUTOMATIC INDEX SELECTION**

Another important default Access has applied to the PublisherID field is its indexing property. Notice that the Indexed property at this point reads Yes (Duplicates OK). By default Access indexes any field that ends in ID, key, code, or num. You can, of course, change the Indexed property if Access's choice isn't correct. You can also change the list of field name suffixes which cause this by using the Tools|Options menu item, switching to the Tables/Queries tab of the Options dialog, and modifying the text in the AutoIndex on Import/Create text box.

6. In a similar way, add a new field, WebPage, directly below the CategoryID field. Make its data type Hyperlink. If you want to try something different, try clicking in the YearPublished field and then clicking the Insert Row button in the toolbar. The effect will be the same.

| Do | Don't |
|---|---|
| **DO** use whatever keyboard navigation methods you like. For example, you had a choice of pressing the Enter or Tab key after adding the field name Ethnicity to move the cursor to the Data Type column. What you choose to do depends on how you like to work and how you've worked in the past. The point is to get there, not the road you traveled during the journey. | **DON'T** worry about following the keystrokes in this book precisely. If your preferred method for using Access differs in some minor way from the instructions in this book, use whatever makes you comfortable. |

7. You've just added two new fields to the Publications table. Save the changes by clicking the Save toolbar button, using the File|Save menu item, or pressing Ctrl+S. Close the table either by double-clicking its control menu icon or by clicking the × button.

▲

# Creating a New Table Manually

Sometimes a table you need doesn't resemble anything in the wizard's samples. In these cases, you'll need to create one from scratch. Many database veterans are reluctant to let wizards take over their work, so they opt for manual design even if a good prototype exists in the wizard. No matter how experienced you are, you should get a feel for manual table design since it's only a matter of time until you need to use table design skills.

Actually, if you've already completed the previous two tasks in this chapter, you have a good idea of what it takes to manually design a table in Access.

---

**THE WIZARD STRIKES AGAIN!**

Actually, the Database Wizard has a rather competent sample called Book Collection, which is a database similar in function to the one manually created in *Sams Teach Yourself Access 97 in 21 Days*. However, this sample database is geared toward a home-based collection of books as opposed to an online bookstore.

Still, after completing this book, you'd be well advised to examine the results of this wizard to see how Microsoft tackled a situation similar to the one posed in this book.

---

**NEW TERM**   You need a table to store information about the publishers whose books are sold through the online bookstore. This table will have a primary key field named PublisherID that will serve as the link to the Publications table. *Linking* means that there is a relationship established between the tables. In this case it means that you can link a publication to a publisher. More information on linking and relationships can be found in Day 3.

This table will also need fields for publisher name, address, phone numbers, and contact information. In a more complete bookstore application, you'd probably have a separate table to store information about the various contacts at a given publisher. You'd have a ContactID field that would link the Publishers table to the Contacts table. For our purposes, however, we'll only allow for a single contact at each publisher.

# Creating the Table

After you close the Publications table, your screen should show just the Database window. If it doesn't, close the extra windows and navigate around Access until it does. The following task shows you how to create a table manually.

## Task: Creating a table without a wizard

1. Click the New button to start the table creation process. In the New Table dialog, select Design View and click OK. Access will immediately open a blank table design grid, similar to those you've been working with to this point.

2. Your cursor will be on the first row in the left-most (Field Name) column of the design grid. Take a moment to examine the square in the lower-right corner of the table design grid. Right now, it says A field name can be up to 64 characters long including spaces. Press F1 for help on field names. (Figure

4.6 shows this same message.) As you use Access, the program helps you along with tips (often valuable) such as this. As you work through this task, watch not only the prompts in this box but also those along the status bar at the very bottom of your screen.

3. Enter `PublisherID` for the first field name, and then press Tab or Enter to move to the `Data Type` field. Access will suggest the `Text` data type. Select `AutoNumber` from the Data Type drop-down list. The `PublisherID` field will be the key field for this table. The `AutoNumber` data type means that Access will automatically add unique numbers to this field for each record you create as you use this table. Look down at the bottom section of the screen and note that the `New Values` field is set to `Increment`. This is the default for the `AutoNumber` data type.

**Note**

Access suggested the `Text` data type because that is the Default Field Type setting that Access installs with. You can change the Default Field Type setting by using the Tools|Options menu item, moving to the Tables/Queries tab, and changing the value in the Default Field Type drop-down list box.

4

### UNLIKE NAMES, LIKE DATA

Link fields such as `PublisherID` need to hold like data, but don't necessarily need to be named identically. However, unless you have a business or functional reason to have different names for link fields, keep them the same to eliminate confusion.

| Do | Don't |
|---|---|
| **DO** comment your tables and other database objects with full descriptions if users will be asked to maintain them. Access shows the contents of the field description column in the status bar during data entry for a table. | **DON'T** be cryptic or overly cute when commenting. The comments or descriptions you think are clever today might come back to haunt you tomorrow. |

4. The next step is to define `PublisherID` as the primary key for the table. Note that Access has already divined that the field should be indexed because its name ends with `ID`. To make the field the primary key, right-click over the field's row in the design grid and select Primary Key from the shortcut menu. You can also click the Primary Key toolbar button when the cursor is anywhere on this field. Click in the next row of the design grid.

▼   5.  After moving to the next row, enter `PublisherName`. Again move to the `Data Type`
        column and accept Access's default by tabbing twice to move to the third row in
        the `Field Name` column. Repeat this process for `ContactName`, `ContactEMail`,
        `Address`, `City`, `State`, and `ZIP`. Your screen should now look like Figure 4.11.

**FIGURE 4.11.**

*In the middle of a
manual table design
session.*

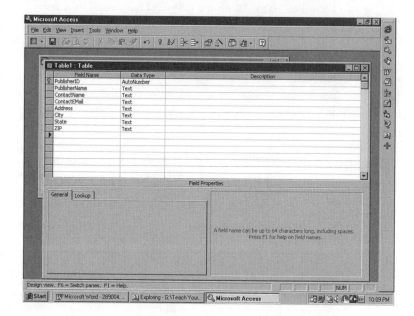

6.  Enter `Active` as the next field name and choose `Yes/No` as its data type. Move to
    the next `Field Name` row.

**Tip**

> When your cursor enters the `Data Type` field, press the Y key on your key-
> board. Access autoscrolls to the `Yes/No` data type. Pressing the A key would
> scroll to `AutoNumber` data type, and so forth. As you move through Access,
> you'll discover dozens of little ways its design speeds and simplifies your
> database chores.

7.  Next, enter `Phone` and leave `Text` as the data type. Since a typical phone number
    won't take more than 13 characters, click on the `Field Size` row in the Field
    Properties section of the table design grid. Change the default value of `50` to `13`.
    Repeat this for a field named `FAX`. Your screen should now look like Figure 4.12. In
    Day 6, "Working with Fields," you'll explore input masks you can use to format
▼   the data to look like a standard phone number. If you want to try this on your own,

▼        click in the row for the Input Mask property and click the Build button (it's the one to the right of the property's text box) to launch the Input Mask Wizard.

**FIGURE 4.12.**

*Changing a field size.*

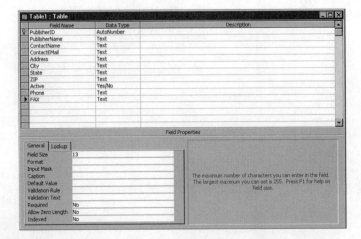

8. Finish this table's field names and data types by entering Comments and changing the data type to Memo.

9. Save and name this table. Click the menu item File and choose Close. Access will respond with a dialog asking you whether you want to save the changes to Table1. Click Yes. When prompted for a table name, enter Publishers and then click OK. Access will save the table and return you to the database window that now contains two tables: Publications and Publishers.

▲

# A Third Way to Create a Table

There's a third way to create a new table—by using the Datasheet View. The following section illustrates how this works, but there's no formal task. Now that you have a feel for manual table design, making a table by using the Datasheet View should be fairly easy, if you want to use this technique instead of Design View or a wizard. In general, however, you won't find much use for this method of creating a table. You'll probably be able to start simple tables with the Datasheet View, but you'll probably have to move to the Design View to finish the table.

To make a new table with the Datasheet View, make sure that the Tables tab is selected in the Database window. Click the New button and then choose Datasheet View from the New Table dialog's list box. See Figure 4.13.

**FIGURE 4.13.**

*Making a new table with the Datasheet View technique.*

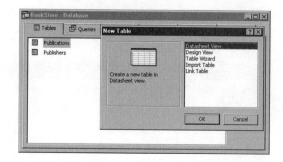

Access will grind away for a second and return with a blank datasheet, as shown in Figure 4.14.

**FIGURE 4.14.**

*The Datasheet View in design phase.*

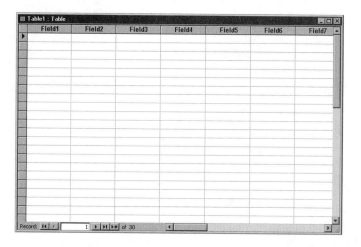

Defining fields is as easy as entering data in each field. Access will make a good guess as to the data type you want to have for each field, based on your initial entries. To name the fields, double-click the column headings—the places that now say Field1, Field2, and so forth. You have 20 columns to work with at first. If you need more, use the Insert|Column menu.

If you need to add a hyperlink column, use the Insert|Hyperlink Column menu item. If a column is a foreign key to another table, that column can be defined as a lookup column by using the Insert|Lookup Column menu item. This will launch the Lookup Wizard, which is discussed in Day 5.

When you're finished designing the table in Datasheet View, click the Save icon in the toolbar or use the File|Save menu. Access will ask whether you want it to add a primary key field to the table. If you haven't included a field appropriate for a primary key, you ought to take it up on its offer. Otherwise, decline and then move to Design View and set the primary key there, as you learned in the previous task.

Figure 4.15 shows the table from 4.16 with some data entered and the field names altered. Mimic these values and field names because this table will become the `Categories` table. Figure 4.16 shows the table in Design View. Note that Access dropped the columns without data and correctly assigned the data type to the fields. Note that you've also assigned the `CategoryID` field to be the primary key field for this table.

**FIGURE 4.15.**

*The table with data added to the fields and appropriate field names based on the contents.*

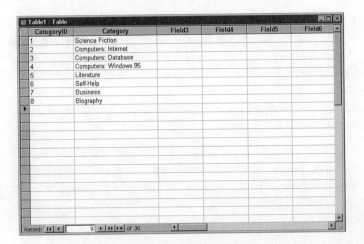

**FIGURE 4.16.**

*The table from Figure 4.15 in Design View, showing how Access automatically assigned the right data type to each field.*

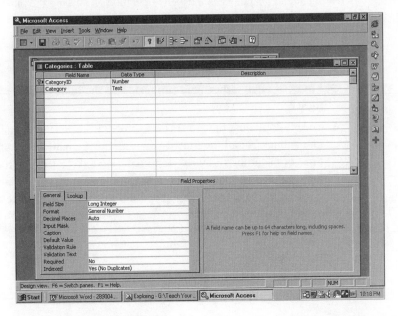

4

# Summary

The ongoing project you're doing in this book is an online bookstore system. Today you created two tables for this database. You created the first table, Publications, by using a New Table Wizard. Since a good prototype apparently didn't exist (or at least, we pretended it didn't), you manually created the second table, Publishers.

Often you'll need to change some elements of a wizard-created table. You can easily do this from the table design grid. For example, to change a field name, just double-click it to select it and then type in the new field name.

It's important to set the right data type for fields. Access defaults to the Text data type (unless you've changed the Default Field Type), which is appropriate for many fields. However, Access also has several less flexible data types, such as Number, and specialized number types, such as Currency. Use one of the Number or Date/Time data types for fields in which you'll need to perform math. If you won't be doing any calculations on a field, the safe approach is to leave it as a Text data type—even if you anticipate that all its entries will be numbers.

Each field also has a set of properties. These properties, such as field size, vary with the data type. Primary key fields always have the Indexed property set to Yes (No Duplicates) because the nature of key fields is that the data for any record can appear only once in a table, and Access indexes (or orders) a table primarily on the key field's entries.

Creating a table manually is the same operation as altering the entries in a wizard-created table. You can also create a table in Datasheet View.

# Q&A

**Q** **I noticed many other field properties in the table design grid. When do you set these?**

**A** The most efficient time to set these properties is during the initial design, but you lose nothing but a little time if you skip this originally and come back to it later. Most of the properties were skipped during today's tasks to focus on basic table-design methods. When you're familiar with Access and making your own applications, try to set as many field properties as you can anticipate during the initial design phase.

**Q I created a field with the Text data type. It accepted date entries such as September 2, 1994, just fine. Why should I bother with the Date/Time data type?**

**A** Date/Time is a specialized number format. You can perform date arithmetic on fields with this data type and, more importantly, Access will automatically verify that any values entered into Date/Time fields represent valid dates and times. Say you have a database with tables tracking loans, and you have fields for the starting and ending dates of those loans. If the data type is Text, you won't be able to use Access to calculate the time between these dates. If the data type is set to Date/Time, performing these calculations is simple. Later in this book, you'll see how handy the Date/Time data type is for this purpose.

**Q Yikes! My Access came without wizards.**

**A** If you chose to install Access in certain configurations, Setup won't install your wizards, so you need to re-run Setup and choose a fuller installation. See Appendix B, "Installing Access 97," for instructions on installing Access with all the wizards necessary for this book.

**Q Is there ever a reason to use the Text data type for numbers?**

**A** Yes. A Number data type field cannot start with a zero—since in a Number data type, zeros on the left are meaningless and Access will drop them. If you enter the number 010 into a Number data type field, Access will strip the left zero and enter just 10. For example, some zip codes begin with a zero, so you need to specify the Text data type.

# Workshop

Here's where you can test and apply the lessons you learned today.

## Quiz

1. What's the first step in creating a new Access table?
2. Why use a wizard when making a table?
3. What's the maximum size of a field with the data type set to Text?
4. What is the maximum number of characters (including spaces) for a field name in an Access table?
5. Say you're going to export a table called A List of My Friends to an old database system that can't handle white space in table names. What do you suppose will happen when you try to use this table in the older database system?

## Exercises

1. During the exercise, you entered a field named ISBNNumber in the Publications table. The field property Field Size was left at 50. Typically ISBN numbers are ten digits with three hyphens thrown in the mix. Open the Publications table in Design View and change the Field Size property for the ISBNNumber field to 13.

2. Add a field named CatalogCardNumber to the Publications table. Set the data-type format to Text and the Field Size to 20. This field will hold the Library of Congress Catalog Card Number, if known.

3. Use the New Table Wizard to create an Authors table. Include all fields suggested by the wizard. See if you can figure out what the proper action is when the wizard prompts you about the table's relationship to existing tables.

4. Your database should now have four tables: Publications, Publishers, Categories, and Authors. The database as it stands now is available on the CD-ROM that accompanies this book. The filename is DAY4FINAL.MDB.

# DAY 5

# Linking Tables with Relationships

Today you are going to go into relationships and some of the methods used to create them. Remember, relationships are how different tables of information are related to one another, and nothing more. If you can keep this basic concept in mind, you'll find working with table relationships straightforward.

There are four methods for creating relationships between tables of information:

- You can use the Table Wizard and it will question you as to how the tables you create are related.
- You can use the Lookup Wizard and define the relationship at the table level.
- You can use the Relationship window and establish relationships between tables.
- And, last, you can define them in VBA code.

Today's lesson will demonstrate the first three methods. Don't worry if you don't understand the last one completely. This method is mentioned to show that there are still places in Access 97 where VBA code can perform the same function as the user interface.

**Note** The material in this chapter relies heavily upon the concepts learned in Day 3, "Designing an Access Database." If you're a little rusty on that material, this would be a good time to skim that lesson, particularly the sections that discuss the various types of keys and relationships.

# Creating Relationships While Creating Tables

You should have already stumbled across the first method for creating relationships if you completed the "Exercises" section of Day 4, "Creating a New Database From Scratch."

In the following task, you are going to create a new table named `Reviews` and create a relationship between it and the `Publications` table that you created in Day 4. You'll do all this by using the now familiar Table Wizard.

### Task: Create a relationship while using the Table Wizard

1. The first step is to open the `BookStore` database. Click the Tables tab of the Database window.

2. Click the New button to launch the New Table dialog. Click Table Wizard in the list box and then click OK. The Table Wizard will start.

3. In the Wizard's first dialog, click the Personal option button. Then select Books in the Sample Tables list box.

**Note** Wait a minute. I thought we were creating a `Reviews` table. Why did I just select Books? Well, there is no sample table for `Reviews`, so you're going to use the next best thing and modify the Wizard's suggested fields, as you'll see in the next step.

4. In the Sample Fields list, double-click the `BookID` field twice, the `PublisherName` field twice, and the `Notes` field once.

5. In the Sample Tables list, click Diet Log (just bear with me). Then double-click the `DateAcquired` field to add it as well.

▼  6. Now you've got enough fields to construct the Reviews table, but obviously you need to work on those field names. Use the Rename Field button to rename each of the fields as shown:

| Old Field Name | New Field Name |
|---|---|
| BookID | ReviewID |
| BookID1 | PublicationID |
| PublisherName | AuthorName |
| PublisherName | AuthorEMail |
| Notes | ReviewText |
| DateAcquired | ReviewDate |

7. When you've finished renaming the fields, click Next. Enter Reviews as the table name and leave the Yes, Set a Primary Key for Me option button selected. Click Next.

8. Finally, you come to the point of this task: the dialog that allows you to define relationships. This dialog is shown in Figure 5.1. Notice that the Wizard has anticipated your next move and assumed that the new Reviews table is, indeed, related to the existing Publications table. Select the Related to 'Publications' entry in the list box and click the Relationships button.

**FIGURE 5.1.**

*The Table Wizard's relationship creation dialog.*

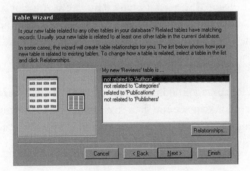

5

9. The Relationships dialog, shown in Figure 5.2, appears. Again, the wizard has anticipated your intentions and the chosen the correct option, One Record in the 'Publications' Table Will Match many Records in the 'Reviews' Table. This means that each publication can have many reviews. Click the middle option button and

▼

▼ notice the text that's displayed in the pane at the bottom of the dialog. If you were creating this type of relationship instead, the wizard can reach out and touch the related table, adding the field necessary to create the relationship.

**FIGURE 5.2.**

*The Relationships dialog.*

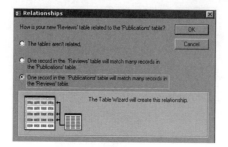

10. Click Cancel to close the Relationships dialog—you don't need to do anything here. Click Next. In the final dialog of the Table Wizard, select the first option, Modify the Table Design. Click Finish.

11. The table appears in design view. Click the row for `PublicationID` and then click the Lookup tab. You'll notice that the Lookup tab is pretty empty and, if you're like me, you'll be a little surprised. After all, didn't the Table Wizard say it was going to create the relationship? In the next task, you'll learn how to create this lookup. For now, close the Design View.

12. To prove that a relationship was created, open the Relationships window by using the Tools|Relationships menu item. Make sure all relationships are displayed by using the Relationships|Show All menu item. Now you can see that the wizard did its job: there is indeed a relationship between the `Reviews` and the `Publications`

▲ table. Leave the Relationships window open for the next task.

Try out this new relationship by doing the following:

1. Open both the `Reviews` and `Publications` tables in Datasheet View. Arrange these two windows so you can see the data from both onscreen (minimize the Database and Relationships windows and use the Window|Tile Horizontally menu).

**Note**

Leave the `PublisherID` field empty unless you know the ID of any publishers you may have entered. Later in this chapter you'll create a relationship that requires that data in the `PublisherID` field match between the `Publications` and `Publishers` tables.

2. If you don't have any data in your `Publications` table yet, enter a publication or two.

3. Make the Reviews Datasheet window the active window. Click in the `PublicationID` column. Now attempt to enter a number that does not appear in the `Publications` table's `PublicationID` column. Use a large number such as `100000`.

4. For now don't worry about entering other data. Click second row of the `Reviews` table to save this row.

**ANALYSIS** Nothing out of the ordinary seems to happen. However, part of the point of making a relationship between two tables is to insure that there is matching data (recall Day 3, "Designing an Access Database," where you learned about foreign key fields). Obviously there is no Publications record where `PublicationID = 100000`, so why did Access let you enter such data? The answer is that the Table Wizard's relationship didn't specify to enforce this data integrity rule. You'll correct this in the following task.

Now that you've got a `Reviews` table and it's somewhat related to the `Publications` table, look at another way to establish relationships while creating tables. This method involves using the Lookup Wizard. The Lookup Wizard assists you in creating a dropdown list for the field for which values will be drawn from another table. In the case of the `Reviews` table, you want to get values for the `PublicationID` field from the `Publications` table. The Lookup Wizard will set the field's properties to make this happen.

**Note** Before you begin the next task, if you entered data into your `Reviews` table, delete those rows now and then close the two Datasheet windows. And, because you'll be recreating the same relationship as in the previous task, delete the relationship by clicking the line that joins the `Reviews` and `Publications` tables and pressing the Del key. Close the Relationships window, saving changes should Access prompt you to do so.

The following task steps you through the process of using the Lookup Wizard.

## Task: Create a relationship with the Lookup Wizard

1. Return to the Database window's Tables tab. Click the `Reviews` table in the list of tables and then click the Design button.

2. In the design grid, click in the `PublicationID` row's `Data Type` column and drop down the list of available data types. Select Lookup Wizard from the list.

▼   3. The Lookup Wizard launches. In the first dialog, leave the default option, I Want
       the Lookup Column to Look Up the Values in a Table or Query, selected. The
       PublicationID values will be drawn from the Publications table, so this option is
       correct. Click the Next button.

    4. The Lookup Wizard presents you with a list of all of the tables in the database.
       Select the Publications table in the list. You could also view a list of queries by
       selecting either the Queries or the Both option button. Click Next.

    5. In the dialog that appears next, shown in Figure 5.3, you select which fields will
       appear in the drop-down list box the Lookup Wizard will create. Double-click the
       Title and EditionNumber fields to add them to the Selected Fields list box. Click
       Next.

**FIGURE 5.3.**

*The Lookup Wizard's
field selection dialog.*

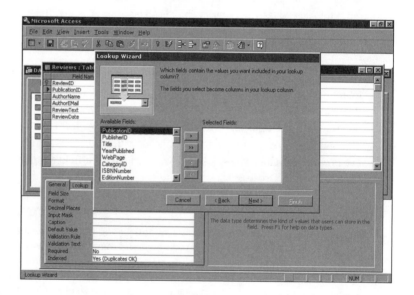

    6. In the next dialog you can specify the widths of the columns and whether or not the
       key column (the primary key from the related table) should be displayed. Expand
       the Title column by clicking the mouse between the column headers for Title
       and EditionNumber and dragging the column to the right.

       If you think that the check box is unnecessary because you didn't select the prima-
       ry key column from the Publications table in the previous step, think again. Clear
       the check box and you'll see that the wizard has automatically selected that field.
       In fact, if you click the Back button now, you'll see that PublicationID is in the
▼      Selected Fields list. Make sure the check box is checked and click Next.

7. In the wizard's final dialog you define the caption for the lookup column. Change the suggested caption to `Publication` and click Finish.

8. Access will prompt you to save the table before creating the relationship. Click Yes in this dialog.

9. Now, with the `PublicationID` field selected in the design grid, click the Lookup tab. Your screen should appear similar to Figure 5.4.

**FIGURE 5.4.**

*The results of the Lookup Wizard's work.*

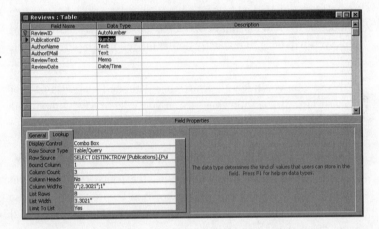

10. To see the lookup in action, you'll need some records in your `Publications` table. If you don't have any, add them now. Simply having the `Title`, `EditionNumber`, and `Pages` fields populated will be enough for now.

11. Open the Datasheet View for the `Reviews` table. Click in the `PublicationID` column and drop down the list. You should see the publications from your `Publications` table!

**Tip**

By default, the Lookup Wizard turns off the column headers for the drop-down lists it creates. In many cases where there are multiple columns in the drop-down list (as there are in the drop-down list created with the previous task), it's easy to forget what each column represents. To turn on the column headers, open the table in Design View, select the field in question, and go to the Lookup tab at the bottom of the Design View window. Change the `Column Heads` property from No to Yes and voilá! column headers appear in the drop-down list.

5

Although this task appears in a section describing how to create relationships while creating tables, there's nothing to prevent you from using the Lookup Wizard with an existing table. For existing tables, however, there are several more elegant ways to create relationships, as the next section demonstrates.

# Setting Up Relationships for Existing Tables

Sometimes, you will add a new table to an existing database and the wizards cannot help you define the relationship between the existing tables and the new one. When this happens, you will have to manually define the relationship by using the Relationships window.

In this section you'll learn how to work with the Relationships window to create new relationships. In the following section you'll learn how to modify the properties of a relationship.

## Working with the Relationships Window

To launch the Relationships window, use the Tools|Relationships menu item. The Relationships window launches, as shown in Figure 5.5. If you didn't complete the first task in this chapter, your window may be empty. Do not panic! In this section you learn how to view the existing relationships.

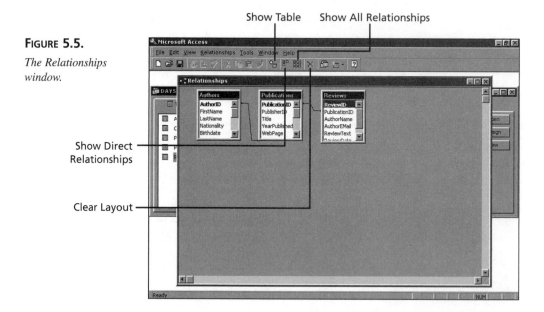

**FIGURE 5.5.**

*The Relationships window.*

Show Table     Show All Relationships

Show Direct Relationships

Clear Layout

Notice the new toolbar that appears immediately under the menu bar? This is the Relationship toolbar. The buttons specific to the Relationships window start at the middle of the toolbar. The first is the Show Table button. That's the one with the plus sign. You use this button to add tables to the Relationships window. Immediately to the right is the Show Direct Relationships button. Use this to view only the relationships defined for a particular table. Next to that one is Show All Relationships, which will show you all of the relationships defined for the database. Finally there's the Clear Layout button. This one is disguised as a Delete toolbar button, but the Relationship toolbar doesn't have a delete relationship button. Use this button to clear the workspace provided by the Relationships window. It has no effect on existing relationships, despite what the button's icon leads you to believe.

To remove an individual table from the Relationships window (which, like the Clear Layout button, has no effect on existing relationships), simply click in the table's field list and press the Del key. You can then use any of the appropriate Show buttons discussed in the previous paragraph to return the table to the Relationships window.

To delete an existing relationship, click the relationship line that joins the two tables in question. Then either press the Del key or use the Edit|Delete menu item. Access will verify that you want to delete the relationship before actually doing so, so try it now if you dare.

## Using Drag-and-Drop to Establish New Relationships

Now that you've seen how easy it is to get to and get around in the Relationships window, it's time to create a new relationship. The process goes something like this (as demonstrated in the next task):

1. If necessary, add the tables to the Relationships window using the Show Table button.
2. Drag the foreign key field from the first table to the primary key field in the related table.
3. Set the properties of the relationship and click Create.

Now for a specific example.

### Task: Create a relationship with drag-and-drop

1. Open the Relationships window. Click the Show Table button. Double-click the Publishers table in the Show Table dialog's list box. If the Publications table is not present in the Relationships window, double-click it as well. Close the Show Table dialog.

▼    2.  Back in the Relationships window, click the `PublisherID` field in the
         `Publications` table's field list. Drag this field and drop it on the `PublisherID` field
         in the `Publishers` table's field list.

     3.  The relationship properties dialog, shown in Figure 5.6, appears. Check the box
         labeled Enforce Referential Integrity. Doing so ensures that PublisherID data added
         to the `Publications` table matches a `PublisherID` in the `Publishers` table. You'll
         learn about the cascade properties in the next section.

**FIGURE 5.6.**

*The Relationships
properties dialog.*

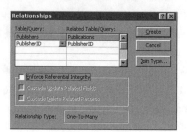

     4.  Click the Join Type button. The Join Properties dialog appears. The join properties
         are used by the Query designer and other tools to help you construct `JOIN` queries
         between the related tables. Select the third option button, which specifies that you
         want queries to return all of the records from the `Publications` table even if there
         is no matching record in the `Publishers` table. Click OK.

     5.  Finally, click the Create button. As long as there is no data in the `Publications`
         table that conflicts with the relationship you're creating, the relationship will be
         created and a line will join the two tables. If there is conflicting data, Access will
         inform you of this fact and refuse to create the relationship. In this case, you'll
▲        have to fix the data before proceeding.

     That's all there is to it. You now have a new relationship that will keep your Publications
     data in line with the `Publishers` table.

## Setting the Relationship's Properties

Now that you can relate tables, you're going to go into the properties associated with that
relationship. Looking back at Figure 5.6, you will see the window used to define the relationship properties.

Double-click the join line between the `Authors` and `Publications` tables. This will bring
up the Relationships properties dialog window.

## Setting the Type of Join

To set the type of join between the tables, click the Join Type button. The window shown in Figure 5.7 shows the kind of joins you can create between the tables.

**FIGURE 5.7.**

*Table Join Properties window.*

**NEW TERM** The first join, and the default, is called an *inner join*. This join only shows records that are related between the two tables. The other two joins are called *outer joins*, one left and one right. A *left outer join* is simply when all of the information in the left table is shown and only those records that are related in the right table are shown. The opposite is true for the *right outer join*. Click the OK button to go back to the relationship definition window.

## Enforcing Referential Integrity

In the middle, you will see a check box labeled Enforce Referential Integrity. By checking this box, you are telling Access that you don't want to be able to specify authors in the `Publications` table that do not exist in the `Authors` table. After you click it, two other check boxes are activated: Cascade Update Related Records and Cascade Delete Related Records.

**NEW TERM** *Cascade update* means that if you change the `AuthorID` in the `Authors` table, the publications that use that `AuthorID` in the `Publications` table will automatically be updated to the value.

**NEW TERM** *Cascade delete* means that if you delete an author from the `Authors` table, the books written by that author will be deleted from the `Publications` table. Be careful when defining a cascading delete. You do not always want to delete records in the related tables.

5

# Summary

Today you've learned the basics of creating relationships between tables. You've learned how to the Table Wizard creates relationships while creating tables, how to use the Lookup Wizard to not only create a relationship but also turn the foreign key field into a drop-down list box, and how to manually establish relationships with the Relationships window.

# Q&A

**Q Sometimes when I attempt to edit or delete a relationship, I get a message box informing me that one of the tables is in use by another person or process. How do I resolve this problem?**

**A** More than likely, the table specified in the message box is opened in Design view. Use the Window menu to see if the table has an open window. If it does, click its entry in the Window menu and close its window.

**Q I'm using the Relationships window to create a relationship and I've accidentally created the relationship between the wrong fields. Can I change the related fields?**

**A** Yes. Double-click the relationship line to open the properties dialog. You can use the grid on this dialog to change the fields or add new fields to the relationship.

**Q If I rearrange the relationships to a more aesthetic arrangement, will my changes be lost when I close the window?**

**A** No. Access will prompt you to save the modified layout. Click Yes in this confirmation dialog and the layout will be maintained for you.

# Workshop

Here's where you can test and apply the lessons you learned today.

## Quiz

1. Do the Table Wizard–created relationships specify to Enforce Referential Integrity?

2. What are the fields that match two tables in a relationship called? (You may have to review Day 3 to answer this one.)

3. How do you prevent unmatched records between two unrelated tables?

## Exercise

To test your newly learned skills, create a relationship between the Publications table and the Categories table. The process involves determining the appropriate fields, dragging and dropping in the Relationships window, and setting the new relationship's properties properly. As you'll see, defining relationships for additional tables is typically just a repeat performance of other relationships you've defined.

5

# DAY 6

# Working with Fields

On Day 4, "Creating a New Database from Scratch," you received an introduction to table field properties. Day 5, "Linking Tables with Relationships," was devoted to the basics of creating relationships. Today's lesson builds directly on that foundation. Today, you'll learn about the following:

- Using an input mask
- The `Field Size` property
- Rearranging field order in a table
- Altering the apparent size of a field
- List and combo boxes in tables
- The field properties for different data types
- Setting a default value for a field
- The `Format` property
- Using the `Validation Rule` and `Validation Text` properties

This might seem like a lot of territory to cover, but each new technique follows logically from the one that precedes it. The material about data validation, defaults, and input masks directly addresses the integrity of your data, so pay particular attention to those sections—especially if you're planning on creating a database application for others to use. Keep in mind that although much of this is rather dry, it's important.

To get started, open the database that you were working on yesterday, the BookStore.mdb file you've been building as you work your way through this book. If you haven't been working along with us (shame on you), you can get the database from the CD-ROM. It'll be named DAY5FINAL.MDB.

## Quality Assurance, Data-Entry Style

If the only thing you want Access to do is store raw data, you need go no further, but it's capable of much more. One of the ways in which an electronic storage system such as Access is superior to a paper-based system is that the electronic system can examine input and then, based on rules you supply, accept or reject it.

You can edit data in an Access table in much the same way you edit field names during the table design phase. For example, open the Publishers table in Datasheet View and enter the number 12345 in the Year Published column. Although that will be a valid year 10,000-plus years or so from now, it's not quite realistic to believe your BookStore database will be around then (I can hear the hisses now from all those who are working to solve the Year 2000 problem). You really only need concern yourselves with four digit years.

**Note**

> For those of you who have been locked away in Siberia for the last decade, the Year 2000 problem involves converting those computer programs that were designed to use two digit years (where 1998 is represented simply with "98") to ones which use four digit years. Computer programmers from the 60s and 70s never imagined their programs would still be living at the turn of the century, and to conserve valuable storage space, decided to drop the century from date fields. After the turn of the century, many programs will think that 00 represents not the year 2000 but the year 1900. I think you can see the problems this can cause!

 **NEW TERM** The reason Access accepted 12345 as a YearPublished value is because you didn't tell it not to. You can solve the problem of inappropriate entries by using an *input mask*. Also called a field template, an input mask is a set of literals and placeholders that control the data that is entered into a field. For example, the input mask that appears (###)###-#### uses the () and the – characters as literals. The # is a place-holder for a number. As you likely can see, this input mask limits entry into this field to U.S.-style phone numbers.

Before moving on, reset the record you edited to its original value.

 **New Term** Access heavily utilizes the word *view*, which replaces the more descriptive term *mode* for many Access activities. So, although you might think you are in Table Design *mode*, Access's term for this is Table Design View. The term view is certainly overused in Access, but once you get used to it…well, you'll be used to it.

The following task shows how to add an input mask.

## Task: Adding an input mask

1. If you didn't follow along in the earlier example, open the Publications table in Table Design View. If you did follow along, you should have the Publications table opened in Datasheet View. Locate the Design View button on the toolbar (the button to the far left). When you're in Datasheet View, as now, this button has a pencil and a triangle on it. When you're in Design View, it has a representation of a datasheet on it. At any time, you can click this button's pull-down list to see all your current view options. Click the Design View button to switch from the table's Datasheet View to Design View. After the switch, your screen should look like Figure 6.1.

**FIGURE 6.1.**

*The table returned to Design View.*

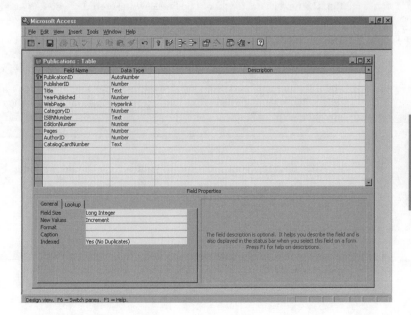

▼     2. Click the field name `YearPublished` because you'll initially be setting a field property for this field.

       3. Examine the field properties at the lower part of the Table Design View window. One of the properties is labeled `Input Mask`. Click in the now empty text box just to the right of the `Input Mask` property label.

          Note that when you clicked the text box for `Input Mask`, a button with three dots appeared to the right of the field. This is a *builder button*, and there are many of them scattered through Access. Clicking a builder button brings up an appropriate builder or wizard. Unfortunately, because you're on a field with the data type `Number`, clicking this button or the toolbar's build button displays a dialog informing you that the Input Mask Builder Wizard only works with `Text` and `Date` data types. So this exercise will create the input mask manually.

       4. Enter `0000;1;"-"` for an input mask. The *0*s in the input mask are placeholders indicating that you must enter a total of four numbers for this field, no more, no less. Press Tab to move to the next field.

---

**ACCESS INPUT MASKS**

Access input masks have three parts. The first part is the look of the mask. Entering `??-??` enables the acceptance of any four characters but separates them with a dash. Access will add a backslash before the dash in this case because the backslash indicates to Access that the next character should be literally interpreted. If you had an input mask such as `?\??`, Access would accept any two characters separated by a question mark.

The second part of the input mask comes after the semicolon. This can be blank, a numeral 1, or a 0 (a zero). A blank or a 1 in this space tells Access to store only the field's data; a 0 tells Access to store not only the input data, but also the formatting characters.

The third and final part of an input mask tells Access what character to use as a placeholder. This example uses `"-"` to tell Access that you want to use the minus sign as a placeholder.

---

▼     After entering your input mask, your screen should resemble Figure 6.2.

FIGURE 6.2.

*An input mask.*

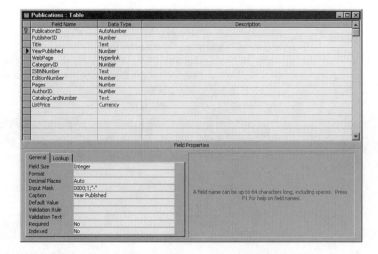

# Trying Out the Input Mask

Return to Datasheet View by either clicking the Datasheet View button in the toolbar—it's the one second from the left—or choosing View|Datasheet View from the menu. Access will tell you that you must save your changes before entering Datasheet View. Since that's what you want, click Yes.

Click the New Record toolbar button to enter a new record. Try to enter 12A45. Two things then happen. First, Access adds dashes throughout the field, and second, it refuses to accept the entire entry. The input mask told Access to use the minus sign as the placeholder and not to accept more than four numbers for this field.

Press Esc to cancel this record's data entry and then add another new row. Click back on the YearPublished field for the new row, enter the incomplete year 198 and then press Tab or Enter. Access displays one of its standard message boxes telling you that your entry doesn't meet the requirement of the input mask you've defined. Click OK to acknowledge this message. Access refuses to accept a Year Published entry shorter than the input mask.

6

**Note**

> YearPublished or Year Published? You might wonder at Access's display of the `YearPublished` field as "Year Published" in the column head. The name of this field is `YearPublished` without spaces. The `Caption` property of the `YearPublished` field is Year Published with a space. Check it out yourself by switching to Design View for Publications and then examining the `Caption` property setting.
>
> The `Caption` property tells Access how to display a field's name in tables and queries or by default in reports and forms.
>
> When referring to this field in queries, reports, forms, code, or macros, use the real name of the field, `YearPublished`. The `Caption` property is only for appearance sake, not internal usage.

Press Esc to cancel data entry and then close the window. Open the `Publishers` table in Table Design View. Click the `Phone` field and then click the `Input Mask` property. Click the Input Mask Wizard button to launch the Input Mask Wizard. Select Phone Number in the Wizard's Input Mask list and click Finish. Now for the `Input Mask` property you'll see `!\(999") "000\-0000;;_`. The big difference between this and the previous input mask is that here Access has `9` *and* `0` as placeholders. The `9` means entry is optional, but must be numeric; the `0` means entry is mandatory and numeric. The `!` tells Access to fill this field from right to left. This means that if you add a phone number without an area code, you'll get 555-1234 rather than (555) 123-4 as the entry for the field. The `!` can appear anywhere in an input mask, but by convention usually appears first. The quotation marks in `")  "` simply wrap the `)` (end parenthesis followed by a space). Save the table design and move to the table's Datasheet View.

**Note**

> Input masks will operate only on newly added data. They won't go back and affect previously entered values.

| **Do** | **Don't** |
| --- | --- |
| **DO** use input masks, especially in applications where you expect a lot of data entry, because they make data-entry chores much easier. | **DON'T** ignore the second part of the input-mask field. Generally speaking, you don't want to embed input-mask literals in your data, but if you do, you must tell Access specifically that you do. |

# Changing Field Order

Changing the order of fields in a table is something you might want to do from time to time. Keep in mind that the order in which fields appear in the design grid doesn't force you to have fields in the same order in Datasheet View, forms, or reports. Typically database designers will group like fields together in an attempt to make the design more self-documenting. For example, system-handled columns such as InsertDate and PublisherID will usually be grouped together while columns for user data will usually be grouped together.

## Moving a Field

Click the Design View button to bring up the table design grid. The following task moves the Active field to just under the FAX field.

### Task: Changing the field order of a table

1. Single-click the gray border just to the left of the field named Active. Access highlights the entire row, just as it did when you inserted or deleted a field.

2. Move the cursor back to the gray area you clicked to highlight the row. Click and drag until the moving dark line appears just below the FAX field.

4. Release the mouse button to drop the field to the space below FAX. Your screen should now look like Figure 6.3.

5. Return to Datasheet View, telling Access it's OK when it reminds you that you must save changes before changing view.

6. Scroll over so you can see the FAX field and the field just to its right. The field to the right of PhoneNumber is now Active rather than Comments.

**FIGURE 6.3.**

*A field moved and dropped to a new location.*

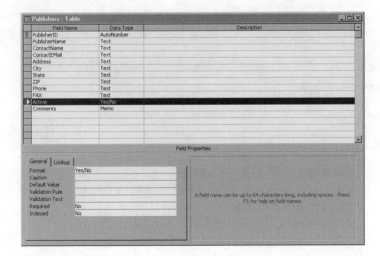

6

## Changing the Apparent Field Order

When you change the field order in the field design grid, you also change the order in which the fields appear in the Datasheet View. However, you can make changes in the Datasheet View that won't change the field order in the Database Design View. The following task illustrates this.

### Task: Changing the apparent field order

1. If you're not in Datasheet View, click the toolbar or use the menu selections in the View menu to make that view current.

2. Click the column header for the Comments field. The entire Comments column will then be selected. (See Figure 6.4.)

**FIGURE 6.4.**

*Getting ready to move a column in Datasheet View.*

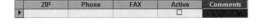

3. Move your cursor over the column header again. You've hit the appropriate place when the cursor changes to look like a left-leaning arrow. Click again without moving the mouse, but this time hold the mouse button down. You'll get a "ghost" rectangle at the base of the cursor. Drag the cursor to the left until a black line appears between the fields FAX and Active, and then release the mouse.

   The Comments field now appears just to the right of the FAX field. Your screen should look like Figure 6.5.

4. Switch to Design View. Note that the Comments field remains below the Active field, just as it did before you moved it in the Datasheet View.

**FIGURE 6.5.**

*A field moved in the Datasheet View, but not in Design View.*

Changing field locations or widths in the Datasheet View *does not* change their location in Design View, but changing field locations in Design View *does* change field locations in the Datasheet View.

# Changing Field Widths and Row Heights

The `Field Size` property for `Text` fields determines the capacity of the fields but doesn't affect how wide they appear in the Datasheet View. Naturally, that leaves some fields looking too small and others too wide in the `default` Datasheet View. Changing apparent field sizes from Access's `default` in the Datasheet View is quite simple, as the following task demonstrates.

## Task: Changing apparent field widths and height

1. Return to Datasheet View, if you haven't already done so.

2. Most street addresses are longer than the default size Access has allowed for fields in the `Publishers` table Datasheet View, so the next step shows you how to make this field look a bit wider.

   Move your cursor into the gray area where field names appear. Now move the cursor to a point between the `Address` and `City` fields. The cursor changes to a wide vertical beam with left- and right-facing arrows.

3. Click and hold the mouse button. Keeping the mouse button down, drag the cursor to the right to widen the `Address` field. When it's roughly one-and-a-half times larger, release the mouse button. The field is now wide enough for most street addresses.

   That's all there is to making a field wider. To make a field *deeper*—to increase row height—use the preceding steps, except move your cursor to the gray area left of the left-most field. Then move the cursor between two rows until the cursor becomes a horizontal bar with up- and down-facing arrows. Click and drag the row to its new height. (See Figure 6.6.)

**FIGURE 6.6.**

*A field made to look wider in the Datasheet View.*

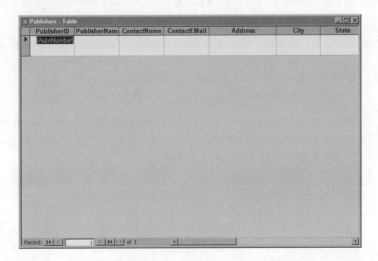

NEW TERM Access calls these appearance changes *layout changes*. When you close a table, Access asks whether you want to save these field width and height layout changes. This gives you the freedom to make layout changes for a session, and then discard them when closing the table. You can also accept Access's offer and make the changes permanent until the next datasheet session, when you again have the option to alter the layout.

You might wonder why you'd ever want to change a row height in a datasheet, but there are two common uses for greater row height. If you store pictures in a database, the standard row height won't show them very well, so increasing it is just the ticket. Also, if you have long Text or Memo field entries, trying to view those entries in one long text row is impractical. If you change the row height to accommodate more than one line, Access wraps the long text entry to fit in as many lines as you want.

Well, that's it for now. Close the Publishers table. When Access asks whether you want to save the layout changes, click No.

## Combo and List Boxes in Tables

It's easier and safer to add or edit table data through forms, but Microsoft responded to user requests and has, in Access 95 and now repeated in Access 97, made entering data directly into tables easier. The reasons to use forms for data entry or editing are discussed in the chapters addressing forms, but if you're determined to manipulate tables directly, here are a few things to make your life easier.

In addition to input masks and other data-validation services covered today, you'll see how Access 97 enables you to look up existing data in another table when entering data directly into a table. Here's a quick look at how this works. Although this isn't an "official" exercise, feel free to follow along with these steps.

You don't want to add data in the Publications table for a nonexistent publisher—that is, one not already entered in the Publishers table. When you established a link between the Publications and Publishers tables yesterday, you made sure this couldn't occur because you checked the Enforce Referential Integrity check box.

However, looking up the right PublisherID when entering data in Publications can be a royal pain. Again, these chores should be handled only through forms, but here's how to simplify the task using only tables.

1. Open the Publications table in Design View. If you're at the database window, click the Publications table and click the Design button.

2. Click in the PublisherID field, and then click the Lookup tab in the Field Properties section. Click the pull-down icon in the Display Control field and select Combo Box. The screen then changes to accommodate the needs of a combo box in a table.

 **Note**

> Several fields in this and other Properties list boxes are toggles—fields with a few possible entries. These entries are often limited to two: Yes and No. To change a Yes/No entry in a Properties list box from one to the other, double-click in the field where the Yes/No entry is.

3. Change the properties for the Lookup tab to match Figure 6.7. Set Row Source to Publishers, Bound Column to 1, Column Count to 2, Column Heads to Yes, and Limit to List set to Yes.

**FIGURE 6.7.**

*Setting the properties for a table combo box.*

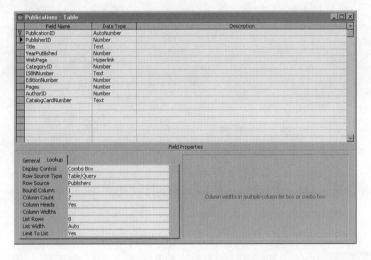

4. Switch to Datasheet View, saving the changes. Widen the PublisherID field to about twice its default size, and then move to the field. Note that a pull-down icon appears when the field has the focus. Click this icon to see all the PublisherIDs currently in Publishers, along with the names of the publishers for each PublisherID (see Figure 6.8).

6

**Note**

If you see no items in the drop-down list it may be that there are no publishers in the `Publishers` table. If this is the case, add a few publishers such as Sams, Macmillan, and Microsoft Press. It could also be that there is a default value of 0 set for the `PublisherID` field in the `Publications` table. Check on the Design View that this is *not* the case because, by default, Access set the `Default` property for `Number` fields to 0.

5. Return to Design View and undo the `Lookup` properties set in the previous three steps to get your database back in sync with the book's. The easiest way to do this is to change the `Display Control` property back to Text Box.

**FIGURE 6.8.**

*A combo box in a table.*

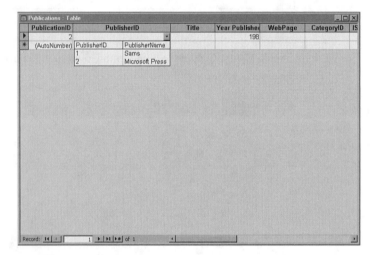

# More on Field Properties

Earlier in this chapter, you saw how adding an input mask to a field can make data entry easier and help make sure the data entered into that field is appropriate.

**NEW TERM** The term *data integrity* is database jargon for ensuring that data entered into a database is correct not only for the field and table, but also for the database in general. There are several other field property settings that can make your data entry easier and/or ensure your data's integrity. Take a look at these properties by doing this: Open the `Authors` table in Design View, click the `FirstName` field, and look at the Field Properties list box. Your screen should resemble Figure 6.9.

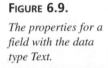

**FIGURE 6.9.**

*The properties for a field with the data type Text.*

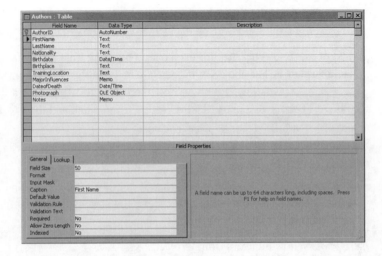

Now click the Notes field. The Properties list box changes to list only those field properties that a Memo field can have. Click the BirthPlace field, and the list box switches back to Text data type properties.

Figure 6.10 shows you the properties for a Number field. Each data type has a particular set of properties associated with it. The Notes field lacks an Index property because you can't index a field with the data type Memo. The best way to learn about the available properties for each data type is to change a field's data type to each of the available types and note the Properties section.

**FIGURE 6.10.**

*The field properties of a Number data type.*

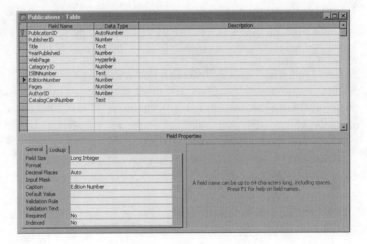

6

The last entry in the Data Type list, Lookup Wizard, isn't strictly a data type; it's a wizard used to have a field look up data existing in another table.

Most of the field properties for each data type are at least somewhat self-explanatory from their labels, but one isn't. In a Text data type, the field size means the amount of space that Access allows for an entry. Therefore, a text field with a field size of 5 can't hold the 11-space text entry "Hello World!" (The blank and the exclamation point each take one space, too.)

Take a look at Figure 6.10, which shows the field properties for a Number data type. There's an entry for field size there too, but in the case of a Number data type, field size has a completely different meaning than it does for a Text data type. Field size in a Number data type means number precision. The various field sizes for a Number data type are as follows:

*Byte*—Whole numbers from 0 to 255.

*Integer*—Whole numbers from -32,768 to 32,767.

*Long Integer*—Whole numbers from -2,147,483,648 to 2,147,483,647.

*Double*—Decimal numbers with 10 places of precision.

*Replication ID*—A very long number used to uniquely identify a record. The length of this number should prevent another record from having the identical number. The common name for a Replication ID is GUID, for Globally Unique Identifier.

*Single*—Decimal numbers with 8 places of precision.

Each of these field sizes requires a different amount of storage in your computer. For example, Access reserves eight bytes of space for a number with a field size of "double," but only a single byte for a number with the field size of "byte."

The reason for having large field-size type numbers, such as single and double, is to ensure precision in calculations. The more precisely a number is stored in Access, the more precise the calculations using that number will be. This is particularly important in repeating calculations (or more precisely, recursive calculations), in which the results of one calculation are fed back in for further iterations. The most common class of recursive calculations are interest calculations, which add a period's interest to the principal to form the basis of the principal for the next period's calculation.

# Default Values of Access

The default value for a field is a handy property; when you specify one, Access automatically supplies that value during data entry. One helpful feature of default values is that you can override them, so setting defaults causes no penalty in your application.

Defaults can be either hard-coded values or can be derived from functions. The typical default value for a field that tracks the date/time a record was inserted into the database is the value =Now().

| Do | Don't |
|---|---|
| DO assign default values liberally in your applications. Even if you override them most of the time, you'll end up saving time overall. | DON'T be concerned about potential penalties or "gotchas" that a default field value might create. There are none. |

Almost all of the books that will be entered into the BookStore database are going to be recently published works. Therefore, you can save a lot of data entry time by entering a default for the YearPublished field. The following task shows how it's done.

### Task: Setting a Default Field property

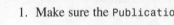

1. Make sure the Publications table is open in Design View.
2. Click the YearPublished field in the Field Name column.
3. Click in the Default Value text box of the Field Properties list box.
4. Enter =Year(Now()) for a value. See Figure 6.11.

**FIGURE 6.11.**

*Creating a default value for a field.*

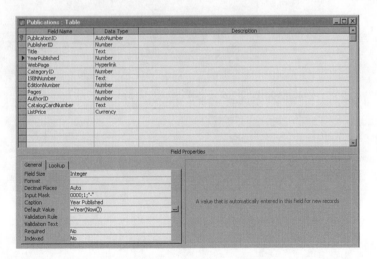

6

▼ It's that easy.

5. Now switch back to Datasheet View, saving the changes when Access reminds you that you must. Enter a record with the following data:

**TABLE 6.1.** DATA FOR Publications TABLE.

| Field | Data |
|---|---|
| Title | Sams Teach Yourself Access 97 in 21 Days |
| YearPublished | 1998 |
| WebPage | http://www.mcp.com |
| ISBNNumber | 0-672-31298-0 |
| EditionNumber | 1 |
| PageCount | 800 |

Did you notice that before you got to the YearPublished field, Access not only filled in this field for the new record but subsequent records as well? Look at Figure 6.12, which shows how Access is now supplying a default value for the State field.

6. Here's how to use a field with a default value. If the record you're entering uses the default value, just press Tab or Enter when you get into this field. If you need to change the default value to another, just tab into the field with the default value and enter the right data.

▲

**FIGURE 6.12.**

*The Default Fields property in action.*

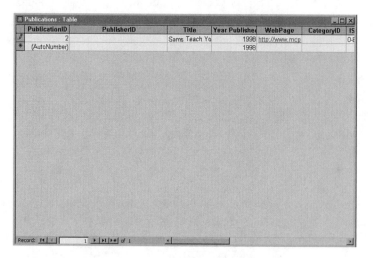

NEW TERM    If you're bothered by the term *default* for a value that's automatically assigned
by Access to a field, you're not alone. Default, which means "failing in an oblig-
ation" to most English speakers, is standard computerese for any automatically assigned
value. This is one term that the Access team didn't make up. It's borrowed from a long-
standing computer tradition.

# Data Validation

In many cases, you'll want to limit field entries to one or a specific group of selections.
One way to do this in Access is to set the `Data Validation` field property. The task that
follows isn't an optimal use of the `Data Validation` property—it was chosen for its
simplicity—but working through it and reviewing the table of data-validation examples
will give you a good idea of this field property's use.

### Task: Setting the `Data Validation` field property

This exercise limits the possible entries for the `Pages` and `EditionNumber` fields in the
`Publications` table to positive values to ensure data consistency.

1. Get the `Publications` table to Design View, if it isn't there already.

2. Click the `EditionNumber` field to let Access know you want to set a field property
   for this field.

3. Click the `Validation Rule` property.

4. Enter `>=0`.

5. Tab to move away from this field.

6. Repeat steps 2 through 5 for the `Pages` field, only enter `>0` as the validation rule
   (after all, your bookstore wouldn't get much money for a book with no pages).

7. Return to Datasheet View, saving the changes when Access reminds you that you
   haven't. Access displays an additional message box reminding you that data-
   validation rules have changed, and some previously entered data might not meet
   the new criteria. It asks permission to search previous field entries to see whether
   they meet the new criteria. Click No, and then move to the `Edition Number` field
   for any row. Enter `-12`.

8. Try to tab away from this field. Access gives a slightly rude and oddly worded, but
   informative, message box saying that the new entry violates the data-validation rule
   for this field. Click OK, and then press Esc to return this value to its original entry.
   Repeat this for the `Page Count` field to make sure you have the validation rule set
   there as well.

▼ TASK

▲

6

In the following exercise, you'll change the error message from Access's choice to a custom one.

## Task: Making a data validation error message

1. Return to Design View, click `EditionNumber`, and then click the field property `Validation Text`.

2. Enter `Please enter a number greater than or equal to 0 for this field`.

3. If it bothers you that you can't see all the text you're entering, press Shift+F2 to enter the Zoom view. This gives you a large editing area for entering this message. When you're done editing and entering your new message, just click OK to exit Zoom view.

4. When you're through entering the validation text for `EditionNumber`, repeat for the `PageCount` field entering `Please enter a number greater than 0 for this field`. Return to Datasheet View. Click OK when Access gives you the save reminder.

5. Repeat the procedure you used when trying to change the `Edition Number` and `Page Count` columns. Access still won't accept the entry because it violates the validation rule you set, but this time it gives you your custom message-box message. Click OK to close the message box, and then press Esc to return the field to its original value.

The following table lists some additional examples of validation rules for table fields:

**TABLE 6.2.** VALIDATION RULE EXAMPLES.

| Example | Meaning |
| --- | --- |
| `=5` | Must be 5. |
| `Between 1 and 5` | Between 1 and 5 inclusive. |
| `Between #2/3/90# AND #1/31/92#` | Any date from February 3, 1990 to January 31, 1992, inclusive. |
| `Like "A[a-z]B"` | Must begin with the letter A, contain any letter from a to z as the second letter, and end with B. |
| `Like "V####"` | Must start with V followed by four digits. Valid entries are `V5888`, `V9023`, or `V0000`, for example. |
| `="USA"` | Must be USA. |
| `In ("Arizona", "New Mexico")` | Can be either New Mexico or Arizona. |
| `Not "New York"` | Any entry that's not New York. |
| `Not Between 1 and 10` | Any number not between 1 and 10 inclusive. |

## The Required Property

The Required property is another field property you'll use extensively. This field property extends for all field types. It's somewhat self-explanatory. Access won't accept a record without an entry in the field or fields where this property is set to Yes.

## A Date-Specific Property

The Date/Time data type has several predefined Format properties. Figure 6.13 is a sample table in Design View with the Format property combo box pulled down to show the different predefined formats along with their examples.

All data types have a Format property, and the Date/Time data type has several predefined formats. These are as many as most people need, but you can create your own formats. For information on this, search online help using "Format" as a search criteria.

**FIGURE 6.13.**

*The formats for the Date/Time data type.*

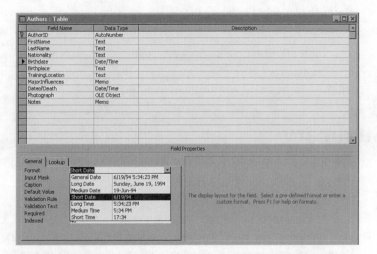

## Two Number-Specific Properties

As discussed previously, the Number data type has a Field Size property, which is different from the Field Size for Text fields. If left to default, Access will choose Long Integer for the field size of a number. This is the most commonly used Number field size and is fairly economical in database resources. If you're sure all your numerical data for a particular number field will be whole (that is, nondecimal numbers), specify Byte or Integer or leave things at Long Integer for this property. If you need decimal precision, use Single or Double, depending on how much precision you need.

6

You can change the default field sizes for Text and Number data types by opening the Options dialog (use the Tools|Options menu item), switching to the Tables/Queries tab, and entering new values in the drop-down list boxes found in the Default Field Sizes frame.

There's only one caution here: When you're going to relate two fields and the key field on the "one" side of a one-to-many relationship is an AutoNumber data type set to Increment, the matching field in that case is Long Integer. Therefore, if your primary field in a relationship is AutoNumber-Increment, make the data type and format of its link field a data type Number with Field Size Long Integer.

The other special property for Number fields, one that they share with the Currency data type, is the Decimal Places property. Access defaults to Auto for the Decimal Places field property. Auto means that the format for the field (that is, what it looks like) determines the number of decimal places shown. Keep in mind that the number of decimal places shown doesn't change the precision of the number. A number with the field size Double will double the precision no matter to what the Decimal Place property is set.

That's it for the discussion of field properties. This is a vital part of Access since tables hold the data for any of your applications. Because of this, any topics relating to tables will have far-reaching ramifications in an Access project.

# Summary

Today you learned how to create an input mask to format data's appearance, and how to change the look of tables by altering the order and width of columns or the height of rows.

You then learned how changing the location of a field in the table design grid changes its location in the Datasheet View. You can also change a field's location and size in the Datasheet, but doing so won't affect either the field's position in the design grid or the Field Size property.

Access has many settings for different field properties. You can specify a default value for a field that you can override or a validation rule that you can't. Access gives you an informative (but abrupt) error message if you try to enter a value in a table that violates data validation rules. You can change this message to one of your own choosing by adding a Validation Text property.

One of the most commonly used field properties is the Required property. If you set this property to Yes, Access requires an entry in this field before accepting a record. Key fields have their Required property set to Yes by inference.

Fields with the Number data type use the property called Field Size to specify how much precision they have. This directly affects the amount of data storage space Access reserves for entries in this field. Although Double is the most precise field size for the Number data type, letting all your number fields remain at the default Long Integer size isn't right for all occasions, even though it's commonly used. Try to use the most economical field size for your numbers consistent with your need for precision.

**Caution**

> Past versions of Access used Double as the default Number data type. If you've used Access in the past, watch out for this "gotcha."

The Number and Currency data types share the property called Decimal Places. This controls how the data appears, not the underlying precision of the field.

Finally, the Date/Time data type has some unique format properties predefined. You can show data in Access by using these predefined format types or you can define your own.

# Q&A

**Q If I change the size and location of a field in Datasheet View, will Access preserve those changes?**

**A** When you close the datasheet, Access asks whether you want to save your layout changes. If you click Yes, those changes will be preserved; otherwise, they'll be discarded.

**Q Can I enter decimal numbers in a field with the data type Integer?**

**A** You can enter them, but Access rounds them off to the next highest whole number.

**Q Can I enter fractions, such as 1/2, in a Number field?**

**A** Access has no native way to accept fractions in a Number field. You can enter 1/2 in a Text field as a text entry, but you can't use it in calculations since it's a text value. However, you can enter the value 1/2 in a Number field by entering its decimal equivalent, .5.

**Q Can I change data type for a field after I've already entered some values?**

**A** Yes, but you might lose data. For example, consider a Text data type field containing numbers for all records except one that reads Sam. Converting the data type from Text to Number will cause you to lose the Sam entry. Access gives plenty of warnings before it discards any of your data, but if you insist, it will go ahead with the conversion.

6

# Workshop

Here's where you can test and apply the lessons you learned today.

## Quiz

1. You're in Datasheet View. How can you tell when your cursor is located in the correct position to change a field's apparent width? Apparent height?

2. Will moving a field in Datasheet View change that field's position in the table design grid?

3. Will the validation rule "A#" accept the value A1?

4. If you set a Default property for a field, can you override it during normal data entry? If not, what must you do to override the default value?

5. Will the validation rule "Between #1/2/90# and #2/1/90#" accept the value 1/5/91?

6. Why bother making input masks?

## Exercises

1. Open the Authors table in Design View.

2. Change the default value for Birthplace from blank to Richmond.

3. Try entering a record using data of your own. Did the default value work? Delete this record by clicking the gray area just to the left of the record (the record selector) and pressing the Delete key. Confirm with Access that you want to delete this record.

4. (This one is a toughie.) Return to Design View. Using the following bits of information, design an input mask that allows up to 12 letters for any entry in the FirstName field, capitalizes the first letter of the name automatically, and enters the rest of the name in lowercase. The following are some characters used in input masks and their meanings:

    > means what follows in the mask is uppercase

    L means you must enter a letter

    < means what follows is lowercase

    ? means any character or space including blanks

   If you need to, search the Online Help system, using the keywords "input mask," or ask the Office Assistant for a hint.

5. If you give up on Number 4, you can find the solution after the quiz answers for this chapter.

6. Delete the input mask for the FirstName field. (Optional.)

7. Close the Authors table, saving or discarding changes (depending on what you chose to do in Step 6). Exit Access.

6

# WEEK 1

# DAY 7

# Creating Simple Queries

Today's topic introduces you to queries in Microsoft Access. Today you'll learn the following:

- What an Access query is
- How to construct simple queries
- How to use criteria in queries
- How to use queries to reorder your data
- How to construct queries using multiple tables
- How links work in queries
- How to use criteria in multitable queries

Queries perform many functions in Access. Relational databases, such as Access, work best when the data they contain is broken into small chunks that are logically grouped. Queries rejoin those small chunks when needed. Primarily, queries in Access perform the following functions:

- Extracting data according to criteria you set (for example, books published by a certain publisher)

- Performing actions on extracted data, such as deleting or updating table information

- Linking several tables or queries to present data the way you want to view it

- Grouping, sorting, and calculating data from tables and other queries

Access Queries represent a large topic, but one that's not particularly difficult to master if taken one step at a time. In short, you use queries to ask Access about your data or tell Access to manipulate it.

 **Note**

Starting with this chapter, *Sams Teach Yourself Access 97 in 21 Days* relies on the book's sample data for the examples shown. The tasks start with the sample data and then build on it for more complex examples. To work with the sample data, simply use the file DAY7START.MDB found on the CD-ROM accompanying the book. To use this database anywhere the BookStore database is referenced, simply copy it to your machine and rename it BookStore.MDB.

# A Simple Query

You can construct a simple query by telling Access you want to create a new query, telling it what fields to include, and then executing the query to view and work with the results. The following task shows you how to construct a simple query.

## Task: The simple query

1. Launch Access and open the BookStore database, if you need to. In the database window select the Queries tab and click the New button to create a new query. Click Design View to bypass the wizards for this exercise, and then click OK.

### DIFFERENT SCREENS

For the sake of simplicity, this chapter shows only those tables and queries relevant to the exercises. Your screens might differ from the book's examples if you are not using the sample data copy of the BookStore database. It's important that you have at least some sample data, though, so you can follow along with these exercises.

▼

▼   2. Access will display the Show Table dialog where you can choose on which tables
       the query will be based. Click the Publications table shown in the list box, and then
       click the Add button. This tells Access that the Publications table is one of the
       tables you want to query. Because this is the only table you want to query at this
       time, click the Close button. Your screen should look like Figure 7.1.

**FIGURE 7.1.**

*The query design grid
with one table added.*

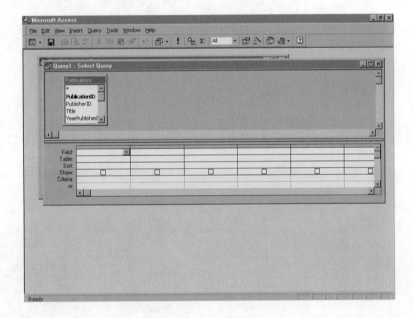

---

**ANOTHER MEANS TO THE END**

Since the Publications table is the only table included in this query, you could
have avoided the Show Table dialog by starting the new query slightly differently.
If you start on the Tables tab of the database window, select the Publications
table, and click the New Query toolbar button (it's on the drop-down toolbar button to the far right of the toolbar, next to the Office Assistant button), you'll find
yourself at the New Query dialog. Select Design View and click OK and you're
taken immediately to the Query Design View with the Publications table visible,
just like Figure 7.1.

---

Now Access knows which table you're querying, but doesn't know which fields
you want to include. To add fields to the query, you'll drag the necessary fields
from the Field list box to the query design grid.

   3. Drag the Title to the first column of the query design grid and drop it there.
▼     Access populates the first column of the design grid with the Title field.

**7**

▼     4. Using the same technique, add the `PublisherID` and `YearPublished` fields to columns two and three. You might have to scroll the list box containing the fields to find the these fields. When you're finished, your screen should look like Figure 7.2.

**FIGURE 7.2.**

*A multifield query.*

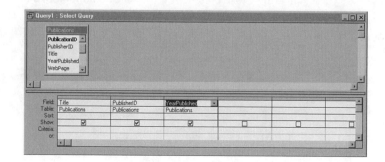

    5. Click the Run button, the one with the exclamation point, in the toolbar. Access
▲     then runs the query, resulting in a screen similar to Figure 7.3.

**FIGURE 7.3.**

*Running the simple query.*

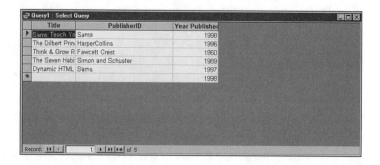

Pat yourself on the back—you've just constructed and successfully run an Access query! Notice something strange in Figure 7.3? The field labeled `PublisherID` isn't an ID value at all, but the *name* of the publisher. This is because the `PublisherID` field in the `Publications` table was defined as a lookup column (see Day 5, "Linking Tables with Relationships," for details on how this was accomplished).

**Note**

Access queries are "live." Changes made to them are reflected in the underlying tables or queries. Look at Figure 7.3. If you were to edit any of the Title fields shown in the query, you'd change the corresponding entry in the Publications table as well.

This is in contrast to most other PC database programs, where queries are dumped into dead tables. Edits into dead tables don't affect the underlying data. If you're used to this type of database, keep the concept of Access's live data queries in mind when editing queries in the Datasheet View.

Also, if you're used to dead table queries, you might, at first glance, feel Access's live queries are a dangerous feature, but it's actually as safe as you make it. It can also greatly increase Access's power and flexibility over those programs that dump queries into dead tables. You'll see examples of Access query power and flexibility as you pursue the subject of queries.

Keep in mind that keeping a backup of your database is vital, especially in a business environment. Many of the changes Access queries make will be permanent.

Well, that was easy—but it wasn't particularly useful. This query just takes some of the fields in an Access table and shows all the records for those fields. Access can do much more.

Return to Design View by clicking the Design View button on the far left in the toolbar.

The following task demonstrates sorting in a query.

| **Do** | **DON'T** |
|---|---|
| **DO** remember that queries keep live links to their underlying tables. | **DON'T** forget how handy that can be when you need to edit data in more than one table at the same time. |

## Task: Sorting in a query

1. Locate the Sort row in the query design grid. It's the third from the top.

2. Click in the first column's Sort row. Access returns a down arrow indicating that this field is a combo box with a pull-down list. Click the down arrow.

3. Click Ascending. You've just told Access to present your data in an ascending order based on the data in the Title field. Choose File | Save from the menu and save this query as Temp. Run the query by clicking the Run button. (See Figure 7.4.)

▼TASK

7

**FIGURE 7.4.**

*A query can use a different sort order than the table on which it's based.*

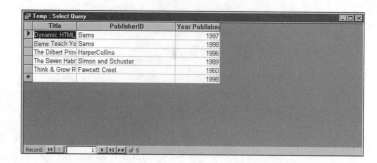

> **Note**
>
> There's an important difference between edits made to Access queries and sorts performed in them. Altering the sort order for fields in an Access query doesn't alter the order of the data in the underlying table.
>
> Occasionally, you'll want to view your data in varying orders. The easiest way to do this is to construct a query for each different sort view you want. Access allows multiple queries on the same table, and each query can have its own criteria and sort order.

# Criteria in Queries

Access queries also perform the important function of extracting subsets of your data. If, for example, you want to view all the records in the Publications table published in 1997, you can easily do so. The following task shows how to convert the general query made in the first two tasks into one with a criterion.

## Task: A criteria query

1. Starting from where you left off in the preceding task, return to Design View.

2. Locate the Criteria row in the query design grid. It's the fourth row down from the top. Enter 1996 in the Criteria row for the YearPublished field. Press the Tab key or click anywhere else in the grid.

3. Save the query using the File | Save menu item or toolbar button.

4. Run the query by clicking the Run button in the toolbar. Your screen should look like Figure 7.5.

**FIGURE 7.5.**

*The criteria query in Datasheet View.*

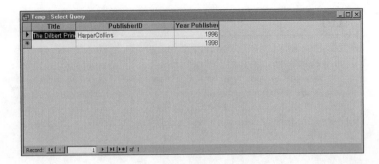

Access ran the query as before, but this time extracted only those records in which the YearPublished field matched the criteria of 1996. In this example, only 1 record had 1996 in the YearPublished field, so Access returned only one record when you ran the query. If your Publications table has different data in it, your query results probably look different. The important thing to concentrate on here is that all records returned, whether one or a million, were published in 1996.

# Some Criteria Variations

Access allows you wide latitude when it comes to criteria you can enter into a query. Using a little imagination and some knowledge, you can extract your data in almost any manner you can think of. The following task goes into some variations on the criteria theme.

## Task: Variations of criteria

1. Click the Design View button to return to Design View for this query.

2. Edit the criteria 1996 to read >=1996 and <=1998. Press Tab. If you have any experience at all writing SQL statements, you're going to think this is a trick step, doomed to failure when you click the Run button. Trust me, it's not. Although you cannot enter this criteria syntax into an Access SQL statement, Access will modify the criteria entered on the Design View to the proper Access SQL syntax of YearPublished >= 1996 and YearPublished <= 1998.

3. Run the query. Your screen should resemble Figure 7.6.

7

| **Do** | **Don't** |
|---|---|
| **DO** experiment with different criteria entries, determining which ones work the way you expect them to and which ones yield unexpected results. Access is unusual when compared with most computer programs because it tries to do what you mean, not just what you say. | **DON'T** assume Access can figure out what you want all the time. Like any application, Access has its limits. Until you're sure you understand query criteria, carefully check Access's output to make sure you got what you expected to get. |

**FIGURE 7.6.**

*Another query criterion.*

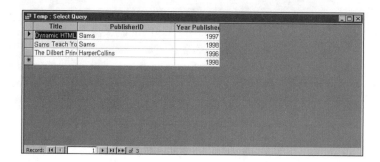

4. Return to Design mode. Here's a way people get wrong data when making criteria queries. Return to Design View and modify the criteria >=1996 and <=1998 to <=1996 and >=1998. Run the query. Access will display an empty datasheet window.

What happened? Your criteria now tells Access to return any records that were published *before* 1996 and *after* 1998. Naturally, no one edition of a book could meet such criteria.

Table 7.1 gives a few examples of other query criteria. Note that criteria expressions closely resemble table validation expressions. In Day 13, "Using Form Control Properties and Subforms," you'll encounter filter expressions, and the expression examples in Table 7.1 work there, too.

**TABLE 7.1.** SOME CRITERIA EXAMPLES.

| Criteria | Return |
|---|---|
| "Cairo" | Field must match Cairo. |
| "Cairo" or "Chicago" | Field can match either Cairo or Chicago. |

| Criteria | Return |
| --- | --- |
| `=#2/20/85#` | Matching the data February 20, 1985. Note that when entering data criteria in Access, you must surround the date with two number signs (#) so Access can recognize you're entering a date rather than the literal. In most cases, Access is smart enough to supply its own # marks, but look to be sure. |
| `Between #1/3/84# And #6/7/85#` | Anything between January 3, 1984, and June 7, 1985, inclusive. |
| `In ("Cairo", "Chicago")` | Another way to match either Cairo or Chicago. A syntactical alternative to or. |
| `Not "Cairo"` | Any record that's not Cairo. The opposite of "Cairo". |
| `< Date()- 30` | Dates more than 30 days old for this field. |
| `Year([Order Date])=1988` | Records that have the Order Date field in 1988. |
| `Like "C*"` | Starts with C; anything else following. |
| `Like "*a"` | Starts with anything; ends with a. |
| `Like "[J-M]*"` | Starts with J through M inclusive, and ends with anything. |
| `Left([City], 1)="O"` | Anything with O in the leftmost position. |

# Using OR and AND Criteria

Say you wanted to see all the data on publishers who's main office is in either Indianapolis or New York; you would ask your assistant to "Get me those files for publishers in New York and Indianapolis." This makes sense in human speech, but the relentless logic of computers interprets this request as "Get me those files where the publisher's main office is in *both* New York and Indianapolis." This clearly isn't what you wanted.

Logically speaking, you should have asked for those files for publishers with an office in New York *or* Indianapolis. This is one important area in which Access does what you tell it to do, rather than what you might mean for it to do. The following task illustrates the distinction.

7

## Task: OR and AND in criteria

1. Close the query from the previous task. Return to the Database window's Queries tab, and click New. Select Design View and click OK. Select the Publishers table, click Add and the Close.

2. Double-click the first entry in the Publishers table field list (the one that's an asterisk). This instructs Access to include all of fields from the table.

3. Now double-click the City field to add it separately to the grid. Next, double-click the PublisherName field.

4. Uncheck the Show Rows check box for each of these new columns in the design grid. This will prevent these columns from appearing twice in the output.

5. In the City field's Criteria row, enter Indianapolis. In the PublisherName criteria, enter S* (this instructs Access to look for data that begins with the letter S, and Access will modify the criteria to read Like "S*" when you tab off of this cell). Your screen should now appear similar to Figure 7.7.

**FIGURE 7.7.**

*Starting the AND criterion query.*

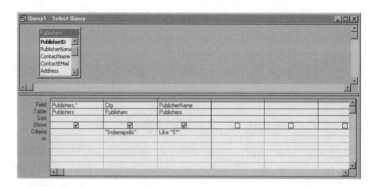

6. Run the query. If you haven't entered any data on your own, Access will display a datasheet with a single record.

   You told Access to extract all those records in which the City field is Indianapolis and the PublisherName starts with S. Only one record in the sample database now meets these criteria. Look what happens when you make a slight change to make this an OR criterion.

7. Return to Design View. Click and drag to highlight the criterion Like "S*" under the PublisherName field.

8. Press Ctrl+X to cut this criteria expression to the Clipboard. Click the second line of the Criteria grid under the PublisherName column next to the word or. Press Ctrl+V to paste your criteria to the new row. Your screen should look like Figure 7.8.

▼

**FIGURE 7.8.**

*Constructing the OR criteria.*

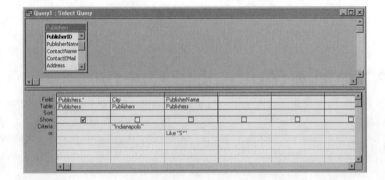

9. Now run the query. Your screen should resemble Figure 7.9.

**FIGURE 7.9.**

*The OR query's return.*

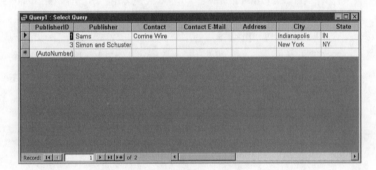

Note the difference between the query results after step 6 and the results shown in Figure 7.9. In the first query's criteria, you told Access to show you all the records in which the city is Indianapolis AND the publisher's name begins with the letter S. Access returns only those records that match *both* criteria.

When you changed the criteria to be on two rows, you told Access to extract all those records in which the PublisherName field begins with S OR those records in which the city is Indianapolis. This query returned all those records for which either criterion was valid, so you also got Simon and Schuster's record, even though their office is located in New York.

# Multitable Queries

Breaking your data into logical chunks makes it much easier for Access to manipulate, but on many occasions you'll want to reconstruct or rearrange your data into larger pieces. For example, the BookStore database contains authors' names in the Authors table, publisher information in the Publishers table, and publications in the Publications table.

7

What if you want to see a bibliography list of all of the publications in the store? All of the necessary information is in the `BookStore` database, but it's scattered throughout these three tables. The way to join all this data into a coherent whole is through a query.

# A Simple Multitable Query

The next task shows you how to manually construct a simple two-table query. Depending on how you like to work, you might prefer, when using Access for your own data, to use one of the New Query wizards for even the simplest queries. However, the right way to learn is to do. After the following task is completed, you'll add another table and enter some criteria to construct a rather sophisticated query.

### Task: A two-table query

1. If you're at the database window, click the Queries tab if necessary. Click the New button. Click the Design View selection to skip the wizards. Click OK. The Show Table dialog appears.

2. Click the `Authors` table in the Show Table list box. Click the Add button.

3. Click the `Publications` table in the Show Table list box. Click the Add button.

4. Click the Close button to close the Show Table list box. (See Figure 7.10.)

**FIGURE 7.10.**

*Starting the two-table query.*

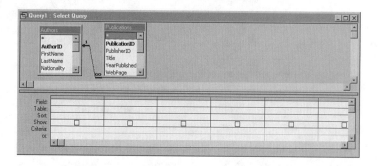

Access remembers that there's a link between these tables and proves to you that it remembers by drawing a line between the tables, illustrating what fields are the link fields as well as which side of the link is the "one" side and which is the "many" side. Remember that you established this link in the Relationships windows in Day 5. Access also remembers that the relationship is a one-to-many, with the `Authors` table being on the one side of the relationship.

5. You want to tell Access to show you the publications written by authors in your database. Drag the following fields from `Authors` into the query design grid, starting with column one: `AuthorID`, `FirstName`, `LastName`, and `Nationality`.

▼ 6. Now to add the publications. Click in the Publications list box on the Title field and drag that into the first empty column.

7. Click the Run button in the toolbar. Access evaluates the query design grid and returns the results shown in Figure 7.11.

**FIGURE 7.11.**

*The multitable query running.*

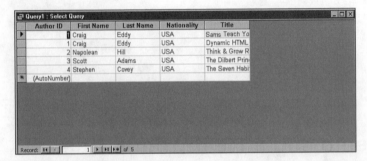

▲

Well, that's all right, but not terribly useful as it sits. For one thing, you wanted only the authors' names, but you also have the AuthorIDs.

Note that although the AuthorID field is in the Publications table, it's not included in the query. Even without the link field, Access has the smarts to link up the right author with his or her publications.

The next section covers removing a field from the query. For now, eliminate the AuthorID field from the query's display by returning to Design mode and clicking the Show check box under the AuthorID field. Your screen should resemble Figure 7.12.

**FIGURE 7.12.**

*Suppressing a field's display in a query.*

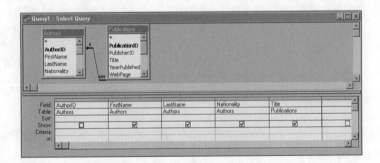

7

Run the query again. Your screen should look like Figure 7.13.

**FIGURE 7.13.**

*The results of suppressing a field's display in a query.*

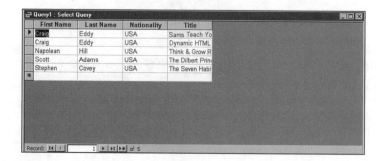

## Removing a Field from a Query

The only reason to include a field in a query while suppressing its display is if you want to include some criteria for that field, but don't want to actually display the field. You don't want to enter a criterion for AuthorID in this query, so you can safely delete it from the query design grid. Save this query by selecting File | Save from the menu, giving it the name `Temp Multi`.

| **Do** | **Don't** |
|---|---|
| **DO** include only those fields in queries you want to either display or enter criteria for. | **DON'T** bother to litter up your query design grid with extraneous fields just for the sake of links. Access can create these links without the field names explicitly called out in the query designer. |

Return to Design View. Move to the `AuthorID` column in the query design grid. Click the column header for the `AuthorID` column. (See Figure 7.14.)

**FIGURE 7.14.**

*Getting ready to delete a field from a query.*

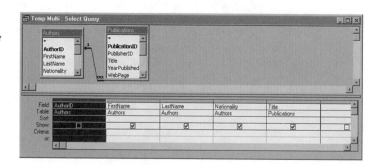

Press Delete or Del to remove this field from the query design grid. Run the query to see that Access still returns the same results even with no `AuthorID` field anywhere in the query. If it doesn't, return your copy of Access and demand your money back.

**Note** | Access doesn't need the inclusion of link fields in a query to know how to link tables in queries. It's smart enough to understand the underlying relationships even with the link fields excluded.

# Adding Another Table

This query is shaping up, but it still doesn't include the publisher information that you want. This information is in the `Publishers` table, which isn't yet part of this query. The following task adds the `Publishers` table to the query.

### Task: The three-table query

1. Return to Design View. Locate the Show Table button in the toolbar and click it. (It's the button with a table and a plus symbol.) Refer to Figure 7.15.

   Access brings up the Show Table list box. Click the `Publishers` table, and then click the Add button. Click Close to close the Show Table list box.

   Notice that Access remembers the link between `Publications` and `Publishers`. This link was established during the creation of the sample database. If you manually generated your sample data, you'll have to establish the link yourself. To do this, close the query, saving changes. Use the Tools|Relationships menu item to open the Relationships window. If necessary, add the `Publishers` to the Relationships window by clicking the Show Table button in the toolbar and dragging `Publishers` to the window. (The Show Table button in the Relationships window is the same as the one in the Query design grid, shown in Figure 7.15.) Drag your cursor from the `PublisherID` field in `Publications` to the `PublisherID` field in `Publishers`. In the Relationships dialog which appears next, click the Join Type button and select option 3. Return to the Relationships dialog and check the Enforce Referential Integrity box. Click Create. Your screen should resemble Figure 7.16. To return to the exercise, close the Relationships window, click the saved query, and click the Design button to open it in Design View.

   Return to the exercise at the point where you add the `Publishers` table to the query design grid. Arrange the new table's list box so that your screen resembles Figure 7.17.

▲ TASK

▼

7

▼    2. Now drag the following fields from the `Publishers` table to the query design grid
and place them in the next available empty columns: `PublisherName`,
`ContactName`, `City`, and `State`. (You might have to scroll horizontally to find
empty columns.) Click the Show box under `Nationality`. You might want to group
or sort by nationality later, so you'll leave this field in the query.

**FIGURE 7.15.**

*Adding a table to a
query.*

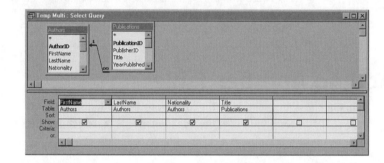

**FIGURE 7.16.**

*Establishing a
relationship.*

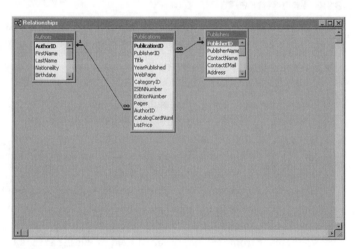

**Note**

Access enables you to dump one field on top of an occupied column and
automatically shifts the new field to a new column. This works all right, but
it's confusing when you see it for the first time.

▼

**FIGURE 7.17.**

*Adding the third table to the query design grid.*

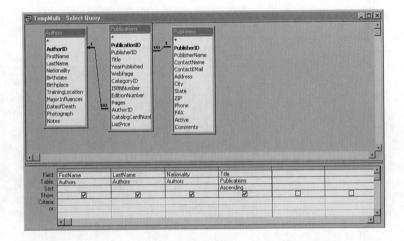

3. After you've dragged the fields into the query design grid, click the Run button. Adjust the widths of the fields in the Datasheet View like you adjusted the column widths in a table. After you adjust the column widths, your screen should resemble Figure 7.18.

**FIGURE 7.18.**

*The completed query.*

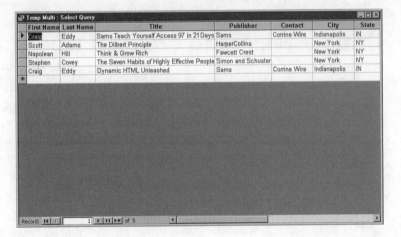

That's more like it. This is getting to be a useful set of information. The only problem is that the query is in sorted in some bizarre order.

4. Return to Design mode. Click the Sort row in the Title field. Pull down the combo box and click Ascending.

5. Click the Run button. Your screen should resemble Figure 7.19, which is the desired query.

7

▼

**FIGURE 7.19.**

*The finished three-table query.*

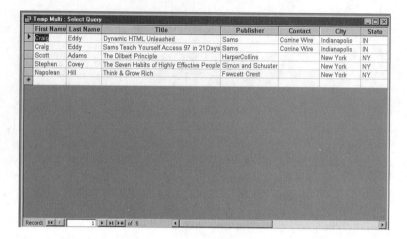

This query shows all the authors and their publications, along with publisher information. Save this query, using the name `Bibliography`, for later work. If you've already saved the query using a different name, use the File | Save As menu item and enter `Bibliography` in the Save As dialog's New Name box under the Within the Current Database option.

# Using a Wizard to Create a Query

Now that you've spent most of the day creating queries by hand, let's see what those wizards we've been avoiding are capable of doing. In the following task you'll re-create the `Bibliography` query using the Simple Query Wizard. While this wizard produces pretty straightforward results that could easily be done manually, the other wizards, particularly the Find Duplicates Query Wizard, produce queries that would take even an accomplished database designer more than a few minutes to create.

Begin by returning to the Queries tab of the Database window.

### Task: Using the Simple Query Wizard

1. Click the New button to invoke the New Query dialog. Select Simple Query Wizard and click OK.

2. Access churns for a few seconds and then the initial dialog of the Simple Query Wizard, shown in Figure 7.20, appears. This dialog is where you'll select the fields from the existing tables and/or queries you'll include in the query you're creating.

**FIGURE 7.20.**

*The initial dialog of the Simple Query Wizard.*

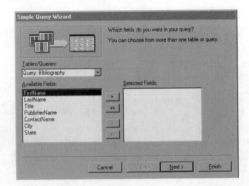

3. Since you're creating a duplicate of the Bibliography query, start by selecting the Authors table in the drop-down list box. Then double-click the FirstName and LastName fields to add them to the Selected Fields list box.

4. Next, select the Publications table and double-click the Title field.

5. Finally, select the Publishers table and double-click PublisherName, ContactName, City, and State. Your screen should now resemble Figure 7.21. Click the Next button.

**FIGURE 7.21.**

*The initial dialog of the Simple Query Wizard loaded with your query's fields.*

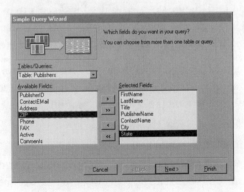

6. In the dialog that appears you can specify whether or not the query contains details or summary information. Details implies a list of records; summary implies a roll-up effect that sums or groups the data in the underlying records. Since you're producing a bibliography listing query, leaving the Detail option button enabled is correct. Click the Next button to continue.

7. In this, the final dialog of the Wizard, you give a name to your new query and tell Access what should happen when you click the Finish button. Name the new query Wizard's Bibliography, leave the Open the Query to View Information option button selected, and click Finish.

7

▼      8. The new query is saved and opened in Datasheet View, shown in Figure 7.22.

**FIGURE 7.22.**

*The completed query
in Datasheet View.*

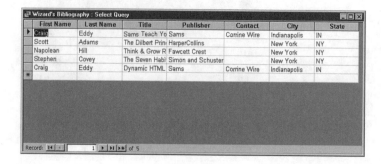

▲

Notice that the sort order isn't quite what you ended up with after completing the previous exercise. That's because the Wizard didn't ask you about any sort orders. This is one of those cases where the Wizard does most, but not all, of the work for you. Still, it's a great start and saved a good deal of time over the manual steps required in the previous tasks.

## Summary

Today you got a good introduction to queries used in Access to extract sets of data from tables or other queries. You can include as many fields as you want in a query, and you can also use criteria in queries to extract records meeting this criteria.

The only tricky thing about this material is the way Access interprets AND and OR query criteria. By placing multiple criteria on one line, you're telling Access you want to use an AND set of criteria; by putting multiple criteria on multiple rows, you're telling Access you want an OR extraction.

Keep in mind the difference between human and computer syntax when creating criteria using the operatives OR and AND. OR tells a computer to widen the criteria; AND tells the computer to narrow the criteria. Humans generally use AND like the computer's OR.

You add tables or other queries to your new query by highlighting the table or query you want to add in the Show Table list box and clicking the Add button.

After you've added the tables you want into your query, you click the Close button in the Show Table list box and start dragging fields from the list boxes to the query design grid.

Finally, until you're comfortable with Access query methods, carefully check what Access returns to you. The expression Like "C*" returns Cairo and Chicago. The expression Like "C" won't return either.

# Q&A

**Q** **You can edit queries, so why bother having tables?**

**A** You need to base a query on either a table or another query, which in turn is based eventually on an underlying table. You can't query nothing. You don't need data entered in a table to base a query on it, but you need some final structure for your data to reside in.

**Q** **I have a table with three entries: Smith, Jones, and Jenkins. I want to return only Smith's and Jones's records. Is it better to make a query with criteria Smith OR Jones, or should I use NOT Jenkins as the criteria?**

**A** Access doesn't care, so use whichever you prefer. The advantage of using Smith OR Jones is that your return will definitely give you only Smith or Jones. NOT Jenkins would also include Jensen, for example, if you were wrong and your table had a fourth entry.

**Q** **The sample data in these tasks seems a little simplistic. Why would I use a computer to manipulate such small amounts of data?**

**A** The data-entry requirements for these examples are intentionally kept small for those readers who have to enter the data manually. The principles apply to any data amount—either the tiny examples used in this book or the thousands of records a real bookstore would use. Also, the complexity of the data relationships is kept low because it only takes a few relationships to demonstrate all the possible convolutions. The data structure shown here would have to be expanded on several levels to operate a real bookstore system.

**Q** **What if I want an OR criteria for a single field?**

**A** Just enter the two criteria separated by the word OR. For example, if you want to modify a query to return records only for those publishers with offices in New York or Indianapolis, edit the first Criteria row under the City column to read Indianapolis or New York, and then run the query. Notice that Access is smart enough to know that New York is a two-word name for a single entity and places quotation marks around the entire city name.

**Q** **Let's say I want to use a different caption for a column in a query's output, such as "Author First Name" instead of "First Name." How can this be done?**

**A** Depending on the design of the Authors table, you may or may not be able to change the label used in the query. If the Authors table has a Caption property defined for the field, you won't be able to change the caption in the query design (change it on the table design). If not, select the first row for the column in question in the query's design grid. Move the pointer to the beginning of the text and type "Author First Name" : in front of the field name.

7

# Workshop

Here's where you can test and apply the lessons you learned today. Because of the length of today's lesson, the query projects will come at the end of tomorrow's lesson.

## Quiz

1. What are the three sort orders available for a field?

2. Can you OR multiple values for the same field?

3. Do you have to learn SQL (Structured Query Language) to design Access queries?

4. Can a query be based upon other queries?

## Exercises

> **Note**
>
> To work through these steps, you should have created the Wizard's Bibliography query detailed in a previous task. If you haven't done so and wish to work through this section, please create the Wizard's Bibliography query before proceeding.

1. Move to the Queries tab of the Database window. Click on Wizard's Bibliography and then click the Design button.

2. To put the sort order in place, click in the Sort row of the Title field in the grid. Select Ascending from the drop-down list box.

3. Click in the Field row for the FirstName column. Press the Home key to move the cursor to just before the word FirstName. Type Author: and press the End key to move the cursor to immediately after the word FirstName. Type + ' ' + LastName. What you've done is created a calculated field in the query. Access will now concatenate the first name and last name for each record and put the result into a column named Author.

4. Click the column header for the LastName column in the grid. Press the Delete key to remove the column from the query. Your design window should now look like Figure 7.23. Save the query.

**FIGURE 7.23.**

*The modified Wizard's Bibliography query in Design view.*

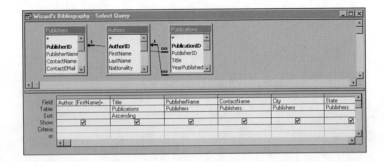

5. Run the query. The results should resemble Figure 7.24 (depending upon your data, of course).

**FIGURE 7.24.**

*The modified Wizard's Bibliography query in Datasheet View.*

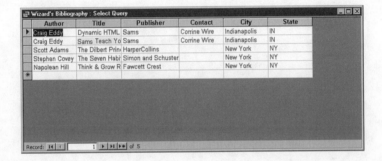

7

# WEEK 1

# In Review

Now that you've completed your first week with Access 97, you should be familiar with the interface, know what the key parts of a database (tables, forms, reports, queries, relationships) are, and have a pretty solid idea of how they work.

You should be able to open an existing database, find tables, open tables to find what their fields are, and even find queries to sort data within tables. If you worked along with the tasks and exercises, you've learned how to create a database, restrict data entry in fields by setting field properties, and how to make Access pull only the resulting data that you want by using simple queries.

Next week, you'll build on all these skills as you move from simply understanding how a database works to building interfaces of your own.

1

2

3

4

5

6

7

# WEEK 2

# At a Glance

This week, you'll learn how to make your data work for you and your end users in the two most basic ways: input and output. You'll work with forms that make entering and updating data easier and faster. You'll also work with creating and printing useful reports based on queries you design to pull the data you want.

Throughout this week you'll learn some of the specific tasks in gradual stages:

- How to work with the various built-in form controls, list and combo boxes, option groups, graphics, and eventually subforms and events within your forms.

- How to modify reports and create mailing labels.

- How to customize reports with report expressions and groups, including building more sophisticated queries.

- How Access 97 handles different date formats and expression (developer-defined) fields.

- How to create parameter queries, range parameter queries, and action queries, append, delete, top, update, crosstab, and union queries.

By the end of this week, you'll know just how to create terrific looking forms that enable your end user to find, update, and use data more efficiently, as well as build useful reports.

8

9

10

11

12

13

14

# DAY 8

# Designing Forms for Data Manipulation

Today's subject—an introduction to forms and form controls—is a lot more interesting and just plain more fun than what came yesterday. Forms are, primarily, attractive ways to show, edit, or enter data. Beyond that, forms are really the right way (as opposed to datasheets) to enter data into tables. Today is a long day, but the topic is light and enjoyable.

Today, you'll learn the following:

- What a form is
- How to make a quick form
- How to navigate in Form and Datasheet Views
- How to use a Form Wizard
- How to manipulate data with the new form
- The meaning of bound, unbound, and calculated controls
- What controls are available for your forms
- What form control properties are

- How to manipulate form controls
- How to select more than one control at a time
- How to add a control to a form
- How to delete form controls
- How to change the appearance of form controls

# What's a Form?

**NEW TERM**   A *form* is a window containing an array of controls with which you view, add, or edit data in Access. You've seen that you can view, add, or edit data in Datasheet View, so you might wonder why you should bother with forms if they only shadow what can be done without them. There are two fundamental reasons to use forms:

- They make the job of editing, adding, and viewing data easier.
- They add many features and capacities beyond what a datasheet can do when it comes to adding, editing, or viewing data.

When you see all the features you can add to your database by using forms, you'll want to use them in even your simplest database applications.

**NEW TERM**   *Controls* are objects on forms or reports that enable you to access data or manage the form or report. Examples of form controls are text boxes, combo boxes, check boxes, and command (push) buttons.

# Making a Form

In the bad old days B.A.—Before Access—creating database forms was something of a chore. It has been said that compared to other database systems, Access requires a lot of computer horsepower to run. That's true, but the reason Access requires so much computer power is that, compared to lesser products, you can do many more things with it. Forms design is one of those areas where Access shines, partially because of its excellent design and partially because it's a native Windows application.

You paid a lot of money for your computer so you could run Access; now you're about to reap some benefits from that investment. Watch how easily Access handles the job of making a simple data-entry form in the following task.

## Task: An instant form

1. Launch Access and open the BookStore database.

2. Open the Authors table in Datasheet View.

3. Locate the New Object button on the toolbar. See Figure 8.1 for help if you have trouble finding it. Pull down this button's list and select AutoForm.

**FIGURE 8.1.**

*Starting an instant form from the Datasheet View.*

4. Access takes some time to process your request. When it's done, your screen should resemble Figure 8.2. If your screen varies somewhat, try maximizing the window.

**FIGURE 8.2.**

*The results of the AutoForm choice from the New Object collection.*

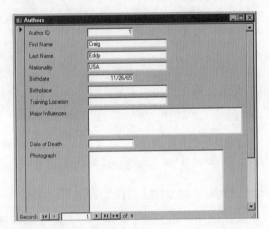

That's it. You've just created a simple form in Access. Congratulations!

# Looking Over the Form

Using the AutoForm button in the toolbar is similar to using any of the AutoForm options on the New Form dialog. Refer back to Figure 8.2 or your screen. You might recognize the data shown in the new form as the first record in the Authors table. Notice that not all the fields are shown because the AutoForm button simply stacks fields and doesn't try to fit them all on one screen.

In this form's case, the `Photograph` and `Notes` fields might be wholly or partially below the form's "horizon" if you're using a screen resolution of 800×600 or less. If you have any fields below the form's horizon, use the vertical scrollbar to scroll the form and reveal the missing fields.

## Moving to New Records

Although while using an Access form you can navigate through your records in several different ways, the simplest method is using the VCR buttons at the bottom of the window. These VCR buttons, or record navigation buttons, are to the right and left of the current record number box. In Figure 8.2, the specific record box tells you that you're at Record 1 of 4. This means the record set supplying the data for this form has four records and you're looking at the first one.

Clicking the inner-right VCR button, the one just to the right of the numeral 4, moves you one record forward in the record set. Try it yourself. After you click this button, your screen will display the record for Napolean Hill, and the current record number box will read "Record 2 of 4." This is the "move one record forward" button. Its equivalent for moving one record back is to the left of the current record number box and looks the same (except it faces in the opposite direction).

The VCR button to the right of the "move one forward" button has a vertical bar added to its graphic. This is the "jump to the last record" button. Similarly, there's an opposite-facing button to the left that moves you to the first record. Try clicking the button that moves you to the end of your records, and then click the left button to move to the first record. Your screen should again look like Figure 8.2. The navigation button to the far right, the one with the asterisk (star), is a "start a new record" button. Clicking this button takes you to a blank record, ready for new data entry.

## Some Alternative Navigation Methods

To navigate quickly around a form, you can use the keyboard, the menus, or the toolbar.

### Keyboard Shortcut

If you know the record number you want to get to, Access has an express train you can ride to it. Press the F5 key and you'll find yourself in the Current Record Number box with the current record number highlighted.

Notice two things. First, the number 1 in the notation "Record: 1 of 4" has the highlight. Second, the status bar directly under this section of the screen reads Enter New Value. Enter a number from 1 to 4, press Enter, and Access will immediately jump to that record.

## Menu Shortcut

Under the Edit menu, click the menu choice Go To. (See Figure 8.3.) Clicking the different choices from this menu enables you to move through your records almost instantaneously.

**FIGURE 8.3.**

*Using the menu to navigate through records.*

## Toolbar Shortcut

The standard toolbar for forms has two buttons used for record navigation. The "move to new record" button is the one with a right-facing triangle and an asterisk; when you click that button, Access moves you to a new blank record. You can enter data in this new blank record just as you can on a blank line in the Datasheet View.

The left-most toolbar button is the View Selection button. The choices on the pull-down menu for this button vary, depending on where you are in Access. When in Form View, you can quickly switch to Datasheet View by pulling down this button and clicking the Datasheet View choice. Figure 8.4 shows the results of clicking the Datasheet View button while viewing Record 2 of 4 in the Authors table's form.

**FIGURE 8.4.**

*The jump to Datasheet View from the Form View.*

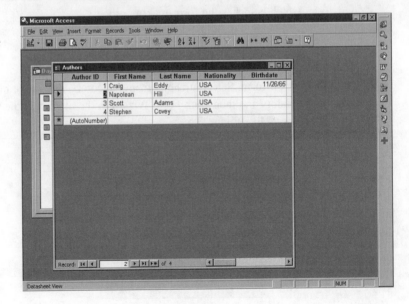

Note that Access kept track of where you were when jumping to that new view. If you were on Record 2 of Authors, you remained there after the jump to Datasheet View. Click the AuthorID field in the last record, the one for Stephen Covey.

| Do | Don't |
|---|---|
| **DO** use whatever navigating method you prefer to move around your records. | **DON'T** think there's an absolute right or wrong way. The right way for you is the way you like; the wrong way is the way you dislike. |

Now pull down the View selector and click the Form View choice. Access returns you to Form View, but with Covey's record (Record 4) now the current one.

# Making a Form by Using a Wizard

Close the AutoForm either by choosing File | Close from the menu or by double-clicking the form's Control menu icon or the X button. When Access asks whether you want to save the form, click No. Close the Authors table if it's open.

Back at the Database window, click on the Forms tab. Click the New button to start a new form, which launches the form-making process.

The following task shows how to use a wizard to make a form.

### Task: Using a wizard to make a form

1. Start a new form. Select Authors from the combo box at the bottom of the New Form dialog, and then click Form Wizard in the list box at the top. Your screen should look like Figure 8.5.

**FIGURE 8.5.**

*The completed New Form dialog.*

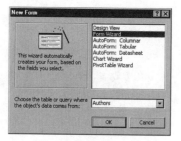

8

▼ 2. Click the OK button to start the wizard process for a form based on the Authors table. The Form Wizard is a general-purpose wizard with more flexibility than the different AutoForm choices. The first dialog in the Wizard is where you'll choose which fields to include in the form. You have the option of including fields from more than one table or query.

> **Note**   There are design and cosmetic differences between the forms made by using the AutoForm toolbar button and those made by choosing any of the AutoForm choices on the New Form dialog. However, the basic function of the AutoForms are quite similar.

3. Forms don't have to include all the fields from the table or query on which they're based. In some cases, you should restrict the fields on a form because you don't want unauthorized viewing of certain fields in a table, or simply because the fields are not germane to the form. You'll be using this form for entering and editing records in all fields, so click the >> button to add all the fields from the Authors table to this new form.

4. Click the Next> button to move on.

5. The next dialog gives you choices about the form's layout. Experiment by clicking the various option buttons in this dialog to see what they mean. When you're satisfied as to what each choice will give you, click the Columnar option button, and then click the Next> button to move on.

6. The next dialog gives you some options as to the look of your form (this example uses Stone). Click the Next> button and edit the suggested name for this form to read Authors Data. Make sure you've chosen or left the Top option button selected.

7. Click the Finish button. When Access finally displays a form, your screen should resemble Figure 8.6.

**FIGURE 8.6.**

*The finished form. Your results will vary, based on your screen resolution and the choice you made for a background.*

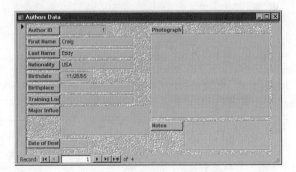

▲

Making a basic form by using a wizard is just that simple. Consider yourself a master of the simple Form Wizard. Leave the form open in Form View for now. The following section discusses entering data into the form. Then you'll take a brief break to investigate form controls, and then return to this form in Design View for the remainder of the chapter.

# Manipulating Data with a Form

Now that you've created a form using a couple of the automatic form creation mechanisms and seen how simple it is, examine how useful forms can be for manipulating the data in your database. After all, one of the assertions made at the start of this day was that forms make data entry easier. Let's find out how.

## Adding Records

Click the menu item, toolbar button, or navigation button of your choice to start a new (blank) record. Enter the record shown in Figure 8.7. After you've entered the data for a field, you can move to the next empty field by pressing either the Tab key or Enter. Don't bother trying to enter anything into the AuthorID field—that's an AutoNumber field and not only will Access supply its value for you, it will also prevent you from entering data into the field. Notice that as soon as you begin typing into one of the other fields Access fills in a value for the AuthorID field.

Notice that Access preserved the input mask for both the Birthdate and DateofDeath fields. Also note the scrollbars that appear when you enter either the MajorInfluence or Notes field.

Try editing Vonnegut's DateofDeath field to 2/29/98 (no, this is not a true fact). Access will give you the same error message it would if you tried doing this in the Datasheet View. Press Esc to return the field to empty. (Vonnegut will be pleased to hear that he didn't die on a non-existent date.)

When you've finished entering the data for this record, use the Records | Save Record menu item or press Shift+Enter to save the record to the Authors table.

**Tip**

> Access preserves your table's field properties when you use the table in a Form View. You also can add many other properties exclusive to a particular form. These form properties are in addition to the underlying properties you already set when designing your table.

**FIGURE 8.7.**

*A new record entered through a form.*

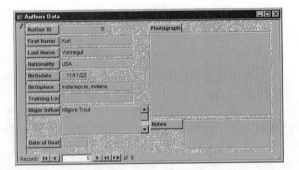

8

> **Note**
>
> Note that you can set a field's Locked property to prevent users of the form from entering or changing data in the field. This can be useful for fields that you want to be display-only on a form for certain or all users.

## Deleting Records

Forms are not only useful for adding and editing records, you can also use them to delete specific records. For example, you might scroll through the records on a form looking for ones with invalid data. You could then delete these records (assuming, of course, that you're positive they should go).

To delete a form's current record, you can use the Edit | Delete Record menu item, the Ctrl+- shortcut key (press the Ctrl and the minus sign keys at the same time), or the Delete Record toolbar button.

Note that this action cannot be undone; the record will be permanently deleted. Also, if you're using the sample data, try to delete the Author record for Craig Eddy. You'll get a message similar to Figure 8.8. This is because there is a relationship specified between the Authors table and the Publications table such that if an author has a related publication, you cannot delete the author. This is the effect of the Enforce Referential Integrity setting on the relationship between Authors and Publications (see Day 5, "Linking Tables with Relationships," for more details on referential integrity).

**FIGURE 8.8.**

*The message displayed when referential integrity is being violated.*

## Further Record Editing Techniques

There are a few more shortcuts you should know about when working with forms. First off, you can reset a field's value to the default value specified in the underlying table by pressing Ctrl+Alt+Spacebar. If you find yourself entering the same data for the same field into several records, use the Ctrl+' (Ctrl+Apostrophe) to copy the field's contents from the previous record to the current record. Finally you can insert the current time by pressing Ctrl+Shift+: (Ctrl+Shift+Colon) or the current date by pressing Ctrl+; (Ctrl+Semicolon).

# Introduction to Form Controls

Using the form from the previous exercise, you've already encountered a few of the available form controls. However, there are many more types of controls beyond those on the Authors Data form. This section introduces you to the various kinds of controls available to you as a forms designer.

This section first discusses the three general types of controls. Then it describes the specific controls available with the standard Access package. Note that Access forms can host any ActiveX control which you have installed on your system, so the list of controls presented here is by no means exhaustive.

## Bound, Unbound, and Calculated Controls

NEW TERM    There are three general categories of controls available in Access: bound, unbound, and calculated. A *bound control* is one that's tied to some underlying element; in Access, this usually means a query or table.

All of the text boxes on the Authors Data form are examples of bound controls. The fields are tied to the Authors table and display and allow update of the data for the current record.

NEW TERM    *Unbound controls* aren't tied to anything; they are generally used for information display, calculations, manipulating or decorating forms, and (as you'll see later in the book) reports. The label Author ID to the left of the AuthorID bound field shown in Figure 8.6 acts as a label, informing you that the text field is showing the AuthorID information.

NEW TERM    *Calculated controls* have a formula or expression as the source of their data. They don't automatically update the data in any table, but you can cause this happen by writing some code for your form. For example, an unbound control on the Authors Data form might calculate the age of the current author by subtracting the author's birthdate from the current date.

## Label Controls

Label controls are used to describe other controls, or to present information to the user of a form. On the Authors Data form there is one label control for each field in the Authors table. The user cannot change the value of a label, but you can change its caption based on varying conditions through Visual Basic code that acts on the form.

**NEW TERM** You can also use labels shortcuts for getting around on a form. By placing an ampersand in the caption while in design mode, the character following the ampersand will be underlined, and the ampersand will not display, when the form is viewed in Form View. If the label control immediately precedes the text box it describes in the *tab order*, pressing Alt plus the underlined character will move the cursor to text box. Tab order is the order in which the fields get focus as you press the Tab key while working with a form. If this is confusing, you'll be using this technique later in the book.

## Text Box Controls

Text boxes are your primary means for entering data. You'll use far more text boxes than any other control. Text boxes can be bound, unbound, or calculated depending upon their intended usage. Text boxes can display data on a single line or on multiple lines, and can even display a scroll bar. You can use a text box for just about any data type, including Memo but excluding OLE Object data.

## List and Combo Boxes

List and combo boxes display their data in, you guessed it, the form of a list. The list box control always displays multiple items—its window is always opened. The combo box displays one item at a time until you click its drop-down button. Doing so causes its list window to open, displaying the contents of the combo box's list.

List boxes can allow for a singe selection, simple multi-selection, and extended multi-selection. Simple multi-select allows the user to select and de-select multiple items in the list by simply clicking the items. Extended multi-select allows the user to select or de-select a single item by pressing the Ctrl key while they click the item. Additionally, the user can select a contiguous selection of items by clicking the first item and then pressing the Shift key while clicking the last item in the contiguous selection.

## Command Buttons

Command buttons are used to initiate some sort of activity. For example, you may place a button on a form to allow the user to print the current form. The button would have a macro or an event procedure (a set of Visual Basic code which fires when the button's click event occurs) that initiates the printing process.

## Check Boxes, Option Buttons, and Toggle Buttons

When the data in a field is Yes/No data, check boxes and toggle buttons make the perfect bound controls for this field. A *check box* is a combination of a small box and a label. The box displays an x, or Yes state, when in the checked. It is empty when in the unchecked or No state. *Toggle buttons* are in either a sunken or a raised state, where the sunken state reflects a Yes value and the raised state a No value.

*Option buttons* (also traditionally known as radio buttons), can also display Yes/No fields. However, they are typically used for choosing one of several options. Option buttons have a label and a circular area that is filled in when the option is selected and empty when it is not. When the choices to be represented come from a fixed list that will not change, option buttons are the way to go. However, if the list of available choices might change in the future, or can be input by the user (such as the Categories table in the BookStore database), you should use a list box or combo box to choose the value.

When these controls are bound to a field in a table or query, they return the value -1 when selected and 0 when not selected. These values conveniently correspond to the actual numeric values stored in Yes/No fields.

Figure 8.9 shows you some examples of check boxes, option buttons, and toggle buttons in action.

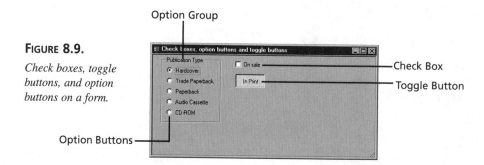

Option Group

**FIGURE 8.9.**

*Check boxes, toggle buttons, and option buttons on a form.*

Check Box

Toggle Button

Option Buttons

## Option Groups

Option groups, also known as frame controls, are used to group other controls into a meaningful collection, which is usually spelled out by the Caption property of the option group control. In Figure 8.9 there is an option group labeled Publication Type. This is used to group the various types of publications (hardcover, paperback, and so on).

When option buttons are placed within an option group, only one of the option buttons can be selected at a time. Therefore, if you have lots of option buttons signifying different types of choices, you'll need to put each type of choice within its own option group.

You can place other controls within the option group frame, but they don't have the same restriction as the option buttons do. In this case, we usually refer to the control as a frame control rather than an option group since it's merely a container for other controls.

8

# Form Control Properties

Just as you can manually design a table, you can manually design a form. The toolbar button on the far left of the toolbar pulls down in Form View just as in the other views you've seen. Click that button now to pull down the list and then choose Design View. (See Figure 8.10.)

Your screen might differ in two basic ways from that of Figure 8.10. Your toolbox— that's the window floating on the far left—might be below the menu bar and across the top of your screen. Additionally, you might not have the floating property window open. Figure 8.10 has the Properties window, open at the bottom-right of the screen.

**FIGURE 8.10.**

*The Form Design View.*

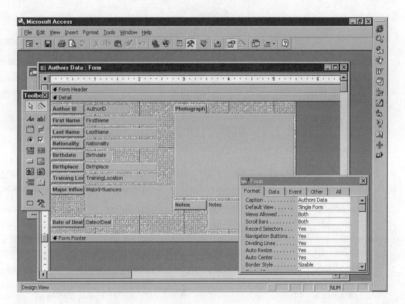

The toolbox is where you select the controls to be placed on the form. To make it appear, click the Toolbox button on the toolbar (the crossed hammer and wrench). You can select any of the controls discussed in the previous section as well as additional controls that you'll learn about later. Hold the mouse over a toolbox button to see which control it represents, or consult Appendix C, "The Toolbox Illustrated," for more information.

If your toolbox isn't oriented as in Figure 8.10, you can click its title bar and drag it to the left side of the screen. Like other toolbars, it'll snap into place as soon as you get it fairly close to the side, top, or bottom of a screen.

Figure 8.11 shows another floating list box. You'll notice that this is the field list for the Authors table, which is the data source for this form. This list was opened by using the Field List toolbar button which is to the left of the Toolbox button, shown in Figure 8.10.

Feel free to close any floating list boxes at this time. You close these boxes by either clicking their X icons or clicking their toggle buttons on the toolbar.

**FIGURE 8.11.**

*Floating property list boxes.*

| **Do** | **Don't** |
|---|---|
| **DO** check the figures from time to time to make sure you're following along with the exercises. | **DON'T** worry if your screen grows out of sync with the book. Some variances can't be helped. As long as you're not lost, you're doing all right. |

Just like fields in a table, each form control has a set of properties that vary from one control to another. Although each type of control has a different set of properties, they all share at least a few properties in common. In many cases, Access automatically sets properties for you as a consequence of another choice you made during form design.

Take a look at Figure 8.12. It displays a partial list of properties for a Text Box control; the properties shown pertain only to formatting the text box.

That's a pretty imposing list, isn't it? Memorizing all those properties for all the controls and all their options would be a daunting task. Luckily, Access makes it fairly easy by doing two basic things.

First, Access has categorized the properties according to function, so you're not overwhelmed with choices. To select a category of properties, click the appropriate tab at the top of the Properties list box. If you want to see all properties at one time, click the All tab. This is a useful when you're not sure to which category a particular property belongs. Some of the properties could arguably be in different categories than the one the designers of Access chose.

**FIGURE 8.12.**

*The format properties
of a Text Box control.*

The second thing Access does to help you with form control properties is to offer you
help setting the value for a property. This is done in the form of drop-down list boxes and
other dialogs. Look at Figure 8.13—it shows the Color dialog used for setting the Back
Color and other color properties in a control. Notice the value currently stored in the
Back Color property. That's a pretty imposing number which has no correlation to any
color I've ever seen. To open the Color dialog, click in the Back Color field and then
click the button that appears to the right of the Back Color property's text box.

Later on, you'll learn some other ways Access helps you when you are setting properties.

**FIGURE 8.13.**

*The Color dialog
assists you in setting
color-oriented proper-
ties.*

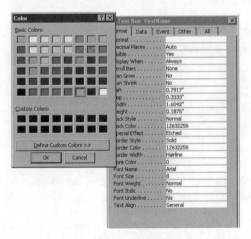

In Day 11, "Working with Form Controls," and Day 13, "Using Form Control Properties
and Subforms," you'll learn a great deal more about control properties.

## Adding and Deleting Controls

You can delete a control from a form by selecting it, and then either pressing the Delete key or choosing the menu selections Edit|Delete. Click the FirstName field to highlight it. When you press the Delete key, Access removes the field from your form. You may have to also delete the corresponding label, depending on how you selected the field.

Click the Form View button in the toolbar to move your form into Form View. Then click the Datasheet View button in the toolbar. Note that Access has eliminated the FirstName field from this view also. Return to Design View.

If the Field List window is not open, click the Field List toolbar button to open it.

Click the Text Box control in the toolbox (the Text Box control is the button with an "abl" on it). Click and hold on the FirstName field in the Authors list box—it's the window that opened when you clicked on the Field List button.

Without releasing the mouse button, drag the FirstName field onto the form, and drop it into roughly the same spot as the field you deleted. Release the mouse button.

You'll learn more about moving controls around in the form a little later in this chapter. One tip for now, though, is that if the Snap To Grid option is turned on, you might not be able to put this field back in its original position. If this is the case, use the Format | Snap To Grid menu item to turn off grid-snapping. Place the FirstName control precisely where you want it, then use Format | Snap To Grid again to reactivate grid-snapping.

## Choosing Multiple Controls

Often you'll want to act on several controls at once. You can choose several controls quickly and easily by using a marquee selection. The following task shows you how.

**Note**

There are many global options you can set in Access, and some of them affect how Access works. Some, if set differently from their defaults, will put your copy of Access at odds with the configuration used for these exercises.

The next exercise requires you to have the Selection Behavior option set to Partially Enclosed. To make sure it is, choose Tools|Options from the menu. Access gives you a tabbed dialog with several choices. Click on the Forms/Reports tab. Locate the property Selection Behavior and, if necessary, change it to Partially Enclosed. Click OK to exit this dialog.

8

| Do | Don't |
|---|---|
| **DO** check your global options if your version of Access seems to be behaving differently from the book's. | **DON'T** be overly worried about experimenting with global options. Most are self-explanatory. It's difficult to get into trouble by altering these options. Feel free to configure Access so it works the way you prefer. |

## Task: Marquee selections

▼ TASK

1. With your screen as you left it after the last section, move your mouse cursor to the right of and slightly above any field. This exercise uses the group of controls that starts with AuthorID and ends with the BirthDate fields. If your screen looks different, use any two or more fields for this exercise.

2. Click and hold your mouse button, and then drag the mouse down and to the left. You'll see a contrasting "rubber band" rectangle that grows as you move your mouse. Note that because of the background, the rubber band selection marquee doesn't show up too well. You can see the effect best by looking at the field labels.

3. Continue dragging the rubber-band box until it covers at least part or all the form controls you've chosen to include for this exercise. Now release the mouse button. All the fields you had covered with the rubber-band box now are highlighted. Your screen should look like Figure 8.14.

4. Move your cursor into any of the highlighted areas. It'll turn into a hand, as shown in Figure 8.14. If you click and drag now, you'll move all these fields at once. This preserves their positions in relation to each other, but not to the form in general or to any other non-highlighted controls. Try dragging this group of controls around. After you're satisfied with how this works, return them to their former location, or if you prefer, drop them anywhere, and then choose the Edit | Undo Move menu item and Access will put them back to their original positions.

**Tip**

You set control properties by first selecting a control or controls, and then altering the relevant properties. You can set the properties for all of a form's controls at the same time by using Edit | Select All menu item or by pressing Ctrl+A. You can affect several adjacent controls by using marquee selections. Finally, you can select any number of nonadjacent controls by holding down the Shift key as you click the controls.

▼

**FIGURE 8.14.**

*The finished marquee highlight.*

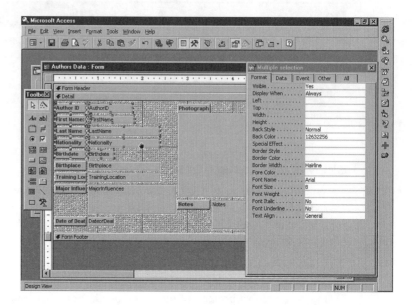

5. Click anywhere outside the areas having the highlight to remove the highlight from these controls.

# Moving and Sizing Controls

When Access inserts Text Box controls into a form through a wizard, it makes a guess based on the `Field Size` property to determine how wide to make that field. Return to Form View and notice that the `AuthorID` and `Last Name` fields are much bigger than they need to be. Also, the Wizard doesn't know how to group controls together based on their meaning. For example, the `Birthdate`, `Birthplace`, and `Date of Death` fields should probably be grouped together but aren't. The following exercises address both these issues.

## Sizing

NEW TERM    To make all the fields or form controls fit on one screen or just to make them the right size for the intended data, you need to both alter the size of overly wide ones and move some of them up from the bottom of the form. Keep in mind that the terms *field* and *form control*, or just *control*, refer to the same thing. A *form control* is the way to show a field on a form.

The following task shows you how to resize a form control.

**▲ TASK**

**8**

## Task: Resizing a form control

1. Click the Design View button to return to Design View.

2. If your screen has some floating list boxes in it, close them by either clicking their X icons or clicking their toggle buttons.

3. Click on the AuthorID field in the text control where the data is displayed when this form is in Form View.

   When you click a control, you highlight it. Take a close look at your screen. A highlighted control gains a series of squares around its periphery, indicating that it's selected. Drag your cursor over the highlighted field. When the cursor changes shape to look like a hand, you can click and move the field.

4. You don't want to move this control, just resize it. The smaller squares around the control's periphery are "hot spots" for resizing controls. Move your cursor to the center square at the right side of the AuthorID control. Your cursor then changes shape to look like a two-sided arrow.

| Do | Don't |
|---|---|
| **DO** proceed slowly and carefully through this and the following sections, especially if you're not comfortable or familiar with mouse actions. Highlighting fields without inadvertently moving them, hitting the right hot spots, and dragging are all difficult for those who are less than expert in mouse operations. | **DON'T** become discouraged if you feel clumsy exercising your form design skills with a mouse. Skill will come in time. Meanwhile, keep in mind the Access Undo facility. If you accidentally move, size, or delete a form control, you can undo it either by pressing Ctrl+Z or choosing the menu items Edit\|Undo. Almost everybody uses this feature when learning about Access form design. |

5. Keeping your cursor over this hot spot, click and hold your mouse. Drag the cursor to the left until the AuthorID field is a little over an inch long. Note the ruler on the top of the form design grid, which indicates the length of the field and the position of the cursor.

6. Release your mouse button and the field snaps into its new size, looking like Figure 8.15.

**▼**

**FIGURE 8.15.**

*The resized field.*

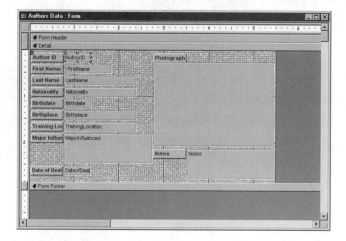

7. Using this same technique, resize the Last Name field so that it's roughly the same size as the First Name field.

**Tip**

You might find that you can't finely adjust the size of your fields because Access snaps them to certain points. Access has the options Grid and Snap To Grid.

**NEW TERM** The *grid* is a series of virtual points in the Design View. You can control how fine this grid is by setting the relevant form properties. When Access is set to Snap To Grid, each control on the form must locate and size to one of these points. When doing this exercise, it makes no difference if your Snap To Grid is on or off. It's not that important to size and locate the controls exactly.

That's all there is to sizing controls. The only other thing to bear in mind is that the other hot spots for resizing work differently. For example, the two hot spots in the lengthwise middle of the controls act to size them vertically, not horizontally like the one you just used.

**Tip**

The two large squares in the upper-left corner of both the control and the field label are not hot spots for sizing; rather, they give you a way to move a control independently of its label or to move a label independently of its control.

## Controls on the Move

You can move controls either with or independently of their field labels. If you moved your cursor around the control in the last exercise, you saw your cursor change to a hand shape, indicating you can now move a field with its label. The following exercise moves two controls with their labels so that the entire form fits on one screen.

### Task: Moving form controls

1. The first step is to make some real estate available for moving the controls around. To do so, move the mouse to just over the horizontal section labeled Form Footer. The pointer will change to show a big plus sign with up/down arrows. While holding the mouse button down, drag down to create an empty area about an inch high at the bottom of the form (the ruler at the left of the form should help you in sizing this area).

2. Click and hold the button down in the DateofDeath field's text box area. Your cursor should change to a hand. Continue to hold your mouse button down; if you let go, click again when the cursor looks like a hand. Your screen should look like Figure 8.16.

**FIGURE 8.16.**

*A form control ready to move.*

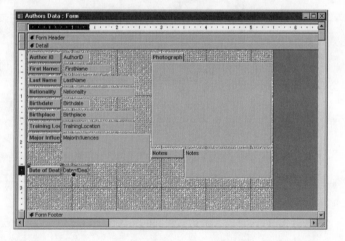

3. Continue to hold the mouse down and drag the field down into the new empty area at the bottom of the form.

4. Use marquee selection to select the Birthdate and Birthplace fields along with their associated labels. Move the mouse into the selected area. Your cursor should change to look like a hand.

▼   5. Continue to hold the mouse button down. Drag the fields to a place directly above the `DateofDeath` field, and then release the mouse button. Click anywhere on the empty area of the form to de-select the controls.

6. Use marquee selection to select the all of the fields from Training Location down to `DateofDeath`. Move the mouse into the selected area. Your cursor should change to look like a hand. Drag the fields upward to fill in most (but not all) of the blank space between `Nationality` and `TrainingInfluence`. Again click outside of the selection.

7. Next, resize the form to return it to its original height using the technique in step 1. Your form should now look like Figure 8.17. Save the form design using the Save toolbar button.

**FIGURE 8.17.**

*Finished with the resizing and moving operations.*

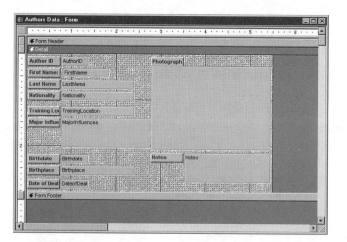

8. Experiment with moving other controls around until you have a good feel for how this works. Arrange and resize the controls until you think you have a pleasing arrangement. Don't forget that if you need more form territory, move your cursor to the sides or bottom of the form. It'll change to look like a double-facing arrow. After the cursor changes, you can drag the form to a new size.

▲   Note that the form itself resizes to accommodate field movements. You don't need to manually resize a form before moving a field, but many people like doing so.

**Tip**

> If you highlight several controls, you can group-align them by choosing Format | Align and then one of the options. This is a tremendous time saver compared to manually aligning several controls with each other.

# Changing Appearances

Today's final topic is how to change the appearance of form elements. This is generally done with the Formatting toolbar, but you can alter these elements, depending on what's happening in an Access application, by using macros or Visual Basic.

Remember how the AutoForm's controls had a sunken look (see Figure 8.2 if you don't remember this)? The following task shows how Access did that.

### Task: Using the Formatting toolbar

1. Start with your form just as you left it after the previous task.
2. Press Ctrl+A to select all the controls on this form.
3. Make sure the Formatting toolbar is active. This is the toolbar that, by default, lies just below the Form Design toolbar. If you don't see it on your screen, right-click the Form Design toolbar and click the Formatting (Form/Report) entry it to make it visible.
4. The sunken option is on a pull-down button called Special Effects. This button is at the far right on the toolbar if you have the standard toolbar. Drop down the button and click the Sunken effect (Refer to Figure 8.18).

**FIGURE 8.18.**

*The Sunken option.*

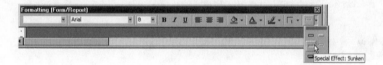

5. Click the Form View button and note that now all the fields or controls on your form have a sunken look.
6. Return to Design View and experiment with changing the color and the look of different controls until you develop a good feel for how the Formatting toolbar works. When you're done, save your changes.

# Summary

A form is an attractive way to enter, edit, or view data stored in tables. There are several ways to create one: You can click the AutoForm button in the toolbar when in Datasheet View, use a wizard, or manually generate one from scratch.

Once you have a form, you can navigate through records by using menu choices, the VCR navigation keys, or direct jumps to record numbers. The Page Up and Page Down keys work as well, but they aren't as convenient, especially if your form takes up more than one vertical screen.

Adding data to a table by using a form can be the same as adding it directly to a table, but keep in mind that there are properties for form fields that can alter data entry with the form. The real power of forms is that they can hide the underlying tables' structures, so that data can be easily entered across multiple tables.

Forms maintain the properties of the underlying tables, plus they can add properties of their own. Forms can contain bound, unbound, and calculate controls. Bound controls are tied to some underlying item, usually inside Access (although in the case of some controls, you can link to applications outside Access).

Forms have three views: Design, Form, and Datasheet. You can design your form in Design View, but the other two views give you access to your data. You change a control in a form by first selecting it, and then applying whatever modifications you want. You can select several controls at once by holding down the Shift key as you click, by using a marquee selection, or by pressing Ctrl+A to choose all form elements.

You delete form controls by selecting those you want to delete and then pressing the Delete key, or you can choose Edit | Delete from the menu. You add bound controls to the form by dragging the fields from the Field list box to the Form Design grid. The Formatting toolbar lets you set the initial display attributes for your form controls. You'll learn later on that you can change certain of these attributes by using macros, Visual Basic, or a combination of the two.

# Q&A

**Q  The text implies you can change a control's display when the form's open in Form View. Why would you want to do this?**

**A  When you review a form's layout properties, you'll see many items you might want to alter, depending on the state of the form or its data. For example, one property that a control has is called Visible. You might want to make some controls visible or not, depending on the current data or the state of another control.**

**Q  Why doesn't Access show a field in Form Datasheet View if that field's not on the form?**

**A  The reason is security. Say you have a form with restricted information. You might clear people to see that form because it lacks the fields containing sensitive data from the underlying table. The way Access works, users of this limited form could not violate security by choosing the Datasheet View. You can also limit the Datasheet View by setting the appropriate form property.**

**Q** Is there any difference between adding, editing, or deleting data through a form rather than doing it directly into a table?

**A** There can be—not in the data, but in how a person can address it. Remember, each control on a form has a slew of properties that act in addition to the properties of the fields in a table and the table's properties. You might not, for example, have any data validation set at the table level, but you might at the form level. This would have the effect of no data validation when entering data directly into a table. Instead, that validation would be effective only when using the form.

One reason to do this is so you can vary the data validation depending on which form is used to enter data into the table. Many forms can be bound to one table. As you'll see later on, one form can contain several tables as well.

**Q** Forms look to me like rearranged table fields. Can they do more than that?

**A** Forms can be very powerful tools in organizing and displaying your data. This chapter covered only the basics. Later you'll learn more about the other form controls (check boxes, option groups, and command buttons), which, when used correctly, greatly enhance your applications.

**Q** Is there a rule of thumb saying when to use a form for data entry and when to do it through the Datasheet View directly?

**A** There's no real rule of thumb, but since most people find data entry to be much easier in Form View than in Datasheet View, why not use forms all the time? Even if you ask Access to generate an AutoForm for each data entry session and then discard the form, you'll probably save time by using a form for data entry. As you learn more about forms, you'll see that they can do many things that are impossible (or at least very awkward) to do from a datasheet.

# Workshop

Here's where you can test and apply the lessons you learned today.

## Quiz

1. How do you know when a form control has the highlight?

2. What visual indication does Access give you so you know when you can move a form control?

3. What does the mouse cursor look like when it's over a hotspot and able to size a field or control on a form?

4. If you delete a field from a form in Form Design View, can you see that field when you switch to Form Datasheet View?

5. How can you select (or give the highlight to) two noncontiguous controls on a form?

6. How can you select (or give the highlight to) four contiguous controls on a form?

## Exercises

1. Launch Access and open the BookStore database, if you haven't already done so. Go to the Tables tab on the Database window.

2. Select the Publishers table and create a form by using the AutoForm choice of the toolbar's New Object button. Your screen might resemble Figure 8.19. Exactly how your AutoForm turns out depends on Access's condition and your Windows setup. The control layout should be similar.

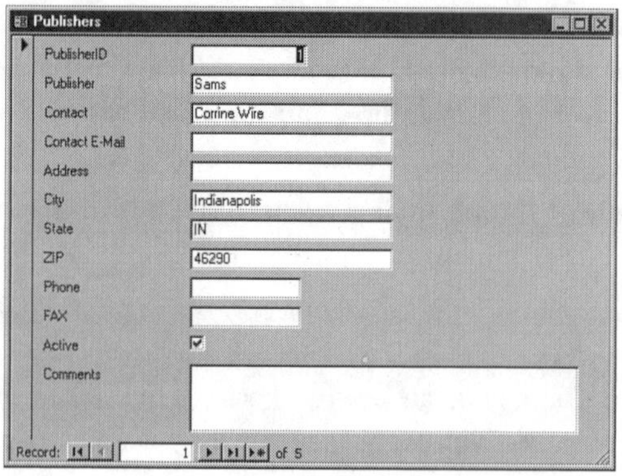

**FIGURE 8.19.**

*An AutoForm created form.*

3. Change to Design View. Rearrange and resize the controls on this form to look like Figure 8.20, which shows the rearranged controls in Form View. Hint: The size of the form itself was shortened vertically. Move your cursor to the bottom of the form and it'll take on the shape you saw when resizing table fields. Click and drag to resize the form itself.

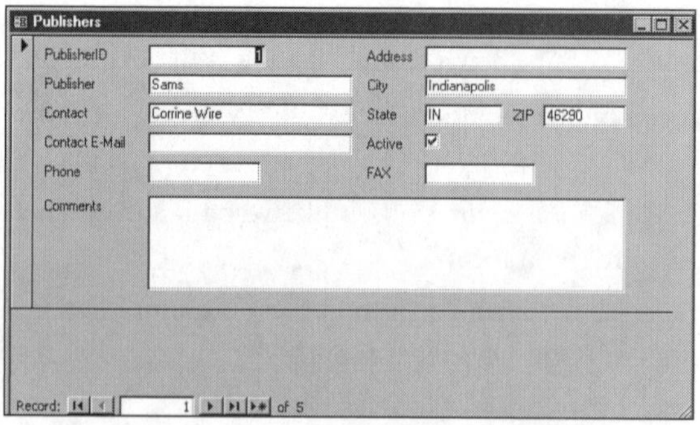

**FIGURE 8.20.**

*The reworked AutoForm.*

8

4. Return to Form Design View and select the Active check box control. Open up the Properties list box and find the `Default Value` property either by scrolling through the All Properties list or choosing the Data tab. Enter `Yes` for a default property, and then return to Form View. What change do you see in the Completed check box? Scroll through all the records to see any changes. Now move to a new (blank) record. Does the default value kick in? Did it kick in with existing records?

5. Save the form. Leave the suggested name (`Publishers`) in place.

# DAY 9

# Creating Functional Reports

Today's lesson covers the following:

- What reports are
- How to use the general Report Wizard for quick results
- How to customize reports
- How to create expressions in reports
- How to group report data

## Report Concepts

Reports are very similar to forms. The main difference between them, as far as application goes, is that reports work much better for data output, especially to printers. Also, Access 97 can present data for viewing over the World Wide Web, and reports perform a vital function in presenting data for this purpose. The primary mission of forms is data entry and display, and the main mission of reports is data output.

Like forms, reports are bound to underlying tables or queries. Access can do much with unbound forms, but most people see little sense to an unbound report, although Access enables you to create one through the Design View option when you tell Access you want to create a new report.

**NEW TERM**    The term *bound* refers to the fact that a report receives its data from the tables or queries to which it is related. The term *unbound* simply means that there is no underlying table or query that provides the object in question with data.

The following task creates a sample report using the Publications table. This report prints out the titles, page counts, year published, and ISBN number data for the publications stored in the table.

## Task: The basic report

1. If necessary, launch Access and open the BookStore database. Click the Report Wizards entry in the list box.

2. Click the Report tab. Click New. Select the Publications table to choose it as the basis of this report. This step is called binding the table to this report. Your screen should resemble Figure 9.1.

**Note**

Note that when you pull down the combo box to bind a query or table, Access doesn't segregate the two types of objects as it does during query design. This is a good illustration of why a naming convention would be useful. For example, if you prefixed all tables with "tbl" and queries with "qry," you could, at a glance, see that you have three tables and one query to choose from for this report.

3. Click OK to tell Access you're ready to go.

4. Access opens up the Publications table and examines it, determining what fields are available. Click the field names, and then click the > button for the following fields: Title, YearPublished, ISBNNumber, and Pages. Your screen should look like Figure 9.2.

5. Click Next>. You could group the report by the year published but we'll save grouping for later in the day, so click Next> again. The dialog shown is where you'll specify the sort order for the report. Specify Title as the sort field by selecting it in the first drop-down list box. Click Next> to move on. Accept Access's defaults for this report, which should be Portrait orientation, a Tabular layout, and Auto adjustments to fit all fields on one page. Click Next>.

**FIGURE 9.1.**

*The Report Wizard just starting out.*

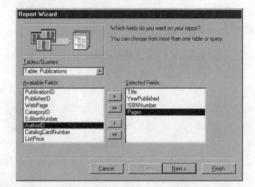

**FIGURE 9.2.**

*Using the Report Wizard to include the fields you want in your report.*

9

6. Select the Compact layout option if it's not already chosen and click Next> to move on.

7. You're almost done now. Edit Access's suggestion for a report title to read: Publications by Title. Make sure you've chosen the option button Preview the Report.

8. Click the Finish button. Access displays the finished report. (See Figure 9.3.)

**FIGURE 9.3.**

*The finished report from a wizard.*

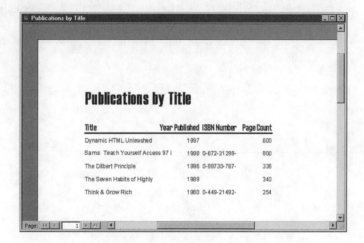

Scroll through this report. If you like, click the Print button in the toolbar to see a printed version of it. All the data is included. There's nothing wrong with this report, but it's not perfect, either.

Although this task uses the general Report Wizard, you can also drag fields onto reports from a field list using the same method you did to drag fields onto forms.

# Altering the Wizard's Output

For most purposes, this report is just fine. However, you can see that the orientation of the Year Published column is a little strange and the Title and ISBN Number columns are too narrow for their contents. You'll correct these problems in the following task.

Note that the all the field labels read alright because Access uses the Caption property for field labels when making forms or reports. Each field you've included in this report has a name and a different caption. For example, the field named YearPublished has a Caption property Year Published. This gives us the best of both worlds. You can use YearPublished for manipulating data (as in queries) where a space might pose problems, but the field displays as Year Published (that is, in good human terms) in forms and reports. Without a Caption property set for a field, Access has to fall back on the actual field name for a label.

The following task shows how to change a report.

## Task: Modifying a report

1. Click the Close Window button in the toolbar. Your screen should look like Figure 9.4, showing the wizard-created report in Design View. If the Formatting toolbar is not shown, turn it on.

   The view you have now is very similar to form Design View. Operating in it is also very similar. You rearrange fields by selecting them and dragging them just as you did in form design. This report is a bit more complex than a simple form because the wizard has left both the report header and footer and the page header and footer sections open.

▼
**FIGURE 9.4.**

*Report Design View.*

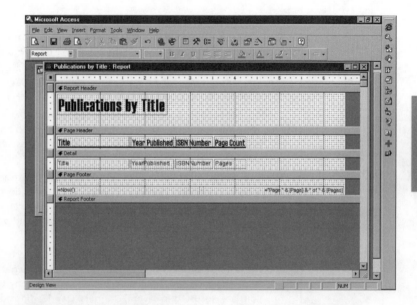

**Note**

**NEW TERM** A *page header* is a section printed at the top of each page. *Page footers* appear at the bottom of each page. Access also can have headers or footers for groups and whole reports. A band is the place in report design where you enter what's to be placed in a header, footer, or the detail section of a report.

In the example shown in Figure 9.4, the words Publications by Title (the name you assigned to the report in the last step of the Wizard) are in the Report header band. These words appear at the top the entire report. The report header band is a place you put things you want to appear at the top of an entire report and only once. Footers, both page and report, appear at the bottom of each page and report respectively.

This Page header band has entries for the report labels. Use the Page header or footer bands to show information (not just labels) that you want to appear at the top and bottom of each page respectively.

2. Select the YearPublished control in the Detail section. If the Properties window is not visible, right-click over the control and select Properties from the shortcut
▼    menu.

**Tip**

A persistent problem people have with visual design program such as Access is selection of individual objects. The problem isn't so much selection as selecting without moving the object at the same time. Access solves this problem quite neatly. Take a look at the Formatting toolbar in Figure 9.4. That's the second or lower toolbar.

The left-most combo box has the word Report in it. That means that at this time the entire report is selected. Pull down the combo box and you'll see all the objects that are on this report. To select one, just choose it from the pull-down list and Access will highlight it.

The Page footer band also has the entry Now() in a text box. This is an Access built-in function that prints the system date or time. The advantage of using a function like Now() in this place is the report picks up the computer's date and time whenever you run this report and places it in the page header.

If you entered a date such as June 1, 1997 for the date field, you'd have to edit the report design each time you ran the report to get the right date in this field. Using the Now() function performs this automatically. Built-in functions are discussed in several chapters. Day 17, "Introduction to Programming in Access," shows you how to create custom functions.

3. Select the Format tab on the Properties window and scroll all the way to the bottom of the tab to find the Text Align property. The default value is General which translates, for numeric data such as a year, into align right. For this report, though, align left would probably look better to most people. Select Left from the drop-down list box. Close the Properties window for now.

4. You can resize or move fields or labels just as you did with forms. Select the Page Count label and the Pages field using marquee selection. Move these fields over to the right side of the report. If you happen to move the fat line below the labels, don't fret; you're going to resize that in a minute anyway.

5. Next, select the ISBN Number label and then hold down the Shift key while clicking the ISBNNumber field. Drag the two fields to the right until they're about half an inch from the Page Count fields. Move the mouse to the right side of the selected controls until the left-right sizing arrow. Click and drag to the right to make the fields wider.

Remember you can resize a field when the cursor changes to look like a double arrow. You move a field when the cursor looks like a hand. These operations work in Report Design just as they did in Form Design.

▼  6. Now select the Year Published label and YearPublished field in the same man-
      ner. Drag these fields to the right. Click the line. Move the mouse to the left-most
      side of the line until it changes to the sizing cursor. Click and drag all the way to
      the left to make the line stretch across the width of the report.

   7. Finally, resize the Title label and field so they stretch all the way to the Year
      Published column. The report should now resemble Figure 9.5.

      As you change your report around, occasionally click the left-most button to switch
      into Report View. If you don't want to chance ruining this report, save and close it,
      and then rerun the wizard to make a clone to experiment with. You might also want
      to experiment with other wizard options.

**FIGURE 9.5.**

*The modified report in
Design View.*

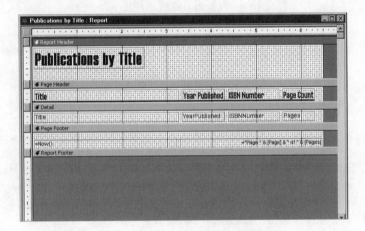

9

> **Tip**
>
> You might find it easier to align your report's fields to look like the exam-
> ple's if you alter the default grid and keep Snap to Grid on. This task used
> the Snap to Grid with a grid set at 10×12.
>
> To change the default grid spacing from 20×24 to a more practical 10×12,
> pull down the Edit menu and choose Select Report. This selects the entire
> report rather than just one object or section.
>
> Click the Properties button in the toolbar. Locate the Grid X and Grid Y
> properties in the Properties list box. Enter 10 for Grid X and 12 for Grid Y.
> Close the Properties list box by clicking its X button. That's all there is to it.

   8. Click the Print Preview button in the toolbar. The screen should resemble Figure
      9.6. You may have to adjust the report window to get it close to what Figure 9.6
      shows. When you run your cursor over this button, Access responds with the
▼     tooltip View. Click the one-page button—third from the left. Now pull down the

▼      combo box that reads Fit or shows a percentage from 10 percent to 200 percent in
       it. This combo box lies two buttons to the right of the one-page button—it's the
       fifth toolbar object from the left. Experiment with other zoom levels in this box.
       Zooming at 75 percent is a good compromise for the report at an 800×600 screen
       resolution.

**FIGURE 9.6.**

*The modified report in*
*Print Preview.*

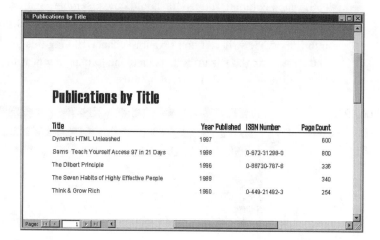

▲

Your report will look different from the screen shots shown here because of screen resolution and font availability. Access chose the Haettenschweiler font for this report's
labels and Arial for the report data. If you don't have those fonts, your report will, naturally, vary from the examples shown.

This is serviceable, but still a bit away from what you'd want to give your bosses or
clients. You'll come back to this report later and spiff it up even more. For now, pull
down the File menu and click Close. Save or discard changes as appropriate if you're
prompted. Your finished report should, when saved, resemble Figure 9.6.

| Do | Don't |
|---|---|
| **DO** use Report Wizards to rough out your reports. | **DON'T** be disappointed if a wizard's output isn't exactly what you desire. That's what manual design is for. In many cases a report should be laid out according to the qualitative content of your database. Access wizards, at least in the current version, aren't capable of making value judgments on your data, so they use general rules to lay out your reports. General rules applied to a specific case often come close, but very rarely hit a bull's-eye. |

9

# Mailing Labels

Since most printers do a poor job of handling envelopes, creating mailing labels from the information in a database is a common and often annoying job. Making these labels poses two problems: getting the text in the center of the individual labels and preventing label creep. Label creep happens when the text prints right on the first set of labels, but then creeps up or down until it starts printing off the labels and onto the space in between them. The truly annoying thing about label creep is that when it occurs, you often have to do much of the printing job over again, wasting a lot of time and materials.

Access has a wizard aimed at making the label printing job quite a bit easier than it would be if you did it manually. The best part of the wizard is that it has programmed into it the most popular label sizes and layouts cataloged by label number. This way you can just tell Access what type of label you're planning to use and the program does the proper layout. No more do you have to calculate how many 2 3/8-inch labels plus header, footer, and interlabel spaces fit on a page. The programmers of the Label Report Wizard have done all of the tedious work for you.

Another difference between the Label Wizard and the standard Report Wizard is that the Label Wizard creates report expressions as you supply it field and punctuation information. The next task illustrates creating a report suitable for labels by using the Label Wizard.

## Task: Making mailing labels

1. You should be on the Database window with the Report tab selected. If you're not, navigate back to that place. Click the New button to start a new report.

2. Select Label Wizard in the list box at the top of the New Report dialog. In the drop-down list box at the bottom of the dialog, select `Publishers` as the source table for this set of mailing labels. Click OK.

3. Choose Avery 5163 as the label type at the next box. If your label selection doesn't show a large variety of labels, click the Show Custom Labels check box to deselect it. Click Next>.

4. Leave the next screen at the defaults, which for this example are Arial font, 8-point type size, and light font weight, black in color. Click Next>.

5. Refer to Figure 9.7. This is where you not only tell Access what fields to include in your mailing labels, but format the labels as you see fit to create a prototype label. The Prototype Label: box will start out empty, and you'll create content for this screen in the next few steps.

**FIGURE 9.7.**

*Designing the mailing label.*

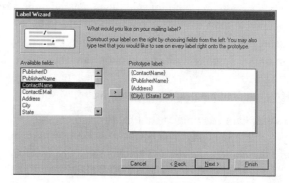

6. Double-click the `ContactName` field in the left list box. Access inserts the `ContactName` field between curly braces (`{}`) to indicate that the data from the `ContactName` field will be inserted in the labels rather than the word ContactName.

7. You're ready to move on to the next line, so click where you think a new line should appear on the label—that is, right below the `{ContactName}` line. Access moves the focus down to the second line of your label template. On this line add the `PublisherName` field.

8. If necessary, scroll the list box until the Address, City, State, and ZIP fields come into view. Add the Address field to the third line of the label. This is the only entry on the third line, so click the fourth line.

9. Add the City field, a comma, a space, the State field, a space, and finally the ZIP field to the mailing label's fourth line.

**Tip**

You can add literals to mailing labels just like field data. The comma after the City field is a literal, for example. If you want such an entry, like the word ATTN:, enter it wherever you want it to appear on the label. Access is happy to accommodate you.

10. Click the Next> button and choose the PublisherName field to sort or order this label report on as shown in Figure 9.8.

**FIGURE 9.8.**

*Specifying a field to sort on for the report.*

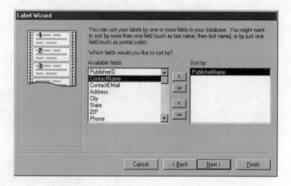

11. Click the Next> button. Here's where you give a name for your label report. Edit Access's choice to Publisher Mailing Labels.

12. Make sure you have the See the Labels As They Will Look Printed option button selected. Click the Finish button to move to Print Preview mode. (See Figure 9.9.)

FIGURE 9.9.

*The mailing labels. Note that the sort order works across then down.*

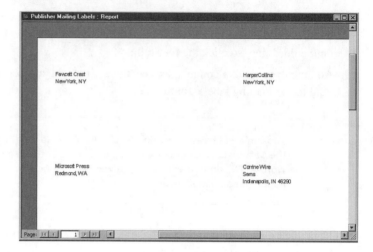

▲

Figure 9.10 shows the Mailing Label Wizard's work in Design View. If you wanted to print these labels for a mailing, you'd only need to tell Access to print this report and feed Avery 5163 or equivalent labels to your printer. Access makes the tedious and often frustrating job of printing mailing labels as simple as using a wizard.

**FIGURE 9.10.**

*The finished mailing label report in Design View.*

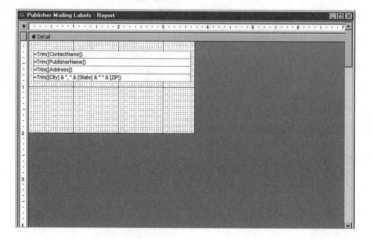

Close this report, canceling any changes you may have inadvertently made while in Design View.

# Looking at Report Expressions

Examine Figure 9.10 and note that the expression =Trim([City] & ", " & [State] & " " & [ZIP]) makes up the last line of this label. Everything included in this label is an expression. You made these expressions when you instructed the wizard in the Prototype label dialog, as shown in Figure 9.8.

In some reports, the field length left by the wizard-generated reports results in rather amateurish-looking output. The fixed-length fields like those in the preceding must be large enough to show all the data that could possibly be entered into them, but then they are too large for some of the entries. If you were to shrink down the fields so that small entries looked good, the longer entries would be truncated, or chopped off.

Here's an example. Fields large enough to show the entire name Constance Jacqueline Fortesque show the name Tom J. Doe like this:

```
Tom          J          Doe
```

Size the fields to fit Tom J. Doe correctly, and Constance Jacqueline Fortesque looks like this:

```
Con J For
```

Neither size compromise is satisfactory. Using expressions based on the data in the fields instead of the fields themselves solves the field size dilemma in this type of report. In this case, an expression is a series of fields, punctuation marks, and spaces that may or may not include some Access-specific instructions. You saw an example of expressions in the Mailing Label Wizard's output. The following task shows how to create a report that includes field expressions.

Field expressions are only one type of expression you can use in Access. You've already seen some Access expressions in queries, the label report, and in tables. The expressions used in the following task show only a few tricks you can do with expressions.

## Task: Field expressions in reports

You might not like the result in this report, but the point of this task is instruction, not making a perfect report. This technique is very useful for a variety of other reporting tasks.

1. Launch Access if necessary and load the BookStore database. Click the Reports tab. Click the New button to design a new report. Select the Authors table in the drop-down list box and click OK. You'll see three bands for header and detail sections.

**Tip**

You might find selecting fields in the narrow header bands to be tedious or difficult. You can increase the size of a band by moving your cursor to the bottom or top of it, and then dragging. If you do this, be sure to return the band back to its original size before running the report, or the report's spacing will look a bit odd.

If you find using the marquee selection awkward, you can also select several fields by Shift+clicking them. Shift+click is Access talk for "extend selection."

2. The first control you'll add to the report will be an unbound text box. You'll bind the text box to some fields later. Click the Text Box tool in the toolbox. This is the tool with abl on it. Click in the report's design grid in the detail band and drag to create a box about 2 inches wide (the ruler at the top can help you size the control). Figure 9.11 shows this operation underway. Be careful not to make the box too tall. If you mess it up, just click the Delete key and repeat the process.

**FIGURE 9.11.**

*Inserting an unbound text field.*

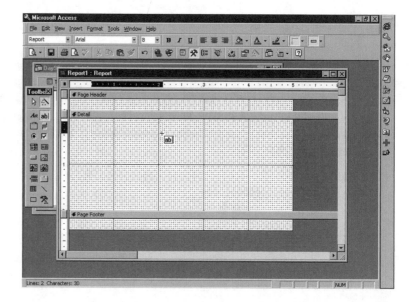

3. Click away from the new field to remove the highlight. Click only on the label part of this field and delete it. The label part of the new field will have text in it saying something like Text 10. You now have a report with a text field. The new text field has the word Unbound in it.

▼    4. It's now time to use an expression to bind this field to the underlying table. Click
        the Properties button in the toolbar. That's the button with a white square and a
        hand on it over toward the right. Click the new text box to bring up its properties in
        the Properties window. Click the Data tab. Locate the `Control Source` property.
        Your screen should resemble Figure 9.12, except the name for your text box (in the
        Properties list box title bar) might be different from that shown in Figure 9.16. The
        text box's name is unimportant for the purposes of this example.

**FIGURE 9.12.**

*The Control Source
property controls what
Access displays in a
text box.*

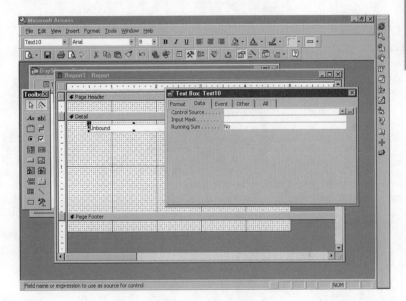

    5. Click in the empty row to the right of the Control Source label. Press Shift+F2 to
        zoom into an editing box. This last step isn't necessary to enter an expression, but
        makes your job much easier. Your screen should look like Figure 9.13.

    6. Enter the expression: `=Trim([FirstName]&" "&[LastName])` in the Zoom box.

    7. Click OK to close the Zoom box. Access will insert the Zoom box's text into the
        Control Source property. Click the Layout View button to see your results. Your
▼        report detail should look like the first lines of the entries in Figure 9.14.

**FIGURE 9.13.**

*Zoom mode for enter-ing expressions.*

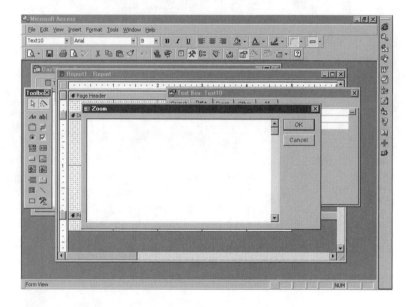

**FIGURE 9.14.**

*The report's output after the inclusion of an expression.*

8.  Return to Design mode. Open the Field List window by clicking the Field List toolbar button. Drag the `Nationality` field and drop it a little to the right of the field you just inserted. Delete its label.

9.  Insert another unbound text box just as you did for the first line of this report. Place this text box immediately below the first, making it about 2-1/2 inches wide. Delete its label. Highlight the now unbound control. Locate the Control Source entry area for this text box and press Shift+F2. Enter the expression

    ```
    =Trim("Born on " & [Birthdate] & " at " & [Birthplace])
    ```

    (See Figure 9.15.)

10. Click the Layout View button in the toolbar. Access runs the report.

**FIGURE 9.15.**

*The expression to con-
catenate the
Birthdate and
Birthplace fields in
the report.*

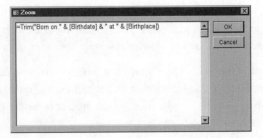

▲

# How Did That Work?

Back when you started this report, you told Access to bind the Authors table to it. This is a key element in how these expressions worked. Return to Design View for this report if you're not there now. Click the Nationality field to highlight it. Look in the Properties list box to see the control source property for this control. It's set to Nationality.

A Control Source is the source of what appears as contents for that control when outside of Design View. In the case of the Nationality control, the contents of the Nationality field in the Authors table is what appears when you print or preview this report. Access knows to look in Authors for the Nationality field because during the initial phase of the Report Wizard, you told Access that Authors is the table bound to this report.

When you enter an equals sign (=) at the beginning of a Control Source, you're telling Access you'll be entering an expression—the same as with Excel. You could edit the Control Source for the Nationality text box to read =[Nationality], which gives you the same results as you have now with this control, but it would serve no practical purpose.

The expressions you added to the unbound text controls for the name and the birth infor-mation are more complex than that. They contain not only the field contents for more than one field, but spaces and other literal text.

**Caution**

Access, like many computer programs, interprets the space character as the end of a string of characters—or delimiter. It is unusual in that it'll let you enter field names containing spaces. These spaces are a problem in expres-sions because Access has no way of knowing when it hits a space if you mean that as an end to the name or a part of the field name.

You can use field names containing spaces by enclosing them in square brack-ets ([  ]) within expressions. It's a good habit to always enter field names within square brackets even if they have one name such as Address. That way you'll get into good habits and won't hit baffling "gotchas" later on.

Look at the expression in the first row of this report's detail band. It reads

```
=Trim([FirstName] & " "  & [LastName])
```

Let's take it apart to see how it works. The first character is the equals sign (=). This indicates to Access that what follows is an expression.

The second element is the word Trim. `Trim()` is a built-in Access function that strips white spaces from the right and left side of a string of characters. Access has two related functions, `LTrim()` and `RTrim()`, which only strip spaces from the left and right of a character string, respectively.

The parentheses that functions come with and are identified by are for function parameters. Parameters represent the data that functions operate upon. In this case, `Trim()`'s parameters are the whole expression. This tells `Trim()` that you want the spaces stripped from the right and left of the whole expression.

 **Note**

> You can use `LTrim()` and `RTrim()` together with results identical to just `Trim()`. In other words, `=LTrim(RTrim([Name]))` results in the same output as `=Trim([Name])`. Access programmers are apparently a wild and crazy bunch.

The third element is the field `FirstName` in square brackets `[FirstName]`. The `Authors` table's field names don't contain spaces, so there's no requirement to include the field name in brackets, but like the sidebar says, it's good practice. There's no penalty for using brackets for field names and two advantages to always doing so: You'll never have an expression with a space misfire due to lack of brackets, and you'll be able to differentiate field names from other elements in expressions.

After `[FirstName]` comes the &, or ampersand operator. This tells Access to concatenate, or join, two elements in a string expression. This first & joins the `[FirstName]` field to the `" "`, which is an open quote, a space, and a close quote. If you didn't include this space in the string at this place, the `FirstName` field would be jammed up against the `LastName` field. The space here prevents Greg Jefferson from looking like GregJefferson.

The rest of the expression follows the first part. The last element is the closed parentheses, indicating the end of the string expression the `Trim()` function applies to.

The birth information expression is almost identical to the first but includes more verbiage. Anything enclosed in double quotation marks in an Access expression appears as a literal. So if you modified the first row to read as follows:

```
=Trim([FirstName] & " Hi! " & [MiddleName] & " " & [LastName])
```

the report would come out:

```
Greg Hi! J. Jefferson
Bill Hi! G. Jones
```

and so forth.

| Do | Don't |
|---|---|
| **DO** use expressions liberally in your reports. In many cases, they look much better than just fields. | **DON'T** neglect to enclose all your field names in square brackets even if Access enables you to get away with skipping this step. Good programming practice always pays off. |

# Groups

Think back to the query done in Day 7, "Creating Simple Queries." This showed publication information sorted or ordered by title. One logical thing you can derive from this query is a report creating a list of all books available at the bookstore, along with the relevant information about those books.

Close the report just created, saving any changes only for your own benefit. The point of the next task is to create a report showing all the publications in the database, plus see the total number of books for each publisher. This is a lot simpler to do than to say, as you'll soon see. The following task bypasses the wizard process. Access includes a wizard that sorts and groups well, but using it will disguise the underlying principles this task is supposed to demonstrate. At this point you should be comfortable enough manipulating Access that you won't have a problem following along with the comparatively faster pace of this task.

## Task: A grouped and totaled report

1. On the Database window's Reports tab, click the New button to start a new report. Scroll through the list of queries and tables Access gives you to locate the three-table query done in Day 7. If you followed the book's examples exactly, this query is called Bibliography. (This query is also part of the sample database.) Click the query's name, click the Design View option, and then click OK.

2. Click the Sorting and Grouping toolbar button to open up the combination list box shown in Figure 9.16.

**FIGURE 9.16.**

*Starting the Sorting and Grouping report.*

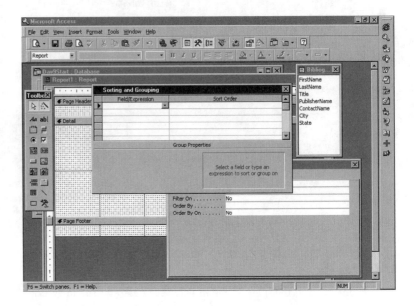

3. Pull down the Field/Expression combo box and click `PublisherName` to tell Access you want to group on this field. Access will default to Ascending order. Leave that as it is.

4. Pull down the combo box for Group Header in the Group Properties section and change that to `Yes`. You can also double-click this field to toggle it. Access will add another band to the report.

**Caution**

> `PublisherName` works for this example because your database hasn't any duplication of names. In a live application, you wouldn't want to group on the `PublisherName` field because duplicate names can easily exist in your data. Instead, you'd use the key field for the `Publishers` table, which is `PublisherID`. While this report and query works with the sample data, grouping on a field that might contain duplicate entries isn't good practice.

5. If the Field list window isn't open, click its toolbar button to open it. If your screen is too cluttered for your tastes, close the Sorting and Grouping box by clicking on its toolbar or X icon. At this point your screen should resemble Figure 9.17.

**FIGURE 9.17.**

*Setting up to add fields for the grouping report.*

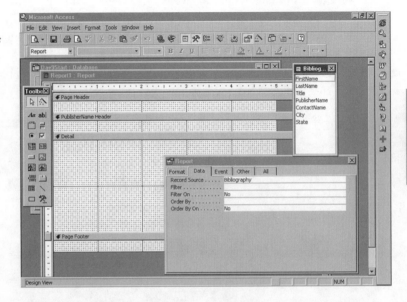

6. Click the `PublisherName` field in the field list box. Drag it to the PublisherName header band. Click away from the `PublisherName` field, and then click its label only. Press Delete to remove the field label from this field. Move the control to position in a decent spot.

7. From the Toolbox, select the Text Box control and place one near the top and at the far right of the Detail section of the report. Go to the `Control Source` property for this control and enter `=Trim([LastName] & ", " & [FirstName])`. Click in the label portion of the control and change the text to read `Author:`.

8. From the Field List, click and drag the `Title` field to the left side of the detail section. Place it so that the bottom lines up with the bottom of the text box you placed in step 7.

9. This next step isn't really tricky, but it's tedious. You need to move the labels and only the labels of the fields in the Detail section from the Detail section to the Group Header section. The Group Header section or band is the band labeled PublisherName Header where you dragged the `PublisherName` field earlier. You will probably have to enlarge this band to accommodate the new field labels. The easiest way to remove and insert the labels is to click the report away from any fields, and then click a field label. Hold down the Shift key and click the other label. Press Ctrl+X to cut the labels to the clipboard. Click in the Group Header section and press Ctrl+V to paste the labels there.

▼  10.  Add a line control above the `PublisherName` field in the PublisherName Header section. Make the line stretch across the width of the report. This will be used to separate the groups from one another.

11.  Arrange the report to look like Figure 9.18. Don't be overly concerned about aligning fields to look good. The focus of this task is grouping, not aligning. You can always prettify your reports after you have the basics down.

**FIGURE 9.18.**

*The arranged report.*

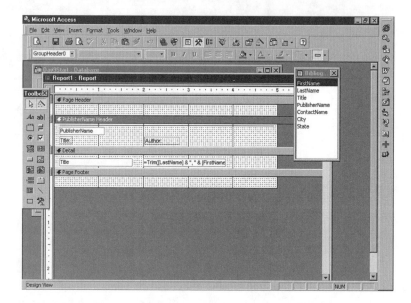

12.  Click the Layout View button on the toolbar. Your report should perform like the one shown in Figure 9.19 even if it doesn't look exactly like it.

**FIGURE 9.19.**

*A grouped report.*

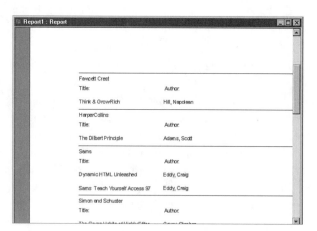

▲

Even the book's example isn't terribly neat looking, but it works and that's what's important. The only two elements missing are a label for the publishers' names and some detail to show the total number of publications for each publisher. The following task shows you how to add these.

## Task: Adding report elements

▼TASK

1. Return to Design View for this report, if necessary, by clicking the Close button in Print Preview. Open up the Sorting and Grouping box if you closed it last task. Locate the Group Footer pull-down field in the Sorting and Grouping box. Double-click this to change its entry to Yes and open up a Group Footer band. Close the Sorting and Grouping box if you choose.

2. Add a text box in the PublisherName Footer band right, all the way to the left side of the band. Open the Properties list box and locate the Control Source for this unbound text box. Enter

   ```
   =Count([Title])
   ```

   as a control source for this text box. Move to the Format tab in the Properties window and change the Text Align property to Left. Edit this control's label to read

   ```
   Titles:
   ```

   Keep in mind that you can edit the label's entry by either clicking within it and then editing the contents, or by locating the Caption property in its Properties list box (labels have them too) and editing the entry there.

3. Move the PublisherName field in the group header to the right a smidge. Locate the Label control in the toolbox. That's the control with the large A on it. Click it and drag to add a label just to the left of the PublisherName field. Enter

   ```
   Publisher:
   ```

   in this label. This example also changed the font size from 8 to 11 and made it bold for both the label and the PublisherName field. You may have to resize these controls when you change the font properties. Your screen should resemble Figure 9.20. This is a bit redundant, as you could have edited the original label that came with the PublisherName field, but this task shows what you can do. You can decide later how you want to do things.

▼

**FIGURE 9.20.**

*Design View of a slightly complex report.*

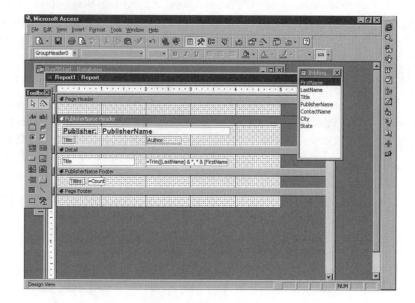

4. Run the report by clicking the Layout or Print Preview button. Then save it (File|Save As/Export) under the name `Titles by Publisher`. When running, your results should look like Figure 9.21, although your alignment probably won't be the same. The important things to focus on are

   - Is your report grouping on the publishers' names?
   - Are your titles summed correctly?

**FIGURE 9.21.**

*Print Preview of a slightly complex report.*

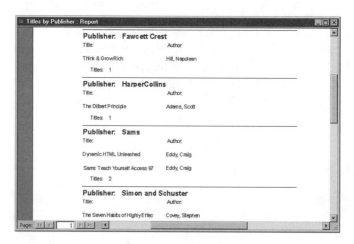

This report doesn't look very good, but could if you changed the fonts and font sizes using the formatting toolbar, added a few lines or boxes from the toolbox, and generally aligned the fields better. If you tell Access to break each page on the group by adding a page break, you have a report that prints out a class card for each student on a new piece of paper. You've seen the fundamentals today. Adding the frills can be time-consuming, but isn't technically difficult. Figure 9.22 shows the same report with some added lines and formatting. It took only about three minutes for an experienced Access user to go from 9.21 to 9.22.

**FIGURE 9.22.**

*The report with a few added frills.*

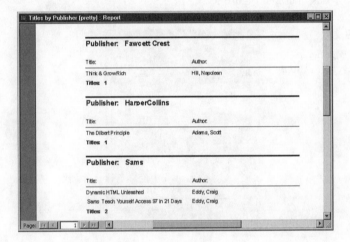

## Summary

Reports present data much as forms do. The biggest difference between forms and reports is that forms work best onscreen, while reports work best printed. You can view report data on the screen and you can print forms, but neither is optimal.

Today you learned how to use the general Report Wizard and how to modify some aspects of the wizard's output. You also got a good run at using the Mailing Label Wizard to design mailing or other labels. Keep in mind that the Label Wizard is good not only for mailing labels, but also for other labels such as folder, record, and book labels. The Mailing Label Wizard can be an enormous time and mood saver. Use it whenever you need to put data precisely on standard size labels or cards.

You didn't see the Sorting and Grouping Wizard in this chapter because it's rather self-explanatory. Instead, you reproduced the work of the wizard manually.

The Mailing Label Wizard has memorized the dimensions of just about all the labels you're likely to encounter, so it'll save you a great deal of layout frustration, too.

# Q&A

**Q** I'm making a mailing label, but don't want to output to an Avery brand label. Can I create my own label size?

**A** Yes. If none of the predefined labels meets your needs, you can create your label either manually or using the wizard. After you're in Design View for the label, choose File|Page Setup from the menu. This brings up a tabbed dialog that enables you to create labels (or other page-related information) to your liking. You can see this dialog in Figure 9.23.

**FIGURE 9.23.**

*The File-Page Setup dialog in report Design View.*

**Q** Can I set a display of the running sum in a report?

**A** Yes, and you are getting a little ahead of where we are. Quickly, you include a running sum by including a bound text box or an unbound text box with an expression in the band to where you want the sum to apply. You then set the `Running Sum` property for that text box to the sum type you wish to calculate.

**Q** I tried printing a mailing label report. The report seems to work all right, but the labels came off in my laser printer. This could have caused real damage. Luckily, none was done. What good is making a mailing label report if I can't use my printer to do output?

**A** You need to buy mailing labels specifically made for laser printers. These work much better than general-purpose labels. Also, if your printer has the option of using a straight paper path, opt for doing the printing that way even if you have to position a tray to catch the output.

**Q** How do you show the report and page header and footer bands? I need to open these bands before I can enter data into them.

**A** In report Design View, click the Layout View menu, and then select either Report Header/Footer or Page Header/Footer.

**Q** **Why can't Access be smart enough to know when field names end and begin without me bothering with square brackets?**

**A** Look at the following: Last Name Street Address. What are the field names? They might be Last Name and Street Address, or there might be three fields here—Last Name, Street, and Address. Placing brackets [Last Name][Street Address] removes any ambiguity.

**Q** **Why not just apply the Trim() function to the fields themselves rather than construct an expression?**

**A** Following your idea, you'd need three `Trim()`s, and, although Access allows this, you wouldn't get your desired result. Look at the Mailing Label Example report's second line. It reads `=Trim([Address])`. The reason your idea won't work is that fields start and end at specific places. If the fields could shift around to make room for non-space characters and squeeze back for trimmed spaces, your technique would be all right. You wouldn't want to do it anyway. It would actually be more effort than just making an expression because you'd need to edit three fields.

# Workshop

Here's where you can test and apply what you have learned today.

## Quiz

1. What is concatenation?

2. Will the expression `=Ltrim(Rtrim([FirstName]))` yield the same output as `=Trim([FirstName])`?

3. How often will a label in the report Header Band appear?

4. If you want a footer on each page, where should you put the label when in Design View?

5. Can a mailing label report be based in a query if that query has expressions included in it? What will be the adverse consequences of doing this?

6. What properties control the grid spacing in the report design grid? (The same properties control the grid spacing in the form design grid.)

7. Why bother with brackets (`[]`) for field names?

8. What built-in function does Access have that totals number fields in a group or a report? Hint: Look at the Class Cards report in Design View.

9. Can you bind a report to another report? To a table? To a query?

## Exercises

1. Start a new query. Bind the `Publications` table to this query.

2. Include the fields for `Title`, `ISBNNumber`, and `Category`.

3. Add a criterion that selects for only those records where the category is Self Help or Business.

4. Save the query by using a name of your choosing.

5. Create a label report based on this query. Use any predefined label type appropriate for this task. Add the three fields on separate lines in the order specified in step 2.

6. Check your output by using the View button.

7. Optionally save this report. This book will not refer to it again. It could be used to print shelf labels for the bookstore's warehouse.

# DAY **10**

# Designing Queries for Dates and Parameters

Today's material covers the following topics:

- Expression (developer-defined) fields in queries
- How Access handles date information
- Date formats
- Date arithmetic
- Constructing a parameter query
- Use of wildcards within parameter queries
- Parameter queries that return a range of values
- Creating a query that prompts users for criteria
- Creating a new table from a query

In many ways, queries form the heart of Access or any other relational database system. Access can take information from one or more query fields, operate on that information, and then create a new field for the output of the operation.

# Manipulating Dates in Queries

Dates are an important part of most databases. Think of all you could do with an information system, even if you could only query it by date. Here are a few examples of questions you could find answers to:

How many and which customers have ordered in the past month?

How many customers haven't bought anything in the past year?

What patients haven't been in for their yearly checkup?

How old are your accounts receivable?

How many of your employees have been here long enough to be vested?

What was your sales volume for each month in 1997?

What products sold the greatest quantity in each month of 1996?

You can imagine that extracting such information from a paper-based filing system would be a great chore. With Access, however, each of those questions could be answered in a few seconds using queries.

Before moving on to dates in queries, this chapter shows you how Access records dates in databases, how it displays dates, and what underlying magic it has to let it perform date-based queries.

The following task works with the BirthDate field in the Authors table and examines how Access can present date information.

## Task: Working with a Date field in a table

1. Launch Access and open the BookStore database if necessary. Click the Authors table to highlight it, and then click the Design button to open this table in Design View.

2. Click the row for the BirthDate field. The field properties at the bottom of the window change to those of the BirthDate field (see Figure 10.1).

**FIGURE 10.1.**

*The field properties for the BirthDate field.*

3. Most of these properties are old friends. The one new property to consider in this section is Format, which is first in the list of field properties. Click in the Format property to give this field the focus. Press F4 to drop down the list section of this combo box. Pressing F4 in a combo box has the same effect as clicking the down arrow. The list of built-in formats for Date/Time data type fields are displayed. This list includes General Date, Long Date, Medium Date, Short Date, Long Time, Medium Time, Short Time.

**Note**

Access stores data in Date/Time data type fields uniformly. The Format property for this data type only affects the display of the data, not its value.

4. Change the value in the property to Long Date. Change the Input Mask to 99/99/0000;0. Edit the Caption property for this field to read Date of Birth. Locate the DateOfDeath. Change its Input Mask to 99/99/0000;0 as well.

Click the Datasheet View button to leave Design View. Click **Yes** when Access reminds you that you must save your table before leaving Design View. The new format is shown in Figure 10.2.

**FIGURE 10.2.**

*The BirthDate field in Long Date format.*

| Author ID | First Name | Last Name | Nationality | Date of Birth | Birt |
|---|---|---|---|---|---|
| 1 Craig | Eddy | USA | Friday, November 26, 1965 | Hampt |
| 2 Napolean | Hill | USA | | |
| 3 Scott | Adams | USA | | |
| 4 Stephen | Covey | USA | | |
| 6 Kurt | Vonnegut | USA | Friday, November 11, 1922 | Indiana |
| * (AutoNumber) | | | | |

5. For the sake of data, enter an Authors table record for Herman Melville. Click in the bottom row of the Datasheet window. Here are the particulars of the data to enter (you'll enter his date of birth and date of death later):

| Field       | Data          |
|-------------|---------------|
| First Name  | Herman        |
| Last Name   | Melville      |
| Nationality | USA           |
| BirthPlace  | New York, NY  |

6. Move to the Date of Birth. Enter 8/1/1819 and tab out of the field. As soon as you do, Access changes this field to the Long Date format as shown in Figure 10.3. Note that the Date of Birth column in this figure has been slightly widened to show all the detail of this field.

**FIGURE 10.3.**

*Access automatically changes the date to* Long Date *format.*

| Author | First Name | Last Name | Nationality | Date of Birth | Birthplace | Trainin |
|--------|------------|-----------|-------------|---------------|------------|---------|
| 1 | Craig | Eddy | USA | Friday, November 26, 1965 | Hampton, VA | |
| 2 | Napolean | Hill | USA | | | |
| 3 | Scott | Adams | USA | | | |
| 4 | Stephen | Covey | USA | | | |
| 6 | Kurt | Vonnegut | USA | Friday, November 11, 1922 | Indianapolis, Indiana | |
| 8 | Herman | Melville | USA | Sunday, August 01, 1819 | New York, NY | |
| (lumber) | | | | | | |

7. Even though you didn't enter the day of week information, Access was able to return the right day of the week for Herman's birth. Move next to the record for Stephen Covey (or any other author) and go to the Date of Birth column. Enter 2/30/1950 for the birthday. Press Tab. Your screen should resemble Figure 10.4.

Access is smart enough to know that there is no February 30 in 1975, or any other year for that matter. It won't accept dates that make no sense in date fields. You are free to enter wrong dates that are valid, but not obviously invalid entries such as 2/30/75. Click OK to clear the message box. Restore the date of birth to its original value by pressing the Esc key.

**FIGURE 10.4.**

*Access refuses to accept incorrect date information.*

Within certain limits, Access doesn't care how you enter dates. You can enter dates as you've done before, 7/8/1974, or in its full format, July 8, 1974. This date is a Monday, but Access won't accept day of week data. It insists on supplying that itself.

If you want, experiment entering dates in different formats. Access gladly accepts 7 Jul 74, July 7, 1974, and Jul 7, 74, to give you an idea.

Return to Design View. Click in the BirthDate field to show the field properties for this field. Change the Format property from Long Date to Medium Date. Return to Datasheet View. Click Yes when Access asks you if you want to save your changes. Your screen should resemble Figure 10.5. Notice that this date format has a serious Year 2000 problem: the birthdate for Herman Melville shows as 01-Aug-19! Return to the design view and change the Format for both BirthDate and DateOfDeath to read mm/dd/yyyy. Switch back to Datasheet view and notice that the date is still correct, it was just displayed incorrectly.

**FIGURE 10.5.**

*The effect of changing the Date Format property.*

| Author | First Name | Last Name | Nationality | Date of Birth | Birthplace | Trainin |
|--------|-----------|-----------|-------------|---------------|-----------|---------|
| 1 Craig | Eddy | USA | | 26-Nov-65 | Hampton, VA | |
| 2 Napolean | Hill | USA | | | | |
| 3 Scott | Adams | USA | | | | |
| 4 Stephen | Covey | USA | | | | |
| 6 Kurt | Vonnegut | USA | | 11-Nov-22 | Indianapolis, Indiana | |
| 8 Herman | Melville | USA | | 01-Aug-19 | New York, NY | |

**10**

**Note**

Changing the format of a date doesn't change the value of the date. If you changed the Format property for the BirthDate field to a time format, Access would have changed all Date of Birth displays to 12:00 a.m., but would still have kept the right data for each record stored in the field.

Close this table.

**Tip**

Even though you told Access to discard changes to the table's layout, Access kept the edits you did to this table. That is, discarding layout changes did not cause you to lose the data you entered for date of birth for the authors.

Access writes data to disk as soon as you leave the last field if the data's valid and in a valid record. Discarding layout changes has nothing to do with the data entered in the table.

# Dates in Queries

Internally, Access stores dates as double precision numbers. The whole part of the number, the part to the left of the decimal place, is for the date. The fractional part of the number is the time. Access dates start with the number 1 for December 31, 1899, and go up to the year 9999. Dates prior to December 31, 1899, are negative. Thus, the number 2.0000 represents January 1, 1900, in Access's method; January 11, 1900, is day 12.0000; and so forth. Each date is really a number.

In human expression, subtracting 1/2/31 from 4/5/65 is a mind-boggling job. Since these dates are reduced to simple numbers internally within Access, the program can do all sorts of manipulations on them quite easily, as you shall see.

The following task shows how you can use dates as criteria for queries.

## Task: Date criteria

1. From the Database window, click the Queries tab. Click New. Select Design View and click OK.

2. Select the `Publications` table in the Show Table dialog's list box. Click Add to add this table to the new query. Select the `Authors` table and add it as well. Click Close.

3. Double-click the `Title`, `YearPublished`, and `ISBNNumber` fields from the Publications list box. The double-click the `FirstName`, `LastName`, and `Birthdate` fields from the `Authors` table. Figure 10.6 shows how your query's Design View window should look now.

**FIGURE 10.6.**

*The new query without criteria.*

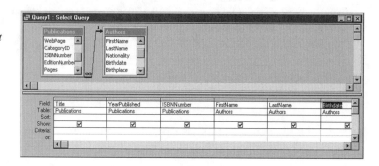

4. Click the Run button in the toolbar. Figure 10.7 shows the results.

**FIGURE 10.7.**

*The new query run-ning.*

▼    5. No surprises here. This query simply extracts all the records for the selected fields.
       Return to Design View. Enter <1/1/1900 in the Criteria row for the DateofBirth
       column. Tab away from this column. Note that Access understands you mean
       1/1/1900 to be a date and surrounds your criteria with the needed number sign (#)
       marks.

**Tip**

> The expression <1/1/1900 reads "less than January 1, 1900" in English. This
> doesn't sound sensible when used in date or time fields. So when using date
> expressions in Access, think of the < operator as *before* and the > operator
> as *after*.

**10**

     6. Again run the query. Access now only returns those records with authors who were
        born prior to the 20th Century. But wait, didn't you just put Herman Melville into
        the Authors table? He should show up, shouldn't he? Well, you didn't enter any
        records in the Publications table for him, so this query won't return his authors
        record—it's returning publications records which have an AuthorID for an author
        born prior to the 20th Century.

     7. Return to the Database window and select the Tables tab. Double-click the
        Publications table to open it in Datasheet View. Enter the information for
        Melville's classic *Moby Dick* (for now, just enter the title, author information, edi-
        tion—use 1, and pages). Close the Publications table.

     8. Return to the query. If you're still in Datasheet View, click over to Design View
        and then back to Datasheet View. The query will now return Melville's Moby Dick,
▲       as shown in Figure 10.8.

**FIGURE 10.8.**

| Title | Year Published | ISBN Number | First Name | Last Name | Date of Birth |
|-------|----------------|-------------|------------|-----------|---------------|
| Moby Dick | 1998 | | Herman | Melville | 08/01/1819 |

*The query returning
some data.*

Access can use dates for query criteria the same as it uses text values or numbers.
Operators like = (equals), < (less than), and > (greater than) work alike with dates, times,
and numbers. You can even combine these operators to read <= (less than or equal to), >=
(greater than or equal to), and <> (which means not equal to, but reads literally as less
than and greater than).

| **Do** | **Don't** |
|---|---|
| **DO** feel free to use expressions to extract your information in creative ways. | **DON'T** rely on your query criteria to return what you expect they will. Be sure to try your queries with known data that will yield results in which you can easily spot errors. Don't rely on complex queries until you're absolutely sure they're working correctly. |

# Date Arithmetic and Developer-Defined Fields

So far, today's material has been rather tame and obvious. Things are about to pick up speed. The following task shows how to use date math. It dynamically calculates the age of each author in years. Dynamic calculation means the computer fetches the current date and does the age calculation based on that date and the fixed value of the author's birthday.

### Task: Date math and expression (developer-defined) fields

1. Return to Design View for the query you did in the second task. Click in the criteria for the `DateOfBirth` field and highlight the entire expression. Press Delete to delete this criteria expression.

2. Click the `Field` row for the column just to the right of the `BirthDate` column (you may have to scroll the Design View window to the right some, as I did). Press Shift+F2 to enter Zoom mode. Enter

   `Age in Years: DateDiff("yyyy",[BirthDate],Date())`

   in the Zoom box. This is one of those occasions where you're really glad the programmers of Microsoft Access thought of the Zoom box!

3. Click OK to leave Zoom mode. Click the Run button in the toolbar. Your screen should resemble Figure 10.9.

**FIGURE 10.9.**

*A field based on a date calculation expression.*

| Title | Year Published | ISBN Number | First Name | Last Name | Date of Birth | Age in Years |
|---|---|---|---|---|---|---|
| Sams Teach Yo | 1998 | 0-672-31298-0 | Craig | Eddy | 11/26/1965 | 33 |
| Dynamic HTML | 1997 | | Craig | Eddy | 11/26/1965 | 33 |
| Think & Grow R | 1960 | 0-449-21492-3 | Napolean | Hill | | |
| The Dilbert Prin | 1996 | 0-88730-787-6 | Scott | Adams | | |
| The Seven Habi | 1989 | | Stephen | Covey | | |
| Moby Dick | 1998 | | Herman | Melville | 08/01/1819 | 179 |

**Note**

> The figures for the Age in Years column will vary depending on the current date. This computer's date was set to early-1998 for this and some other screens. If, for example, if your clock is set to early 1999, the authors will be shown as one year older—because they are! This is dynamic date calculation in action.

**ANALYSIS** Let's take a closer look at what this query does before saving the results. The entire operation of this query depends on the expression

```
Age in Years: DateDiff("yyyy",[BirthDate],Date())
```

The first part of this expression is the label for this developer-defined field. Access knows that from the colon to the right of the field. Anything to the left of the colon in a defined field is interpreted by Access as a label for the column.

The second part of this expression is its heart: DateDiff. DateDiff() is another built-in function that calculates the difference between two dates. The parameters for DateDiff read as follows:

```
interval, date1, date2[,firstdayofweek][,firstweekofyear]
```

The last two parameters in the square brackets ([]) are optional. The interval is how you want the date differences to be expressed. You can enter "ww" for weeks, "d" for days, "m" for month. This example used "yyyy" for year interval. Figure 10.10 is the same query edited to return authors' ages in months.

The second element is the first, or earlier, date that figures in the date math expression. In this case you told Access to fetch the data entered into the BirthDate field to use as the date1 parameter. You should enter the field BirthDate in square brackets even though it's a field name without spaces. It's always a good idea to enclose field names in square brackets because you'll get unpredictable results if your field name contains spaces. Not only do the brackets act as insurance in case your field names do contain spaces, but they show you at a glance that the entry [BirthDate] is a field name and not a function.

The last element of the parameter is the function Date(). This merely tells Access to use the current system date as date2. The two optional functions [,firstdayofweek] and [,firstweekofyear] aren't used in this query. You can set the optional parameters [,firstdayweek] and [,firstweekofyear] to count the specific days or weeks in the interval.

**10**

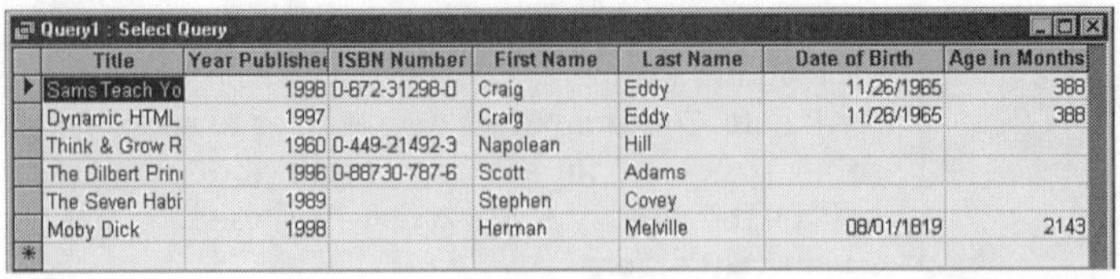

**FIGURE 10.10.**

*The DateDiff() func-
tion returning month
intervals.*

| Title | Year Published | ISBN Number | First Name | Last Name | Date of Birth | Age in Months |
|---|---|---|---|---|---|---|
| Sams Teach Yo | 1998 | 0-672-31298-0 | Craig | Eddy | 11/26/1965 | 388 |
| Dynamic HTML | 1997 | | Craig | Eddy | 11/26/1965 | 388 |
| Think & Grow R | 1960 | 0-449-21492-3 | Napolean | Hill | | |
| The Dilbert Print | 1996 | 0-88730-787-6 | Scott | Adams | | |
| The Seven Habi | 1989 | | Stephen | Covey | | |
| Moby Dick | 1998 | | Herman | Melville | 08/01/1819 | 2143 |

Save the query using the name PublishedAuthorAges. This query is part of the sample
data. You'll use it in the upcoming tasks, so don't bother closing it unless you're going to
take a break here (and if you need one, this is a good time for it because the subject matter is about to change!).

# Other Date Arithmetic Functions

While the DateDiff() is probably one of the most useful date arithmetic functions available in Access 97, there are a few other useful ones as well.

The DatePart() function returns a specified piece of the provided date, such as the
month. The function takes parameters similar to DateDiff(). The parameters are

```
interval, date[,firstdayofweek][,firstweekofyear]
```

The interval parameter uses the same strings as DateDiff() so if you wanted to know
the month for a particular date, you'd use m. The date parameter is the date that you
want to evaluate.

There is also a related WeekDay() function that returns to you the weekday a particular
date falls upon. The parameters for this function are

```
date[,firstdayofweek]
```

both of which have the familiar meanings of the other functions. Similarly, Access provides Year(), Month(), and Day() functions that return the year, month, and day, respectively, for the provided date. These three functions take only the date parameter, though.

# Parameter Queries

So far with all the queries you've done you've established the query criteria at design
time using the Design View window. This isn't always desirable for two reasons. First,
you might not know what criteria you will need when you run the query or you might
want to quickly change criteria for the same query. The second reason is security. You
might want a user to be able to establish query criterion without getting to the Design
View for the query.

NEW TERM The way to enter criteria at the time a query is run, rather than when it's designed, is to convert your query to a parameter query. Access is rather loose when using the words *criteria* and *parameter*. Think of query parameters as criteria entered during the execution of a query.

"The parameter query" task (coming up after the next short task) shows how to construct a simple parameter query. But before trying that, go over the following task to see how the same parameter works in the familiar Design View window. This task shows the parallels between criteria and parameters in queries.

## Task: A different criteria demonstration

1. If you've been away for a bit, launch Access and open the BookStore database if necessary. From the Database window, click the Queries tab, highlight the PublishedAuthorAges query and click Design to open this query in Design View.

2. Locate the Age in Years expression field. Enter: <=50 on the first Criteria row for this field.

3. Click the Run button. Access will run the query and return a screen similar to Figure 10.11.

4. Return to Design View and delete the criteria from this query.

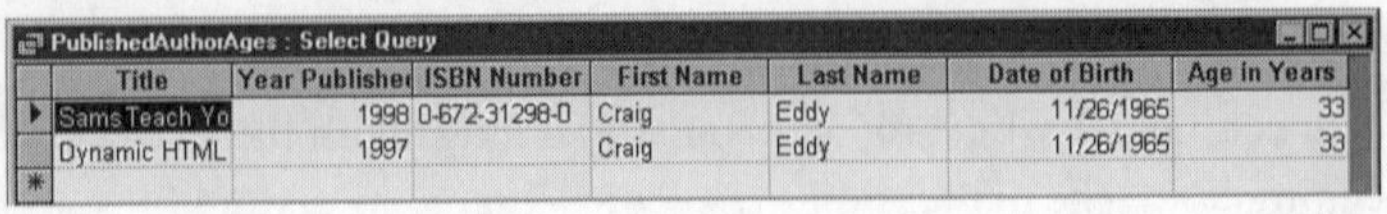

**FIGURE 10.11.**

*The criteria query running.*

| Title | Year Published | ISBN Number | First Name | Last Name | Date of Birth | Age in Years |
|-------|----------------|-------------|------------|-----------|---------------|--------------|
| Sams Teach Yo | 1998 | 0-672-31298-0 | Craig | Eddy | 11/26/1965 | 33 |
| Dynamic HTML | 1997 | | Craig | Eddy | 11/26/1965 | 33 |

That didn't pack much of a surprise. Access had no problems figuring out that you wanted to select authors who are 50 years young or younger. The query might have taken a little longer to run than other queries because Access had a two-step problem; first, it had to do the DateDiff() calculation, and then it had to apply your criteria to filter out the unwanted records. The more you ask an Access query to do, the longer it'll take to run.

The query in preceding task might seem almost trivial, but it's one that's widely used in databases. Imagine you're creating an aging of your accounts receivable and you want to find out which accounts are less than 30 days old, which are between 31 and 60 days old, and finally which are more than 60 days old. One way to do this is to use the DateDiff() function in three columns, and then enter these criteria for the three columns: <=30; Between 31 and 60; and >60.

The beauty of using the DateDiff() function is that any time you run this query, you'll be up-to-date aging your receivables because the query's based on the difference between the date entered in the table or query and the current date.

# The Parameter Query

The following task shows you how to construct a simple parameter query. This query will extract information similar to that extracted in the preceding task, but you'll be able to alter your query criteria without entering Design View.

## Task: The parameter query

1. If you're still in Datasheet View, return to Design View.

2. Enter [Enter First Name:] in the Criteria row for the FirstName column. Remove the criteria for the Age in Years column.

3. Click the Run button. Access responds with a dialog requesting you to enter a value for the first name criteria.

4. Enter Craig in the dialog and click OK. Your screen should resemble Figure 10.12. Although the results of the queries look the same, they do so for different reasons. Try entering other data with a variety of names and ages for varied results.

**FIGURE 10.12.**

*Parameter queries return criteria entered as they are running.*

| Title | Year Published | ISBN Number | First Name | Last Name | Date of Birth | Age in Years |
|---|---|---|---|---|---|---|
| Sams Teach Yo | 1998 | 0-672-31298-0 | Craig | Eddy | 11/26/1965 | 33 |
| Dynamic HTML | 1997 | | Craig | Eddy | 11/26/1965 | 33 |

You can't enter wildcards in parameter dialogs with the query constructed as in the preceding task. The expression Like "C*" entered as a straight (nonparameter) criterion for the FirstName column will, when the query's run, return records for Craig Eddy (and any other authors whose name starts with C, assuming they exist as authors records and have related publications records). Entering C* or Like "C*" in the query dialog for the query done in the preceding task will yield no records returned. The following task shows how to use wildcards in parameter queries.

## Task: Wildcard parameter queries

1. Starting where you left off, return to Design View. Run this query again. Enter C* for a parameter in the parameter dialog. Click OK. The results of running this query are shown in Figure 10.13.

2. Return to Design View. Edit the parameter criterion to read Like [Enter First Name:].

3. Run the query again, this time again entering C* for the parameter. Click OK.

   This time things work like you might have anticipated they'd work earlier. Your screen should resemble Figure 10.14.

PublishedAuthorAges : Select Query
Title | Year Publishe | ISBN Number | First Name | Last Name | Date of Birth | Age in Years

**FIGURE 10.13.**
*The wildcard parameter surprisingly results in no matched records.*

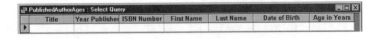

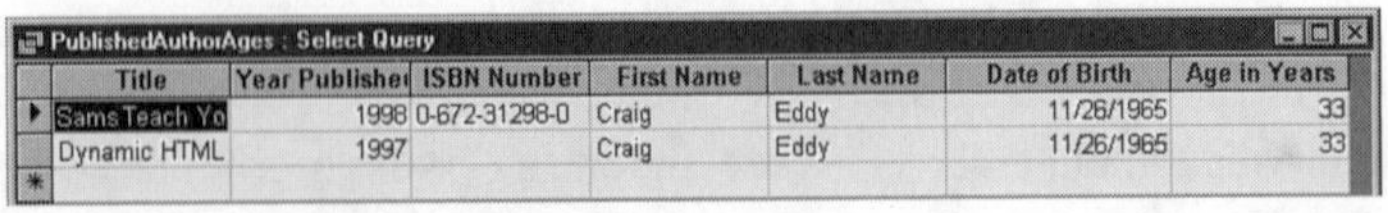
PublishedAuthorAges : Select Query
Title | Year Publishe | ISBN Number | First Name | Last Name | Date of Birth | Age in Years
Sams Teach Yo | 1998 | 0-672-31298-0 | Craig | Eddy | 11/26/1965 | 33
Dynamic HTML | 1997 | | Craig | Eddy | 11/26/1965 | 33

**FIGURE 10.14.**
*The successful wildcard parameter query.*

# Range Parameter Queries

Sometimes you'll want your query to extract information from a table based on a range of information. An example of a criterion for such a query reads `Between #1/1/1800# AND #12/31/1899#`.

This query looks as if it'll return all records where the author was born in the 19th Century. It does just that, as shown in Figure 10.15, where the criterion was used for the `BirthDate` field.

This is a rather constrained query. Sure it's useful, but in many cases you'll want to enter the beginning and ending dates at the time you run the query to ask Access to fetch, for example, all your sales for a particular span of time. Access has, built in, the capacity to do just this. The next task shows you how to construct a parameter query that returns a range of values.

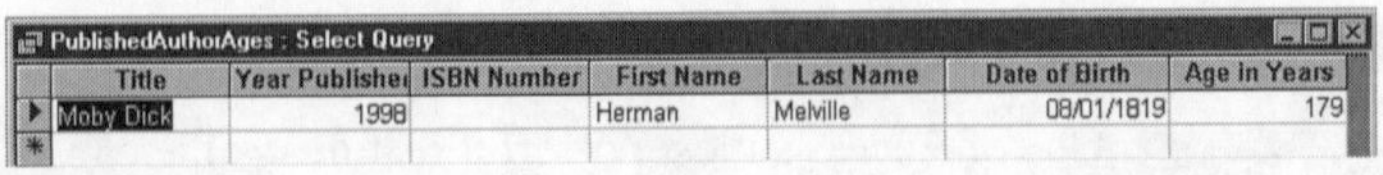
PublishedAuthorAges : Select Query
Title | Year Publishe | ISBN Number | First Name | Last Name | Date of Birth | Age in Years
Moby Dick | 1998 | | Herman | Melville | 08/01/1819 | 179

**FIGURE 10.15.**
*The results of the date range query.*

## Task: The range parameter query

1. Return to Design View for the query you just constructed. Delete any criteria you might have entered either in the task or through your own experimentation. Enter the following on the `Criteria` row for the `BirthDate` column:

   `Between [Enter Earliest Date:] AND [Enter Latest Date:]`

2. You've just told Access that you want two parameter prompts when this query's run. First, Access prompts you with a dialog saying `Enter Earliest Date:`. When you enter a value and click OK, Access will bring up a second dialog prompting you with `Enter Latest Date:`.
3. Click the Run button on the toolbar. Access responds by requesting the first date for the range.

▼   4. Enter 1/1/1900 and click OK. Access next requests the second date in the range.

▲   5. Enter 12/31/1965 and click OK. Access runs the query with these parameters and
       gives you the same screen you saw in Figure 10.14.

Although the results of this run can be identical to those of the fixed range query shown
running in Figure 10.14, the difference is that you can now choose your range of values
for the parameters at the query's runtime rather than in its Design View. Try running this
query again, but enter 1/1/1933 and 03/31/1964 as criteria. This time you'll get no
records returned (unless you've entered some extra authors and publications on your
own, of course, that match this query's criteria).

Close and save the new query using a different name if you wish to preserve your original query, PublishedAuthorAges. The book's example saved the query at this stage using
the name PublishedAuthorAgesParameter.

| **Do** | **Don't** |
|---|---|
| **DO** use parameter queries when you don't want to alter the design of a query to change its criteria. | **DON'T** use a parameter query to construct queries with unchanging criteria such as older than 30 days. This works technically, but it slows down the workflow, as you'll have to enter the same criteria over and over again. |

# Action Queries

NEW TERM   One of Access's most powerful features is the capability to take the results
of a query and do something with them. These queries are called *action*
*queries* because they perform some sort of action. This chapter introduces action queries,
but they'll get full treatment in Day 12, "Creating Action and Union Queries."

The following task shows how you can take the output of a query and have Access automatically create and enter data into a new table. In this task, you convert a select query to
a simple action query that creates a new table containing the query's output.

### Task: Make table action query

1. The default type of query Access creates is called a select query because it selects
   records and fields from a table or another query. To make an action query, first
   construct a select query in the normal way. It's highly recommended that you run
   the query in Select mode to make sure it's running as you think it should.

▼ 2. Return to Design mode after running either the query from the preceding task. If you're using the sample data and didn't save the query from the task, use the query PublishedAuthorAgesParameter as a starting point for this task. Use the Query|Make Table Query menu item. Access responds with a dialog. Enter FirstTrial as a name for your new table. Your screen should resemble Figure 10.16.

**FIGURE 10.16.**

*Creating a make table query.*

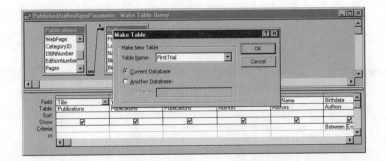

**10**

3. Make sure the Current Database option button is selected. Click OK. That's all there is to it.

4. Click the Run button in the toolbar. Access prompts you for two dates. Enter 1/1/1900 as the earliest date and 12/31/1999 as the latest date.

Access will crank around a while and respond with a confirmation message box, as shown in Figure 10.17. After confirmation from you, Access runs the query and places the contents of it into a new table, FirstTrial.

5. Click Yes to finish running this query. Nothing apparently occurs. Use the File|Save As menu item to save the changes to a new query named PublishedAuthorAgesMakeTable. Back on the Database window's Queries tab, note that this query now has a new icon next to its name in the Database list box, as shown in Figure 10.18. This visually tells you that this query is an action query that will make a new table.

6. Did it work? Click the Tables tab. (See Figure 10.19.)

▲ Click the Open button for the FirstTrial table. (See Figure 10.20.)

**FIGURE 10.17.**

*The confirmation message box for the make table query.*

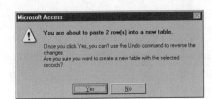

**FIGURE 10.18.**

*The Database window showing different kinds of queries. Most queries here are select ones, but* `PublishedAuthor AgesMakeTable` *is a make table query and it has a different icon.*

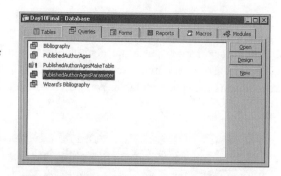

**FIGURE 10.19.**

*The new table at the Database window.*

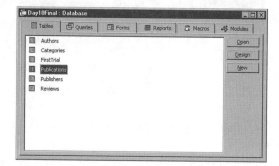

**FIGURE 10.20.**

*The newly created table showing the records automatically entered after being selected from a parameter query.*

| | Do | | Don't |
|---|---|---|---|
| | **DO** make as many action queries as your application requires. This is a very useful capability of Access. | | **DON'T** use these queries as action queries until you've verified their output as select queries. |

# Summary

Today you learned how to include dates in tables, how to format those dates, and how Access stores date information internally. Queries can use dates for criteria, as you saw in the second task. You also saw how to create a complex expression to calculate the difference between today's date and the authors' dates of birth and return the values in years. Further, you learned how to place the results of this calculation into an artificial field called Age in Years.

Access can prompt for a range of values to extract data. This is called the range parameter query. You use the Between...AND operators to construct such a query.

Finally, you learned that Access can use the output of a query to perform some action. To have Access create a table using a query's output, change the query type from Select to Make Table and tell Access what the new query's name is to be.

# Q&A

**Q  Can I use the DateDiff() function to perform time math?**

**A  Yes, it does so whether you ask it to or not. The trick to seeing time intervals between dates is to use h, n, or s for hours, minutes, or seconds. (The n for minutes isn't an error. The m is reserved for months.)**

**Q  If I know a date is, say, a Sunday, should I enter the date like this: Sunday, [the date] where [the date] is the date that's a Sunday?**

**A  No. Format the field as Long Date to show days of the week. Access won't permit you to make entries looking identical to its Long Date format. It's funny that way.**

**Q  Can I enter two parameters on the Criteria row to create an AND query?**

**A  Yes. Access will first prompt you for the parameter on the left, but the query will function just like a standard AND query.**

**Q  What about using parameters to create an OR query?**

**A  It works the same as the AND query. Just enter the parameters on two different rows. Access will prompt for the parameter on the top-most row first. Figure 10.21 shows the PublishedAuthorAgesParameter query modified to be an OR parameter query.**

10

**FIGURE 10.21.**

*Constructing the OR parameter query.*

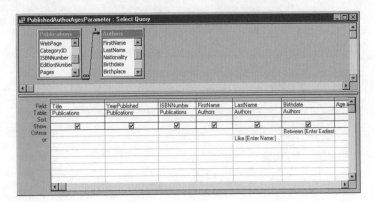

# Workshop

Here's where you can test and apply what you have learned today.

## Quiz

1. If you have a field in a query with the Data Type set to Date/Time, will a criterion of "January" select for those records in the month of January?

2. What does >#1/31/97# mean as a criterion?

3. What function(s) will tell you the year a particular date falls within?

4. Can you use wildcards in a parameter query?

5. Will the parameter Like [Enter a Name:] accept U* as a wildcard criterion?

## Exercises

1. Open the PublishedAuthorAges query in Design View.

2. Delete any criteria for this query.

3. Pull down the Query menu and change this query back to a select one if necessary.

4. Construct a parameter query that will act as an AND query requiring a match on two fields before you can get a return.

5. Modify the query so both parts of the AND query accept wildcards.

6. Modify the query to keep the same parameters, but make it an OR query.

7. Close the query, discarding changes.

# DAY **11**

# Working with Form Controls

Today's material covers the following topics:

- Using list or combo boxes in forms
- Binding combo boxes to lists
- The TabControl for forms
- What an option group is
- How to modify a table to accept the option group's output
- How to place an option group in a form
- Adding graphics with Image Control
- How to include a bound OLE graphic object in a form

# Using List or Combo Boxes in Forms

This chapter introduces you to the online bookstore database's Reviews table. This table is used to store impromptu reviews that browsers of the bookstore's Web site can enter. The schema for the table is rather simple, and is shown in Table 11.1.

**TABLE 11.1.** THE Reviews TABLE.

| Field | Data Type | Usage |
|-------|-----------|-------|
| ReviewID | AutoNumber | The primary key field |
| PublicationID | Number (Long Integer) | Foreign key to Publications table |
| AuthorName | Text (50) | Name of person entering review |
| AuthorEMail | Text (50) | Email address of review author |
| ReviewDate | Date/Time | Date/time review was created |
| ReviewText | Memo | Actual review contents |
| RatingID | Number (Long Integer) | Foreign key to Ratings table |

This table contains information related (linked) to the Publications table. You wouldn't want to enter an incorrect PublicationID into any form that creates or edits records for the Reviews table. Doing so would introduce orphan records in the database. An orphaned record is one with no related records in the related tables.

The Reviews table is linked to Publications, and Access has been told to enforce referential integrity across this link. In this context, referential integrity means that, for example, when you enter a PublicationID in the Reviews table, Access will look in the Publications table to make sure that PublicationID really exists.

Referential integrity enforcement does prevent entry of wrong or nonexistent PublicationID values. However, it does nothing to assist the data entry person in finding the right values for these fields.

Primitive data entry systems gave entry people a paper list of valid entries as a reference. This worked but wasn't particularly efficient. What would be much better is to have Access look up correct values from within a data entry form bound to Reviews. This eliminates the need for paper references and greatly speeds up the data entry process. It also goes a long way toward preventing data entry people from entering a valid, but wrong, value for either of these fields.

Like so many things in personal computers, getting a feeling for how this works is easier when seen than when explained. The tasks that follow create a form for entering data into Reviews. One of the controls on this form looks up existing values from previously entered data.

Most of the controls on the forms shown so far in this book have been text or memo boxes. You can do data entry and basic editing within them. But list and combo boxes are also handy controls for data entry. A list box shows a list of values you can scroll through. A combo box, a combination of a list box and a text box, has a place to enter data and a drop-down list that works exactly like the list box. The following task shows you how to create a form with a combo box.

## Task: A form with combo boxes

▼ **TASK**

1. If necessary, launch Access and open the BookStore database. Click the Forms tab and click the New button to create a new form. Select the Reviews table from the drop-down list at the bottom of the New Table dialog.

2. Be sure to select (or leave selected) the Design View option to bypass the wizards.

**Note**

Although this will be a simple form, you will be using a combo box for one of the fields. There's no way to tell Access to use combo boxes rather than text boxes during a simple form wizard operation. In this case, using the wizard, and then undoing what the wizard left you, would be more work than just going directly to Form Design View. You could, though, run the wizard, and then have Access change the control type from text box to combo box. However, manual design teaches techniques better than running a wizard, and learning the technique is the real point of this task.

3. Click OK and your screen should resemble Figure 11.1. If the Reviews Field List window is not open, click the Field List toolbar button to open it.

4. The review table has a key field (ReviewID) that sports the data type AutoNumber-Increment. Since Access increments this field automatically when you enter records, you don't need to include that in this form. The only fields you need to include on a form are those into which you enter data or those that have information you need to view. You can safely skip ReviewID because it meets neither of these criteria.

| Do | Don't |
|---|---|
| **DO** include only those fields on your forms you need to view, edit, or make entries into. | **DON'T** litter up your forms with unnecessary fields. Doing so serves no useful purpose and will only confuse your users. |

▼

**11**

**FIGURE 11.1.**

*The Form Design View.*

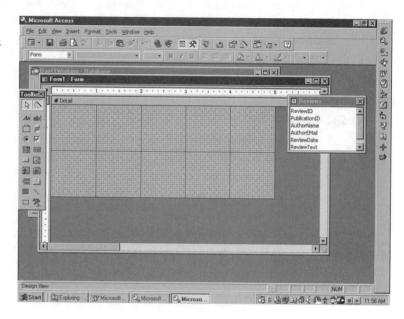

5. Examine the Toolbox in Figure 11.1. Note that the magic wandlike tool is selected, indicating Control Wizards are turned on. Click your Control Wizard toggle, if necessary, to turn it on too.

6. The first field you'll place on this form is PublicationID. You'll use a combo box for this and let a wizard do most of the work. Click the Combo Box tool in the Toolbox. This tells Access that you want to use this control type for the previously selected PublicationID field. Drag the PublicationID field from the Field List window to form design grid. Release the mouse button. Access will automatically start up the Combo Box Wizard. Your screen should resemble Figure 11.2.

**FIGURE 11.2.**

*The Combo Box Wizard that can insert a combo box in a form.*

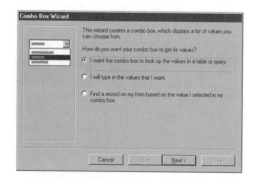

▼ 7. Of course you want the combo box to look up values for you, so leave the top option box checked and click the Next> button.

8. The values for the `PublicationID` field you want to look up are located in the `Publications` table because the purpose of this task is to make sure that no record is added to `Reviews` for a publication not previously entered in `Publications`. Like the Show Table list box in query design, this dialog gives you the option of showing tables, queries, or both. Keep in mind that you can look up values in queries as well as tables. Highlight Publications in the list box. Your screen should resemble Figure 11.3. Click the Next> button.

**FIGURE 11.3.**

*Binding a combo box to a table.*

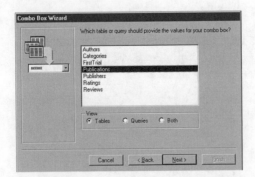

9. You could have only the `PublicationID` field appear in this combo box, but, because this field is an `AutoNumber` field, it won't make any sense to the person entering the review record. It's easier to search a list for text values than to look for an arbitrary number such as the PublicationID. Double-click the `Title`, `EditionNumber`, and `YearPublished` fields (in that order) in the Available Fields list to include each of these fields. Your screen should resemble Figure 11.4. Click the Next> button.

**FIGURE 11.4.**

*Including fields in a combo box.*

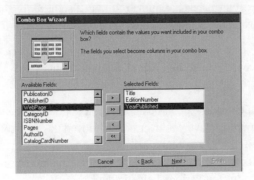

▼

11

▼ 10. This dialog is where you can adjust the field widths that will be shown in the combo box. This example modified the field widths. You should change the width of the drop-down combo box's fields at this screen by clicking between the column headers and dragging to the right, just as you can adjust apparent field widths in Datasheet View. You can also hide the key field. Users will only look up data by title, so leave this check box turned on. Click the Next> button.

11. In the next dialog, you tell Access what to do with the value looked up. Because you want to enter the value in the PublicationID field of the bound table, leave the default option button, Store that Value in this Field, selected as in Figure 11.5. Click the Next> button.

**FIGURE 11.5.**

*Telling Access how to handle a looked-up value.*

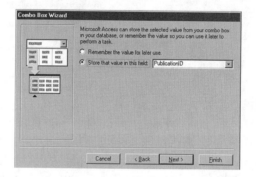

12. Modify the label for this field to read Publication. Click the Finish button to see your results. Access grinds around a bit and ends up placing the now programmed combo box on your form. Click the Form View button to see how this control works. Click this combo box's down arrow. (See Figure 11.6.) If your combo box is too small to show all of the title, open up the Properties list box. Find the List Width property in the Format tab and enter 4. This tells Access to make the entire drop-down box four inches in width. You may also have to adjust the width of the control itself using the sizing handles. Save the form, giving it the name Reviews.

Now entering correct values in this form for the PublicationID field is as simple as pulling down the combo box and clicking the value you want from the supplied list.

A multicolumn combo box can be an important option if you create applications that serve the public. Have you ever been annoyed that someone you're doing business with required that you remember your customer identification number before you could be located in the business's records? A multicolumn combo box enables
▼ you to locate people by various fields in their records.

**FIGURE 11.6.**

*The programmed combo box.*

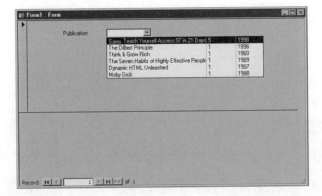

▲

# Auto Expanding

Access will try to locate values already in a combo box list as you make an entry into the text portion of the combo box. By using the partly completed form created in the preceding task, move to a new record (if necessary, which it probably isn't since this table is pretty new to the book's discussion) by clicking the New Record toolbar button, and then try this: pull down the combo box to show the list portion of the combo box. Enter D. Access immediately knows that there's only one value in the list that begins with the letter D, and it not only goes to that value in the list portion, but fills in the text section of the combo box with this value for you, as shown in Figure 11.7.

**FIGURE 11.7.**

*Auto Expand in action.*

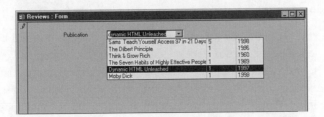

Try the same procedure (you'll have to press the Esc key first to cancel the current edits), but enter T instead of D. Access immediately moves to the top of the section where Publications start with a T and fills the text portion of the combo box with the value located there. Next enter H. This still doesn't give Access any more limiting information because there are at least two publications starting with TH. Now enter I. Access immediately knows you must mean *Think and Grow Rich* because that's the only one that starts with THI.

Combo box Auto Expand works the same with numbers as with text. The property that controls whether or not a combo box auto expands is the Auto Expand property under the Data tab in the control's Properties window.

11

> If you set the Limit to List (next to Auto Expand in the Properties window) property to Yes, you're telling Access to limit the entries in a field to those entries already entered in the field specified as a Row Source.

Return to Design View after you're satisfied that you are familiar with combo box operations.

> If you change the Limit to List property to No, you can alter the data in the PublicationID field on this form for an existing record. In this example this would be incorrect, and would result in a nasty error message when you attempt to save the new Reviews record (because referential integrity is being enforced and checking that bogus PublicationID). So, leave Limit to List set to Yes.

# Manual Combo or List Box Programming

The wizard works fine for programming list or combo boxes, but it is also important to learn the reason for the wizard's decisions. Just as you should use a calculator only after you know how to add, you should know what a wizard is doing with these controls before you use it. The following task shows how to manually program a combo or list box, using the RatingID field as its source.

You use the same method for programming both a combo box and a list box. Whether you use a list or combo box depends on your aesthetic sense and your specific application. List boxes remain full size—there's no pulling them down. List boxes work well when you want to show a value selection all the time or when you don't want a pull-down control. Figure 11.8 shows the RatingID field as it would appear on this form in a list box. Note that, although the Publication field has a drop-down arrow at the left end, the Rating ID box is permanently open without such an arrow.

The following task creates a combo box for the RatingID field. If you prefer the list box, you can use that for this application as well.

FIGURE **11.8.**

*A list box on a form.*

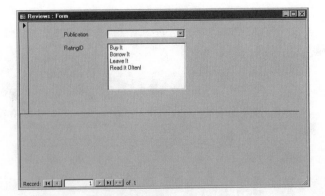

## Task: Manual combo box programming

1. Return to Design View for the form started in the previous task. Click the Control Wizards button in the toolbox to turn off Control Wizards.

2. Click the Combo Box control in the toolbox, and then drag the `RatingID` field onto the form just under the `PublicationID` field. If the field doesn't change to a combo box, you forgot to click the Combo Box control in the Toolbox. Press the Delete key and try again.

   This time Access didn't start up a Combo Box Wizard because you turned off the Control Wizards. If you failed to do this and the wizard started anyway, just click the Cancel button to end the wizard's participation in this task.

3. Programming this combo box amounts to setting certain properties for it in the Properties window. In this task you'll use an SQL (Structured Query Language) statement to set these properties.

   If the Properties window is not visible, click the Properties toolbar button—the button with the icon showing a hand holding a white square. Find the `Row Source` property (it's on the Properties window's Data tab), and click its row. Enter `SELECT Ratings.Rating, Ratings.RatingID FROM Ratings` into the text box. Remember, the values you want to look up for this field reside in the `Ratings` table. Set the `Bound Column` property to `2`. This tells Access to bind the `Reviews.RatingID` column to the `Ratings.RatingID` value for the selected rating (when you dragged the field from the Field list box, you told Access to store the looked-up value in the `RatingID` field within the `Reviews` table). Your screen should resemble Figure 11.9.

11

**FIGURE 11.9.**

*Binding the combo box to a table.*

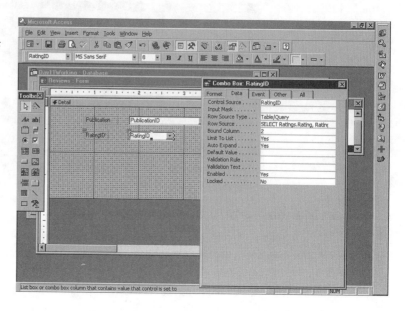

> **Note**
>
> Access, by default, binds the first column of a table or query specified in the Row Source property of a list or combo box. In this case, you want Access to bind to the RatingID field in Ratings, which is why you entered 2 in the Bound Column property.

4. Set the Limit to List and Auto Expand properties to Yes.

5. Click the Form View button and then pull down the combo box to see the operation of this control. Your screen should resemble what you see in Figure 11.10.

**FIGURE 11.10.**

*The finished combo box.*

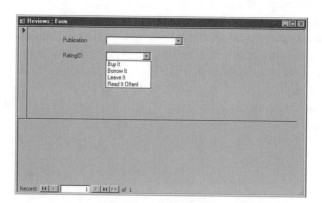

**Note**

You can activate a combo or list box by pointing and clicking as in the preceding example. However, Access is a program firmly based on SQL, and many prefer to perform look-ups using this language, which also forms the underpinnings of Access queries.

SQL is a subject worthy of its own book, and there's not room enough in this chapter for even a primer on this language. Later on you'll get a small introduction to it. SQL is really just plain English (although a bit stilted), and not all that tough to pick up.

To get a quick course in SQL, create a few queries, pull down the combo box attached to the left-most button, and choose SQL View. Access will respond by showing you the underlying SQL statement that forms the query.

Another good idea is to let the Combo Box Wizard or List Box Wizard run a few times and examine the SQL statement it constructs for a Row Source property. Remember, when you are addressing fields in Access tables you use the field's name, not its Caption property. If you pull down the combo box you made manually, you'll see the Caption property for column heads, not the actual field names.

11

# Finishing Up

Finishing this form takes a little more effort. Return to Design View. Move the two combo boxes to the top-left corner of the form. Then drag the AuthorName, AuthorEMail, ReviewDate, and ReviewText fields from the Field List window to the form. Rearrange the fields to make your form look like Figure 11.11.

Change the Text Align properties of all of the labels to Right. Select the ReviewDate text box (by itself), go to the Properties window, select the Data tab, and set the Locked property to Yes (this will prevent the user from changing the field's default). Then move to the Format tab and set the Format property to Short Date.

Click the Properties toolbar button to move to the form's Properties. On the Format tab, set the Caption property to Reviews. Change the Border Style to Dialog (there's no need to resize this form).

The only thing left is to enter a label for this form. Click the View menu. Click the Form Header/Footer selection to show this section of the form design grid. Click the label control in the toolbox. Click in the form header band and enter the label: Reviews Form. Press Enter or click outside the edit box to leave Edit mode.

**FIGURE 11.11.**

*Finishing up the form.*

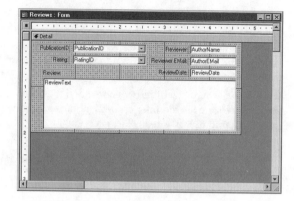

Pull down the Font Size combo box and select 18 as the point size for this label. Click the Bold button to change the font to bold. Resize the label box and the form header section to accommodate the new size and style font. Make the width of the label match the width of the form. Set the label's `Text Align` property to `Center`. Click the Form View button. Your screen should resemble Figure 11.12.

**FIGURE 11.12.**

*The finished Reviews form.*

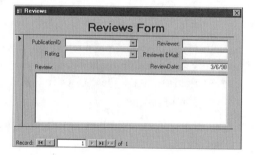

Save this form as `Reviews` if you didn't already save it. The form's not perfect, but it's workable. You'll probably want to change the `Tab Index` and `Status Bar Text` properties for some of the controls to make the form a little easier to use by a data entry clerk.

# The Tabbed Form

Access 97 includes a TabControl as one of the tools in the toolbox. The TabControl makes it possible for you to use one form for several views by using a format identical to what Microsoft itself uses in its complex dialogs.

The Database window is an example of a tabbed form. Each tab has on it a different selection of objects. The advantages of such a tabbed form are the following:

- You can stack data in the Z axis as well as the X and Y axes as on usual forms, so you can include more data on a form.

- You can group data or form controls according to some logic you wish to include in your application.

- You can give your application a sophisticated look that matches what users will see in Microsoft applications.

Using a TabControl is fairly simple. You add a TabControl from the toolbox to the form, add the controls you want, and then do some simple formatting to make the tabbed form look as you wish. You can also use macros or Visual Basic for Applications to manipulate TabControls. This example sticks to the basics. Once you see how to use macros and Visual Basic in your applications, you'll have no difficulty applying those skills to TabControls.

The following task shows you how to create a tabbed form for Publications data. The task creates a form with three pages—one for the publication's information, one for the author's information, and one for the publisher's information.

## Task: The tabbed form

1. Open Access if necessary. Click the Forms tab, and then click New. Leave Design View selected and click OK. Do not select a table/query in the drop-down list, you'll be creating a SQL statement to use as the form's Record Source property.

2. The form's Design View window opens. If the Properties window is not open, use the Properties toolbar button to open it. Click on the Data tab of the Properties window, click in the Record Source property, and finally click the ellipses button that appears to the right of the text box.

3. A window entitled SQL Statement: Query Builder appears. It's the familiar Query Design View window you've worked with previously. In the Show Table dialog, double click Publications, Authors, and Publishers (in that order) to add those tables to the design grid. Click the Close button. Double-click the asterisk entry in each of the three tables' field lists (again, in the order you added the tables). That's all you need to make this SQL statement work, so click the X button to close the Query Builder window. Access will question you about saving your changes. If everything is correct, click Yes. If you missed a step or two, click Cancel and make the necessary corrections. After saving the SQL statement, you'll find yourself back in the Properties window of the Form Design View.

4. Locate the TabControl in the Toolbox—that's the control that looks like two stacked manila folders—and click it. Note that the tooltip for the TabControl is Tab Control. Click in the Detail area of the form. A new instance of the tab control is added to the form at the spot where you clicked.

▼

11

5. You'll need a larger TabControl to accommodate all the controls, so increase the size of the TabControl to be roughly the size of the entire form. If you want to add or remove pages to your tabbed form, right-click the last tab, and then choose Delete Page or Insert Page, depending on what you want to do. You need three tabs, so use the right-click Insert Page menu item to add the third page. You choose which page of a TabControl is active by clicking the page or its tab. Click the tab labeled Page1.

> **Tip**
>
> Click around on the tab control. Notice that each page (or tab) has its own set of properties (watch the Properties window as you click around). The overall tab control properties can be viewed by clicking in the area at the top of the tab control but not on an individual tab. Make sure you're back on the Page1 tab before continuing with the task.

6. Open the Field list box by clicking its icon in the toolbar. Notice that the fields are listed in the order that the tables were added to the SQL Statement builder.

7. Drag the fields starting with Title and ending with ListPrice (but excluding Publications.AuthorID) onto the first page of the TabControl. Drop them into the upper-right corner of the tab control—Access will grow the form and the control if necessary to fit the bottom-most field you're dropping, and this can be an annoyance. Arrange your fields in any manner you like, or follow the book's example as shown in Figure 11.13.

**FIGURE 11.13.**

*Adding fields to a tab page.*

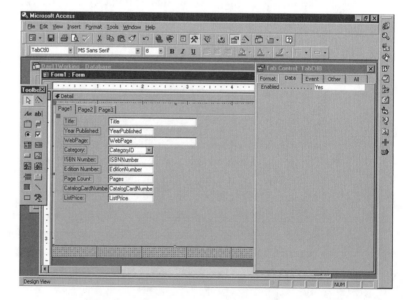

▼   8. Click the tab that says Page2 to make page 2 of the TabControl active. Drag the
       fields from `FirstName` down to `Notes` (but excluding `Photograph` for now) to this
       page, arranging them as you see fit. Figure 11.14 shows the book's arrangement.

**FIGURE 11.14.**

*Adding fields to the
second tab page.*

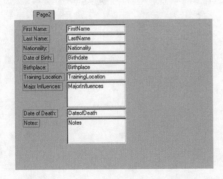

9. Finally, click on Page3 and drag the fields from `PublisherName` down to `Comments`
   (the last field in the Field List) onto the tab control. Arrange your fields in any
   manner you like, or follow the book's example as shown in Figure 11.15.

**11**

**FIGURE 11.15.**

*Adding the publisher
fields to the third tab
page.*

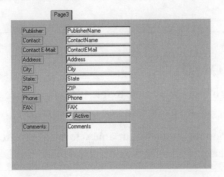

10. The form is almost finished. The only thing left is to add meaningful captions to
    the tabs. Click the Format tab in the Properties list box. Click the tab that now says
    Page1. Locate the `Caption` property and enter `Publication` as a caption for this
    page. Press the tab key to move to a different property and Access will add the new
    caption to the TabControl.

11. Now use the same method to change the caption for Page2 to read `Author`
    `Information` and Page3 to `Publisher Information`.

▲  12. That's it— you're done. Save this form as `TabbedBibliography`.

Switch to Form View. Try clicking on each tab to see the different views of your data. Figure 11.16 shows how the sample form turned out.

**FIGURE 11.16.**

*The tabbed form in action.*

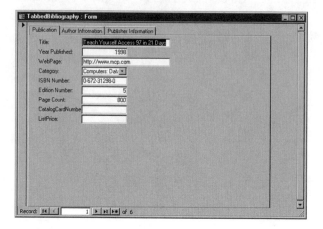

> **Note**  You can add any kind of control to a TabControl page except another TabControl.

# The Option Group

An *option group* is a set of option buttons, toggle buttons, or check boxes in which one control *must* be selected, and no more than one control in a group *can* be selected.

To quickly get a feel for option groups, start a new form. When Access asks you for a binding table or query, leave the combo box blank and click the Design View option, and then click OK.

Locate these two controls in the toolbox: the Option Button and the Option Group. The Option Group icon is a square with the letters *x y z* on the top. The Option Button is a solid circle within another circle. Click the Option Group and click somewhere on the form to place an option group on it.

Click the Option Button tool, and then click in the option group box. Repeat until you have two or three option buttons inside the option group and two or three option buttons outside the group. Your screen should resemble Figure 11.17. Don't be concerned if your form objects have different label numbers than the ones shown here.

FIGURE 11.17.

*The option group demo form with buttons added.*

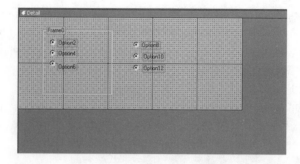

Click the Form View button. Try choosing more than one option button in the option group. Try making no button in the option group selected. Now try the same thing with the buttons outside of the group.

Your form might open with no option group buttons selected, but the minute you do select one, you won't be able to return the group to having none selected. The option buttons outside of an option group can toggle on and off unrelated to their neighbors.

# What's It Good For?

11

In many cases you'll want to give your users a choice from several options. Option buttons work well for this. If you want to force a choice of one from a group of selections, the option group is the easiest way. Take a look at Figure 11.18. This is the form from Figure 11.17 with labels, showing how you might use option buttons in and out of an option group.

**FIGURE 11.18.**

*A practical use for an option group.*

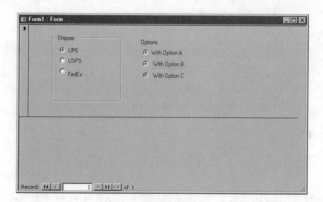

This is another fictional example—a mail order company where management needs to ship all sales. Each shipment might include Option A, B, or C, but doesn't have to include any of these options; these choices appear outside of an option group. However, all orders need to be shipped via some carrier, so the Shipper option buttons are in an option group.

Our fictional online bookstore sells publications on three different media types: Book, AudioBook, and CD-ROM. Each publication must be one of these, and none can be more than one. This is a great application for an option group.

The value for media type will be stored in the `Publications` table. The first thing you need to do is modify the table to accept this new data. The following task simply adds a new field to `Publications` to store a 1, 2, or 3 corresponding to the media type.

## Task: Modifying an existing table

**▼TASK**

1. Close the Option Demo form, discarding changes.

2. Back on the Database window, click the Tables tab. Highlight the `Publications` table and click the Design button to enter Design View for this table.

3. Click in the first empty row at the bottom of the design grid.

4. Click in the `Field Name` column of the blank row and enter `MediaType` as a field name. Move to the `Data Type` column and enter `Number` as a data type. Move to the `Field Properties` section of the table design grid and change the field size to `Byte`. Finally, change the `Default Value` property to `1`.

**Note**

> The values in the `MediaType` field will be limited to 1, 2, or 3, as you'll soon see. The `Number` data type with field size `Byte` is a very efficient way to store information in Access; however, entries in this type of field are limited to positive integers no greater than 255. This fits our projected data perfectly.
>
> The general rule of using a `Text` data type field, unless you're sure you'll be doing math on a field's contents, was overridden here for the sake of efficiency and in the sure knowledge that no text will ever be entered in this field.

▲    5. Close this table, saving changes.

You need a form to place the option group in. As luck would have it, you saved the `TabbedBibliography` form from an earlier task. This form in its completed state is part of the sample data.

The following task makes room on the TabbedBibliography form for the new option group and then installs the option group on it.

## Task: Creating and programming the option group

1. At the Database window, click the Forms tab. Click the TabbedBibliography form, and then open it in Design View.

2. Click the Publication tab to activate page 1 of the tab control (if it's not already activated). Resize and rearrange the fields until your form resembles Figure 11.19. Don't worry if your form doesn't look identical to Figure 11.19. Close is good enough here.

**FIGURE 11.19.**

*The rearranged form ready for the option group.*

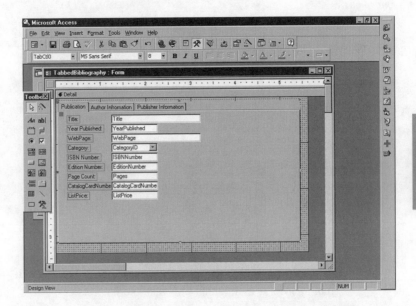

**11**

3. Make sure the Wizard button in the Toolbox isn't enabled. Click the Option Group button in the toolbox. Click in the lower-right portion of the form to insert the option group there.

**Tip**

Making an option group is easier if you use a wizard. This task avoids the wizard to show you the underlying principles of an option group. You might want to redo the task using a wizard to see how Microsoft has automated the process for you. When using Access for production chores, you'll probably use the Option Group Wizard rather than bothering to do these tasks manually.

▼     4. Insert three option buttons in the option group box, as shown in Figure 11.20.
         Remember that you can drag a control and its label separately by dragging on the
         large square in the upper-left corner of the control or label when the control is
         highlighted.

         Don't be concerned if your controls are numbered differently than the example's.
         You'll take care of that next.

**FIGURE 11.20.**

*The option buttons
placed in the Option
group box.*

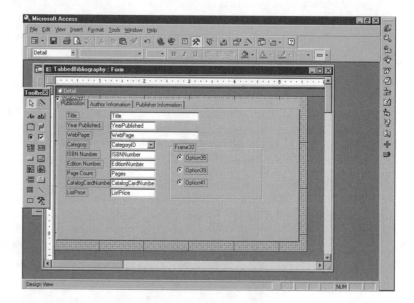

      5. If the Properties window is not visible, click the Properties toolbar button to it.
         Click the top option button in the option group. Make sure the option button and
         not its label is highlighted (this takes some practice).

      6. Locate the `Option Value` property in the Data tab for this control. If necessary,
         edit it to 1. If this is the first option button you added to the form, it should already
         have this value. Figure 11.21 shows this control and its Properties list box with the
         proper value entered for the Option Value.

      7. Highlight the label (this is even trickier than highlighting the option button portion
         of the control) for this option button and enter `Book` for its `Caption` property. (You
         edit the label for this control either directly on the form or by changing its `Caption`
         property on the Format tab of the Properties list box.) If you want to, you can
▼        resize the label box to accommodate this new value for its caption.

**FIGURE 11.21.**

*Setting the* Option
Value *property for an
option button.*

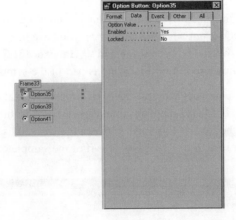

8. Similarly, set the Option Value property for the middle option button to 2 and the bottom one to 3. You should find that Access has anticipated your needs and set these values for you when you placed the option buttons within the group. Set their labels' Caption properties to AudioBook and CD-ROM, respectively. (See Figure 11.22.)

**FIGURE 11.22.**

*Finishing up the option
group.*

9. Finally, bind this option group to the MediaType field in the Publications table. Click the option group itself by clicking one of the frame's lines. Look in the Properties list box for the Control Source property. Either pull down the combo box and click MediaType, or enter MediaType for this property. Edit the label for this option group to read Media Type.

10. Switch to Form View. The first record appears. Click the Book option button for this publication. Scroll through the records one by one, clicking the Book option button until you hit the last record.

11. Close the form, saving changes. Click the Tables tab and open the Publications table in Datasheet View. Scroll to the MediaType column and note the values you entered at the option group are reflected here.

**11**

# What Good Are Numbers?

Option values must be numbers. Because you want to know if a publication is a book, an audio book, or a CD-ROM, not what the number is, you have to do a final step. Construct a table with two fields: MediaType and MediaDescription. This table, MediaTypeLookup, is shown in Figure 11.23 and is part of the sample data.

The next thing to do is construct a simple query linking the MediaType field's data in Publications with the MediaTypeLookup table. Figure 11.24 is the ShowMediaType in Design View showing the relationship links between the two tables of the query. Figure 11.25 shows this query in action. This query is part of the sample data.

**FIGURE 11.23.**

*The* MediaTypeLookup *table.*

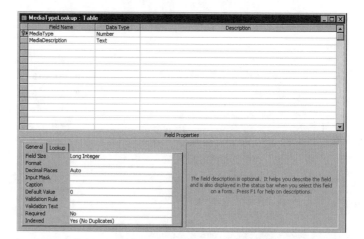

**FIGURE 11.24.**

*The Design View of the* ShowMediaType *query.*

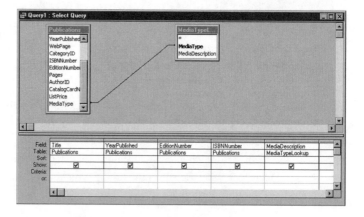

11

**FIGURE 11.25.**

*The results of running the* ShowMediaType *query.*

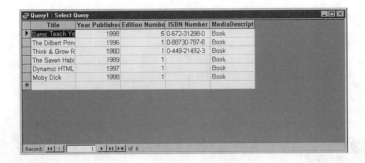

# The Image Control

Access 97 includes a control that makes it very easy to include graphics on forms and reports. Using this control is quite simple, as the following example illustrates. While this isn't a formal task, you can treat it as such.

This demonstration adds the graphic galore.bmp (part of the sample data) to the TabbedBibliography form.

Open the form in Design View. Move the tab control down to make room for the image. Click the Image control in the toolbox. Click anywhere in the tab control. Access will bring up the Insert Picture dialog asking you which graphic file to open.

Locate the graphic you wish to include on the form. Move the graphic to a reasonable location where it doesn't cover the fields. Figure 11.26 shows the finished form in Form View.

**FIGURE 11.26.**

*The tabbed form with a graphic added.*

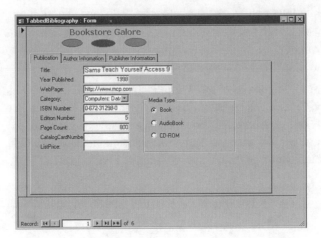

> The Internet is a great source for free, pubic domain graphics which you can
> use in your databases. One such site is http://www.iconbazaar.com/ (just
> be sure to review the sites Conditions of Use page). A great source for pho-
> tographic images is PhotoDisc (http://www.photodisc.com). You'll have
> to pay for these images, but they're high-quality.

# Images as Part of Data Within Databases

The last thing to cover today is how to embed graphic images in forms and reports when
those images are part of the data. The previous section demonstrated how easy it is to
include decorative graphics in a form or a report using the Image control. Access can
include graphic objects, such as photographs of students, as part of its dataset. Such data
are called bound OLE objects. The next task shows you how to embed this type graphic
in your form. The same principles apply to including graphics in both forms and reports.

The fictional bookstore includes photographs of authors (when available). The following
task adds a picture control to the TabbedBibliography form to demonstrate the concept
of bound OLE objects within the dataset.

### Task: Embedding a graphic in a form

1. The first step is to have a place in a table to put a picture. This type of field has the
   data type OLE Object. The Authors table has such a field included. Open this table
   in Datasheet view.

   To insert a picture while in Datasheet View, select the author whose picture you're
   inserting, right-click the Photograph field, and choose Insert Object from the shortcut menu. Select one of the supplied bitmaps or use your own.

2. After you've added some pictures, close the table and return to the Design View
   window for the TabbedBibliography form.

3. Move to the Author Information tab on this form. If the Field List window is not
   visible, activate it by clicking the Field List toolbar button. Click the Bound Object
   Frame control in the Toolbox, and then drag the Photograph field from the Field
   List window onto the Author Information tab. Drop the field at the right side of the
   tab. Rearrange the control to resemble Figure 11.27.

**FIGURE 11.27.**

*The*
TabbedBibliography
*form with the*
Photograph *field.*

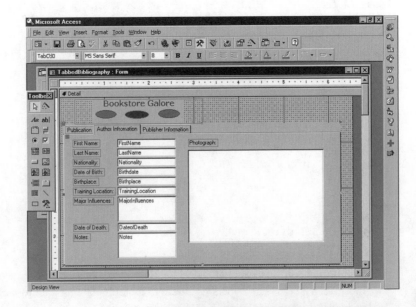

| Do | DON'T |
|---|---|
| **DO** use OLE to use the tools of other applications you may have, such as Excel or Word 8, in your Access databases. You can have a lot of fun and make a much more effective database using OLE, especially on a multimedia machine. | **DON'T** try using OLE on a marginal system, that is, a computer with 16MB or less. Although it works, you'll be disappointed in the performance. |

11

4. Switch to Form View. The screen should resemble Figure 11.28. While in Form View, scroll through the records. You'll see that the picture changes for each record (assuming you've put some pictures into the Authors table) while the Image control graphic from earlier stays the same for each record. You can right-click over the Photograph field and use the Insert Object shortcut menu in Form View just like you could in the Author table's Datasheet view. Close this form, saving the changes.

FIGURE 11.28.

*The*
TabbedBibliography
*form in Form View.*

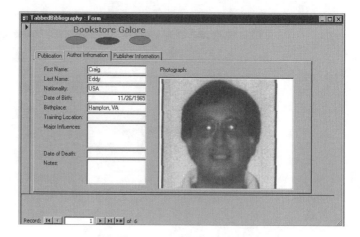

▲

# Summary

Combo and list boxes show a list of data. Although these controls have a variety of uses, most often Access developers use them to look up existing data to make data entry easier or to help in data validation. You can insert and program these controls both manually and with a wizard.

The trick to making these controls work properly is to bind their Row Source property to a proper source. This source can be an entered list or a previously existing query or table. After you've set this property to point to the right source, all that remains of the list or combo box programming is to improve its aesthetics or its ease of use.

The TabControl can add a Z axis dimension to your forms. There are three steps in this process. First, add the control to a form. Second, add the controls to the individual pages. Third, format the pages as you see fit.

Option groups are boxes containing check boxes, option buttons, or toggle buttons. The distinguishing characteristics of an option group are that only one control in the group can be selected and one must be selected. If you wish to use many unrelated option buttons, check boxes, or toggle buttons on your form, you can do so, but don't place them within an option group.

Using the Image control, you can easily include existing graphics files in reports and forms. Simply add the control to a form or report, then tell Access which graphic to use for that control.

Access stores graphics, sounds, or other OLE type objects as data in a database. These objects are called bound objects. You can show unbound objects in forms and reports as decorative items. With Access you can either create objects at the time you insert them into a form or report, as the task this morning demonstrated, or use a pre-existing file such as a bitmap.

# Q&A

**Q  I don't like the manila file look of the TabControl, but I like its function. Can I change the appearance of this control?**

**A** You can to some extent. The TabControl has a `Style` property (under Format) which will allow you to substitute buttons for tabs in this control.

**Q  What's the difference between Row Source and Control Source in a combo box?**

**A** Row Source is the source for the data in the list portion of a combo or list box. Control Source is where the data entered in this form will end up in the bound table or query.

**Q  Can I use OLE to edit pictures in the Image Control?**

**A** No. You need to edit the picture outside of the Image control.

**Q  What's an OLE object?**

**A** Certain Windows applications support Object Linking and Embedding (OLE). Applications that allow objects they create to be used by another application are called OLE server programs. Access 97 is an OLE client application. It can use objects created by an OLE server but cannot share objects it creates with another OLE client. For example, take an OLE image embedded in an Access form. Paintbrush can act as an OLE server program and Access the OLE client, so Access can use an object created in Paintbrush for its own purpose. However, Paintbrush cannot use objects created by Access in its applications, in part because Access isn't an OLE server.

**Q  What other kinds of OLE objects are there?**

**A** There are as many OLE objects as application programs that can act as an OLE server. For example, Word and Excel are OLE servers, so you can embed Word documents and Excel spreadsheets in your Access database. This gives you all the financial and numerical analysis powers of Excel or the editing power of Word in Access. The downside of this is you must own either Word or Excel to use this tool.

Windows comes with all the tools you need to play WAV sound files if your computer is sound capable. Using the same techniques as shown in this chapter, you can embed WAV sound files in forms or tables to give your databases some real flair.

11

Additionally, OLE is resource-demanding. A 386/33 with 12MB of RAM works all right for Access alone. Using OLE on this machine would be slow going indeed.

**Q** **I created a combo box and set the `Column Widths` property to `1 in; 1 in; 2 in`, yet the combo box just stays small, showing part of only one column. Why?**

**A** A combo box will stay the size it is during Design View unless you set the `List Width` property to the total of what's in your `Column Widths` property. The `List Width` property can be as wide as you want, but cannot be smaller than the combo box is during Design View.

**Q** **Why create an unbound form?**

**A** You'll see the use for this later on. Unbound forms work very well for such things as button menu forms (Switchboards). You can also create an unbound form, and then bind it using a SQL statement if you prefer to work this way.

# Workshop

Here's where you can test and apply what you have learned today.

## Quiz

1. What character tells Access an entry in the `Control Source` property list box is an expression?

2. What two controls make up a combo box?

3. If you place an Image control image on page 3 of a tabbed form, will you be able to see that image on page 1?

4. What property binds an option group to a table field?

5. You have a form `MyForm` bound to the table `MyTable`. You want to enter a combo box, MyCombo, on this form that will look up values in a table called `MyLookup`. Do you enter `MyLookup` as the control source or row source for MyCombo?

6. What property must be set to `Yes` to limit the possible entries to those already entered as a row source for the combo box?

## Exercises

1. Launch Access and open the `BookStore` database if necessary.

2. Open the `TabbedBibliography` form in Design View.

3. Add a new option button to the option group on the Publication tab. Label this button `Online/Download` (to represent publications available for purchase in an electronic form on the bookstore's Web site). You might have to adjust the position of the existing buttons, resize the group, or both.

4. Make sure Access has set the `Option Value` property for this new control to 4.

> You can change the label for a control by either directly editing the label or altering its `Caption` property from within the Properties list box.

5. Close the form, saving changes. Edit the `MediaTypeLookup` table to add a number 4 for `MediaType` and `Online/Download` for `MediaTypeDescription`.

6. Close the table. Access will automatically save the table edits you made.

**11**

DAY **12**

# Creating Action and Union Queries

Today you'll learn

- What append action queries are
- What delete action queries are
- How to construct and run these two action queries
- Why and how to compact databases
- What top queries are and how to use them
- What crosstab queries are and how to use them
- What update queries are and how to use them
- How to use UNION queries
- The purpose and usage of data definition queries

# Delete and Append Queries

Deleting a single record from a table is quite easy. You open the table in Datasheet View, locate the record you want to eliminate, and click the row header for the row containing the record to be deleted. This highlights the row. Press the Delete key to eliminate the record.

What do you do if you want to eliminate many records, such as all those publications for a particular publisher? You could go through your table record-by-record to locate and then delete these records. You could also create a query, sort on the PublisherID field, and then delete the records by highlighting them and pressing the Delete key.

The second method might sound ingenious, but it's more cumbersome than just doing a delete query.

The following task, which demonstrates the delete action query, deletes all of the publications for JimBob Publishing Company (a fictional publisher I've added to the database that accompanies this chapter). In the third task, append query, you'll add them back to the Publications table (there's a temporary table named JimBob's Books in this chapter's database that has all of the titles for JimBob in it; you'll append to the Publications table by selecting from this temporary table).

## Task: The delete query

1. Launch Access and open the BookStore database for Day 12. Click the Queries tab. Click the New button to start a new query. Bypass the wizard by clicking the Design View option and clicking OK. Add the Publications and Publishers tables to the query. Close the Show Table list box.

2. Drag the PublisherName field to the first column of the query design grid. Add the parameter [Enter Publisher Name:] to the first criteria row for this query.

3. Run the query by clicking on the Run button on the toolbar. Enter JimBob Publishing Company when prompted. The query will return four rows, all of which contain the same data. Your screen should resemble Figure 12.1.

**FIGURE 12.1.**

*The trial run for the delete action query is a select query.*

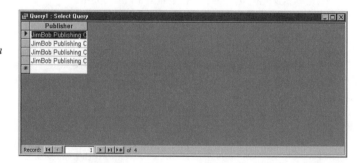

▼ The point of running this query first as a select query is to make sure it's running right, extracting all the records you want and none that you don't. This query is working correctly, so it's time to alter it to a delete action query.

4. Return to Design View. Click the Query menu and click Delete Query. (You can also click the Query button in the toolbar and choose the Delete option from that.) After you've told Access to change the query from a select one to a delete one, your title bar will change to reflect the new type of query. Also, a Delete line will replace the Sort line in the query design grid. (See Figure 12.2.)

**FIGURE 12.2.**

*The title bar along with the Delete line in the design grid indicates that this query is a delete one.*

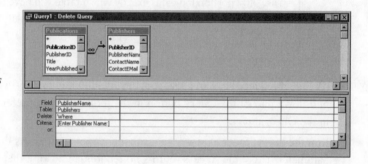

5. Because you want to delete rows from the Publications table, not the Publishers table used for the criteria, you must now double-click the asterisk in the Publishers table's field list. This will add a column to the design grid and set the Delete row for this new column to From, indicating that this is the table from which rows will be deleted.

6. Click the Run button in the toolbar. Access again prompts you for a parameter, just as it did when this was a select query. Enter JimBob Publishing Company again. Click OK. A warning message, showing in Figure 12.3, appears.

**12**

**FIGURE 12.3.**

*Access displays a warning message box when you run a delete action query.*

▼ Click Yes. Note that even though the query only returns one column of figures, the PublisherName, Access warns you that it will delete four rows.

▼

> **Note**
>
> Delete action queries work on entire rows or records even if the same query running as a select query returns only part of a row or record. Here is the SQL code behind this query.
>
> ```
> DELETE Publishers.PublisherName, Publications.*
> FROM Publishers RIGHT JOIN Publications ON Publishers.PublisherID =
> Publications.PublisherID
> WHERE (((Publishers.PublisherName)=[Enter Publisher Name:]));
> ```
>
> The FROM portion indicates exactly which table will have rows deleted. You can open the Publishers table and see that JimBob Publishing Company is still there.

7. Change the query back to a select query by clicking the Select choice from the pull-down part of the Query button in the toolbar. If you prefer, click Select Query in the Query menu.

8. Run the query. Enter JimBob Publishing Company again as the PublisherName parameter. This time Access returns no records, indicating that there are no longer any records for JimBob Publishing Company in the Publications table.

9. Return to Design View and change this query back to a delete action query. Close this query, saving it as Deleter. Note the special icon on the Queries tab of the Database window that Access assigned to this query, which visually clues you that this is a delete type query.

▲

# Compacting the Database

In many operations, Access leaves "holes" in its databases. For example, when you add a table or query to Access, Access will enlarge the MDB file to accommodate this new object. However, if you later delete these objects, Access won't dynamically shrink the MDB file to its initial size.

After running the action query from the preceding task, Access continues to hold open room for the deleted records, even though they aren't included in the table. Access's wasted space grows worse as you add and then delete database objects such as forms, reports, and queries.

Compacting a database immediately gets rid of these empty spaces or holes that Access leaves in its file structure and only recovers at its leisure. The following task shows how to compact a database and the results of doing so.

**Tip**

There is no difference between switching query types using the menu or toolbar selections. How you work is up to you.

You could, for example, manually edit the SQL statement in SQL View to change query types that way.

If you want to see how flexible Access 97 can be, try this. Go to SQL View using the View toolbar button. Access will respond by showing you a screen with the following SQL code:

```
DELETE Publishers.PublisherName, Publications.*
FROM Publishers RIGHT JOIN Publications ON Publishers.PublisherID =
Publications.PublisherID
WHERE (((Publishers.PublisherName)=[Enter Publisher Name:]));
```

Edit this to read

```
SELECT Publishers.PublisherName, Publications.*
FROM Publishers RIGHT JOIN Publications ON Publishers.PublisherID =
Publications.PublisherID
WHERE (((Publishers.PublisherName)=[Enter Publisher Name:]));
```

by changing the first word, DELETE, to SELECT. Now switch back to Design View. Access has reflected the edits you made in SQL to its design grid.

The all capital letters in the SQL keywords, DELETE, SELECT, and so forth, are a convention for SQL keywords. SQL and Access work just fine if you enter mixed case.

## Task: Compacting a database

1. Return to the Database window. Use the File | Database Properties menu item. Switch to the General tab on the dialog that appears and note the Size indicated. Click the OK button to close the dialog.

2. Choose Tools | Database Utilities | Compact Database from the menu.

3. Access will close the database, grind away a while, and then re-open the compacted database. Again use the File | Database Properties menu item. Switch to the General tab on the dialog that appears and note the Size indicated. It should be smaller than the original size. Also notice that the Modified date (shown in the section just below the file's size) has changed to the current date. Click the OK button to close the dialog.

The amount of reduction you see when compacting depends on many factors, such as how often you issue the Compile All and Save All commands that enable Access to recover space without the Compact action.

**12**

# The Append Action Query

The append action query extracts data from one table or query and appends, or attaches, it to another table. The target table therefore grows to include all the records it had initially, plus those records extracted by the query. The following task takes the records from the JimBob's Books table shown in Figure 12.4 (included in the sample data) and appends those records to the Publications table. Obviously this is a somewhat contrived example, but art does imitate life, doesn't it?

**FIGURE 12.4.**

*The table supplied to simplify this task.*

| | Publicatio | PublisherID | Title | YearPublished | WebPage | CategoryID | ISBNNu | EditionNumbe | F |
|---|---|---|---|---|---|---|---|---|---|
| | 9 | 6 | JimBob Etiquett | 1998 | http://www.jimb | 6 | | 1 | |
| ▶ | 10 | 6 | JimBob for Pres | 1998 | http://www.jimb | 6 | | 1 | |
| | 11 | 6 | JimBob's Guide | 1998 | http://www.jimb | 2 | | 1 | |
| | 12 | 6 | JimBob's Caree | 1998 | http://www.jimb | 7 | | 1 | |
| * | utoNumber) | | | | | | | | |

Open the Publications table in Datasheet View. Notice that there are no records that have JimBob Publishing Company as the publisher. Of course, if you didn't do the first task, delete query, there might be some such records in the table. If there are, either work through the first task (recommended) or simply delete those records now.

The purpose of the query you'll create in the following task is to extract records from the JimBob's Books table and append them to the Publications table. To see the effect of this task, you don't need to have these exact records in JimBob's Books. Any records that are validated through the Publications table will work.

## Task: The append query

1. Close all open tables and queries to clear the work area. Start a new query by moving to the Database window, clicking the Queries tab, and clicking on the New button. Choose the Design View option to bypass the wizards and click OK.

2. Double-click the JimBob's Books table in the Show Table window's list box to add this table to the query. Click Close to shut down the Show Table window.

3. Drag the asterisk from the Field list box to the Field row of the first column of the query design grid.

4. Access changes the asterisk to JimBob's Books.*, which is Access shorthand for "include all the fields from JimBob's Books in this query." Click the Run button in the toolbar to see how this query runs. Your screen should resemble Figure 12.5.

**FIGURE 12.5.**

*The effect of the
JimBob's Books.\* field
in a query.*

| PublicationID | PublisherID | Title | YearPublished | WebPage | CategoryID | ISBNNumber |
|---|---|---|---|---|---|---|
| 9 | 6 | JimBob Etiquett | 1998 | http://www.jimb | 6 | |
| 10 | 6 | JimBob for Pres | 1998 | http://www.jimb | 6 | |
| 11 | 6 | JimBob's Guide | 1998 | http://www.jimb | 2 | |
| 12 | 6 | JimBob's Caree | 1998 | http://www.jimb | 7 | |
| (AutoNumber) | | | | | | |

> **Tip**
>
> When you move the \* from the a table's Field list box into a query, Access
> automatically includes all the fields from that table in the query.

This particular query includes all the records from the `JimBob's Books` table
because you've entered no restricting criteria.

5. Return to Design View. Click the Query Type button in the toolbar and choose
   Append from the drop-down menu. If you prefer, make these choices from the
   main menu. The Append query button is the one with the green cross in the pull-
   down. The Append dialog, shown in Figure 12.6, appears.

**FIGURE 12.6.**

*The Append dialog.*

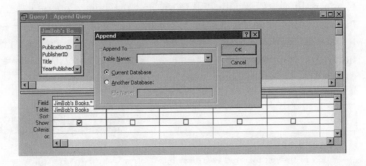

6. Pull down the combo box in the Append dialog and choose the `Publications` table
   to append to. Click OK.

7. Look how the query design grid has changed. Not only has the title bar changed to
   indicate this is an append query, but the design grid itself changed to include rows
   needed by append queries.

8. Click the Run button on the toolbar. Access presents you with a message box
   warning you that continuing to run this query will append four rows to the target
   table, `Publications`. Click Yes. As with the delete and make table queries, nothing
   seems to occur, but it has. Access has added the records from JimBob's Books to
   the `Publications` table.

9. Close this query, saving it as `Appender`. Back at the Database window, note how
   Access clues you that this is an append action query by using the green cross icon
   next to the query's name.

12

▼ 10. Now open the `Publications` table again. This time you'll see new records for JimBob Publishing Company. These are the records appended from `JimBob's Books`. The results of this query are shown in Figure 12.7.

**FIGURE 12.7.**

*The appended records.*

| PublicationID | PublisherID | Title | Year Published | WebPage | |
| --- | --- | --- | --- | --- | --- |
| 3 | Sams | Sams Teach Yo | 1998 | http://www.mcp | Computers: D |
| 4 | HarperCollins | The Dilbert Prin | 1996 | | Business |
| 5 | Fawcett Crest | Think & Grow R | 1960 | | Self-Help |
| 6 | Simon and Schuster | The Seven Habi | 1989 | | Business |
| 7 | Sams | Dynamic HTML | 1997 | | Computers: I |
| 8 | | Moby Dick | 1998 | | |
| 9 | JimBob Publishing Company | JimBob Etiquett | 1998 | http://www.jimbi | Self-Help |
| 10 | JimBob Publishing Company | JimBob for Pres | 1998 | http://www.jimbi | Self-Help |
| 11 | JimBob Publishing Company | JimBob's Guide | 1998 | http://www.jimbi | Computers: I |
| 12 | JimBob Publishing Company | JimBob's Caree | 1998 | http://www.jimbi | Business |
| (AutoNumber) | | | 1998 | | |

**Note** Access is a tightly integrated program. The icons shown for the various query types in the Database window are the same as the icons shown in the toolbar for these same queries.

▲

Compare Figure 12.7 with 12.4 to see how the append query added records to the `Publications` table. Notice that all of the records from `JimBob's Books` were appended to the `Publications` table. That's because you didn't specify any criteria for the append query. You could have only appended a certain set of records from the source table (`JimBob's Books`) by using some criteria on this query.

| **Do** | **Don't** |
| --- | --- |
| **DO** use action queries regularly. An append query combined with a delete query on the same records can act as a powerful archiving tool. | **DON'T** fail to back up your data. Access will always follow your criteria for action queries perfectly. Sometimes, unless you're very careful, you'll enter defective criteria that will extract and delete the wrong data. The best defense is a solid backup system that's used regularly. |

# Top Queries

Take a look at Figure 12.8, which shows some data from the `OrderDetails` table for the bookstore. This table contains an entry for each book ordered from the bookstore. It would be a little difficult to determine the top five selling books by looking at this set of data.

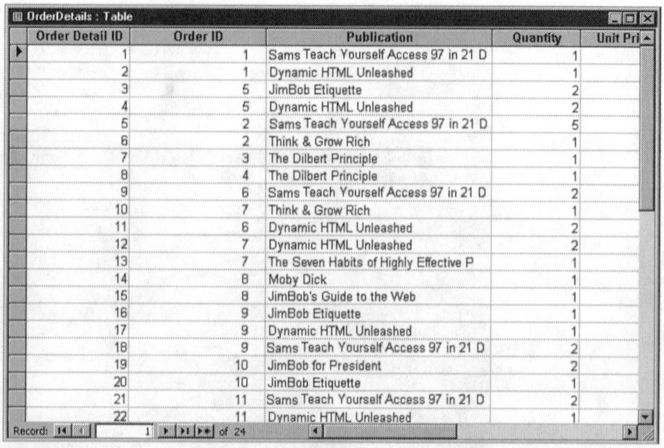

OrderDetails : Table

| Order Detail ID | Order ID | Publication | Quantity | Unit Pri |
|---|---|---|---|---|
| 1 | 1 | Sams Teach Yourself Access 97 in 21 D | 1 | |
| 2 | 1 | Dynamic HTML Unleashed | 1 | |
| 3 | 5 | JimBob Etiquette | 2 | |
| 4 | 5 | Dynamic HTML Unleashed | 2 | |
| 5 | 2 | Sams Teach Yourself Access 97 in 21 D | 5 | |
| 6 | 2 | Think & Grow Rich | 1 | |
| 7 | 3 | The Dilbert Principle | 1 | |
| 8 | 4 | The Dilbert Principle | 1 | |
| 9 | 6 | Sams Teach Yourself Access 97 in 21 D | 2 | |
| 10 | 7 | Think & Grow Rich | 1 | |
| 11 | 6 | Dynamic HTML Unleashed | 2 | |
| 12 | 7 | Dynamic HTML Unleashed | 2 | |
| 13 | 7 | The Seven Habits of Highly Effective P | 1 | |
| 14 | 8 | Moby Dick | 1 | |
| 15 | 8 | JimBob's Guide to the Web | 1 | |
| 16 | 9 | JimBob Etiquette | 1 | |
| 17 | 9 | Dynamic HTML Unleashed | 1 | |
| 18 | 9 | Sams Teach Yourself Access 97 in 21 D | 2 | |
| 19 | 10 | JimBob for President | 2 | |
| 20 | 10 | JimBob Etiquette | 1 | |
| 21 | 11 | Sams Teach Yourself Access 97 in 21 D | 2 | |
| 22 | 11 | Dynamic HTML Unleashed | 1 | |

Record: 1 of 24

**FIGURE 12.8.**
*The OrderDetails table.*

You've probably guessed by now that Access 97 has an easy way to do this. Actually, this capability has been in previous Access versions, but wasn't discovered by many users who don't program in SQL. Microsoft, beginning with Access 97, made things simpler.

To find the top five selling books, construct a new query and include the `OrderDetails` table. Add the `PublicationID` and `Quantity` fields to the query design grid.

Run the query. At this point it just returns all records in any order. Well, so far this is a big "duh." Here's where things start to get interesting.

Return to the query's Design View. Pull down the Sort combo box under the `Quantity` column and change it to Descending. Locate the Top Values drop-down combo box as shown in Figure 12.9.

Pull down the box and select 5. Run the query again. This time Access will return all of the `OrderDetail` rows that make it in the top five for the `Quantity` field. Pretty neat! Except for one thing—what you were looking for was the top five selling *books*, not the top five order quantities. Return to Design View.

Click the Totals button on the toolbar (it's the one immediately to the left of the Top Values drop-down list). A new row labeled `Total:` appears in the design grid. For the `Quantity` field's column, set the value in this row to Sum. This instructs Access to add up all of the quantities. Notice that `PublicationID` has Group By in its Total cell. This means that the query's output will be grouped by `PublicationID`—that is, there will be one row for each `PublicationID` value found in the `OrderDetails` table.

**FIGURE 12.9.**

*The Top Values box.*

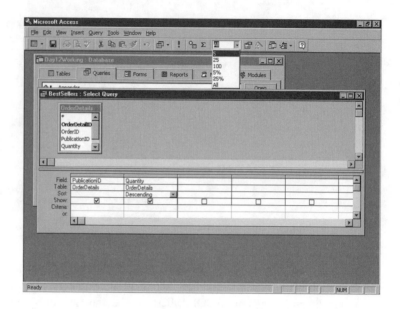

Run the query. The results are shown in Figure 12.10. Notice that now there are only five rows, and they are indeed the top selling books according to the OrderDetails table.

**FIGURE 12.10.**

*The correct results of the Top 5 Books query.*

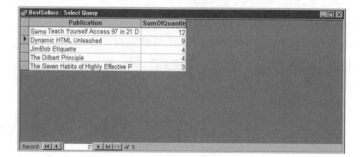

## The Secret Behind the Top

The sort order told Access that you wanted the top five summed quantity values. Had you sorted the query in Ascending order, Access would have returned the bottom five books. Also, Access selects the top from the left-most column that's sorted. Had you not pulled down the Sort combo box and told Access to sort on Quantity, Access would have, by default, selected the top values from the PublicationID field.

Keep in mind that Access works from the left in queries. You don't have to include fields from other queries or tables in the order they are in the table. You could have placed the

`Quantity` field to the left of the `PublicationID` field and then executed the `Top` statement without a Sort order and your results would have been valid.

 **Caution**

> Be very careful. When executing top queries you are extracting the top of the field you intend. A good safety measure is to include a dummy record much larger or smaller than any other in the table, and then run your top query to see if the record is included. If it is, you have some assurance that your top query is working right. You can then delete this record from either the underlying table/query or directly from the top query itself.
>
> Remember to rerun the query if you delete records from it.

You can also select top percentages using a method similar to selecting the top five. Just change the value of the Top combo box to a percentage rather than a number and re-run the query.

# Two Sophisticated Queries

This lesson is a little long, so if you're trying to do this chapter in one sitting, this is a good time to take a break. The following subjects are very important in Access. The importance of the crosstab query varies with the database in question, but the update query is called upon by database users on a regular basis.

## Update Queries

An update query is a query that, when run, alters the fields of target records. This is the only action query that acts on fields rather than on entire records. For example, if you wanted to delete an entire record or set of records, you could perform a delete action query. If you wanted to delete a field or set of fields in a record (change them to blank), the delete query won't work but the update query will.

The bookstore has received word from JimBob Publishing that the Web address for all of its books should be changed to one central URL instead of the individual URLs each book now has. The following task shows how to make this change using an update action query in Access.

This task creates an update query that looks for all publications published by JimBob Publishing Company (`PublisherID` = 6) and changes the URL to `http://www.jimbob.com/Books`.

**12**

## Task: Update queries

1. Starting from the Database window, click the Queries tab. Click the New button to start a new query. Skip any wizard. Add the Publications table to the query design grid from the Show Table window and then close the window.

2. Click the menu selections File|Save As and save this query as qryUpdater. Add the PublisherID and WebPage fields from the list box to the query design grid.

3. Run the query. As expected, Access returns all the records from the Publications table because no criteria have been specified. (See Figure 12.11.)

4. Return to Design View. Add the criterion 6 to the PublisherID field's criteria row.

**FIGURE 12.11.**

*Running the select query.*

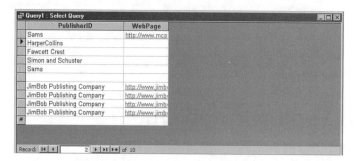

 **Note**

Running this query in Select mode before changing to the action update query might seem overly cautious. However, in most live cases you can't see an overview of your data, and running it as a select query first is important.

When you run the query, Access now extracts only those publications published by JimBob Publishing. If this is not the case, open the Publishers table and verify the value of PublisherID for JimBob Publishing.

5. Return to Design View. Pull down the Query type button on the toolbar. (That's the button just to the left of the Run (!) button.) It has an icon of two grids on it. Select Update from the pull-down list. It's the one with the pencil on it. If you prefer, you can change to an update type query by choosing that option from within the Query menu. Either way, Access changes the third row of the query design grid to read Update To: and also changes the title bar to indicate this is an update query. Add http://www.jimbob.com/Books as the value to update to in the WebPage column.

6. Click the Run button on the toolbar. Access gives you the message box shown in Figure 12.12.

7. Click Yes. Access runs the query. Close this query, saving changes.

**Figure 12.12.**

*The Update Query
message box.*

▲

Back at the Database window, notice how the new query qryUpdater has a distinctive
icon showing you that not only is it an action query, but an update one.

Click the Tables tab. Open the Publications Demo table in Datasheet View. Your screen
should resemble Figure 12.13.

The four records for JimBob Publishing Company now all have the same WebPage value.
Note that unlike other action queries, nothing in the record was touched except for the
specific field you chose to update. Close this table to clear the decks for what comes
next.

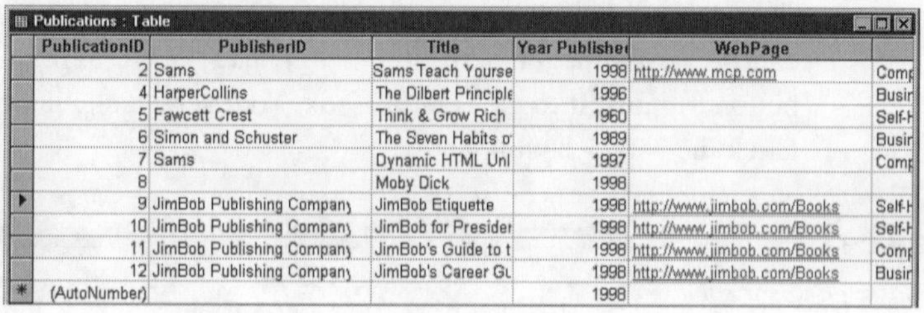

**Figure 12.13.**

*The update query's
results.*

| PublicationID | PublisherID | Title | Year Published | WebPage | |
|---|---|---|---|---|---|
| 2 | Sams | Sams Teach Yourse | 1998 | http://www.mcp.com | Comp |
| 4 | HarperCollins | The Dilbert Principle | 1996 | | Busir |
| 5 | Fawcett Crest | Think & Grow Rich | 1960 | | Self-H |
| 6 | Simon and Schuster | The Seven Habits o | 1989 | | Busir |
| 7 | Sams | Dynamic HTML Unl | 1997 | | Comp |
| 8 | | Moby Dick | 1998 | | |
| 9 | JimBob Publishing Company | JimBob Etiquette | 1998 | http://www.jimbob.com/Books | Self-H |
| 10 | JimBob Publishing Company | JimBob for Presider | 1998 | http://www.jimbob.com/Books | Self-H |
| 11 | JimBob Publishing Company | JimBob's Guide to t | 1998 | http://www.jimbob.com/Books | Comp |
| 12 | JimBob Publishing Company | JimBob's Career Gu | 1998 | http://www.jimbob.com/Books | Busir |
| (AutoNumber) | | | 1998 | | |

## The Crosstab Query

People have a hard time understanding and designing crosstab queries. However, these
queries can be quite important when you are analyzing your data. Microsoft has gone to
great lengths in both Access 97 and Excel 97 to make the creation of these queries quite
simple. The Excel term for a crosstab query is a Pivot Table.

Technically speaking, a crosstab query is a two-dimensional matrix with a mathematical
operation performed at each intersection. Once again, a crosstab is much easier to understand in the concrete than in the abstract. Take a look at Figure 12.14. This is the
Publications table arranged as a crosstab to show the number of books published by
year by each publisher.

12

**FIGURE 12.14.**

*The* Crosstab Demo *table.*

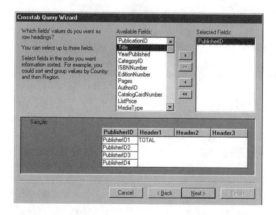

| PublisherID | Total | 1960 | 1989 | 1996 | 1997 | 1998 |
|---|---|---|---|---|---|---|
|  | 1 |  |  |  |  | 1 |
| Sams | 2 |  |  |  | 1 | 1 |
| Simon and Schuster | 1 |  |  | 1 |  |  |
| Fawcett Crest | 1 | 1 |  |  |  |  |
| HarperCollins | 1 |  |  |  | 1 |  |
| JimBob Publishing Company | 4 |  |  |  |  | 4 |

The following task creates this crosstab output. If at any time you want to see this query in action, the sample data includes a query called Publications_Crosstab which, when run, will duplicate the results of the following task.

## Task: The crosstab query

1. Click the Queries tab. Click the New button. Select the Crosstab Query Wizard option and click OK.

2. The Crosstab Query Wizard appears. On this initial dialog you select the table or query on which the crosstab query will be based. Click the Publications table in the next list box. Click the Next> button.

3. This query should list the publishers in the rows and the count of each years publications across the top. Click the field PublisherID to highlight it and click the > button to move it to the right list box. Your screen should resemble Figure 12.15. Click the Next> button.

**FIGURE 12.15.**

*Choosing fields for the rows in a crosstab.*

4. This dialog sets up the column headers. The column heads are the count of the number of publications per year, so highlight YearPublished in the list box. See Figure 12.16. Click Next>.

**FIGURE 12.16.**

*Choosing fields for the columns in a crosstab.*

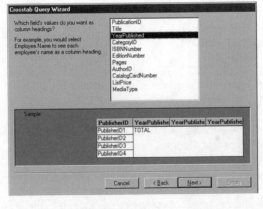

5. The column to count for each publisher in each year is `PublicationID`, so highlight that in the left list box and Count in the right list box, as shown in Figure 12.17. Click the Next> button.

**FIGURE 12.17.**

*Choosing the field to count.*

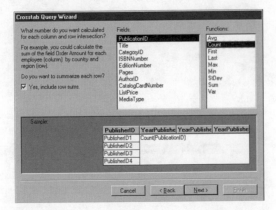

6. Accept the Access defaults by clicking the Finish button. Access will grind away a while and eventually will finish constructing and running the query. Your screen should look like Figure 12.18 (after resizing a few columns).

**FIGURE 12.18.**

*The finished crosstab query running.*

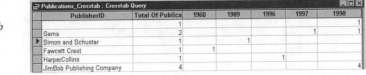

| PublisherID | Total Of Publica | 1960 | 1989 | 1996 | 1997 | 1998 |
|---|---|---|---|---|---|---|
|  | 1 |  |  |  |  | 1 |
| Sams | 2 |  |  |  | 1 | 1 |
| Simon and Schuster | 1 |  | 1 |  |  |  |
| Fawcett Crest | 1 | 1 |  |  |  |  |
| HarperCollins | 1 |  |  | 1 |  |  |
| JimBob Publishing Company | 4 |  |  |  |  | 4 |

12

Look how handy the results are. At a glance you can see which publisher published the most books in a given year and overall. The dataset was a little small, so a trained eye could have seen this by examining the raw data in the table, but what happens when there are hundreds or even thousands of books in our bookstore? That's what computers are for.

Switch to Design View. Your screen should resemble Figure 12.19.

The underlying design of a crosstab query isn't very obvious. That's why Microsoft went to the trouble of making a special wizard for it. The heart of this query is in the third and fourth columns. Notice that the Total row has the word Count in it for the third and fourth columns. This tells Access to count the PublicationIDs for the crosstab.

To see the number of books from each category published in each year, change the Field row in the first column to CategoryID and run the query again. Your results should resemble Figure 12.20.

**FIGURE 12.19.**

*The Design View of a crosstab query.*

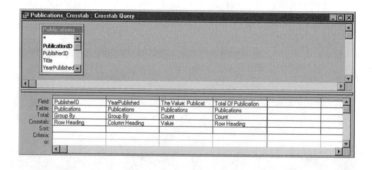

**FIGURE 12.20.**

*Changing a crosstab's grouping field.*

> **Tip**
>
> You can make one crosstab and then use many operatives in the same frame by changing the operative (count, sum, avg, and so on) and selecting File I Save As for each operative. This gives you a series of crosstabs that show different aspects of the same data.

# UNION Queries

The final type of query you'll examine today is the UNION query. This is a query that combines the row sets from different tables into a single result set. For example, you could use a UNION query to produce a list of all of the publishers and authors stored in the database.

The following task walks you through creating this list using a UNION query.

### Task: The UNION query

1. Return to the Database window's Queries tab. Click the New button and then click OK to open a new query in Design View.

2. Click the Close button to close the Show Tables window—you cannot use the design grid to create UNION queries.

3. Use the Query | SQL Specific | Union menu item to start the UNION query. The Design View changes to a SQL entry window because you cannot use the design grid to create a UNION query.

4. Enter the following SQL statement into the window:

```
SELECT FirstName + ' ' + LastName AS Name FROM Authors
UNION
SELECT PublisherName AS Name FROM Publishers
```

   This uses an expression to create the authors' names and simply selects the PublisherName field from the Publishers table.

> **Note**
>
> UNION queries require that the same number of fields be returned from each SELECT statement and that corresponding fields in each SELECT have compatible data types. However, you can use number and text fields in the same field position.

5. Run the query. The results should resemble Figure 12.21. Notice that the authors and publishers are intermixed within the datasheet, and that the results are sorted in an ascending order.

6. To sort the results in the descending order (and, more importantly, to demonstrate the ORDER BY clause in a UNION query), return to the SQL view and enter ORDER BY Name DESC on a new line after the second SELECT statement.

**12**

**FIGURE 12.21.**

*Running the UNION query.*

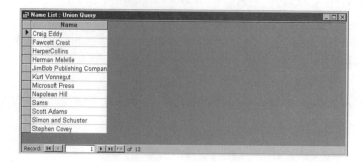

7. Run the query again and notice that the record order is reversed. Also note that you need only a single ORDER BY clause for the entire UNION query and that it should appear at the end of the SQL statement.

8. Remove the ORDER BY and save the query as Name List. Notice its icon on the queries tab.

# Summary

Today you learned how to delete records in groups by using a delete action query. You also learned how to append records from one table to another using an append action query. You saw how Access can leave "holes" or dead space in its files that can be eliminated with the Compact Database utility built into Access. Finally, you learned how to find top or bottom values in numbers or percentages from a query.

Update queries alter data according to your criteria. The updates occur to the queried table or query.

Crosstab queries are complex enough that Access has a specially designed wizard just for them. You need to tell the wizard four essential things: what's the source for the query, what's to be in the rows, what's to be in the columns, and what operation to perform at the intersections and for a row summary.

Union queries allow you to view lists of like data from different tables within the same datasheet. This is mostly useful for producing phone lists, Web listings, and so on across tables with common fields.

# Q&A

**Q** **When I update a table a crosstab is bound to, does the crosstab query get updated too?**

**A** Yes, the next time the query is run. If you have both the `Publications` table and the `Publications_Crosstab` query open at the same time and you edit the table, the query won't reflect the edits until it's run again (or queried again).

**Q** **Can I base a form on a crosstab query?**

**A** Sure. Look at Figure 12.22. This is a form based on the `Publications_Crosstab` query done in the fifth task. The advantage of using a form to view crosstab data is that you have all the form services available to you.

**FIGURE 12.22.**

*A form based on a crosstab.*

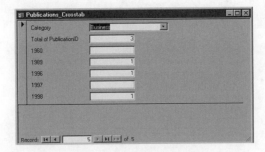

**Q** **How do crosstabs differ from subtotals?**

**A** Crosstabs act on two dimensions, across and down. Subtotals only operate on one, either across or down.

# Workshop

Here's where you can test and apply the lessons you learned today.

## Quiz

1. Can you undo (Ctrl+Z) the action of a delete action query? An append action query?

2. If you have a query selecting the top 25 percent of a field, how can you change it to show the bottom 25 percent?

3. Can you use criteria in top queries?

4. Can you make a crosstab that finds average values?

12

5. Can the update query act on individual fields in a table, or must it work on entire rows, like the delete query?

6. What are the two requirements for the SELECT field list in a UNION query?

## Exercises

By now you're probably sick of the query designer, so I'll let you off the hook today for the Exercise section. But rest up, because tomorrow you tackle more form control properties and work on subforms. Rest assured that there'll be a big assignment in this section for Day 13!

# DAY 13

# Using Form Control Properties and Subforms

Today you learn about the following:

- What a form control property is
- The meaning of enabled and locked controls
- A better way to find records
- How to filter records
- The need for forms with subforms
- The steps to create a form with a subform
- Creating the subform
- Drag-and-drop subforms
- How to synchronize main and subforms with control properties

# Control Properties

To a great extent, using Access depends on understanding and setting properties for database objects or controls. You can use the program successfully for minor applications such as simple list management even if you know very little about properties, but when your needs grow even slightly complex, your time spent learning this subject will pay off tremendously.

 **Note** — Much of what applies to form control properties also applies to reports. Form design and report design are very similar subjects, only diverging where the applications of forms and reports divide. For example, you make no data entry in reports, so there's no reason to have combo boxes there.

Many of the basic property settings can be handled by wizards, so why reinvent the wheel? Let wizards do what they do so well. However, there's a huge world of capability in Access that the wizards don't even attempt to address. In some cases, venturing into these worlds will call up other wizards or Access helpers called *builders*, so you don't need to do it all yourself. For example, in Day 11, "Working with Form Controls," you bypassed the Form Wizard because it wasn't sharp enough to know when a combo box made sense for a form's field (since the lookup properties weren't set properly). But, as soon as you put a combo box onto the form, the Combo Box Wizard appeared, making the job of setting the combo box's properties much easier.

Take a look at Figure 13.1. This is the Property dialog for a form control (or field, if you prefer). Each of the tabs across the top exposes a different set of properties.

Here are the tabs available in the Property list box, with a short explanation of each set of properties:

- **Format**—Format properties control the appearance of the data on the form or report.
- **Data**—Data properties determine what can be done to and the source for the data that is bound to the control.
- **Event**—Event properties determine how a control behaves in response to an event. Examples of events in Access: when the cursor moves over the control, when a control is clicked, when the control gets the focus, and when the control loses the focus.
- **Other**—Here you'll find the properties that don't fit in any of the other classifications. Don't think just because these are classed as "other" that they are unimportant. Some of the most used and needed properties are in this list.
- **All**—All properties from all classifications are listed here.

**FIGURE 13.1.**

*The various types of properties for a control.*

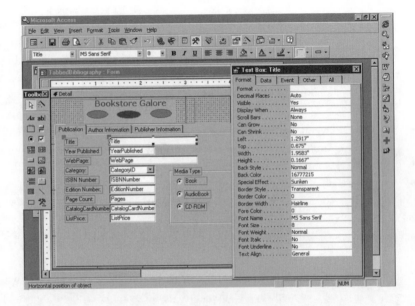

The first few sections of this chapter discuss a few valuable field control properties. Two other important control properties, Link Child Fields and Link Master Fields, are the topic of the second half of this chapter.

# Enabled and Locked

In many situations you'll want to protect your data from being altered. You may have some people doing data entry who only need to enter data into a few specific fields, but also need to be able to view other data on the form.

For example, once the ISBN and Library of Congress Card Catalog Number are assigned to a publication, it's unlikely that data will ever change. It is necessary to see such information, but it's rare you'll ever want to edit the data. Therefore, you should modify your forms to disable editing in any controls bound to such fields.

The following task, which demonstrates the use and limitations of the Locked and Enabled properties, addresses this need.

### Task: Locked and Enabled properties

1. Start Access and open the BookStore database, if necessary. On the **Forms** tab, select the TabbedBibliography form and click the **Design** button to edit the form in Design View.

13

▼ 2. Using the Shift+click method, select the YearPublished, ISBNNumber, EditionNumber, and CardCatalogNumber fields in the **Publication** tab. If your Properties list box isn't on Data, change that to make it so. Locate the Enabled property in the list box. Click in the Enabled field. Pull down the combo box and choose No or double-click on this field to toggle it from Yes to No.

Did you catch Access changing the color scheme of the fields in the main form when you switched the property to No? This is Access's visual clue that these fields aren't enabled. Move to Form View. Your screen should resemble Figure 13.2.

> **Tip**
>
> Access enables you to set the common properties for many controls at the same time. Just select as many controls as you want to set the same property to, change the common property in the list box, and let Access do the rest.

Try clicking in any of the fields you disabled. You can't get your cursor in them at all. In some applications this would be quite efficient. Setting the Enabled property for a control or group of controls to No prevents not only data entry into the field(s), but also prevents you from giving the fields the focus.

> **Note**
>
> Well, that's ugly and hard to read. If you're like many people, you don't like the way the Enabled set to No makes the form look. If you don't want people to change the values in a form, you can prevent them by either setting the Enabled property to No or the Locked property to Yes, as you'll see later in this task. Locked-Yes has several advantages over Enabled-No, including the way controls look.

**FIGURE 13.2.**

*Some fields in the form disabled.*

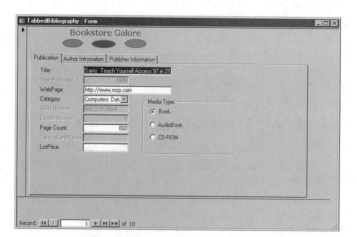

▼

▼  However, there's a drawback to using this form with some of the form's controls disabled. How do you use this form to find the record for a particular ISBN? The only way is to scroll through the records until you hit the one you want. You could click in the Record selector section and enter the particular record you want, but that won't work unless you know the record number for a particular publication in the Publications table.

Setting the Enabled property to No did safeguard the data, but at too great a cost. It would be better to let users work with these fields so they can use Access's search capacity, but prevent them from altering data. The answer is the Locked property.

3. Return to Design View mode. Select the same group of fields (if they're not already selected) using the Shift+click method. Change the Enabled property back to Yes. Locate the Locked property, right below Enabled. Set that property to Yes.

| Do | Don't |
|---|---|
| DO use the marquee or Shift+click method to select multiple fields to set their properties. | DON'T choose the Edit I Select All menu selections. That chooses not only the field, but all the controls associated with this form. |

4. Return to Form View. Try editing any of these fields. You can't edit the fields, but you can give them the focus. You can also copy from, but not paste to, locked fields. You can't do anything with fields for which Enabled is set to No.

# The Obscure Auto Properties

There are two control properties available on text box control that can produce some pretty cool behavior. These are the Allow AutoCorrect and the Auto Tab properties.

## The Allow AutoCorrect Property

The Allow AutoCorrect property is available for both text box and combo box controls. You'll find the property on the Other tab of the Properties window.

If you've used Microsoft Word 97, you're familiar with the AutoCorrect feature. This feature automatically corrects or replaces what you type based upon a pre-defined list replacements. For example, the default AutoCorrect for the character sequence (c) is the copyright symbol. Similarly, AutoCorrect can fix capitalization mistakes that are made as you type.

13

To specify what actions AutoCorrect takes (or doesn't take, as the case may be), use the Tools|AutoCorrect menu item. Access will display the AutoCorrect dialog, shown in Figure 13.3. By clicking the Exceptions button, you can specify exceptions to the AutoCorrect rules.

**FIGURE 13.3.**

*The AutoCorrect options dialog.*

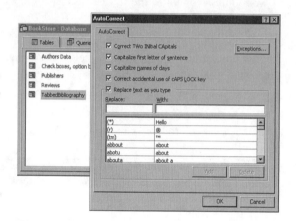

Note that AutoCorrect is a shared tool—all Microsoft Office applications that offer an AutoCorrect feature work from the same set of AutoCorrect rules. Any changes you make to the rules while using Access will also affect how AutoCorrect behaves when you're using Microsoft Word.

## Using Auto Tab

The Auto Tab feature will be familiar to users of some older data entry systems. When enabled, this feature will cause the focus to move from the current text box to the next one in the tab order as the user completes the entry into the first text box.

For example, you may have an Input Mask set for a text box that forces the user to enter a date in mm/dd/yyyy. When the user completes entry of the date and Auto Tab is set to No for the entry box, the focus will stay in the date's box. If Auto Tab is set as Yes, however, once the user enters the last digit of the year, the focus will move to the next field in the tab order. (You'll learn more about tab order tomorrow, "Putting the Finishing Touches on Forms.")

The Auto Tab feature works only on controls where the Input Mask property is set either for the control or the underlying field (in the case of a bound control).

# Searching About

Keep the form from this task open. If you're not on Form View, go there. Move to the first record if it's not already current and click the **Author Information** tab. Click in the LastName field, and then click on the **Find** button in the toolbar. This is the button with the picture of a pair of binoculars. Access will bring up the Find in Field dialog. Your screen should resemble Figure 13.4.

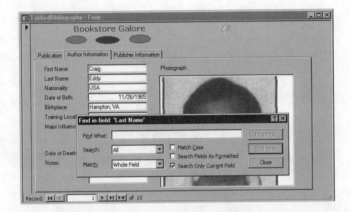

Enter Melville as a Last Name to search for. Click the **Find First** button. Access will move to the first record that matches the criteria of Last Name being Melville. Look carefully at the bottom of your screen toward the left of the status bar. Access quietly tells you that your search was successful. Your screen should resemble Figure 13.7.

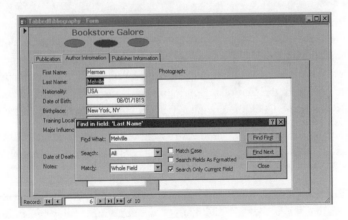

13

## Filtering Records Using Filter by Form

That worked, but because Access obscured part of the view of the main part of the form, it was a pretty subtle success. Try this as a better way to search. Close the Find in Field dialog and again move to the first record by clicking the **Record** button at the bottom of the screen. If you prefer, you can use the Edit|Go To|First menu item. (This last step isn't really necessary, but is included to set things up identically to the original find you performed.)

Click the **Records|Filter|Filter By Form** menu item or click the **Filter by Form** toolbar button. Access brings up a blank form with two tabs at the bottom. Here is where you can enter criteria to restrict which records Access displays. Your screen should look like Figure 13.6.

**FIGURE 13.6.**

*The blank Filter by Form window.*

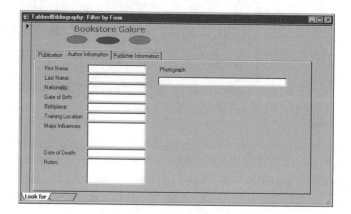

Move down to the Last Name field and enter Melville. As you enter the name, Access tries to help you by Auto Expanding your entry to match the data already entered in the bound table or query. If you wanted to add more than one criteria to the filter using AND logic, simply enter that criteria in the appropriate field. If you wanted to add more than one criteria to the filter using OR logic, you'd click the Or tab, which will bring up another blank form. Click the **Or** tab. After clicking the Or tab, enter Covey as another criteria.

To apply the filter—that is, to restrict the display of records to only those where the Last Name field is Melville or Covey—click the **Apply Filter** toolbar button (that's the one with a picture of a funnel on it).

After applying the filter, you'll find you have only two records to choose from. Access hints that this is the case and that you are applying a filter, by adding the word Filtered to the record number enunciator at the bottom of the screen. Your screen should look like Figure 13.7.

**FIGURE 13.7.**

*Records displayed limited by the filter.*

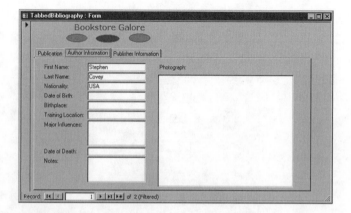

You can add in as much criteria as you need to in order to limit the filtered record set by returning to the Filter by Form design screen.

For now, remove the filter by clicking the **Remove Filter** toolbar button. It's the same button as the Apply Filter button, but now it serves the opposite purpose.

**Note**

If your users will have to locate records by querying or filtering, make sure when you design your forms that you include fields sufficient to cover all possible eventualities.

## Filtering Records by Selection

Sometimes you'll only want to see a subset of your data based on the data currently being displayed on the form. Say you have a publication on screen that's of a particular category and you want to see only those publications in the same category. Access contains a shortcut to get you there on the express track.

### Task: Filter by selection

1. If the TabbedBibliography form isn't running in Form View, make it so. Click in the **Record** number box at the lower-left portion of your screen. Click the **Publication** tab and move to the record for *The Dilbert Principle*.

2. Click in the Category field. Next, click the **Filter by Selection** toolbar button (it's the one with the funnel and a lightning bolt on it). Access will restrict the records to those publications in the Business category. The results of this are shown in Figure 13.8.

13

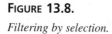

**Figure 13.8.**

*Filtering by selection.*

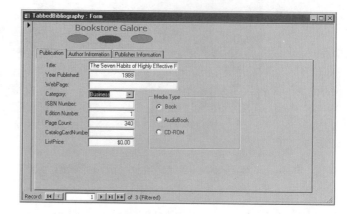

3. That's it! Remove the filter by clicking the **Remove Filter** toolbar button, just as you did when you used the Filter by Form method. Access will save this filter for quick use next time.

## Quick Sorts

The only other thing to note in this area are those two buttons to the left of the filter buttons. They have arrows pointing up or down with the letters Z A or A Z on them.

These two buttons will sort the records underlying the form by any field that currently has the focus. After clicking in the FirstName field, click the left-most button, **Sort Ascending**, and you'll sort the form's results by the author's first name, as shown in Figure 13.9.

**Figure 13.9.**

*Sorted results.*

**Note**

Sorting the records using Form View's sort buttons does not change the order of the records in the underlying query or table.

# Why You Need Forms with Subforms

Access is a relational database system. In any system such as Access, there are relationships between records in various tables; in other words, one record in a table can be related to many other records in other tables. Here are some examples:

One customer has many orders.

One order has many line items.

One author has many publications.

In a hospital, one doctor has many patients.

In that same hospital, one patient has many medicines required to be given daily.

One person has many CD-ROMs.

One CD-ROM has many tracks.

One salesperson has many sales.

One company has many salespeople.

One department has many sales items.

One store has many departments.

In each of the preceding examples, and many more you can likely think of, there are one and many sides to a relationship. The link, or common field, in both tables has one occurrence in the one table and potentially an unlimited number of occurrences in the other table.

How do you enter a series of occurrences on the many side of the relationship? For example, you want to enter a series of sales for a particular salesman. The combo box task in Day 11, "Working with Form Controls," shows how you can look up a publication ID to make sure the value you added to the PublicationID field in the Reviews table is correct.

The technique shown in Day works, but it's slightly cumbersome. It has two drawbacks. First, you can't just enter a series of occurrences for a particular publication, but must look up the right publication ID for each record or use Ctrl+'—this key combination, the repeat key for Access, repeats the value from the last record in the current field. Also, you can't see an author's information along with all of his or her publications at the same time without making a query and a form to host the query.

13

Forms with subforms are a very convenient and aesthetically pleasing way to show or enter occurrences on the many side of a one-to-many relationship. There's no reason the same form can't be used to create new records on the one side of the relationship, but that's not the most common use of this technique.

You can easily get lost in the following task unless you have a good idea of the goal shown in Figure 13.10. Take a look at Figure 13.10 to see the finished form with a subform. The following steps shows how you're going to get there. This task is also a good reference if you need to manually create a form with one or more subforms. Like so much else, the job goes much faster with a wizard.

## Task: Designing a subform

1. Determine the one and the many sides of the relationship to see if the two tables or queries you want to include are right for the form with subform technique. If necessary, construct the needed queries or tables.

2. Design the subform. This is where the many table or query will appear. In most cases the subform will be a form using the Datasheet View, but it doesn't have to be.

3. Save the subform, giving it a distinctive name. Access users and developers have adopted a set of naming conventions for objects in their databases. Using these conventions, if a form is to be named `ClassEntry`, the subform is generally called `subClassEntry`, but you can make up your own naming convention or not use one at all.

4. Design the (container) form, leaving room for the subform in your design.

5. Drag the subform into the container form.

6. Test the new form with subform with known data to make sure it's working right.

**FIGURE 13.10.**

*The finished form with subform example.*

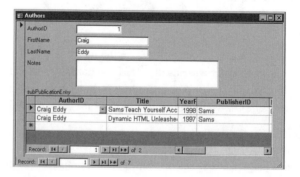

# Preparing for the Form

The subform part of this form makes it possible to enter, edit, or display all of the publications currently available for an individual author. This requires a change to the Publications table to add the field holding such information. This will be taken care of in the following task, along with setting up a query to bind the subform to.

The following task uses a query for this subform with a criterion to return or display only those records for which the Available field is equal to Yes. The task uses a query instead of the original table because if this form were bound to the table, it would show all of the publications, available or not. This isn't a fatal error, but it would make for an inconveniently long scroll through irrelevant records in the case of authors who have many unavailable publications.

Also, you're going to join to the MediaTypeLookup table in order to get the descriptions for the Media Type column in the Publications table. Although this can be done using a field's lookup properties, your table is not set up for this feature. To comply with Access' requirements when adding a new record using the subform, you must also add the MediaType field from Publications to the query. But, as you'll see in the task, Access has a data entry/validation shortcut that really comes in handy.

## Task: Making the subform's query

**◄ TASK**

1. Launch Access and open the BookStore database if necessary. Click the Tables tab, select the Publications table, and click the Design button. Click the first empty row to add a new field. Name this field Available and make its Data Type Yes/No. Set the Default Value property to Yes. Close the table design view, saving the changes.

2. Next, you need to update the existing rows in the Publications table for this new field. You can either do this on the Publications datasheet or by creating a new update action query with the SQL UPDATE Publications SET Available = Yes. This will update all of the rows in one fell swoop. There's no need to save this query if you take this route.

3. Click the Queries tab and then the New button to start a new query. Select the Design View option and click OK. Add the Publications and MediaTypeLookup tables to the query design grid and close the Show Table window.

4. Drag the MediaType field from the Publications field list and drop it on the MediaType field in the MediaTypeLookup field list. This instructs the query to join these two tables using matching data in the MediaType fields.

**13**

▼

▼    5. Double-click the `AuthorID`, `Title`, `EditionNumber`, `YearPublished`, `Pages`, `ISBNNumber`, `PublisherID`, `CategoryID`, `MediaType`, and `Available` fields (in that order) from the Publications list box to add them to the query design grid. Uncheck the Show check box for `Available` and enter `Yes` for this field's criteria.

6. Double-click the `MediaDescription` field from the `MediaTypeLookup` table to add it to the query design grid. Your screen should resemble Figure 13.11.

**FIGURE 13.11.**

*Setting up the query.*

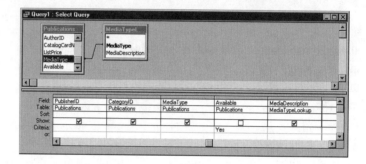

7. Click the Run button in the toolbar. Your screen should resemble Figure 13.12. Remember that the actual return you get when you run this query depends upon the data in your database.

**FIGURE 13.12.**

*Running the new query.*

| Author | Title | Edition Numbe | Year Publishe | Page Count | ISBN Number | Pu |
|---|---|---|---|---|---|---|
| Craig Eddy | Sams Teach Yourse | 5 | 1998 | 800 | 0-672-31298-0 | Sams |
| Scott Adams | The Dilbert Principle | 1 | 1996 | 336 | 0-88730-787-6 | HarperCollin |
| Napolean Hill | Think & Grow Rich | 1 | 1960 | 254 | 0-449-21492-3 | Fawcett Cre |
| Stephen Cove | The Seven Habits o | 1 | 1989 | 340 | | Simon and |
| Craig Eddy | Dynamic HTML Unl | 1 | 1997 | 600 | | Sams |
| Herman Melvil | Moby Dick | 1 | 1998 | 300 | | |
| JimBob Jones | JimBob Etiquette | 1 | 1998 | 50 | | JimBob Pub |
| JimBob Jones | JimBob for Presider | 1 | 1998 | 500 | | JimBob Pub |
| JimBob Jones | JimBob's Guide to t | 1 | 1998 | 25 | | JimBob Pub |
| JimBob Jones | JimBob's Career Gu | 1 | 1998 | 25 | | JimBob Pub |

Record: 14 ◄ [ 1 ] ► ►I ►* of 10

8. Now for that shortcut. Select one of the JimBob books and move over to the `Media Type` column. Change the value to 3 and press the Tab key. Did you see that? Access automatically filled in the value for the joined field (`MediaDescription`) to CD-ROM. Pretty cool feature.

9. Close the query, saving it and using the name `subPublicationEntry`. This is also ▲    the name it has in the sample data.

# The Form with Subform

You are now ready to create the main form with a contained subform. There are two ways to do this—the easy way and the hard way. You've probably guessed by now that the easy way is to use a wizard, so that's the way to proceed. After creating this form with a subform and seeing it in action, you'll learn the secret of the magic acts the wizard performed so you can manually design the same thing if the need arises. For now, just concentrate on making and using the form with subform. The following task uses a wizard to create a form with a subform.

### Task: The form with subform

1. From the database window, click the Forms tab and then click the New button. Pull down the combo box and choose Authors as the bound table. Select the Form Wizard option to use the wizard. Click OK to start the process of creating the new form.

**Note**

When planning a form with a subform, you must know ahead of time which form will contain the other. The container, or main form, is the form you initially bind to the new form when starting the wizard, as in step 1.

2. Here's the central place where the Access wizard shows its intelligence. Add the AuthorID, FirstName, LastName, and Notes fields to the Selected Fields list by double-clicking each field in the Available Fields list or by selecting each field and clicking the > button.

   Now pull down the combo box labeled Tables/Queries. Locate the subPublicationEntry query you created in the third task, "Making the subform's query." Click it so that it's highlighted. Access populates the Available Fields list box with the fields returned by this query.

3. Add all the fields from this query to the Selected Fields list by clicking the >> button. Your screen should resemble Figure 13.13.

13

**FIGURE 13.13.**

*Adding the fields that will appear on the sub-form.*

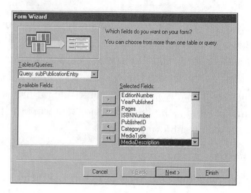

**Note**

The main, or container, form needs only a few fields from Authors—the table it's bound to. These fields—AuthorID, FirstName, LastName, and Notes—are all that's required to locate a student from Authors. The Notes field was included to allow for notes about the author to be entered as new publications are entered into the subform.

The balance of the fields in Authors aren't relevant for the purposes of this form. Remember, this form will only be used to look up existing records in Authors, not to create new ones. If this form were also going to do double duty as a new record-creating form, it would have to contain all the fields from Authors.

At this point you have two fields with the same name, AuthorID, as part of this form/subform. Access associates these fields with their table or query by using the dot notation that's also used throughout Access. So Authors.AuthorID identifies the AuthorID field from the Authors table and subPublicationEntry.AuthorID identifies the AuthorID field from the subPublicationEntry query.

4. Click the Next > button to move on. Here you tell the wizard which is the form and which is the subform, but not quite in those words. Access asks the question in plain English: How do you want to view your data? Since you want to view the authors and their publications, select By Authors in the list box. Leave the Form with Subform(s) option button selected. If you wanted to see the authors and publications all combined on one form, you'd choose subPublicationEntry. This part of the wizard is a little tough conceptually, but the preview window at the left of the dialog gives you a good indication of what each option will produce. Just follow along for now. If you have the time and inclination after finishing, run the wizard again, but view your records by subPublicationEntry.

▼   At this point your screen should resemble Figure 13.14. Make sure the Form with Subform(s) option button is selected. The other choice is Linked Forms. Linked forms are, as you might guess, two forms that share a common field and remain in sync. If you have the time, run this wizard again doing the same steps, but choose Linked Forms at this step to see the differences between linked forms and a form/subform.

**FIGURE 13.14.**

*Telling Access how you want to view your data within the form/sub-form.*

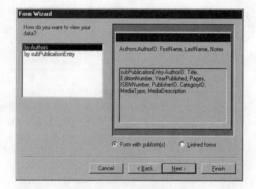

5. Click the Next> button to move on. This dialog is where you define the style for the subform. Leave Access's default, Datasheet, selected. The usual layout for a form/subform is for the form to be in Form View while the subform is in Datasheet View. This isn't a hard and fast rule, however. Your specific needs might include having a Form View subform. Click Next>.

6. Here is where you can give your form an artistic look. Give this form the Windows 95/98 look by clicking the Standard entry in the list box. Click the Next> button.

7. Use the name `Author's Publication Entry Form` for the Form and change the Subform text box to `subPublicationEntry`. The process is now finished, so click the Finish button. Click the Record Advance button. As you advance through the authors, you'll also see their publications (see Figure 13.15).

▼

13

**FIGURE 13.15.**

*The running form.*

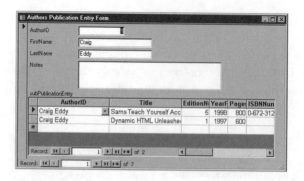

> **Note**
>
> Look again at Figure 13.15. Notice that the Author ID column in the subform shows the author's actual name, not his or her ID value. If your form shows a number here instead, you've run across what seems to be a bug in the Form Wizard. It seems that every other time I created this form/subform combination, the subform would display the actual data instead of the lookup data. If you were to look at the subform in Design View, you'd see that the wizard had chosen text boxes for these fields. On the times when the wizard correctly displays the value (as opposed to the ID), the fields were given combo box controls.
>
> So, if you have a form with IDs, simply recreate the form.

The Main/Subform Wizard creates two forms during its run. The main form is the one you initially bound even before calling on the wizard. The contained, or subform, is the form you told the wizard to bind to the subform in the middle part of the wizard's run. After finishing its run, the wizard called on for the fourth task, "The form with subform" should leave you with two forms, Author's Publication Entry Form and subPublicationEntry, as shown in the Database window in Figure 13.16.

**FIGURE 13.16.**

*The two forms the wizard made in one pass.*

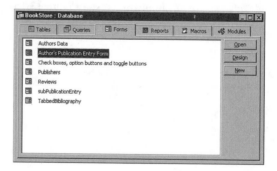

Refer to Figure 13.17, which is the wizard-created form from the last task in Design View.

**FIGURE 13.17.**

*The Design View of a form/subform created by a wizard.*

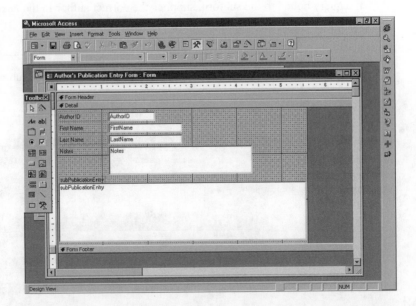

The keys to forms with subforms are the two properties Link Child Fields and Link Master Fields. These properties tell Access how to keep the form and subform in sync. Access, in the subform, shows only those publications for a particular author by filtering the subform according to the AuthorID in the master form. If you are in Design View for the wizard-created form, move back to Form View. The first record, the one for Craig Eddy, shows two publications.

Move to the next record in the form, the one for Napolean Hill, by clicking the right-facing arrow at the bottom of your screen. The subform portion of this form shows only one publication, *Think & Grow Rich*, for Hill.

If you want to check out Access's accuracy, you can open the relevant tables to view similar data. Although the data in your dataset might be different from the samples shown in the book, your data should agree internally.

The query that the subform is tied to is an Access query. These queries are so powerful that even the inclusion of the AuthorID field in this form isn't necessary. The fourth task included it only so you could see how the AuthorID fields remain coordinated in the main and subform.

13

Try entering a new book for Hill. Click in the Title column in the first empty row in the subform portion of the form. Enter Master Key to Riches. As soon as you start to type, the query bound to the subform supplies the correct author in the AuthorID field. Your screen should resemble Figure 13.18.

**Note** It is impossible to enter uncoordinated data into the subform of a properly constructed main/subform.

**FIGURE 13.18.**

*Access will not enter uncoordinated data if you construct your forms correctly.*

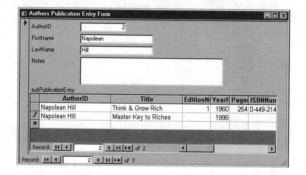

Continue to enter data for this book, making up required entries you're unsure of (EditionNumber and Pages).

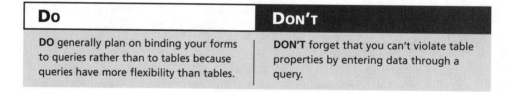

| **Do** | **DON'T** |
| --- | --- |
| **DO** generally plan on binding your forms to queries rather than to tables because queries have more flexibility than tables. | **DON'T** forget that you can't violate table properties by entering data through a query. |

Close this form. Run the Wizard's Bibliography query. You'll see that your new entry in Hill's form/subform is reflected in the database's data. The running query is shown in Figure 13.19.

**FIGURE 13.19.**

*If done right, all data presentations in Access can be of live data.*

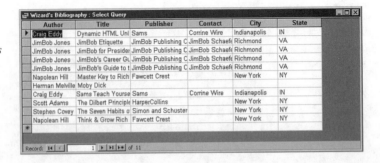

| Author | Title | Publisher | Contact | City | State |
|--------|-------|-----------|---------|------|-------|
| Craig Eddy | Dynamic HTML Unl | Sams | Corrine Wire | Indianapolis | IN |
| JimBob Jones | JimBob Etiquette | JimBob Publishing C | JimBob Schaefe | Richmond | VA |
| JimBob Jones | JimBob for Presider | JimBob Publishing C | JimBob Schaefe | Richmond | VA |
| JimBob Jones | JimBob's Career Gu | JimBob Publishing C | JimBob Schaefe | Richmond | VA |
| JimBob Jones | JimBob's Guide to t | JimBob Publishing C | JimBob Schaefe | Richmond | VA |
| Napolean Hill | Master Key to Rich | Fawcett Crest | | New York | NY |
| Herman Melville | Moby Dick | | | | |
| Craig Eddy | Sams Teach Yourse | Sams | Corrine Wire | Indianapolis | IN |
| Scott Adams | The Dilbert Principle | HarperCollins | | New York | NY |
| Stephen Covey | The Seven Habits o | Simon and Schuster | | New York | NY |
| Napolean Hill | Think & Grow Rich | Fawcett Crest | | New York | NY |

**Note**

Structure is everything. If you structure your database logically, you'll likely have all things go right with your database project. The links in BookStore make it so data entered in the form/subform is reflected throughout the entire database because tables contain all data and all objects refer to those tables.

The fact that entering data in one place results in its appearing everywhere might, at this point, seem a little baffling to you, but as you go along the advantages will become clear. The *point* of Access is that data entered anywhere by anyone through any means is available anywhere else.

# Dragging and Dropping Your Way to Subforms

There is a simple alternative to using the wizard for the design of forms with subforms. This section shows you how to embed a form within another form using the drag-and-drop capability of Access 97. Although this is not a formal task, if you choose to go along you can use the sample data forms DDAuthorPub Entry and subPublicationEntry. DDAuthorPub is the same form as from the previous task, but has the form/subform removed.

Figure 13.20 shows DDAuthorPub Entry form in Design View. If you want to follow along, open this form in Design View.

**13**

**FIGURE 13.20.**

*A form opened in Design View ready for insertion of a subform.*

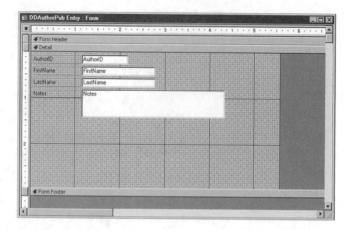

To get the subform `subPublicationEntry` into the form, drag the form from the Database window to the design grid of the host form. Figure 13.21 shows the two windows, database and form design, tiled so each shows on the screen. To tile your windows, click the Restore Window buttons for all of the windows you want to tile. Then make use the Window | Tile Horizontally or Window | Tile Vertically menu items to tile the windows.

**FIGURE 13.21.**

*Tiling the windows to make both visible at the same time.*

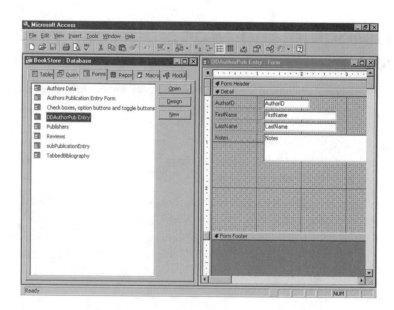

Drag the `subPublicationEntry` form from the database window to the form design window right below the existing four fields shown in Figure 13.21.

When you drop the form onto the DDAuthorPub Entry form, your screen should resemble Figure 13.22.

**FIGURE 13.22.**

*Dropping the dragged form places it into the host form.*

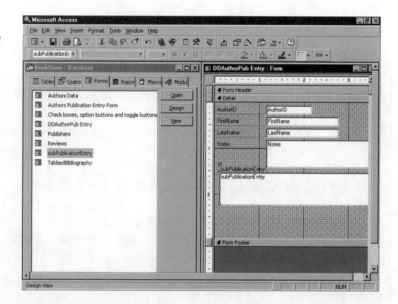

Figure 13.23 shows the form from Figure 13.22 running. If you try this yourself you'll see that Access has the brains to link the forms so that the records for each author's publications remain in sync with the author's record from the host form. When you've finished this mini-task, close the form—do not save your changes.

**FIGURE 13.23.**

*The finished form/subform works just like the form/subform created by the wizard.*

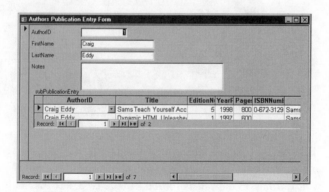

13

# A Working Example

Now that you've seen two ways to create a form/subform combination, play with the main form in Form Design View to see how this all works. There are two field control properties for the subform control (there is an actual subform control, as you'll see in the upcoming task) that dictate how the subform is to be linked to the main form—Link Child Fields and Link Master Fields.

The following task reviews these field control properties.

## Task: Field control properties

1. Open the DDAuthorPub Entry form used in the previous section in Design View. Make sure the Control Wizard option is off (using the wizard is cheating—it does the majority of these steps for you).

2. Click on the Subform/Subreport control in the toolbox and click in the bottom portion of the form's design grid to create the subform control. Size the subform control to take up most of the space available.

3. Open the Properties window (if necessary) by clicking its button in the toolbar. Click the Data tab. Your screen should look like Figure 13.24.

FIGURE 13.24.

*The Properties window's Data tab for a subform/subreport.*

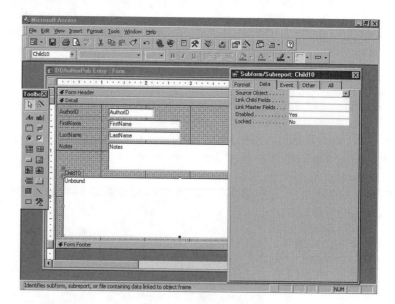

4. Click the Source Object property and select subPublicationEntry from the drop-down list for this property. When you do so, Access displays its intelligence by also filling in the values for the Link Child Fields and Link Master Fields properties, and correctly at that!

5. Switch to Form View. Your screen should look like Figure 13.25.

**FIGURE 13.25.**

*The form with sub-form/subreport.*

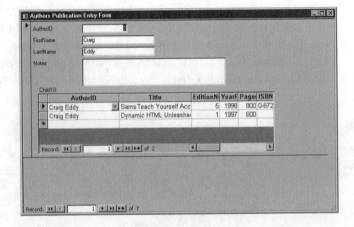

6. This looks familiar, doesn't it? Return to Design View and see what happens when you break some things. Click the subform/subreport control to set the Properties window to the proper context. On the Data tab, delete the values in the `Link Child Fields` and `Link Master Fields` properties.

7. Open the Form View once again. The results are shown in Figure 13.26.

The effect of the link breakage is apparent: you can see that all publications for all the authors are dumped here rather than just the ones that are associated with the record in the main form. Scrolling to another author record has no effect on the contents of the subform.

**FIGURE 13.26.**

*The effect of breaking the link.*

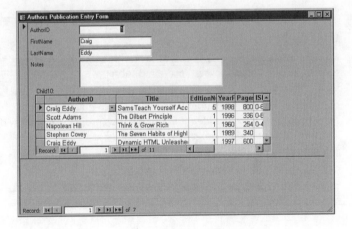

**13**

▼    8. Return to Design View. Again go to the Properties window's Data tab for the sub-
        form control. Select the `Link Child Fields` property and click the ellipses button.
        This will bring up the Subform Field Linker dialog, shown in Figure 13.27. Notice
        that this dialog has correctly suggested the proper field names. You can click the
        Suggest button to see an explanation of why these fields were chosen. Click OK on
        the Subform Field Linker dialog. Switch back to Form View. Your screen should
        again resemble Figure 13.25.

**FIGURE 13.27.**

*The Subform Field
Linker dialog.*

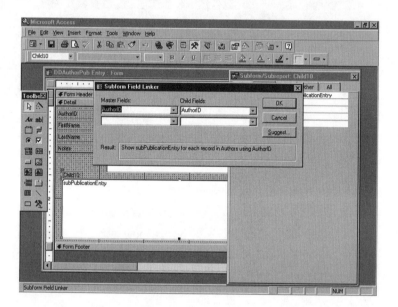

▲

---

**UGH! I'M SICK OF THIS!**

If you're the counting type, you've now hit three sections in a row dealing with the one
topic of linking fields between forms and subforms.

It's not that this itself is a terribly difficult topic, but rather the entire concept of links is
quite important in the relational model. I've been pounding on this topic almost ad nau-
seam to communicate the idea that using Access properly means dividing data into pieces
and then reassembling those pieces by using links.

The links have been form field links, but the same general principles apply to links in
queries, or for that matter, reports.

# Summary

Access controls have many different classes of properties. These properties can be set during the design phase, and in many cases during runtime. These properties affect how a control behaves, reacts, or looks, and where a control gets its data from or outputs it to. It's fair to say a control is the sum of its properties.

Four important properties are `Link Child Fields`, `Link Master Fields`, `Enabled`, and `Locked`. The first two properties determine which fields in the main form and subform are in common, or linked. The last two properties control entry and editing of the fields and data. The more you know about properties, the better off you are. Feel free to click various properties, keeping an eye out for the status bar text changes to see what they do. If you want to explore deeper, use online help. More properties are discussed in Day 14, "Putting the Finishing Touches on Forms."

You can filter or sort the underlying data shown in a form (or report) by clicking the appropriate toolbar buttons or by making menu selections. You can filter by criteria, complete with a series of `OR`s if necessary; you can filter by more than one field and more than one `OR` if you want to. You can filter by selection and sort the filtered or unfiltered records in ascending or descending order.

Forms with subforms or linked forms make a handy way to show related data. The easiest way to create a form with a subform is to use the wizard, but you can drag a subform from the database window onto a form when that form is in Design View.

# Q&A

**Q Why not just use a form based on a query to do what a form with a subform does?**

**A** Subforms are much more efficient in situations such as those outlined for the fourth task. If you want to enter many publications for an author using the form/subform, you simply add the publications in the subform portion while the main part of the form remains static.

NEW TERM  If you used a *unitary* form (a form without a subform) based on the query, you'd have to navigate through all the fields on the form to make each new record. There are shortcuts making that last statement not precisely true, but that doesn't alter the fact that forms and subforms are much more efficient for entering records to the many side of the one-to-many relationship than any unitary form.

13

**Q** I didn't understand how Access knows what records in the subform belong to the main form. That part wasn't made clear to me.

**A** The properties that link form with subform data are the `Link Master Fields` and `Link Child Fields` located in the Data tab of the subform's Property list box. Access's wizard is good at making guesses as to which fields are link fields when you include these fields in the wizard process.

**Q** Can I customize a form with a subform or must I accept what the wizard created?

**A** You can customize forms with subforms just as you can any other forms and, when you've finished customizing it, drag and drop that subform onto the form.

**Q** Can I use greater- or lesser-than operatives as filter criteria?

**A** Yes. The < and > operators, just like all the rest, work the same in filters as in queries. For example, `Not "IL"` returns all those records that don't have `IL` as their data.

**Q** How do I apply a sort without a filter to records shown in a form?

**A** Click in the field on which you want to sort, and then click the Sort Ascending or Sort Descending toolbar button.

# Workshop

Here's where you can test and apply the lessons you learned today.

## Quiz

1. Which property should be set to `True` if you want to allow users of your form to copy data from a Text Box control but not modify its contents?

2. How do you display only Data properties from the Properties list box?

3. You have a main and subform with a link field `SSN`. How do you tell Access to synchronize the main and subform using the `SSN` field?

## Exercise

1. Create a form for the `Publishers` table using the AutoForm: Columnar Wizard.

2. Add the `subPublicationEntry` subform to this form using drag-and-drop.

3. Switch to Form View, click in the subform's `YearPublished` field for a row where `YearPublished` is 1998.

4. Click the Filter By Selection button. Now scroll through the different publishers. What publications are displayed in the subform?

5. Remove the filter. Click the Filter by Form toolbar button.

6. Filter the Publications records to limit the records shown to those in the category Computers: Database. Again scroll through all of the publishers.

7. Close the form, saving it if you choose. The book does not come back to it.

13

# DAY **14**

# Putting the Finishing Touches on Forms

Today you'll learn

- How to place event-only controls on a form
- How to have a picture-perfect command button
- How to use a wizard to program controls that respond to certain events
- How to clean up a form's look
- What tab order is and how to change it
- How to alter the design of a subform
- How to use graphic elements in form design
- About form page layout considerations

## Instantly Smarter Forms

You might have heard that programming computers is a job for brilliant social misfits. Personally, I take offense at that remark but do recognize the image that exists does portray programmers in such a light.

Some programming tasks are best handled by social misfits, but you can do quite a bit of programming in Access with little effort and without losing your social skills. Today's lessons show you how. If you're a user/designer, much of what you need to do in Access is simplicity itself. However, Access has the power to facilitate its use as a professional development tool as well. Thousands of professional applications demonstrate this to anybody's satisfaction. However, using the more esoteric Access functions does take at least a little work.

## The First Programmed Command Button

So far you've made use of Access's excellent design to create static forms and reports. You can open and display data by using supplied controls, and you can edit data when you are using forms. Your needs to this point probably haven't gone beyond using Access's supplied tools. However, this chapter starts you on the path of being able to design your own tools.

The following task shows you how to make controls that scroll through records.

### Task: Record manipulation

1. Launch Access and open the BookStore database if necessary. Open the Author's Publication Entry form in Design View. If you're picking up where Day 13, "Using Form Control Properties and Subforms," left off, clear any filters and return to Design View for the form.

2. Rearrange and resize the controls on your form to resemble Figure 14.1. The point of the rearrangement is to create some room at the bottom of the form for some new controls. Your screen doesn't have to look exactly like Figure 14.1; just allow for some room for two new controls. If you prefer, you can just open up a little space at the bottom of the form by enlarging the form itself and leaving the controls where they are.

   Refer to Figure 14.1 and note that the Control Wizard toggle button is selected in the Toolbox. Make sure your Control Wizard button is similarly selected, or the following steps in this exercise won't work the same for you as they do in this example.

3. Click the Command Button control in the Toolbox. (It looks like a small, blank button.) Move your cursor on the form and click just below and toward the left of the subform section. The Command Button Wizard starts.

4. Select Record Navigation from the Categories list and the Go to Next Record entry in the Actions list. Click the Next> button.

**FIGURE 14.1.**

*The rearranged form.*

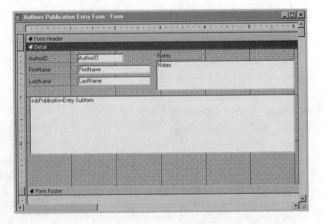

> **Tip**
>
> As you'll see later in this chapter, you can manually program command buttons, but it makes little sense to do so if what you want is available from this wizard. Look over the lists to get a feel for what's available. When you need a service that is available from these lists, invoke the wizard. Unlike some things, the way the wizard handles programming command buttons is at least as good as most programmers' methods.

5. The next dialog in the wizard is where you define the style of the command button. The new button can have a simple caption or it can sport a picture (the default setting). For this button, leave the Picture option selected.

   The standard left- and right-facing VCR-style controls Access uses for record navigation make sense as analogs for tape operation when the movement is horizontal, but most people think of moving up and down in a record set for navigating records. To place an icon on this button that fits these people's conceptions, check the Show All Pictures check box, find Down Arrow (Blue) in the list, and click this entry (the best way to find it in the list is to click in the list, type the letter d, and then scroll down until you locate the entry). Click the Next> button.

6. You can name this command button just about anything you want, but as I have preached in past chapters, it's best to use descriptive labels. A common naming convention for command buttons is to prefix them with the three-letter mnemonic cmd. Further, you should include a descriptive part of the control name so you or anybody else can tell at a glance what this control is supposed to do. Name this button cmdNextRecord. This name tells the world that this is a command button (cmd) that moves to the next record (NextRecord). Click the Finish button.

**14**

**Note**

Unlike Visual Basic, which allows you to create indexed arrays of controls, Access provides no such mechanism. In Visual Basic, you can have a group of command buttons all named cmdAction with each having a unique value for its Index property. In Access, all command buttons must be named uniquely.

7. Your screen should look like Figure 14.2. Switch to Form View to try out the new command button. Your results should be similar to Figure 14.3.

**FIGURE 14.2.**

*The finished command button.*

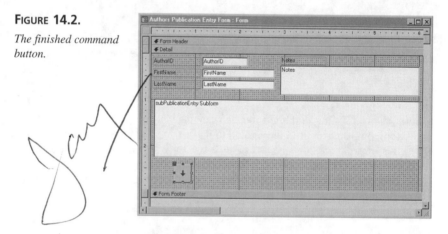

**FIGURE 14.3.**

*The new command button awaiting a command.*

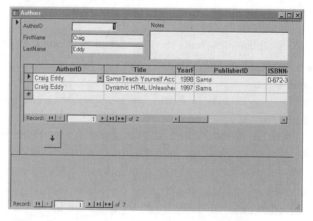

Click the new button twice. Access scrolls down through the records until record 3 shows up. (See Figure 14.4.) Your button works to navigate through the records. Although this button duplicates the Record Navigation button down at the record selector's area of the screen, the size and icon on the button make it much easier for people to understand and use.

**FIGURE 14.4.**

*The new command button in use.*

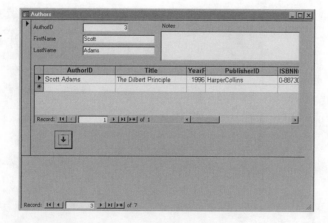

## A Complementary Command Button

The following task creates a command button that is similar to the one you created in the preceding task. This second button complements the first one.

### Task: Another command button

1. Return to Design View.

2. Click the Command Button control in the toolbox. Click the form, next to the first button you created.

3. Choose Record Navigation and Go to Previous Record from the wizard's list boxes. Click the Next> button.

4. Again check the Show All Pictures check box. Select the Up Arrow (Blue) from the list. Click Next>.

5. Give the button the name cmdPreviousRecord.

6. Click Finish. Move the new control if necessary to line up its top with the other command button. Your screen should look like Figure 14.5.

**▼ TASK**

**14**

▼ 7. Open the Properties window. Locate the `ControlTip Text` property on the Other tab. Edit the entry to read `Previous Author` for cmdPreviousRecord and `Next Author` for cmdNextRecord.

**FIGURE 14.5.**

*The do-it-yourself command button.*

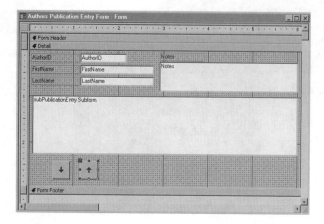

▲

Return to Form View. Try using your new command buttons to navigate around your records. They work just fine. Congratulations—you're a computer programmer!

## Your Own Tools

Having record navigation tools both on the form and below it uses up extra space and is redundant because the form already has navigation buttons at the bottom. The next exercise extends the subject of control properties to eliminate this duplication.

The following task demonstrates the placement of record selectors and navigation buttons in forms.

### Task: Record selectors and navigation buttons

1. Return to Design View. Open the Property list box. Click the Format tab. The Default View property for this form is set to Single Form. This means that by default Access will only show one record at a time. This makes sense for this form because it includes a subform. There's no practical way to show many records bound to the main form and also show the records bound to the subform.

2. Pull down the left-most button in the toolbar and click the Datasheet View option (see Figure 14.6).

As you can see, it is possible to view the form in Datasheet View, but, because all the publication information from the subform is lost in this view, it isn't very useful for displaying this form. The Datasheet View is useful for quickly scanning

▼ through the records in the master form, however. After locating a record, switch to Form View again. The found record is in the master form and the related data is in the subform. Additionally, it makes little sense to have record selectors (the gray bars at the far left in Form View) for this form, because only one record is ever going to show at one time.

**FIGURE 14.6.**

*The form in Datasheet View.*

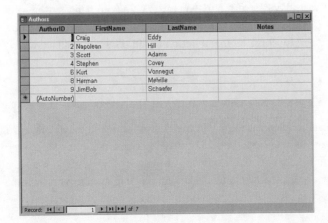

3. Return to Design View. Change both the `Record Selectors` and `Navigation Buttons` properties to `No`. Record selectors do nothing but litter the screen in Form View.

4. Switch to Form View. Notice how much cleaner your screen looks without record selectors or navigation buttons in the main part of the form/subform. Because you've made no changes to the subform, the record selectors and navigation buttons remain there. There's no loss in function as long as you want to move through the records one-by-one because the buttons added through the wizard replace the navigation buttons. If you wanted to come close to the functionality of the standard Access navigation buttons, you'd have to add some more command buttons to jump

▲ to first and last records.

# Event Properties

The Command Button Wizard from these two tasks actually wrote Visual Basic code. This section takes a look at what that code is.

Return to Design View and open the Properties window if it's not already open. Click the Event tab. Click the first command button you made, the one that moves down one record at a time.

14

The On Click property has been set to [Event Procedure] by the wizard. This means that the wizard has created some Visual Basic code that will be called into action whenever the control is clicked.

Examine the other event properties for on this tab. Command buttons can react to such events as Got Focus, On Mouse Move, On Enter, and other such odd-sounding events, but the vast majority of things you program a command button to do are in response to the On Click event. The wizard you used in the first two tasks programmed the On Click event for this command button based on what you told it to do during the wizard process.

Take a look at Figure 14.7. This shows the events to which a form (not a command button) can react. This is only a partial list. The screen isn't large enough to hold them all.

Keep in mind that Figure 14.7 only shows the event properties associated with a form. There are also Format, Data, and Other properties. Don't be concerned if some of these properties' behaviors aren't obvious to you by their names. And don't worry about memorizing all of these properties. The Online Help system in Access has all of them memorized for you.

**FIGURE 14.7.**

*A partial list of Event properties for a form.*

## Context-Sensitive Help to the Rescue

Here's an example of how to get help about any property. Click the Format tab and then click in the entry area next to the Caption property. You should have a good idea of what the Caption property does—it's the label for a control. In the case of the command buttons you just created, the caption is invisible because that space is occupied by a picture.

If you look right below the Caption property in the list box, you'll see the property Picture. An entry in the Picture property will override the caption text.

You can get some idea of what this or any property means because Access gives you a limited explanation in the status bar at the bottom of the screen. But these status bar hints really only refresh your memory; they aren't comprehensive enough to teach you how to use a property or event in your application.

To get more information, press F1 with your cursor in the Caption property field to call up context-sensitive help. Access responds with the help screen shown in Figure 14.8.

This section provides comprehensive information about the Caption property. It tells you what objects have the property and how Access will act if you don't supply a caption. Across the top of the screen you'll see entries for See Also, Example, and Applies to. These entries vary depending on the help topic and help's contents. Down toward the bottom of the screen note the underlined words Access Key. The broken underline means that when clicked, Windows help will bring up a pop-up explanation box. Move to these words with your cursor. Your cursor will change to look like a hand. Click once. Help pops up an explanation of what an access key is.

**FIGURE 14.8.**

*A context-sensitive help screen about one property, the* Caption *property.*

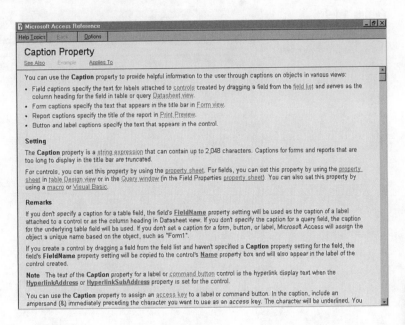

14

Notice the three topics at the very top of Figure 14.8 (See Also, Example, and Applies To)? Pay special attention to the See Also entry. This is an effective cross-reference to other related Access or Windows topics. As you use Access, you'll find online help—and especially the cross-reference—invaluable.

**Note**

Microsoft took an informal poll of about 40 well-known and high-profile professional Access programmers to learn how often and in what manner they used the Access Help system.

The response Microsoft got was overwhelming. This group of dyed-in-the-wool professional programmers used Help regularly (every day) and especially praised the cross-reference. So if you think that only wimps use Help and real programmers memorize, think again.

## Back to the Event Procedure

Close the help system for now, and see what an event procedure is like. While viewing the properties for the first command button you created, click in the entry area that now contains [Event Procedure], next to the On Click property. Access responds by showing two icons at the right side of the line: a combo box down arrow and an ellipsis (...) button. Click the ellipsis button. This action calls up the Visual Basic code that runs when you click this button. Your screen should resemble Figure 14.9.

**FIGURE 14.9.**

*The code attached to the On Click event of a command button.*

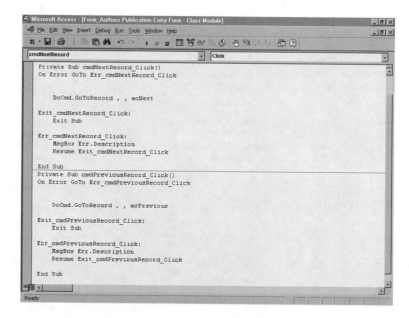

> **Tip**
>
> Clicking the ellipsis in this context brings up the code builder, where you can enter your own code or edit code already associated with the Event property. Access also has an expression builder that helps you build complex expressions.

**ANALYSIS** If you're unfamiliar with Visual Basic or VBA, this might, at first glance, look like some arcane and imposing foreign language. Like so many things that look complex at first, however, it's really quite simple when it's taken apart. Although you obviously didn't need to know what this code does to create it, here is the same code, taken line-by-line with a short, non-technical explanation for each line, which are numbered to make it easier for you to follow.

```
1: Private Sub cmdNextRecord_Click ()
2: On Error GoTo Err_cmdNextRecord_Click
3: DoCmd GoToRecord , , acNext
4: Exit_cmdNextRecord_Click:
5: Exit Sub
6: Err_cmdNextRecord_Click:
7: MsgBox Err.Description
8: Resume Exit_cmdNextRecord_Click
9: End Sub
```

```
1: Private Sub cmdNextRecord_Click ()
```

This first line declares the start of a new routine (known in Access as a "sub," which is short for subprocedure) that's going to run when the `cmdNextRecord` command button is clicked. Remember that you named your control `cmdNextRecord` at the end of the wizard process. Had you named your control `cmdHelloThere`, this line would read `Private Sub cmdHelloThere_Click ()`. The `Private` keyword states to Access that this procedure is only available (read "visible") from within this module. All the subs within this exercise are part of a module that's bound to this form. Declaring this procedure as `Private` keeps it private to the code within the module for this form and this form only.

```
2: On Error GoTo Err_cmdNextRecord_Click
```

Line 2 instructs the computer in the case of an error condition—which means something unforeseen has occurred—to jump down to the line `Err_cmdNextRecord_Click:` (line 6) and continue execution from there.

```
3: DoCmd GoToRecord , , acNext
```

DoCmd is the Visual Basic code that essentially invokes a macro. There are many macro actions, such as changing cursors, moving through records, opening and closing forms,

14

and dozens of others. The two commas are placeholders for optional parameters that are unneeded by this On Click sub. The `acNext` tells the `GoToRecord` command to go to the next record.

```
4: Exit_cmdNextRecord_Click:
```

This is a label used as a location for code to jump to in case the routine that handles a trapped error gets called. You can tell at a glance that it's a label because it ends with a colon (:). In this code fragment, line 8 will jump here if it does run.

```
5: Exit Sub
```

Exit this routine.

```
6: Err_cmdNextRecord_Click:
```

Another label. This is where line 2 instructs VBA to jump to if something goes awry. This entire section of code runs only in the case of an error condition.

```
7: MsgBox Err.Description
```

Display a message box telling the user the specific description of the type of error that occurred.

```
8: Resume Exit_cmdNextRecord_Click
```

After the message box closes (the user clicks a button), jump to line 4.

```
9: End Sub
```

Line 9 signals Access that this code segment ends here.

## Learning Code Is Optional

Don't be concerned if, even after that explanation, you still don't feel confident about your understanding of this code. Remember, you programmed the cmdNextRecord command button without knowing a line of code. You did it once, you can do it again.

| Do | Don't |
|---|---|
| DO feel free to experiment with this code to see what changes you can make. | DON'T worry if what you do results in obscure complaints from Access. Just remember what you did so you can undo it. If things get totally out of hand, delete the entire code section and delete the offending control; then use the wizard to re-create it. That will put all things right again. |

For now, close the code window if it's open, and close the form, saving the changes you made.

# Pretty Pictures on Buttons

Some people like pictures; other prefer icons; others still like text. You can tailor your command buttons as well as other Access objects to appear as you want. Microsoft supplies a variety of icons for use on objects. To see a list of these objects, open a form or report in Design View, click any object—like a command button—that has a Picture property, and then click the Picture property. Click the Build button—the one with the ellipsis on it. The Picture Builder dialog appears, complete with a large variety of icons you can use within your own projects.

You can go further than this, however. By clicking the Browse button on the Picture Builder dialog, you can browse for and include bitmap images beyond what Microsoft supplies.

Take a look at Figure 14.10. This is an unbound form with four unbound command buttons inserted. As you can see, you can add a lot of variety to your command buttons by changing the Picture property and adding a few bitmaps. The bitmap files used to make these buttons are part of the sample data, but the form isn't.

**FIGURE 14.10.**

*Adding a few bitmaps to your objects can make them look more than lively.*

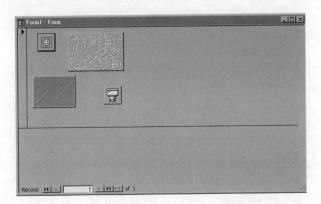

If that's not enough, you can change the Picture property for the form itself. This gives the form a background similar to what the Access Form wizard itself does. Figure 14.11 shows how adding a picture to the Picture property of a form can change the form's look quite a bit. This form is the Reviews form with a picture added.

Take it easy using graphics in your forms and reports. A little decoration goes a long way.

14

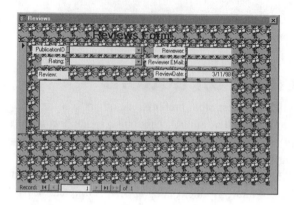

**FIGURE 14.11.**

*Adding a picture to a form can help or hurt the look of the form.*

# Tab Order

Open the Reviews form in Form View. Click in the PublicationID combo box and press the Tab key five times. When you tab through a form, you expect to move either from left to right and then back to the far left and down (this is the way we read English), or down the left column to the bottom and then wrap back up to the top of the right column. However, in this case, the tab moves in this order: PublicationID, Rating, Reviewer, Reviewer EMail, Review, and then Review Date. Tab action such as this is sure to annoy users, so get ready to change it to a more intuitive pattern.

The following task shows how to alter the tab order in a form and eliminate controls from the tab order.

## Task: Changing the tab order

▲ TASK

1. Move to Design View for the Reviews form. Click the View | Tab Order menu item.

2. Figure 14.12 shows the Tab Order dialog. This dialog shows the order in which controls receive the focus when you tab through a form. By default, Access places the first inserted control at the top of the Tab Order dialog's list box. When you made this form you placed the PublicationID field first and the ReviewDate last. The only change needed at this point is to swap the ReviewDate and ReviewText fields in the tab order.

3. Click just to the left of the ReviewDate entry in the list box, on the gray area that looks like a record selector (the cursor becomes a right-facing arrow when it's hovering over this area).

4. Click again on the now-pressed gray square. Your cursor should change to gain a box at its end, indicating that the cursor is in Move mode. Drag the ReviewDate
▼   field until it's just above the ReviewText field. Release the mouse button. Your

▼ screen should resemble Figure 14.13. Click OK to close the Tab Order dialog and save your changes.

**FIGURE 14.12.**

*The Tab Order dialog.*

Tip

The technique for changing the order of controls in the Tab Order dialog is the same as changing the order of almost anything in Access. It is a bit tricky at first, but once you get the hang of it for any function (such as changing column order in a query), you have it made for them all.

**FIGURE 14.13.**

*Moving a field to change the tab order.*

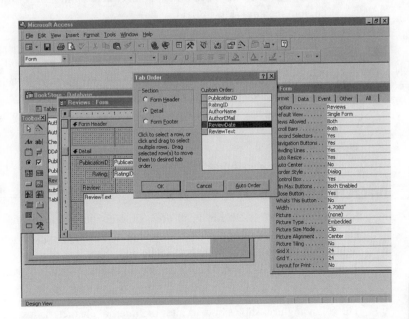

5. Return to Form View and click in the PublicationID field. Again, press the Tab five times. Due to your efforts, the cursor now behaves like people expect it should.

▼ 6. But wait a second. If you'll remember, the ReviewDate column has its Locked

▼

property set to Yes. This means that the user cannot edit any text in this field. So perhaps the user shouldn't be able to Tab into it at all. There's another important tab characteristic called Tab Stop. This property determines if a control ever receives the focus when a form is tabbed through.

---

**PROGRAMMER'S REVENGE**

I can hear the user-interface and accessibility purists now: you should always provide a keyboard method to access every field. While this might be true, most programmers I know are far from being user-interface purists. While it is an admirable goal to attempt to design your Access forms to be accessible to all users, it's not always practical to do so. This case is used as a teaching example and, in general, I would not remove this field from the tab order.

7. Return to Design View. Select the ReviewDate text box. Open the Properties

---

window if necessary and select Other. Change the Tab Stop property to No.

8. Return to Form View. Start tabbing anywhere on the form. Notice that you never tab into the ReviewDate field.

9. Close this form, saving changes.

▲

Another note about tabbing. At the last field, Access will, by default, move to the next record (or to a new, blank record if you're on the last record) when you press Tab. If you wish to Tab from the last field to the first (instead of to the next record), change the form's Cycle property from All Records to Current Record. This will keep the tab cycle within the current record and is probably the behavior most users would expect to experience.

# Modifying Subforms

Return now to look at the form/subform combination. While the main form is open in Design View, the subform is only available as a white rectangle. You can click it to highlight it, but the only properties that can be edited are those that relate to its functioning as a control in the main form. There's no way to alter the subform itself. Additionally, there's no way to get to the subform's controls and their properties.

The following task shows how to alter the internal characteristics of a subform.

## Task: Altering a subform

1. From the Database window, locate the form subPublicationEntry subform. This form serves as the subform for the Author's Publication Entry form. Open it in Design View. Your screen should look like Figure 14.14.

**FIGURE 14.14.**

*The subform opened in Design View.*

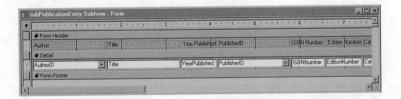

This wizard-generated form probably appears just about as you thought it would. Open the Properties window. Click the Format tab and look at the Default View property. This property sets how the form appears when its host or main form is in Form View. Access assigned the default view of this form to Datasheet, which is a logical choice because the records bound to this form are on the many side of the one-to-many relationship.

2. Staying on the Format tab, change the Navigation Buttons property to No and the Border Style property to Thin.

3. Click in the form detail section on the AuthorID field to give this control the highlight. This field doesn't need to be displayed, so press the Delete key to eliminate it from the subform. Click its label in the form header section and delete that.

4. You could adjust the remaining fields to take over the vacant spot left by deleting the AuthorID field, but since this form will almost always be viewed in Datasheet mode, there's really no point (Access will correctly format the datasheet's columns despite this gaping hole you've left on the form's Design View.

5. Close this form, saving changes.

Your form now has a cleaner look after the elimination of the unnecessary controls. From the Database window, open the Author's Publication Entry form. Your screen should resemble Figure 14.15.

**Tip**

You can also edit a subform by opening a form/subform in Design View and double-clicking the subform. This saves you from having to locate the subform in the Database window.

14

**FIGURE 14.15.**

*The main form reflects the changes made in the subform.*

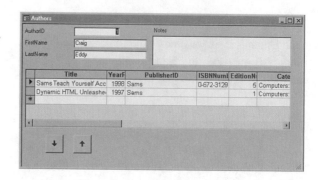

 **Caution**

If you size a subform to fit exactly inside its container within a main form, you might hit a problem when the data within the subform exceeds the vertical space you allotted for the subform. Access will automatically add a scrollbar to the side of the subform when this occurs. The scrollbar will take up real estate you need to display the data.

To eliminate this problem, you can either set the Scroll Bars property for the subform to None or Horizontal, or you can allow sufficient room for the scrollbars when you design the subform container.

# Graphic Elements in Forms

Access provides two graphic elements you can use to spruce up your forms: lines and rectangles. By changing the properties of these elements, you can radically alter your form's looks. Use these elements to isolate form controls into logical groupings, to enhance the aesthetic appeal of your forms, and to break your forms into sections.

The following exercise takes the rather barren-looking Author's Publication Entry form and gives it some fancy elements. It's up to you how ornate to make your forms. Remember, because you can embed any graphic in your form, you have no effective limit as to how elaborate you can be. The problem with forms containing too much fru-fru is that they might appear frivolous. Also, keep in mind your target audience. What's overly baroque for financial analysts might be overly stark for children.

The following task shows some uses for graphic elements in forms and illustrates how these elements' properties affect their appearance.

## Task: Graphic elements in forms

1. Open the `Author's Publication Entry` form in Design View, or if it's already open, switch to Design View. Locate the Rectangle tool in the Toolbox.

2. Depending on the exact layout of your form, you might need to move all the controls away from the form design grid's border to complete this action. Figure 14.16 shows the form with its controls moved to allow for easy rectangle making. After you've made some room, click the Rectangle tool, and then move your cursor to slightly above and to the left of the `AuthorID` field label and drag the rectangle to just below and to the right of the `Notes` field. Your screen should look like Figure 14.16. Keep an eye on the rulers to monitor the progress of your rectangle as you drag.

**FIGURE 14.16.**

*Adding a rectangle to a form.*

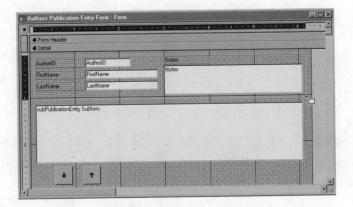

If the rectangle Access adds is a solid one obscuring the fields and labels, locate the Back Color button on the Formatting toolbar. Click the button to activate the pull-down menu, and then click the Transparent choice.

3. Click the Border Width button in the Formatting toolbar (it's the second one from the right) and change the width to 1. Click the Special Effect button (the right-most one) and choose Shadowed from the pull-down menu.

4. Click the Border Color button to activate the pull-down menu and change the color from black to deep blue.

   Because *Sams Teach Yourself Access 97 in 21 Days'* figures are grayscale, these figures only approximate the look of the form with its added color.

5. The command button section of this form is separate in function from either of the other two sections, so set it apart visually. Click the Line tool in the Toolbox. Move to the form's detail area and draw a horizontal line between the subform and the buttons, spanning the entire width of the form.

14

▼ 6. In the Formatting toolbar, click deep blue as this line's color and 3 as its border
width. Shrink the form if necessary to be appropriate to the number and location of
the controls. Your screen should resemble Figure 14.17.

**FIGURE 14.17.**

*Adding a line to a
form.*

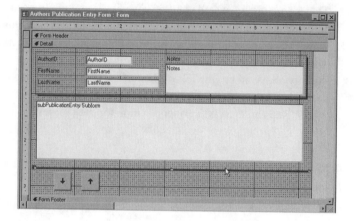

7. Switch to Form View. Your screen should look like Figure 14.18 if you have your
form in a window rather than maximized.

**FIGURE 14.18.**

*The finished form.*

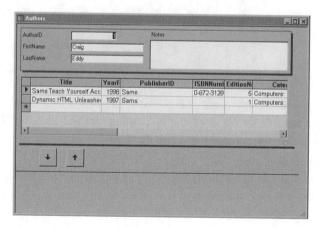

▲

While hardly a work of art, this form does reflect many design goals. It contains all the
information needed, with nothing extra. People using the form won't be confused by
excessive design elements, yet will clearly be able to determine the three separate form
areas. Close this form, saving changes.

All Windows 95 native applications such as Access 97 have inherently good-looking
designs. You have to make an effort to produce a lousy-looking form. You might think

that the final exercises today have taken a nice, clean, grayscale form and dolled it up to the point of being grotesque. Or you might think the design still is too conservative for your tastes.

The beauty of personal computers is that they are, well, personal. It's your copy of Access, it's your computer, and it should be your design decision (unless of course you work for a large Information Technology department that feels it's necessary to dictate both function and style).

# Page Layout Considerations

This form's only view is Single Form, so it doesn't make any difference where the command buttons appear. If this form could be displayed as a series of continuous forms, each detail section would have its own command buttons, which just take up room with no added function. Figure 14.19 is the form from Figure 14.18, with the subform deleted and the view changed to Continuous Forms. This figure shows the command button duplication that would occur in Continuous Forms View.

The safe way to handle controls you want to see only once on a form is to locate them in the form header or footer sections. Figure 14.20 is the form from Figure 14.19, with the command buttons located in the form footer.

**FIGURE 14.19.**

*Command buttons in the detail section don't work right in continuous forms.*

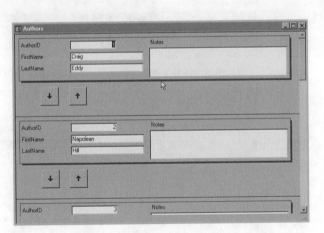

Locating the command buttons in the form's footer recovers lost room and makes for a better overall form than locating them in the detail section. If you'd like to examine the form shown in Figure 14.20, it's saved as Continuous Author's Publication Entry as part of today's sample data. The buttons aren't attached to any Event procedure in this form.

14

**FIGURE 14.20.**

*Moving the command buttons to the form's footer solves the problem.*

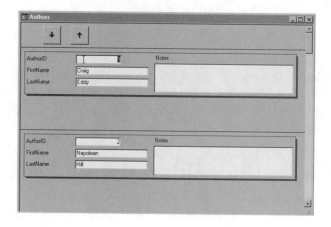

## Further Fancy Forms

This short section sprints through some form creation options. By this time you should have a good idea of how to use menus and toolbars, so the steps will come faster than in previous sections.

Take a look at Figure 14.21. This is an unbound form containing an unbound text box.

**FIGURE 14.21.**

*A form for experimentation with formatting options.*

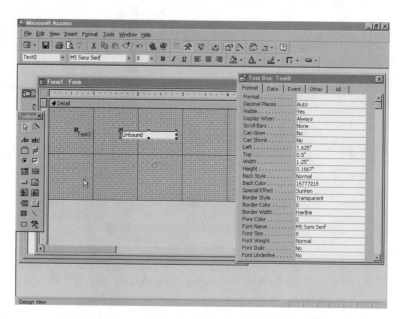

If you want to play along, create the unbound form by clicking the Forms tab at the Database window, and then clicking New. Choose Design View with no table or query showing in the combo box.

Add an unbound text control to the form, as in Figure 14.21. By using the Formatting toolbar's appropriate buttons, change the text box to a raised look with blue text and a light gray background. Now pull down the Format menu and choose Set Control Defaults. This sets the default control style to that of the selected control. Add another unbound text box and note that this one has the same formats as the first one.

Try adding a label control. Note the new default only applies to text boxes.

Now click either one of the text box controls and then the toolbar button with the paintbrush. Move back to the form design area and note your cursor changes to look like a paintbrush in a circle. Click the label control to "paint" it like the text boxes.

## Sinking and Rising

You can combine several sunken or raised looks to yield interesting results. Add three rectangles to the form, as shown in Figure 14.22.

**FIGURE 14.22.**

*Setting up for a deep sunken look.*

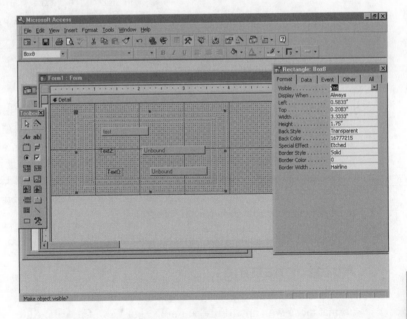

Now highlight all the rectangles either by a marquee selection or by the Shift+Click method. Pull down the Special Effect button and choose the Sunken look. Figure 14.23 shows the results of this in Form View.

14

**FIGURE 14.23.**

*Applying a special effect to layered form elements.*

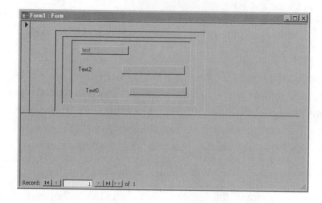

Figure 14.24 is the same form in Form View but with the rectangles given a raised look.

**FIGURE 14.24.**

*Applying a different special effect to con-centric form elements.*

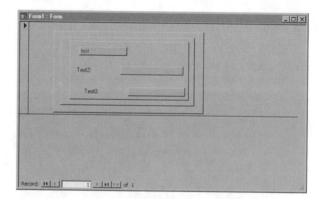

Add the date and time to the form by clicking in the detail section while in Design View. Use the Insert | Date and Time menu item. Access displays a dialog prompting you for the format of the date/time label to place on the form. Access plunks a text box into the form header section. Because the date and time are part of a text box, Access uses your newly created default style for this control.

You can save or discard your forms at this point. The book does come back to them.

## Autoformatting

One final thing before leaving the section on formatting fancy forms. Pull down the Format menu with any form open in Design View. Click the AutoFormat entry. This will enable you to add those fancy formats and backgrounds you saw in the wizard-generated forms to your own.

Some people think that fancy formatting distracts from the utility of a form. Others think formats such as these make a good form great. Just remember not to get carried away with frivolity and always keep your target market in mind when playing with these fancy options, and you won't go wrong.

# Summary

Access controls have many different properties. Each item in Access has its own set of control properties. For example, the form itself has an On Resize property that makes sense for it, but doesn't apply or appear for the command button control.

Event properties describe how controls respond to certain events, such as being clicked or double-clicked. One class of Event properties is the Event procedure. Event procedures are Visual Basic code that activates when the Event property it's attached to fires.

---

### VISUAL BASIC? I THOUGHT THIS WAS ACCESS

Both *Sams Teach Yourself Access 97 in 21 Days* and the Microsoft documentation make liberal mention of Visual Basic.

This is both a Microsoft product and one of the languages used by Access, the other one being Structured Query Language (SQL). The "real" name for the Basic language in Access is Visual Basic for Applications (VBA), and the independent product is Microsoft Visual Basic. Both seem to be called just Visual Basic, so this book follows that convention.

---

Control wizards can save you a lot of programming headaches and, equally important, won't make any typographic errors when writing Access Basic code. To save a lot of time and possible grief, use the wizard if one exists for your purposes.

By default, Access equips forms with a complete set of selectors, scrollbars, and navigation tools. In many cases you can delete one or all of these items. In doing so, you can simplify your forms, making more room for data display without decreasing your form's functionality (if you're careful).

You can add either an icon or a picture to objects. Just be careful not to get overly enthusiastic when doing so. A little bit of a bitmapping goes a long way.

The tab order is the order in which controls get focus as you tab around your form. Access assigns tab order in the same order in which controls are placed on a form. You can change the tab order to one of your choosing. Additionally, you can leave a control out of the tab order by setting its Tab Stop property to No.

**14**

Creative use of lines and rectangles can highlight or separate sections of forms. Remember, you can assign lines and rectangles to be in the foreground or background, according to your needs.

The final part of the chapter was a fast sprint through several options of roughly one scadzillion combinations you can apply to your forms to give them a custom look. Use these options sparingly and keeping your target audience in mind.

# Q&A

**Q**  Can I attach more than one `DoCmd` action to an event?

**A**  Yes. You can attach as many as you like.

**Q**  I have many forms with the same look, only differing in details. Is there some way I can define a generic form as a template for others?

**A**  Yes. You can do this two ways. The first is to just create the template form, and then use Copy/Paste in the Database window to create other identical copes of the form. You can then modify the copies to fit your needs. Alternatively, you can define your template form as the standard form by selecting Tools I Options from the menu. Once there, click the Forms/Reports tab, and then change the Form Template option from Normal to the name of your form.

**Q**  Is there a list of all the actions I can do with the `DoCmd` I found in the wizard-generated code for command buttons?

**A**  Access's Online Help has all these actions grouped both by name and by function. Search on `DoCmd`.

**Q**  Can I vector graphics files for form backgrounds?

**A**  You'll have to convert them to a bitmap before you do so. A shortcut to bitmap conversion is to copy them to the Windows  clipboard, and then pastes them either into your form or into a program such as Windows Paint.

**Q**  Can I use my own pictures on button faces?

**A**  Yes. You can use any program that can create a bitmap file that Access can understand. Create your artwork, save it, and then use the Browse button in the wizard to set the button's face with your creation. You can also set the button face by directly entering your filename in the `Picture` property of the button's layout properties.

# Workshop

Here's where you can test and apply the lessons you learned today.

## Quiz

1. Are the types of control properties the same no matter what type the control?

2. If you want to repeat a small picture throughout your form, which property must be set to Yes in the form's properties list box?

3. How would the code line Sub cmdNextRecord_Click() change if the event you wanted the sub for was named Clack?

4. Will the filter Like "Ka" let the name Kaplan through? What about Kramer? Will the filter Like "Ka*" let the name Kaplan through? What about Kramer?

## Exercises

1. Open the Author's Publication Entry form in Design View.

2. Make sure the Control Wizards button is enabled in the toolbox.

3. Place a command button on the form at the right side, under the subform section.

4. Use the wizard to set this button's On Click property to an event procedure that will, when clicked, close the form. Hint: Look under Form Operations in the wizard.

5. Give the button a stop sign icon and name it cmdExit. Position it just to the right of the existing command buttons. Switch to Form View. Your screen should resemble Figure 14.25.

**FIGURE 14.25.**

*The form with an Exit button added.*

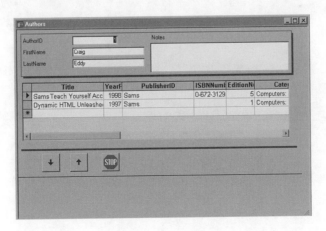

6. Save the form by selecting File | Save from the menu. Click the button to see if it works.

14

# WEEK 2

## In Review

This week you have learned how to build the look and feel of useful reports. You've gone behind the interface you'll present to your user and learned how to create complex queries that will enable you to present strong and useful reports to your user.

You have gained a lot of valuable experience working with the "front end" of what your user will see and what it takes to make that interface work effectively to manage data.

Next, you'll dig even deeper as you learn more about control—not just the kind you place on a form—the kind of control that programs reactions to events and steers your user through an Access application.

8

9

10

11

12

13

14

# WEEK 3

## 16

## At a Glance

This week is the week you've been working for! During week 3, you'll begin moving beyond the simple acts of inputting and outputting data to creating the "glue" to hold together a user-friendly and intuitive application. You'll do this by learning more about the behind-the-scenes work that creates the nuances and features your users will appreciate.

This week, you'll work toward building an application by practicing the following tasks:

- How to use expressions, dynamic controls, and advanced layout design in your reports.
- How to leverage simple and complex macros to automate routine tasks.
- How to use simple Visual Basic for Applications code, including reacting to events, functions, or general procedures, and error trapping.

- How to add ActiveX controls to your Access application.
- How to begin programming with Data Access Objects.
- How to maintain, secure, and replicate your database.
- How to use Office Links to integrate Access 97 with other applications in the Office 97 suite to create a useful end product.

- How to publish to the World Wide Web or your company's intranet.

DAY **15**

# Using Expressions and Creating Advanced Reports

Today you learn the following methods:

- How to create a complex query with an expression
- What joins are
- How to add a table to a query
- How to manually design a report
- How to group records in a report
- How to use expressions in reports
- How to enter calculation expressions in reports
- How Access evaluates expressions
- How to create better report layouts
- How to create dynamic report controls

# Expressions in Reports and Queries

The previous lesson, "Putting the Finishing Touches on Forms," showed you some advanced form design techniques. Today you learn some advanced query and reporting techniques. The first technique you learn about is using expressions in queries and reports.

As you'll recall, an expression is a combination of identifiers (which may be fields in a table or controls on a form, for example), constant values, and operators that combine to produce some result. You've seen expressions in previous chapters, and you'll continue working with them well beyond this one. Expressions are one of the most powerful features available to help you customize and fine-tune your Access application to meet your needs.

In today's lesson, you'll deal primarily with the `OrderDetails` table. You'll see how to relate this table back to the `Authors` and `Publishers` tables, as well as how to produce reports based on the table. In the following task, you'll create a query that uses the `OrderDetails` table as its basis. This query includes an expression or two to produce its output.

## Task: Expressions in queries

**◄ TASK**

1. Launch Access and open the `BookStore` database, if necessary. Click the Queries tab, and then click the New button to start a new query. Click the Design View selection and click OK to bypass the wizards. Add the `OrderDetails`, `Orders`, `Publications`, `Authors`, `Categories`, and `MediaTypeLookup` tables to the query, and then click Close. Your screen should look like Figure 15.1.

   Access knows there's a link between `Publications` and `Authors` because a one-to-many relationship has been established for these tables, with `Authors` on the one side. This relationship ensures that you can only enter records in `Publications` for those records that existed previously in `Authors`. So far, no relationship has been created that tells Access whether any link exists between `Publications` and `MediaTypeLookups`.

   The common, or link, fields are `MediaType` in `Publications` and `MediaType` in `MediaTypeLookup`. Access should be smart enough to know the two `MediaType` fields are related and show that by a link line. If it fails to do so, it's up to you to tell Access about this link so it can synchronize records from both tables in this query.

2. Sometimes Access misses. If you don't show a link line between the two `MediaType` fields, do step 3. If you already have that link, skip to step 5.

**▼**

**FIGURE 15.1.**

*The new query just starting.*

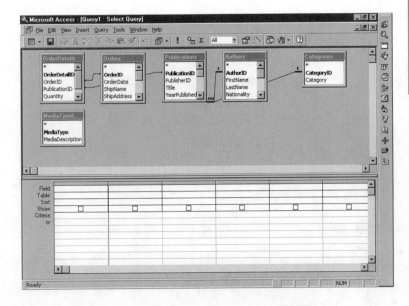

3. Click the MediaType field in Publications (you'll have to scroll the Publications field list to find it). Drag the field until it's over the MediaType field in the MediaTypeLookup table, and then release the mouse button. Your screen should resemble Figure 15.2.

**FIGURE 15.2.**

*Manually establishing a link.*

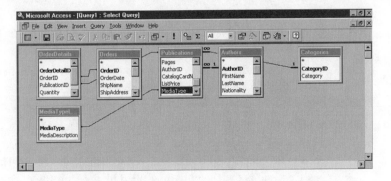

4. Double-click the line Access just added to the design view. The Join Properties dialog, shown in Figure 15.3, appears. Click 2: Include ALL Records from 'Publications' and Only Those Records from 'MediaTypeLookup' Where the Joined Fields Are Equal. This ensures that Access will include all of the Publications records, even if the value in their MediaType field doesn't match a value in the MediaType field in the MediaTypeLookup table. Click the OK button.

**FIGURE 15.3.**

*The Join Properties dialog.*

**Tip**

Linking tables within a query links those tables only for the query. If you want to link tables globally, you must use the Tools|Relationships window.

5. Drag the `Title`, `EditionNumber`, and `ISBNNumber` fields from `Publications` to the query design grid.

6. Next, drag the `OrderDate` and `ShipPostalCode` fields from the `Orders` table to the next columns in the query design grid. These fields are good candidates for grouping and sorting.

7. Add the `PublicationID`, `Quantity`, and `UnitPrice` fields from the `OrderDetails` table and the `MediaDescription` and `Category` fields from the `MediaTypeLookup` tables, respectively.

8. Finally, scroll to the first empty column and type `Author: [LastName] + ', ' + [FirstName]` on the `Field` line (that's the first row) of the column. You don't need to specify a table in the second row because there is only one table with the `FirstName` and `LastName` fields, but it's a good idea to do so anyway.

9. Scroll back to the `Title` field, click in the sort row for this field, and choose Ascending for a sort order. Run your query now to make sure it's working properly. Figure 15.4, which shows this query running, has been scrolled to show the query's last columns.

   There's one more thing to do. This query shows the unit price and quantity for each order detail, but not the total value of the order detail. That value is called the Net Cost and is the Quantity multiplied by the Unit Price. You need to add an expression to calculate this value.

10. Return to Design View and scroll until you see an empty column to the right of the `Author` expression field (yes, that's an expression as well). Click in the first row and press Shift+F2 to open the Zoom window. Enter `Net Cost: [UnitPrice]*[Quantity]` in the Zoom window's text box. This tells Access to create a column called `Net Cost` and insert the value of the `UnitPrice` field multiplied the `Quantity` field into that column.

**Figure 15.4.**

*The raw query in operation.*

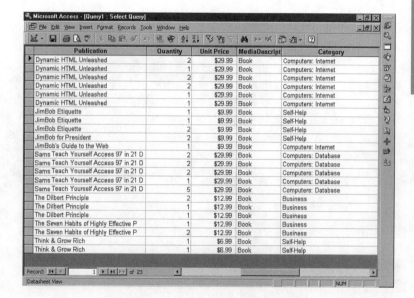

11. Click OK to close Zoom. Run the query again to make sure all's right with it. Check the right-most field, Net Cost, to make sure it's calculating correctly. If it's not, check to make sure you entered the expression correctly. Close and save this query as SalesReport.

After finishing this task, you have a query on which sales reports can be based. This is the first step needed for the finished report. The next task picks up where this one left off. Designing the actual report would be easier with a wizard to do some of the work, but the following task doesn't use one so that you can learn some important details about report design. This exercise manually creates a grouped report with several expressions and a secondary sort order.

## Task: Grouping and sorting in reports

1. On the Database window, click the Reports tab to move to the Reports section of your database, and then click the New button to start a new report. Choose SalesReport as the query to bind to this report.

2. Click the Design View option, and then click OK. If necessary, click the Field List button in the Report Design toolbar (the standard one for this view). Access moves you into the report design grid. Increase the height of the page header area to about 1.5 inches to give yourself some working room. Click and drag the Title field from the Field list box to the page header area. Widen the field somewhat so that your screen looks like Figure 15.5.

**Figure 15.5.**

*Starting to place fields in a report.*

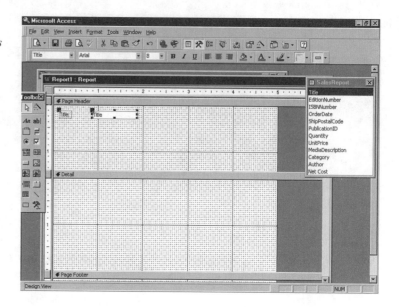

This report will have the title, author's name, and other information about the publication in the page header area. Details about individual sales of the publication will be in the details area. And, when finished at the end of this lesson, summary information will be in the group footer area.

**Note**

Remember Access can appear many different ways in any view. Your screen might look quite different from the book's, as shown in Figure 15.5. For example, you might not have the Toolbox toolbar in view, or it might be docked at the left side of the screen instead of floating. You might not have the grid checked in the View menu. If you don't, you won't see the dots shown in this exercise. Even if you do, your dots might be finer or coarser than the book's.

If you want to come as close to the book as possible, arrange the screen as shown in Figure 15.5, open up the Properties window. Locate the Grid X and Grid Y properties on the Format tab and change each to 12. Then pull down the View menu and select Grid if it doesn't have a check mark next to it.

3. Create an expression for the author's name by inserting an unbound text box right below the `Title` field. Delete the label for this field and enter the following expression:

```
=Trim([Author])
```

This expression is shown in Figure 15.6 as the Control Source property for this unbound field. If you prefer, you can add this line directly into the unbound text field itself, which automatically assigns it to the Control Source property.

**FIGURE 15.6.**

*Inserting an expression in a text box.*

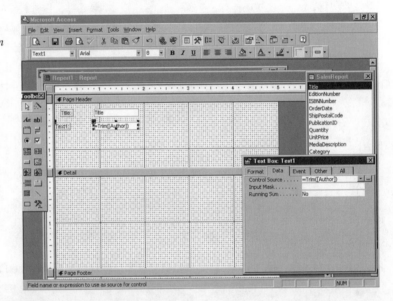

4. Next, add the EditionNumber, ISBNNumber, Category, and MediaDescription fields, stacked on top of each other down the right hand side of the report. Your screen should resemble Figure 15.7 (rearrange and resize the controls if necessary).

**Tip**

Report designing is a skill acquired over time. Rather than finish your report only to find that something at the start has gone awry, switch back and forth between Design and Layout or Print Preview Views to see your progress and to catch any misdirection early.

5. These next two steps are a little tricky. You want the order details information for each ordered publication in the detail section of the form, but the labels for the information should appear in the page header. This prevents repeating these labels for each order. Drag the fields OrderDate, ShipPostalCode, UnitPrice, Quantity, and Net Cost onto the Detail section of the form. Using either a marquee or Shift+mouse click, highlight only the labels for these fields. (See Figure 15.8.)

**FIGURE 15.7.**

*Finishing up the page header section.*

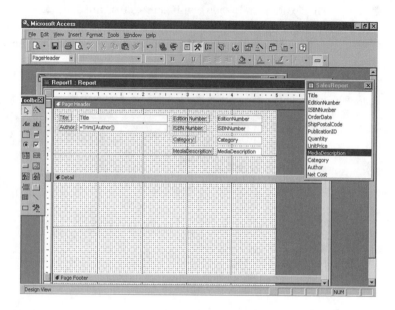

6. Press Ctrl+X to cut these fields to the Clipboard. Click in the Page Header section of the report design grid, and then press Ctrl+V to paste the label fields into this section of the report. Arrange all the fields so they resemble Figure 15.9.

**FIGURE 15.8.**

*Moving the field labels to the page header starts by highlighting them.*

**FIGURE 15.9.**

*Placing proper elements in the header and detail sections.*

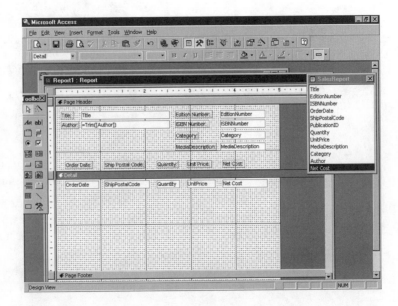

7. You need to tell Access to group the details of the report according to
   `PublicationID`. You could also have used `ISBNNumber`, but since there's no real
   guarantee an ISBN will be entered for a publication, you'll stick to the field you
   know will have valid, unique data. Click the Sorting and Grouping button in the
   toolbar. Next, click in the first column in the grid on the window that pops up.
   Either enter or scroll to `PublicationID` as a field to group on. Access will, by
   default, set `Sort Order` column to `Ascending`. Make sure the `Group On` and `Keep`
   `Together` properties are set to `Each Value` and `Whole Group` respectively, as
   shown in Figure 15.10. The `Keep Together` setting tells Access to keep the group
   on a single page, if at all possible. Click the Sorting and Grouping button in the
   toolbar again to close the list box.

**FIGURE 15.10.**

*Creating a sorted grouping for the report.*

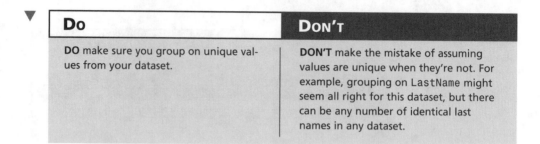

| Do | Don't |
|----|-------|
| **DO** make sure you group on unique values from your dataset. | **DON'T** make the mistake of assuming values are unique when they're not. For example, grouping on LastName might seem all right for this dataset, but there can be any number of identical last names in any dataset. |

At this point, it's a good idea to check the progress of your report. Shrink the Details section of your report to be just large enough to accommodate one line of fields. Click the Print Preview button to see how the report's coming along. Your screen should look like Figure 15.11.

Well, that's not exactly what you had planned. This report seems to attach all the orders to one publication, *Sams Teach Yourself Access in 21 Days*. Actually, this report does have the orders grouped by title, but it lacks the breaks needed to make that obvious.

**FIGURE 15.11.**

*The report still needs some work.*

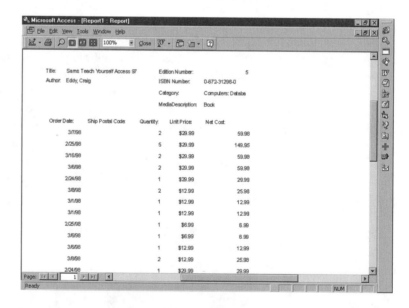

8. Return to Design View. If you have the Sorting and Grouping list box closed, open it by clicking the Sorting and Grouping button in the toolbar. Add a group header and footer section for PublicationID by selecting that row and changing the

▼ Group Header and Group Footer properties for it to Yes. Then add Orderdate on the second row of the list box. This makes OrderDate the sort order field in the Details section (see Figure 15.12).

**FIGURE 15.12.**

*Creating a secondary sort order and adding group headers and footers.*

Try switching to Print Preview View again. Your screen should resemble Figure 15.13.

**FIGURE 15.13.**

*The groups are now visible.*

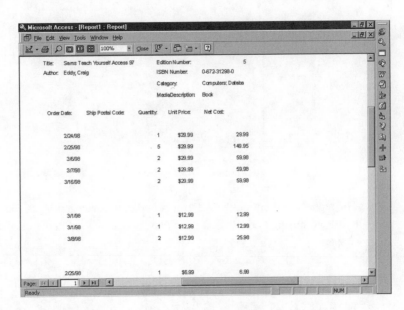

The only thing needed to finish this report's basic structure is to break the report's page on each group and add the right header to the groups.

9. Return to Design View. Click in the PublicationID Header section to make it current. Open the Properties window and locate the Force New Page property under Format Properties. Change this property from None to Before Section.

▼

▼ 10. Click the Print Preview button in the toolbar and scroll through several pages. Access finally has it right, thanks to your efforts. The orders for each publication are grouped with the publication's information, the orders are sorted according to order date, and each publication's information is contained on a single page. Figure 15.14 shows a portion of the results of placing a group on each page. As you scroll through the report at this time you'll see one publication on each page.

11. Close this report, saving it with the name SalesReport.

**FIGURE 15.14.**

*The first record of the grouped report.*

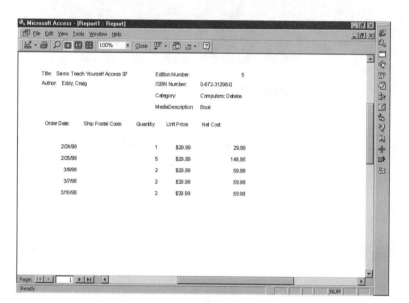

▲

The report's still not quite ready for prime time because it lacks some calculations and is a little confusing to read. These problems are addressed in the third task later in the chapter.

# Calculations in Reports

The SalesReport report does several things needed for the fictional bookstore.

• Groups the orders with the right publication

• Puts publication information and orders on separate pages

• Reports the orders by showing quantity, unit cost, and net cost for each order for each publication

This is fine, but the bookstore needs some summary information from this report as well. You can do this by placing an unbound text field where you want these figures to print (or appear), and then entering an expression to calculate these values.

> **Note**
>
> Many calculations can be performed at either the query or report level. In some cases, it's a toss-up as to where you choose to place your expressions. Keep in mind that you can query queries, so you can create several in-query expressions or totals-type queries (that yield sums, counts, and other math or statistical functions from query contents), and then create a "master" query that queries the queries and base your report on that.
>
> Generally speaking, the shorter the chain of queries behind your reports, the faster the reports will run. If performance is your goal, try to use as many expressions in your reports as you can instead of having multiple queries. However, if you want your calculations to be viewed from the Datasheet View of queries themselves, you'll have to include the expressions there.

The following task demonstrates how to create calculations in reports. The technique shown is identical to the technique used for forms. All the material in this exercise applies to forms also.

## Task: Calculation expressions in reports

1. Launch Access and open the BookStore database, if necessary. Open the `SalesReport` report in Design View. Your screen should look like Figure 15.15.

**FIGURE 15.15.**

*The SalesReport report in Design View.*

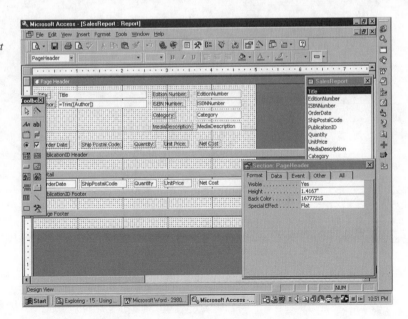

▼    The first thing to do with this report is calculate the total number of each publica-
     tion ordered, which is simply the sum of the Quantity field from the SalesReport
     query. This and other calculations will appear in the group footer band because
     you want the total to be for each publication. Remember, this report groups on
     PublicationID. If you need a refresher, click the Sorting and Grouping button in
     the toolbar and note that the group icon is to the immediate left of the
     PublicationID field in the list box.

2.   If you don't have a band called PublicationID Footer in your report from the earlier
     exercise, you'll need to reveal one now. If you have such a band, open it slightly to
     give you some working room and skip to step 3. Open the Sorting and Grouping
     list box and click in the PublicationID field. Locate the Group Footer property
     and change it to Yes to open up a narrow group footer band in your report. Now
     that you have the band opened, widen it to give yourself some working room.

3.   Add an unbound text box control to the PublicationID group footer band. Edit the
     label for this unbound text control to read Units Ordered. (See Figure 15.16.)

     Access can do calculations using any field in the bound query or table, not just

**FIGURE 15.16.**

*Adding the unbound
control to the group
footer.*

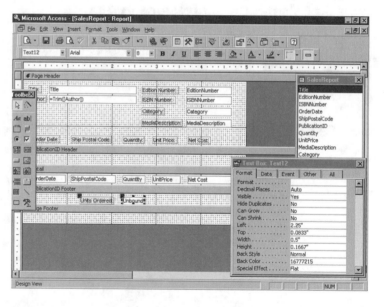

those showing in the report. In this way, reports are similar to queries because
queries can filter, sort, or use criteria based on fields not included or showing in the
query. The following step uses the Access built-in function Sum() to calculate the
total number of books that have been ordered. Access knows you want the sum of
units for a group based on PublicationID, and not the entire table of publications,

▼    because the Sum() expression is in the PublicationID group footer band, rather than

▼          the report footer band.

4. If necessary, move the text box so it's just below the Quantity field in the Details

**Tip**

If, for example, you wanted to calculate the sum of all orders for all publications in this report, you would locate the Sum() statement in the Report Footer band. If you wanted to calculate the sum of anything on a page, you would locate the Sum() function in the Page Footer band. You can include multiple Sum() (or other) functions in a report, so you can calculate the sum for each publication and also for the entire collection of publications.

section. Open the Properties window, click the Data properties tab and edit the Control Source property for the unbound text box to read =Sum([Quantity]). Remember, you can also add this expression directly into the control, or you can use the Zoom view (Shift+F2) to do the entry. Whichever method you choose, the expression appears in the control on the form and in the properties box.

5. Click the Other tab and edit the Name property for this unbound control to read txtTotalUnits. Switch to Print Preview View; your screen should resemble Figure 15.17. The Name property is how you can refer to controls from other expressions. You'll see the need for this soon.

The exact calculations of your report and query might differ from the book's examples if you've added or removed records during your learning process. What's important isn't that your data matches the book's, but that your data is internally consistent.

**Tip**

Remember, you can press the F11 key to bring up the database window and from there click the Queries tab and run the SalesReport query. You don't need to shut down the SalesReport report to run the query to check your results.

**Caution**

Access is a computer program. As such, it's incapable of making math errors, but you can enter the wrong expression, which Access will correctly calculate to yield the wrong answer. Always check Access's output against known data before committing critical applications to the computer. This applies to any computer program, not just to Access.

▼

**FIGURE 15.17.**

*The report now calcu-
lates totals.*

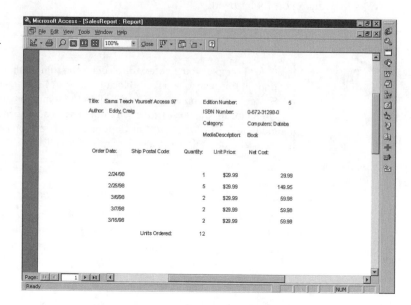

The next step is to calculate the total number of dollars taken in for each book.

6. Switch back to Design View and enter a new unbound text box to the right of
   the txtTotalUnits one. Edit its Name property (from the Other tab) to read
   txtTotalRevenue and its label to read Total Revenue:. Enter =Sum([Net Cost])
   as the Control Source property for this control.

   Again switch back to Print Preview mode to check whether the report's doing the
   calculations correctly. You should now see a dollar figure total at the bottom of the
   right column.

7. Return to Design View. Click the Format tab in the list box, making sure the text
   box, txtTotalRevenue, has the highlight. The first property is called Format (to help
   in the confusion). Pull down the combo box for the Format property on the Format
   tab. Locate the Currency entry and click it. This will format the contents of the text
   box to display as a monetary figure. While you're at it, select the Net Cost control
   in the Details section and set its Format to Currency as well.

8. Return to Print Preview mode to see the effect of altering the Format property. You
   should now see that all the figures in the right column have the dollar sign to indicate currency amounts.

9. The form is complete (for now). Save the changes you've made, but keep the report
   open if you're continuing on in the chapter.

**Caution** | Avoid using circular expressions, which happen when you have the input of expression B set to the output of expression A, and the input of expression A set to the output of expression B. Setting up such references results in infinite regression—something worth avoiding because Access can't resolve the loop.

15

# A Few Handy Expressions

Access is loaded with built-in functions (such as Sum()) and expressions. Table 15.1 shows some of the more handy ones:

**TABLE 15.1.** ACCESS BUILT-IN EXPRESSIONS.

| Function | What It Does |
| --- | --- |
| IsNull() | Tests to see whether a field is blank. null is not the same as a zero value. Access will treat an expression as null if it finds any null values as part of that expression. |
| IIF() | Immediate If. Tests a value and evaluates to one of two possible returns, depending on what if finds. A very simple If...Then...Else construct you can use in an expression. |
| DateDiff() | Determines the interval between two dates or times. |
| Left() | Returns the left part of a string. How much is returned depends on the entered parameter. For example, Left([MyField],2) returns the two left-most characters in the MyField field. Similar functions are Right() and Mid(). |
| Count() | Returns the count (number of entries) in a set. |
| Avg() | Returns the average of a set of numbers. |
| Now() | Returns the date and time of the system. |
| DateAdd() | Returns a future date. |
| NZ() | Converts any nulls it finds to the value 0. |

# How Access Evaluates Arithmetic Expressions

Access uses the standard algebraic hierarchy to evaluate expressions. Take the following expression:

6 + 3 * 4 = ?

If you add 6 to 3 and then multiply by 4, the answer is 36. If you multiply 3 by 4 and then add the 6, the answer is 18. Which is right? Well, there's no right answer unless you tell Access what you want. In this case, Access does the multiplication first and then the addition because it adheres to the standard algebraic hierarchy, which says do calculations in the following order:

1. Exponential
2. Multiplication
3. Division
4. Addition
5. Subtraction

These words form the acronym EMDAS. The mnemonic for remembering this is "Eeks—My Dear Aunt Sally!" If you want Access to evaluate expressions out of the standard hierarchy, enclose your expressions in parentheses, such as in the following example contrast:

```
(6 + 3) * 4 = 36
with6 + 3 * 4 = 18
```

Expressions within parentheses are always evaluated first and separately. The expression `=(Sum([Weighted Value]))/(Sum([Units])` uses parentheses to make sure each sum is evaluated first; only then does Access perform the division. This is, strictly speaking, unnecessary here because these particular expressions aren't sensitive to order. The placing of the parentheses is just a good habit, like enclosing all control names in square brackets.

| Do | Don't |
|---|---|
| **DO** create expressions in queries for values needed in the queries. | **DON'T** create expressions in queries for values needed only in the bound forms or reports. The SalesReport report violates this rule by including the Net Cost expression in a query. The reason for the violation was to demonstrate technique, not to show the right way to create a report. |

# Layouts for Reports

**15**

At the end of the previous task, the SalesReport report is functionally all right, but not very attractive. The method for adding layout elements to a report is identical to that for forms. Reports can have more bands, which add slightly to possible complexity, but it's hardly overwhelming.

The next task adds some graphics to the SalesReport report.

### Task: Graphic elements in reports

▼ TASK

1.  Starting where you left off, return to Design View. Rearrange your report controls to resemble Figure 15.18. If you followed the previous task literally, you shouldn't need to do much rearranging.

**FIGURE 15.18.**

*Getting ready to add graphics to a report.*

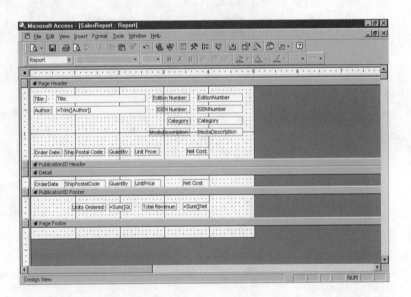

2.  Add a rectangle around the controls in the PublicationID group footer area. Send it to the back by using the Format|Send to Back menu item. (Refer to Figure 15.19, which shows this step and the next.)

3.  Add a line under the column titles in the Page Header area. Open the Formatting toolbar and increase the line width to 2. (See Figure 15.19.)

▼

**FIGURE 15.19.**

*Adding a box and lines to column heads in a report.*

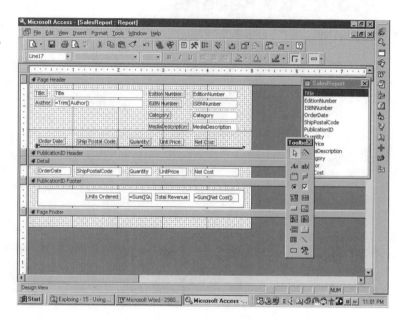

4. Change the alignment for the OrderDate text boxes to Left by selecting the control in the Details section and clicking the Align Left button in the Formatting toolbar.

5. Switch to Print Preview. Your screen should look like Figure 15.20.

**FIGURE 15.20.**

*The report with graphic elements.*

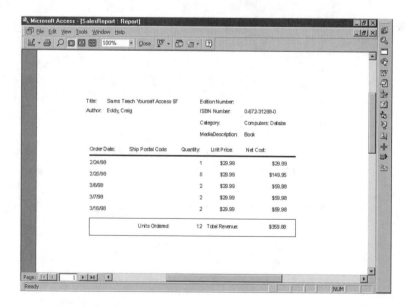

15

This report is a bit easier to read now. It's still not anyone's idea of a work of art, but its sections are at least set off from each other.

# Dynamic Controls on Reports

The Publications table has a field named MediaType, which describes the media on which the publication is published. This is currently displayed as a text box on the SalesReport report. However, you can make it stand out more by replacing the text box with an option group.

The following task places an option group on the report that evaluates the MediaType column and highlights the appropriate button. This is the same table you've used before. Remember its contents are the following:

1   Book

2   for Audio Book

3   for CD-ROM

4   for Online/Download

### Task: A dynamic control

1. Picking up where you just left off, return to Design View. Delete the MediaDescription text box and its associated label.

2. Place an unbound option button control in the Page Header section just below the Author text box. Edit the label for the new option button to read Book. Repeat this three times, arranging the option buttons in a 2×2 matrix, as shown in Figure 15.21. This figure also shows the controls in place and the expressions that control their behavior (which you'll set in the next step). Change the Caption properties to match Figure 15.21 as well. (The BackStyle property for these labels was changed to Normal to get this appearance in Design View.)

3. Click the control portion (rather than the label) of the Book option button. Locate the Control Source property and enter the expression =[MediaType]=1. Repeat this for the other three option buttons, modifying the expression to match the MediaType values from the MediaTypeLookup table. (See Figure 15.21.)

   This expression tells Access to examine the MediaType field, and if the value of that field matches one of the option buttons' programmed values, to change the value of the option button to True. Otherwise, the option button's value is False.

**FIGURE 15.21.**

*Adding the option
group to the report.*

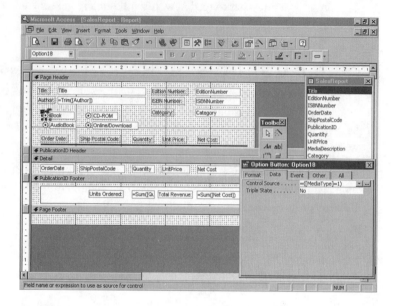

4. Switch to Print Preview. Oops—you're prompted for a value for MediaType. Why? Because, if you remember from your first task in this chapter, you didn't include the MediaType field in the query. Instead, you used the MediaDescription field from MediaTypeLookup.

5. Click Cancel on this dialog to return to Design View (you can leave the report open). Return to the Database window and open the SalesReport query in Design View. Drag the MediaType column from the Publications table onto the design grid. Close the query, saving your changes.

6. Now return to the report and click the Print Preview button. The screen should resemble Figure 15.22. Scroll to through the records, observing the option button for any changes.

Close this report, saving the changes. The report at this stage is included in the sample data as ReportCards1.

**FIGURE 15.22.**

*The report running with the dynamic controls.*

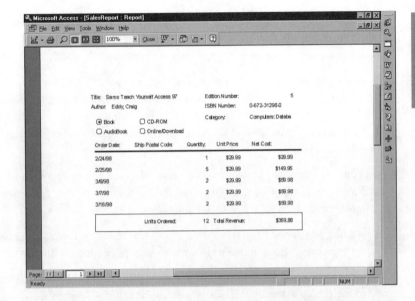

15

> **Note**
>
> Using an option button to visibly show the media type isn't a great idea because you'll have to change the report every time you add or change a media type. Still, this is only an example and does work very well.

## Summary

Access has no trouble creating a query from many tables. The report card query needed four to work correctly and also needed an Expression field. You create Expression fields in a query by adding Field Name:[Expression] to an otherwise empty column in the query design grid. Field Name is the name you want to appear at the top of the column and the expression is any valid Access expression. Be sure to end your field name with a colon (:), as this tells Access the string to the left of the colon is the column label.

The first field placed in the Grouping and Sorting box while in the report's Design View is the field Access will group on. Subsequent fields placed in this box are fields to sort on within a group. Access's grouping isn't particularly obvious unless you break the groups with a group header, group footer, or both. If you want your groups one to a page, you have to set the group's Force Page Break property to anything other than None, the default.

Access, by default, gives you an inner join, but you can also choose an outer join, either right- or left-handed. An inner join returns only matching records; outer joins add to the flexibility of Access's queries as they will return both matched and unmatched rows.

Adding expressions to reports is as simple as entering them in unbound text boxes. It's vital to check with known data to determine that these expressions are working as you think they should. Access can neither make a mathematical mistake nor read your mind to determine what you mean. An expression in Access is only as accurate as the person who designed it.

You can format the appearance of a text box's data by altering the Format property in the Properties list box. Access gives you almost unlimited ways to format fields. You can make your fields look just about any way you choose.

Adding boxes and lines to a report works exactly as it does in forms. Because most printers are grayscale, using color in a report generally makes little sense.

You create a simple dynamic control in a report or form by entering an unbound control to the report—usually a check box or option button—and then entering an evaluating expression as that control's Control Source.

# Q&A

**Q How can I set the page size for my reports?**

A Use the Print Setup dialog in the File menu to change the defaults. Remember, Access's wizards use these defaults when making a report. If your wizard made reports that seem to be aimed at bizarre paper sizes, the fault's in the Print Setup settings under the File menu selection.

**Q Can I calculate on a calculated field in a query?**

A Yes. The calculated values in query are just as accessible to your reports and forms as any other value. Therefore, what you can do with a table field output from the query, you can also do with a calculated field output from the query.

**Q Could I have put the labels from the Page Header of the SalesReport into the PublicationID group header band?**

A Yes, and your results would have been effectively identical. This method is actually better, but because of the exercise's flow, the headers for the detail band were placed in the Page Header band.

**Q Could I have created a report with a subreport as I did in forms?**

A Yes, and the method is almost identical. Access gives you many ways to get to the same place. For example, the calculation done in the SalesReport query could have been done in the report itself.

# Workshop

Here's where you can test and apply the lessons you learned today.

## Quiz

1. What's the significance of the colon in the query column label Net Cost:?

2. How often will a label in the Report Header band print in a report?

3. Refer to the SalesReport query. If the expression Author:[FirstName]&" "&[LastName] were entered in a column's Field row, would it be valid?

4. Does the PublicationID field need to appear on a report for the report to group on it?

5. Name two ways to change the width of a line or box in reports or forms.

6. Refer to Figure 15.12. What icon does Access use to distinguish the grouping field from a sort within the group field?

## Exercises

Modify the SalesReport report to display an overall total number of units and total revenue. There are several ways to accomplish this feat, some faster than others. If you want a real challenge, also display the average dollars per-publication sold.

As another exercise, add your company's logo to this report. If you need a hint, recall that working on a report's design is very similar to working on a form's design. Still need more help? Refer to Day 11, "Working with Form Controls," where the process of adding a picture to a form is described.

# DAY 16

# Working with Macros

Today you'll learn the following:

- What a macro is
- What three programming languages Access supports
- More about Structured Query Language (SQL)
- How to use the macro design grid
- How to make a switchboard form
- About conditional branching
- How to program branching or conditional macros
- Practical uses for conditional macros
- How to create a macro that changes control values

# Macros

NEW TERM    A *macro*, as far as Access is concerned, is a simple programming language that enables you to automate certain tasks. Fundamentally, a macro is a series of actions executed either linearly in response to an event or upon certain conditions being met after an event. Like so many computer topics, macros are easier to understand after you've seen one or two in action than from abstract text.

You can use macros for many tasks; here are some of the more common uses:

- Programming buttons to do a series of actions, such as opening or closing forms
- Setting or removing filters or sort orders in forms and reports
- Changing the properties or values of controls during runtime
- Helping ensure accurate data entry by watching the data entered and advising data entry people of any errors they're making
- Automating tasks that you do often

# Access's Three Programming Languages

NEW TERM    Access supports three programming languages: Visual Basic, macros, and *Structured Query Language*. Structured Query Language, used mostly in queries, is often abbreviated to SQL—pronounced "sequel." If you care to split hairs, you can add a fourth language, expressions, to the list, but few people do.

Keep in mind that every query you construct "by example" by using the query design grid is "backed up" by SQL. Take a look at Figure 16.1, the Bibliography query's SQL code.

NEW TERM    To see the SQL code that makes up a query, enter Design View for a query, pull down the left-most menu button on the toolbar, and click on the SQL View item. If you chose to, you could construct an Access query by using native SQL rather than the query design grid, which uses a technique called *QBE (Query By Example)*. Few people use native SQL exclusively in Access queries because QBE is much easier. However, there may come a day when you find it's quicker to construct simple queries "manually" in the SQL View than by using the user interface provided by the Design View.

Take a look at the simple query shown in Design View in Figure 16.2. This query contains the fields AuthorID, FirstName, LastName from the Authors table and returns only the first name and last name because the Show row's checkbox for AuthorID is unchecked. Figure 16.3 shows the query running, and Figure 16.4 illustrates the SQL that makes up this query.

**FIGURE 16.1.**

*The SQL code from a moderately complex query.*

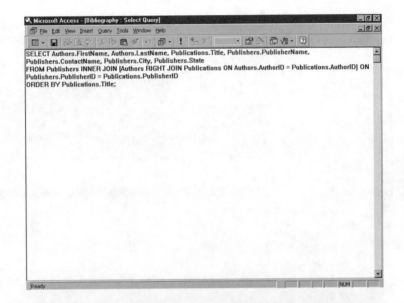

**FIGURE 16.2.**

*A simple query to demonstrate SQL.*

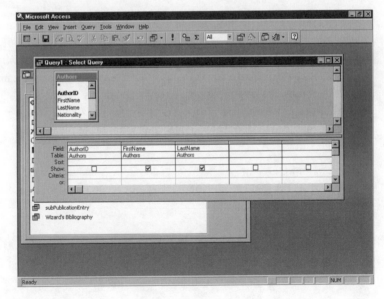

16

**Figure 16.3.**

*The simple query in action.*

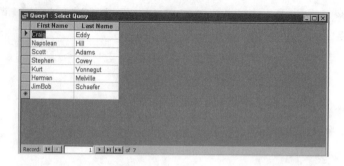

**Figure 16.4.**

*The SQL code behind the simple query.*

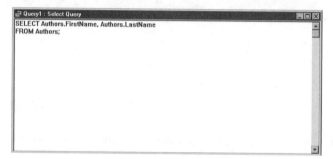

**ANALYSIS** The SQL code should seem fairly obvious—it's English with some operators or keywords to provide the action. The SELECT statement means, well, "select" or "choose from," so this query states to choose (or display) the FirstName field within the Authors table from the set that includes the Authors table. Yes, it's slightly redundant, but the duplication of Authors is necessary for clarity when more than one table comes into play in a query.

Criteria in SQL comes from the WHERE clause. Look at Figure 16.5, the query design grid with a criterion added. Now look at Figure 16.6, the same query's SQL, and note the change from Figure 16.4.

**Figure 16.5.**

*Adding a criterion to Access's QBE.*

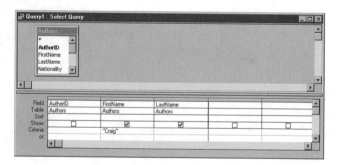

**FIGURE 16.6.**

*The effect of adding a criterion as seen in SQL.*

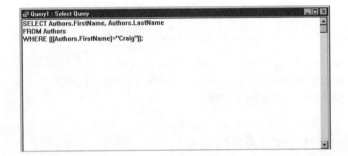

16

Access has added the line WHERE ((Not (Authors.FirstName)="Craig")); to the query in SQL. By this point in the book you know that if you run this query you'll see all of the authors except those whose first name is Craig.

SQL is a topic that's simple in details yet huge in scope. It has very few operatives, or keywords, but by combining these few operatives you can query SQL-compliant databases in almost any way imaginable.

# Using SQL

There's little reason for most people to write SQL in Access queries. A hand-entered SQL query isn't superior to a QBE one done by using the query design grid. The SQL capability of Access isn't even known to most users. Some database systems require SQL to query them, and Access acts as a good front-end for those systems. It's also a great training ground for those who want to learn SQL.

One area where some people use SQL natively is in constructing code in Visual Basic to be used for querying Access databases. We'll touch some on this topic in Day 18, "Advanced Programming with Data Access Objects and ActiveX Controls." This topic is also well-covered in other texts. If you're planning on using Access as a professional developer, it's a topic with which you need at least basic familiarity.

Also keep in mind that you use SQL in places other than the query design process. Forms and reports can use SQL as their control source properties to control displayed data. If you use the database wizards to create frameworks for your own applications, you'll find that Microsoft uses SQL for control sources on forms extensively. You'll see this technique also used in the sample files, such as Northwind, that Microsoft supplies with Access. Studying these control sources is a good way to learn practical SQL.

If you want to see SQL in action, construct the simple query from Figure 16.6, and then edit it in SQL view to read

```
SELECT Authors.*
FROM Authors
WHERE ((Not (Authors.FirstName)="Craig"));
```

What do you suppose the change from ...Authors.FirstName to ...Authors.* will bring? That's right: instead of returning only the FirstName field, the query will now return *all* fields from the Authors table.

# Looking at Macros

The earlier part of this chapter gives you a brief introduction to SQL. Day 14, "Putting the Finishing Touches on Forms," introduces you to Visual Basic with an exercise that programs a command button to respond to an event. Now it's time for the third Access language, macros—what they look like and how they work.

You construct macros in a macro design grid, just like many other Access objects. Also, like many other parts of Access, making macros consists mainly of selecting from lists and choosing options. Take a look at macros yourself by following along with the first task, which shows the macro design grid and constructs a simple macro.

Macro actions are the heart of the macro. In some cases, macro actions take no arguments or parameters; in others, macro actions require rather elaborate and specific parameters or arguments. To start, make a simple macro that just causes your computer to beep.

## Task: The macro design grid

▼ TASK

1. From the database window, click the Macros tab, and then click the New button to start a new macro. On the blank screen click the down arrow for the combo box in the Action column (see Figure 16.7).

   Now you'll create the macro.

2. Pull down the Action combo box, click Beep, and then click the Run button in the toolbar, the one with the exclamation point, just like on the query design toolbar.

3. Access prompts you to save the macro before running it. Click Yes and save the macro, naming it macBeeper. After you save it, the macro runs, beeping your system once. Try clicking the Run button several times to cause Access to beep your computer several times. If you have a special sound assigned to beep in Windows, you'll hear your assigned sound. Congratulations! You've just programmed your first macro.

▼

FIGURE **16.7.**

*The list of macro actions.*

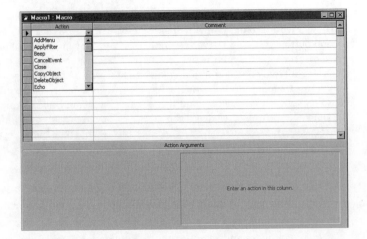

16

**Caution**

That was awfully easy and so are most macro tasks. There's no real way to run a macro with an error trap like the Event Procedure in Day 14. For this reason, some professional programmers frown on using a lot of (or even any) macros in Access applications. If there's no error trap, Access doesn't know what to do in case of an error condition and generally exits rather ungracefully. The lack of an error trap in macros is a disadvantage. However, error traps are mostly a concern for those distributing applications to others, especially outside the developer's organization. Most internal or for-your-own-use Access applications seem to survive without error traps. The ease of programming macros counteracts the lack of traps in macros for the vast majority of Access users. However, any system lacking these traps, or ways to handle things once something unexpected happens, is significantly more prone to crashing, data losses, and other woes than one that's programmed to anticipate that something will go wrong. Worse, the unexpected and uncontrolled behavior of untrapped errors will cause you, the developer's, phone to ring with irate users on the other end. Of all problems with unexpected errors, this is the worst.

There are too many Access applications merrily running along on macros alone to condemn the practice of using macros extensively, but keep in mind that you're safer using properly constructed Visual Basic code than you are using just macros.

| Do | Don't |
|---|---|
| **DO** use a wizard to program your command buttons when you have the right wizard. This will give you the best of both worlds: easy button programming and error trapping through Visual Basic. Also remember that you can modify the "canned" error traps the wizard produces. | **DON'T** get overly worried if you find programming in Visual Basic to be overwhelming and you choose to use macros for actions where no wizard exists. Most noncommercial Access applications do just fine while lacking a few error traps, even though this practice is roundly condemned by the Access elite corps. |

4. Now for a little more work. Pull down the combo box in the second row of the Action column. Scroll to and select OpenForm. Access automatically brings up the Action Arguments section at the bottom of the screen. Click next to the Form Name argument and select Author's Publication Entry Form as the form to open. Your screen should resemble Figure 16.8, depending on the state of your form.

**FIGURE 16.8.**

*The OpenForm macro.*

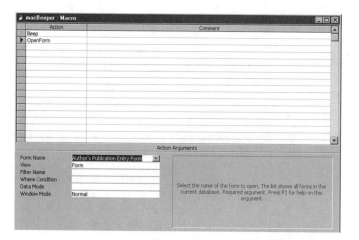

5. Again, click the Run button in the toolbar. Access again reminds you that you must save the macro, so click Yes. Access lets fly with another beep in response to your programmed beep line as the first action in this macro, and then opens the form, responding to the second.

6. Click the cmdExit button to exit this form—that's the one with the stop sign on it. If you don't have a cmdExit button on your form, exit the form by clicking its close (X) icon or choose File|Close from the menu.

7. Close the beeper macro. Back at the database window, you can delete it by clicking it, pressing the Delete key, and confirming to Access that you want to delete this macro. *Sams Teach Yourself Access 97 in 21 Days* won't come back to macBeeper, but you might want to keep it around for experimentation.

**Tip**

> The "mac" prefix is a popular naming convention for macros. Using it here is an example of using naming conventions for Access objects. Although many Access developers use this convention, not all do so. You should, however, adopt a naming convention and stick to it. Doing so will help you make sense out of your work when you return to it in the future.

16

# Creating a Switchboard Form

You saw how easy it was to create a macro that, when run, opens a form. Doing many other things with macros is equally as easy. The following task shows you how to make a switchboard form. This specialized unbound form has command buttons that act as a menu system for your applications.

## Task: The switchboard or menu form

▼ TASK

1. With Access launched and the Bookstore database open, click the Forms tab, and then click the New button to start a new form.

2. Leave the Design View option selected and don't bind any table or query to the new form. Click OK to launch the form in Design View. Move the cursor to the lower-right corner of the form design area. When you hit the corner, the cursor will change to a box with four arrows sticking out from it. Click your mouse button and drag the form until it's about 6 by 6 (according to the ruler on the form design window).

These next steps give the form its basic design elements, as shown in Figure 16.9.

**FIGURE 16.9.**

*Placing command buttons and inserting a Label control in the form.*

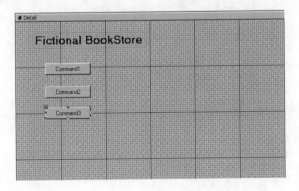

▼

▼   3. Click the Label control in the Toolbox and click again in the upper-left corner of
       the form design grid. Enter Fictional BookStore as the caption for the label.
       Next, change the font size to 18 and the style to bold. You will have to resize your
       label to make the new font fit.

    4. Make sure the Control Wizard's button in the Toolbox is deselected, and then
       double-click the Command Button control in the toolbox. This locks the Command
       Button control choice, allowing you to place more than one control without
       reselecting it. Unlock a control selection by pressing Esc. Place three command
       buttons on the form; you can place them as shown in Figure 16.9 or wherever you
       think they look good.

       The next step is to name and caption the Command Button controls.

    5. Press Esc to remove the control lock. Open the Properties window if necessary.
       Highlight each command button in turn and change its Name property (on the Other
       tab) to cmdOpenAuthorPubEntry, cmdOpenBiblioReport, and cmdExit, respective-
       ly. While in the Properties window, change the buttons' Caption property (on the
       Format tab) to Publication Entry Form, Bibliography Report, and E&xit,
       respectively. Make the buttons slightly taller to fit the Caption properties. Figure
       16.10 shows what your screen should look like after changing the last button's
       Name and Caption properties.

**FIGURE 16.10.**

*Altering the command
buttons' properties.*

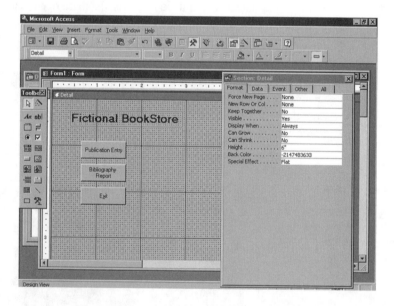

    6. Choose File|Save from the menu and name this form Switchboard. Keep this
▲      form open for your next task.

# Creating the Switchboard's Macros

The next task creates a macro for the Switchboard form you completed in the preceding section.

## Task: The compound macro

1. If the Switchboard form is still open, press the F11 key to bring the database window forward. If you're looking at the database window already, you don't need to press F11 (naturally). Click the Macros tab, and then click New. Locate the Macro Names button in the toolbar and click it.

   Macros have one overall name that appears in the database window, but they can also have sub-names that appear in the Macro Name column. When you attach this macro to the Switchboard form, you'll see how it works. Figure 16.11 gives you a guide for the next three, related steps.

**FIGURE 16.11.**

*The OpenForm, OpenReport, and Exit macros.*

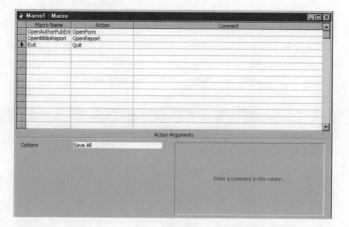

2. Click in the first row of the Macro Name column and enter `OpenAuthorPubEntry` for a name. Move to the Actions column, pull down the combo box, and click `OpenForm`. In the Action Arguments section, specify the Author's Publication Entry Form as the one to be opened.

3. Click in the second row of the Macro Name column. Enter `OpenBiblioReport`. Move to the Action column and enter `OpenReport`. Specify `BiblioReport` as the Report Name and make sure the view is Print Preview.

4. Click in the third row of the Macro Name column. Enter `Exit` as a name, move to the Action column, and then enter `Quit` as an action.

▲  5. Close and save this macro, giving it the name `macSwitchboard`.

# Putting It All Together

All's ready now to attach the `macSwitchboard` macro you just created to the Switchboard form. The next task shows you how.

## Task: Activating the form

1. Open up the Switchboard form in Design View, either by switching to it (Ctrl+F6) or clicking the Forms tab, and then clicking Design after highlighting the Switchboard form. Your screen should look like Figure 16.10.

2. Click the Publication Entry command button and open the Properties window (if necessary). Click the Event tab to show only the events associated with this command button. Locate the `On Click` event, pull down the combo box, and then find and click the `macSwitchboard.OpenAuthorPubEntry` entry.

3. Click the Bibliography Report button, and assign the `macSwitchboard.OpenBiblioReport` macro to its `On Click` property.

4. Using the same technique, attach the `macSwitchboard.Exit` macro to the Exit button.

5. Click the Save button on the toolbar and then switch to Form View. Your form should resemble the one shown in Figure 16.12.

**FIGURE 16.12.**

*The new Switchboard form up and running.*

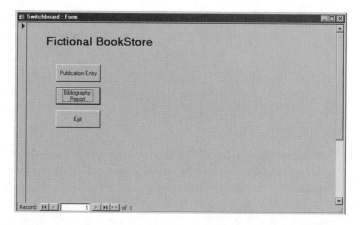

Try clicking the button labeled Publication Entry. You'll switch to the Author's Publication Entry Form. Click the button with the stop sign on it or exit this form in some other way. You'll return to the Switchboard form.

Experiment with these buttons, starting and ending the Author's Publication Entry Form and the Bibliography Report report. One caution: The button labeled Exit exits you from Access. Try pressing Alt+X to use this button.

# Conditional Branching in Macros

All but the simplest computer programs rely at times on evaluating a condition, and then taking action based on the results of that evaluation. You created a program that evaluated a condition and reacted accordingly in Day 15, "Using Expressions and Creating Advanced Reports," when you added a dynamic control to a report.

On their own, controls can do only limited things, but team them up with macros and the field widens quite a bit. The problem is how to get the macro, rather than the control, to evaluate a condition and act on what it finds. As you've probably guessed by now, Access gives you a simple way to do this evaluation. The second problem to address is how to decide when the macro should do the evaluation.

16

**NEW TERM** Take a look at Figure 16.13. This is the macro design grid with all the possible columns showing. Note that in addition to the Macro Name column, there's also a Condition column. By default, macros execute under any condition when called. If you make an entry in the Condition column, the macro starts, does the evaluation, and executes, depending on the results of the evaluation. In other words, it *branches*.

One handy thing a macro can do is flash a message box informing data entry people of just about anything, from a credit overrun to an error condition to a sales suggestion. The following task creates a macro that brings up a message box if certain conditions are met. It evaluates the contents of the YearPublished field when a new publication is entered, and responds with a confirmation message box if the year is later than the current year.

## Task: Conditional message box macro

1. Launch Access and open the BookStore database, if necessary. Click the Macros tab, and click New. Click both the Macro Names and the Condition buttons in the toolbar to open both these columns. If you're a menu enthusiast, you can choose both columns from the View menu. Your screen should resemble Figure 16.13.

   Generally speaking, the first thing to do with a macro is to give it a name, unless the macro will have only one routine. It's good practice to group macros according to usage.

2. Click in the first row of the Macro Names column and add the name YearVerification.

3. Click in the Condition column and enter [YearPublished] > Year(Now()). This means you want to have the macro evaluate the entry in the YearPublished field and spring into action if the condition's met. In this case, the condition the macro looks for is the text in a text box control. Your screen should look like Figure 16.13.

**Tip**

Remember, you can expand or contract macro columns just as you can other columns (such as in a table or query). You can also Zoom by pressing Shift+F2 to enter criteria or data within the macro design grid.

**FIGURE 16.13.**

*Entering a condition for the macro to evaluate.*

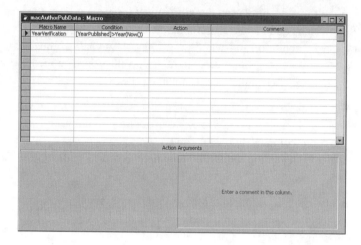

Now you need to enter the action to be taken in case the condition is met. This macro will inform the data-entry person that the year this publication is published in is later than the current year, just as a precaution against a typo.

4. Click in the `Action` column of the second row, pull down the action combo box list, and click MsgBox.

5. Enter the text `You entered a year published value that is after the current year. Is this correct?` as the Message argument. Edit the message box type to be `Warning?` and the Title argument to be `Alert!`. Figure 16.14 shows what your screen will look like when you're done.

6. Close this macro, saving the macro as `macAuthorPubData`.

**FIGURE 16.14.**

*Specifying that the macro action is to show a message box.*

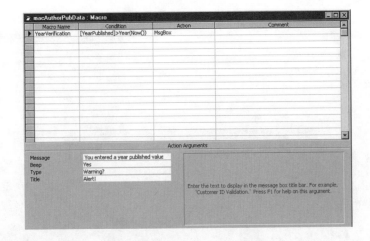

16

## Attaching the Macro to the Form Control

One more thing needs to be done at this point. The macAuthorPubData. YearVerification macro must be attached to the form in just the right way so it will spring into action at an appropriate time.

In the following task, you attach the macro to the form.

### Task: Attaching macros

▲ TASK

1. Back in the database window, click the Forms tab, highlight the subPublicationEntry SubForm, and click the Design button to open this form in Design View.

2. Click the YearPublished field to highlight it. Make sure you click the field itself, not the label for the field. After finding the After Update property in the Properties window, click it and pull down its combo box. Next, locate the macAuthoPubData.YearVerification macro and click it. This macro will "fire" after the data in the text box has been edited. Your screen should look like Figure 16.15.

3. Close this form, saving the changes.

▼

4. Open the Author's Publication Entry Form in Form View.

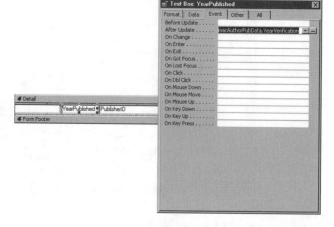

**FIGURE 16.15.**

*Adding a macro to the
After Update property
of a text box.*

| Do | DON'T |
|---|---|
| **DO** make sure to have the field itself highlighted when trying to enter event-driven macros. | **DON'T** highlight the field's label or you won't see the events for the control shown in the list box. No events can happen to a label. |

## Macros in Action

Now take a look at how this new macro works. Click the first empty row in the sub-form's grid. Enter a title of your own choosing. Tab to the Year Published column and enter the current year. Enter information for the EditionNumber and Pages fields as well since these are required fields. Notice that no message box popped up when you edited the YearPublished field.

Now start another new publication. But enter any year *after* the current year in the YearPublished field.

Press Enter or tab out of this field. Access looks at the entry, finds it's after the current year, and executes the macro, now that the condition's met. Your screen should look like Figure 16.16.

It works just as it should, so click OK to close the message box. Return to the YearPublished field by clicking it, and again tab out. The message box doesn't appear because the macro executes only when the field's been updated. That's the meaning of the After Update event. Close this form.

**FIGURE 16.16.**

*The macro executing.*

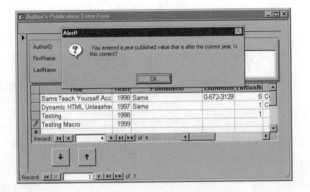

**16**

> **Note**
>
> This macro could have been successfully added to the On Exit property of this control. However, the fictional bookstore wanted this macro to be executed only when a new publication is entered. If the macro executed each time the field was exited, it would execute every time someone tabbed through this field. This macro will also fire when the YearPublished field is edited or updated.

# Macros That Alter Properties

A macro can have an action that alters control properties. The next two exercises show how this works. The form and the controls that have their properties altered aren't terribly useful, but the technique is. The reasons for the rather "hokey" example are simplicity and a desire to focus only on the issues, rather than on irrelevant details.

The following task creates a simple form with four controls. Two of the controls respond to events by altering the other two controls' properties with a macro. Each macro in this exercise is a multiline one and represents an increase in complexity in several areas.

## Task: The form

1. If you have any Access objects open, close them, saving the changes if you want. From the database window, click the Forms tab, and then click the New button. Click the Design View option without binding the form to any table or query and click OK. Increase the size of the form design grid to give yourself some working room.

2. Place a Label control on the form with the caption I'm Green in 18-point font. Open the Formatting toolbar and set the background color of this label to green.

3. Open the Properties window, click the Format tab, and set the Visible property to No. Your screen should look like Figure 16.17.

**FIGURE 16.17.**

*The Green label control.*

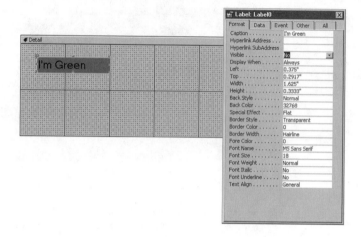

4. Create another Label control exactly the same size and location as the one in step 2. You can right-click the existing label and choose Copy the right-click and Paste to duplicate this control. You'll need to move the two controls over each other if you use this technique. Give this label the caption I'm Red in 18-point font. Set the background color to red and the Visible property to No.

**Tip**

> Another shortcut to step 4 is to choose Edit | Duplicate from the menu, and then edit the caption and the background color of the new control.
>
> If you were making this form for your use, you'd probably also change the Name properties for this and other controls on this form to conform to a naming convention. This exercise skips these steps to remain focused on the goal: the macro that alters control properties.

5. Switch to Form View. Since both label controls have their Visible properties set to No, the screen looks blank.

6. Return to Design View and add two command buttons. Edit the caption of one to read Green and the other Red (see Figure 16.18).

**FIGURE 16.18.**

*Adding two command buttons to the form.*

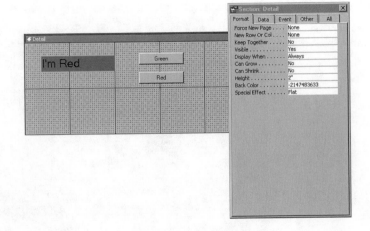

16

7. Close this form, saving it as RedGreen.

In the next task, you create a macro that changes the control properties when called by the command buttons. It creates one macro that has two macro names. When called by its command button, this macro changes the labels' Visible properties.

## Task: Control property macros

**▼ TASK**

1. From the Database window, click the Macros tab, and then click New to start a new macro. Open the Macro Name column. This macro doesn't evaluate conditions, so you can have that column open or shut. Choose File | Save from the menu and name this macro macRedGreen.

2. The first part of this macro makes the Red label visible. Enter the macro name ShowRed in the Macro Name column, and then tab to the Action column and select SetValue as an action. Click in the Item line of the Action Arguments section to bring up the three-dot ellipsis ... builder button. Click it to bring up the Expression Builder (see Figure 16.19).

These macros do the same thing, but work in opposition. One positively sets the Green label's Visible property to No and the Red label's Visible property to Yes; the other sets the Red label's Visible property to No and the Green label's Visible property to Yes.

▼

**FIGURE 16.19.**

*Getting ready to use the Expression Builder.*

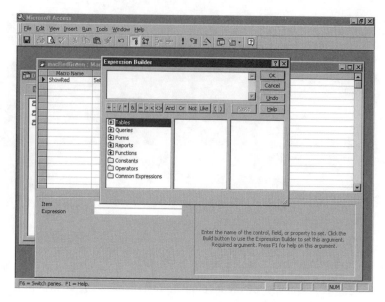

3. In the Expression Builder dialog, double-click Forms and All Forms, and then click RedGreen to tell the Expression Builder you're interested in this form. Locate the Label0 field in the second column and click that. If you've renamed the Green label to something else, find that name and click it. Next, click the `Visible` property in column three (you'll have to scroll the list to find it), and then click the Paste button to paste this argument into the Expression Builder (see Figure 16.20).

**FIGURE 16.20.**

*Using the Expression Builder.*

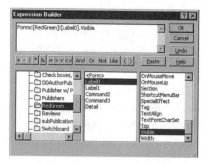

**Note**

Access, in this context, might not construct the entire expression shown in Figure 16.20 when you click the Paste button. If it doesn't, edit the expression to be the same as the one shown in the figure. You can freely edit expressions pasted into the Expression Builder's text box.

4. Click OK to place your expression in the Item line of the Action Arguments. Because Label0 is the Green label, the ShowRed macro should set its Visible property to No. Click the second line of the Action Arguments section and set the expression to No.

5. Click in the second row of the Action column (in the grid) and again choose SetValue as an action. Click in the Item section and again bring up the Expression Builder. This time, choose Forms![RedGreen]![Label1].Visible by clicking those items as they appear in the columns, and then paste them to the Expression Builder area.

6. Click OK, and then click the Expression line of the Action Arguments section and enter Yes.

7. Create a new macro name, ShowGreen, on the third line of the Macro Name column. Enter two SetValue actions for this macro, too. This time set them to just the opposite of the ShowRed macro.

> **Tip**
>
> A shortcut to doing step 7 is to click in the Item line for the first SetValue, press Shift+F2 to enter Zoom, copy the expression to the Clipboard, close Zoom, click the new SetValue, and paste the expression into the new Item line. Do this for both SetValues in the ShowGreen macro, and then set the expressions for each SetValue to the opposite of those for ShowRed.

Have the Label0 Visible property set to Yes and the Label1 Visible property set to No. After you enter these two values, your screen should look like Figure 16.21.

**FIGURE 16.21.**

*Settings to reveal the Green label.*

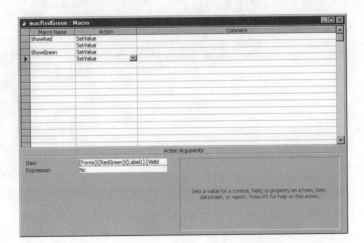

▲     8. Close this macro, saving the changes.

You've just created the macros that will operate on the form. In the next section you'll attach these macros to the form itself.

# Placing the Macros on the Form

You now have a demonstration form and the macros that will, when invoked, change the label control's Visible property—or so you hope. Although this set of exercises focuses on the Visible property, you can change many other properties while a form is running.

Next, you'll attach the macros done in the preceding task to controls in the RedGreen form.

## Task: Putting it all together

1. From the database window, click the Forms tab and open the RedGreen form in Design View (see Figure 16.18).

2. Open the Properties window if necessary and click the Event tab to display only the events. Click the Green command button to highlight it. In the Properties window, click the On Click event and select the macRedGreen.ShowGreen macro from the drop-down list (see Figure 16.22).

**FIGURE 16.22.**

*Programming the Green button.*

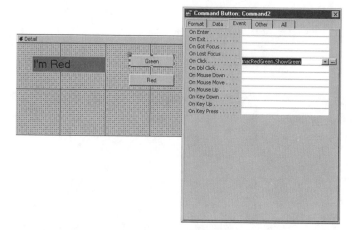

3. Similarly, click the Red button to highlight it and set its On Click property to macRedGreen.ShowRed.

4. Switch to Form View. When launched, each label control has its Visible property set to No, so you see a screen like the one in Figure 16.23.

▼

**FIGURE 16.23.**

*The RedGreen form at launch time.*

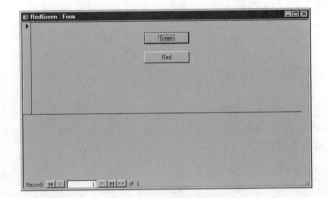

5. Click the Green button. This sets the I'm Red label's (Label1) Visible property to No and the I'm Green (Label0) to Yes. Setting a Visible property to No when it's already at No, as with the I'm Red label, has no effect, but it's important, as you'll see later. After clicking the Green button, your screen should look like Figure 16.24.

**FIGURE 16.24.**

*The effect of clicking the Green button.*

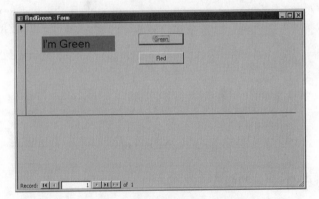

6. Click the Red button; you should be seeing Red!

The Red button's ShowRed macro sets the Visible property for the Red label to Yes and the Visible property for the Green label to No. Try clicking each button. The colors and labels switch, just as you would expect them to. If the macros left out switching the "off" label's Visible property to No, both labels would be visible after clicking both buttons, and only the one to the front would actually show up in the form. Close this form, saving the changes.

16

# Access Identifiers

The Expression Builder (or your edits) placed constructions such as the following in the macros:

```
[Forms]![Red Green]![Label0].[Visible]
```

The exclamation points and periods are Access identifiers that help find the controls and properties you want to address. In the preceding expression, you're telling Access that the control you want to address is named Label0, it's located in (or on) an object called Red Green, and that object is one of Access's forms.

You must be explicit when telling Access where to find the control you're interested in because controls can have the same names on different forms or reports; for that matter, forms and reports (for example) can have the same names. Therefore, the field Label0 might appear on two or more forms and two or more reports. Look at the following expressions:

```
Reports![CaseStudy]![Label0].Visible
Forms![CaseStudy]![Label0].Visible
```

Both expressions refer to discrete controls that have the same name and are on a same-named report and form. Access will have no trouble finding the correct control because you've told it to look for one Label0 in the reports and one in the forms.

 **Note**  | Access uses the Me expression to refer to the current object. So the expression Me![MyControl].Visible refers to the Visible property of the control, MyControl, located on the currently active form, report, subform, or subreport.

# Dots and Bangs

Generally speaking, the exclamation point is followed by a user-named Access object, and the period is followed by an Access-named object or property. For example, in the following expression, [RedGreen] and [Label0] are user-named objects (or can be), but [Visible] is Access-named:

```
[Forms]![RedGreen]![Label0].[Visible]
```

Also (generally speaking), you don't need to use full identifiers in macros. Access automatically looks on the current form or report for the named controls. This exercise forced the use of full identifiers to introduce you to them. When using Visual Basic, you must use fully qualified and syntactically correct identifiers, with the exception of the Me identifier discussed in the preceding note.

Access is intentionally programmed not to need full identifiers in macros, so you can construct more macros for very generalized use. For example, the same macro works on [Label0]-named fields on both the report CaseStudy and the form CaseStudy when called from within those objects.

# Summary

Access has three programming languages—Visual Basic, macros, and SQL. SQL is the basis of all Access queries, and you can use SQL statements for control sources in forms and reports. Macros are a simple point-and-shoot method to program Access, with the disadvantage of not having any error-trapping capacity. However, many of the macro actions are fairly simple and don't suffer too much from operating without an error trap. Even so, many professional Access developers prefer to avoid macros for Visual Basic whenever possible.

Macros have two parts: Actions and Action Arguments. Simple macro actions, such as the Beep, take no arguments, but most others do. Programming Access macros can be as simple as clicking the macro action, and then clicking the right arguments.

Macros can evaluate a situation, such as a text entry or numeric value, and take action accordingly. One of the exercises evaluates a text box field when it's updated and responds with a message box if it finds the entry to meet a certain condition.

Macros can also change control properties. You saw how to create a macro that set two controls' properties from Visible = True to Visible = False when called.

You can combine the capabilities of macros. For example, you could create a macro that evaluates a condition and alters properties, rather than one that flashes a message box.

Access uses the exclamation point and period as identifiers. Exclamation points precede user-defined objects, and periods precede Access-defined ones, generally speaking. Be sure to use square brackets in your identifying expressions to maintain consistency and to make sure that Access always knows to what you're referring.

# Q&A

**Q Why bother to learn and use SQL?**

**A** If you'll be using Access only for querying Access tables, there might not be any reason. SQL is a common query language used by professional database managers to query many different databases, and many large system databases need SQL to extract information. Access can provide a convenient front-end for these database systems, but most Access users aren't even aware that Access includes an SQL capacity. You can greatly extend Access's flexibility by learning SQL, though.

**Q** Can I enter lines such as `Forms!RedGreen![FirstName].Visible` directly in the Item line in the macro design grid instead of using the Expression Builder?

**A** Yes. The reason to use the Expression Builder is to make sure you don't make an error by typo. It's easy to make one, like this:

```
Forms![RebGreen]![FirstName].Visible
```

If you entered that line, the macro would misfire. A typo like RebGreen for RedGreen is easy to make and difficult to spot.

**Q** Can I use the `On Click` event with controls other than command buttons?

**A** Yes. Any control having an `On Click` event can respond to mouse clicks like command buttons. Most people think of command buttons when they think of clicking, though.

# Workshop

Here's where you can test and apply the lessons you learned today.

## Quiz

1. Look at the way the second task in this chapter, "The switchboard or menu form," had you enter the `Caption` property for the cmdExit button—E&xit—in step 5. Now look at the way the button appears in Design or Form View. What do you suppose the ampersand (&) does?

2. If the View option for the `macSwitchboard.OpenBiblioReport` macro was changed to Print, what do you suppose would happen if you ran the macro?

3. What does the period do in a macro name?

4. The word *Not* works as a criteria in queries, but won't work in mathematical expressions. How can you specify a Not or Not Equal To operator in an Access expression? Hint: *Not* is the same as "not equal to."

## Exercises

1. Start a new macro and enter `Close` as a macro action.

2. Click in the Action Arguments section. Pull down the Object Type combo box and enter `Form` as an object type.

3. Click in the Object Name section and enter `TabbedBibliography` as an object name. This form is part of the sample data.

4. Close the macro, saving it as `macTabbedBibliography`.

5. Open the `TabbedBibliography` form in Design View. Place a command button in the footer section toward the right side of the form. Name the button `cmdCloseForm` and give it the caption `&Close Form`.

6. Assign the macro `macTabbedBibliography` to the `On Click` event for this button.

7. Choose File | Save to save your changes, and then switch to Form View.

8. Click the new command button. Did it work as you anticipated?

9. Reopen the form in Form View and press Alt+C. What happened? Why do you suppose it happened?

**16**

---

**THE ACCESS WAY**

If you'd like to see something interesting, try this. Create a simple macro with one action—close the TabbedBibliography form if you don't have the macro already made. A macro, macDragMe, that does this is part of the sample data. Close everything except the database window. Open the TabbedBibliography form in Design View. Make sure the Form Footer section is visible. Use the Window | Tile Vertically menu item. Click the Database window's Macros tab and find the macro you just made. Click that name and drag it to the form's footer section (see Figure 16.25). Switch to Form View and try the new command button.

In some ways, Access makes things almost *too* easy. After all, database programming is supposed to be a challenge, right?

---

**FIGURE 16.25.**

*Drag-and-drop pro-gramming.*

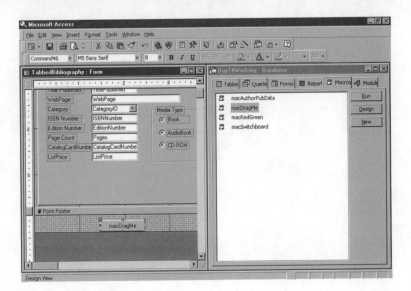

# DAY 17

# Introduction to Programming in Access

You may be thinking to yourself, "Introduction to Programming? Why just an introduction? Why not the whole kit-and-kaboodle?" Access programming is a vast topic that is, in and of itself, the subject of entire books. However, consider the following:

- Programming in Access is subject to the 80/20 rule: 80 percent of everything you need to do is contained in 20 percent of the scope of Access programming.

- The balance of programming knowledge in Access relates to advanced topics, such as manipulating or addressing Windows itself, multiuser applications, and manipulating the JET database engine directly. These topics interest only a limited number of professional developers, and they are beyond the intended scope of this book. These topics are important and several good books cover them, but this book doesn't try to.

Most of what people need to do when programming Access boils down to handling these few circumstances, which are covered in today's chapter:

- When to use Visual Basic
- Springing into action upon an event
- Sensing a value and optionally manipulating it
- Error trapping
- Making a custom function
- Variables, loops, and other programming concepts
- Identifiers
- Message boxes
- Input boxes

This chapter presents several examples of these techniques. In addition to these topics, there's the broad topic of ActiveX controls, but it's large enough to warrant its own chapter: Day 18, "Advanced Programming with Data Access Objects and ActiveX Controls."

Obviously, no example can come close to including every nuance that can crop up for each of these techniques, but you should be able to extrapolate from the specific examples here to the general case, and then back to what applies to your specific needs.

Visual Basic (technically, Visual Basic for Applications, or VBA) is the fully functional programming language for the Access database program. Using it is more difficult than using Access itself or the macro extensions of Access. Microsoft has made it a design goal that using Access shouldn't require programming in VBA for most database chores. However, some tasks simply require its use.

---

**PROGRAMMING IN VBA**

This chapter is heavy on discussion and is tough going in spots because it covers a lot of theory in a short amount of time. These aren't easy topics, so give yourself plenty of time with them. The chapter starts with some simple concepts, and then expands on some of them later in the chapter.

---

# When to Use Visual Basic

The simple answer to such a complicated question is that you use Visual Basic when nothing else will do the job. Here are some examples of those situations:

- You need to create a custom function that's not possible (or practical) through an expression.

- You need to get complex input from your user. Macros and parameter queries allow simple data input, but these tools are limited to a single-input data line with an OK and Cancel button. You need Visual Basic for a more complex input.

- You need to perform a conditional loop. Macros cannot, for example, use loops like WHILE...WEND. WHILE...WEND means WHILE [a certain condition exists perform a certain task and] WEND [end when the condition fails to exist or ends].

- You need to trap errors; if an error occurs when the macro is running, the results can be unpredictable. Writing VBA code makes it possible to determine what to do when an unexpected error occurs; those who use your applications will appreciate this.

- You need to invoke Windows API (Application Program Interface). The Windows API is a library of functions used to interact with the Windows environment. This extends the already powerful Access environment.

**17**

## Custom Functions

You've seen several built-in Access functions such as Now() and Sum() in previous chapters. As you design your forms, you might find yourself repeatedly typing a long, calculated expression. Rather than continue to do this, you could create a custom function that does the same thing. In a module, you'd type something like the following:

```
Function Repeat(AnyField)
Repeat = That long expression
End Function
```

In this case, the name of the function is Repeat. It will apply to some field represented by AnyField, and the entry That long expression is the long expression you're converting to a custom function.

This is similar to elementary algebra. One of the first things you learn with algebra is to use letter symbols to replace certain numeric quantities. For example, you might read the following in algebra:

Let A = 2+3+4+5

If you then saw the following expression, you'd understand that the quantity B is equal to 17:

B = A + 3

In the preceding code example, you take the long expression and assign it to the function Repeat.

## Complex Input

Macros have to work with what they find already entered into Access. You can't poke new information into them when they run. In some cases, you might want to have your user enter information during a database operation or put it into jargon at runtime. You've seen how queries can act on user-entered parameters, but, by using Visual Basic, you can go further. You can develop a program that asks users for information, and then executes an action based on what they enter.

## Conditional Loops

NEW TERM   A conditional loop executes, or fails to execute, a particular action until some other condition exists. Using macro conditions you can, in some cases, test to see whether a certain thing is true and act accordingly. That's a *static test*—it checks once to see whether something's true and moves on. Say you want to get a user input, test to see whether it's between 1 and 35, and then take different actions depending on whether the input's from 1 to 10, 11 to 21, 22 to 30, or 31 to 35. Doing this in Visual Basic is quite easy.

NEW TERM   A *conditional loop* is a feature available in Visual Basic that repeats a group of statements as long as a certain condition is true. For example, you might create a conditional loop to keep prompting the user for new records as long as he or she doesn't press the Esc key, telling Access that "as long as the Esc key isn't pressed, keep on doing this." This is similar to the Condition section of the macro design grid, but Visual Basic allows for the possibility of dynamic conditions.

You might force macros to test these conditions, but the process is rather laborious. However, you can't use a macro to retrieve user input at runtime.

# Reacting to an Event

You saw how you can conditionally respond to an event in Day 16, "Working with Macros," when you constructed a macro to open a message box when the YearPublished field was edited to contain a year after the current year. You can do the same thing using Visual Basic with greater clarity and an increased number of options.

Take a look at Figure 17.1. This is a form named frmInventoryBalance that's part of the sample data for this chapter. At this point, it's still under construction.

**FIGURE 17.1.**

*A form under construction.*

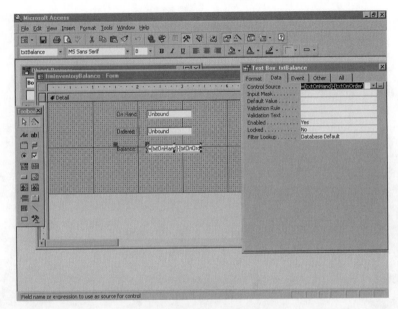

This is a simplified example with all the unnecessary elements stripped away for the sake of clarity. This form has a field for number of books on hand, the number of books on order, and the calculated surplus/shortfall. In a working example, these fields would be connected to queries that checked an Inventory table and an Orders table. The value in txtBalance is calculated from the other two fields (notice the Control Source property in the Properties window shown in Figure 17.1). The example has been shortened so you can see clearly how things work; a "real" working example would have to be more complex, detracting from the focus of this example.

The purpose of this example is to alter the color characteristics of the text box showing the inventory balance.

The way to do this (well, one way) is to create a routine that, when certain events happen, examines the value of the control txtBalance and alters its colors accordingly. Figure 17.2 shows the code that does this.

**FIGURE 17.2.**

*The code for the form.*

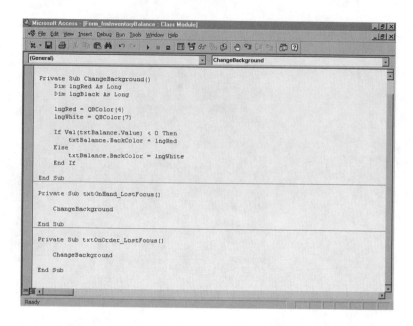

> **Note**
>
> The code shown in Figure 17.2 has no error handling. Like other elements of this example, it has been left out intentionally for the sake of clarity. Because one of the benefits of using Visual Basic in Access is to trap errors, a real-world application written without at least a rudimentary error trapping mechanism isn't a good idea. Later in this chapter, you'll learn about errors and how to trap them.

You can probably make better sense of the code shown in Figure 17.2 if you open the event procedure and examine it within Access because remarks (at least) are color-coded.

The code shown in Figures 17.2 "fires" when the LostFocus event triggers in either control, txtOnHand or txtOnOrder. To see the code, open the form in Design View, open the Properties window, click the Event tab, and then click the [Event Handler] entry to bring up the ellipsis button. Click that button and you'll be taken right to the code.

To try this code out for yourself, switch to Form View and enter differing amounts in either of the top two controls. After you press Enter or Tab to leave the control, Access examines the resulting sum in the txtBalance control and colors it according to the rules in the code. Try entering a negative number in both the top controls. What happens? Welcome to the world of a computer programmer, where you have to anticipate what your users will do.

## Is That It?

The preceding example shows the essentials of responding to events and changing properties at runtime. Naturally, the scope of the events and properties you can respond to and alter are enormous, but the following steps outline the generic solution to this problem:

1. Determine on what you want to base your action, such as the value of a control's contents.

2. Decide what event will trigger the examination—FormLoad, AfterUpdate, Change, something else?

3. Try to anticipate anything your users will do and make sure your routine will handle it.

4. If your actions are conditional, tell Access what to do when it finds differing conditions (Select Case, If...Then...Else).

## How Can I Learn All These Keywords?

In a way, you shouldn't. Once you have the generic solution down, you can always open up Online Help, look up the specific topic you're interested in (often with an example you can copy), and refresh your memory or learn something new. Figure 17.3 shows part of the Online Help when queried about the BackColor keyword. The figure shows part of the sample Visual Basic code supplied with this topic. Even if you have no idea how to set the BackColor property for an Access object, you can learn how by reading the help text and example code. After you've absorbed the information, you can copy and paste the example code from the help system to your application.

Are you surprised that the code fragment looks quite similar to the sample in the book? Well, you shouldn't be. The lng prefix for variables declared as Long Integer is widely accepted Access practice. As to the rest—well, there are only so many ways you can make ham and beans. If you open Online Help to the place in Figure 17.3, you'll see the example uses If...Then...Else rather than Select Case. Either one works all right, but most people prefer If...Then...Else for short statements and Select Case for longer ones.

Don't knock yourself out trying to memorize all the properties for all the different controls. There's no need—that's what Online Help is for. Instead, focus on learning the generic solutions for each situation as you run into them, and use Access's help system to find the specific answers you need when writing your code. Don't be shy about copying Microsoft's sample code and inserting your own control names and variables for Microsoft's. That's what the Edit|Replace entry in the code window is for (see Figure 17.4).

**17**

**FIGURE 17.3.**

*An entry from Online Help with sample code.*

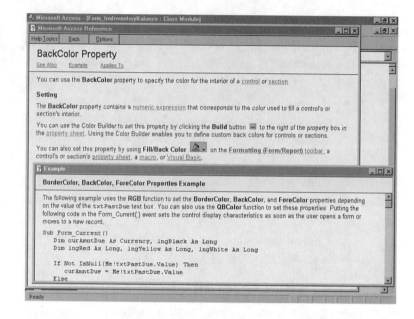

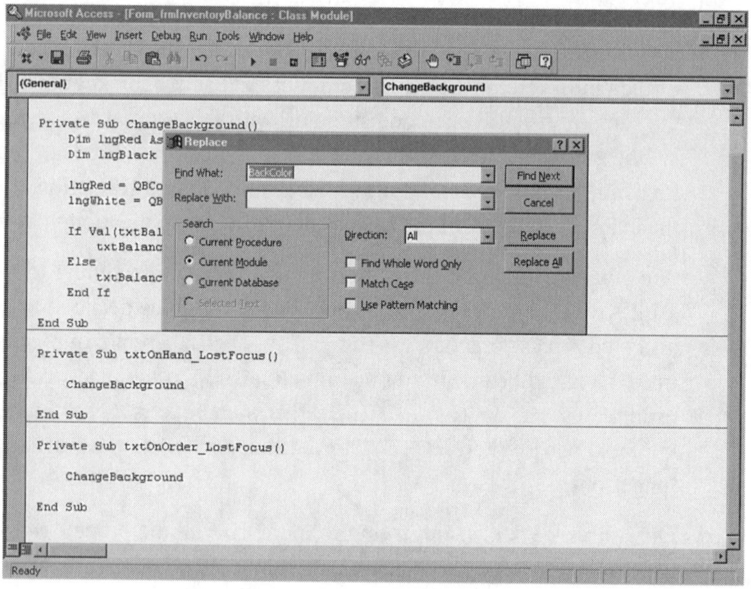

**FIGURE 17.4.**

*Edit|Replace—a programmer's best friend after Copy and Paste.*

# Functions

**NEW TERM**   The previous section dealt with Visual Basic procedures called *subs*. A *subprocedure* is called into action in response to some event. You use subprocedures when you want to do something, but they have certain limitations. First, you can't use a sub in an expression (actually, it'd make little sense), and a sub can't return a value (which is why it cannot be used in an expression). This section shows you how to create procedures called *functions* that can do both. If you're a bit hazy on subs and functions, that's all right; this section illustrates the differences.

Before you begin a more complex example, though, look at the basic steps for a much simpler example that creates a function that will accept data and return the thing you want. For example, if you wanted to create a function that would return the hypotenuse of any right triangle, you would follow these steps:

1. First, you need a formula—in this case, it's $a^2 + b^2 = c^2$.

2. Next, you have to determine what inputs you'll get. Assume you'll know a and b.

3. In a new or existing module, declare the function, telling Access what data type the inputs will be and what data type the function will return. Remember to use appropriate placeholders for each input. The following is one possible way to declare this function.

   ```
   Function Hypotenuse(intSideOne as Integer,
   ➥intSideTwo as Integer) as Integer
   ```

4. Create the Visual Basic code from the equation or formula.

   ```
   Hypotenuse = intSideOne ^2 + intSideTwo ^ 2
   ```

5. Finally, tell Access where the function ends.

   ```
   End Function
   ```

6. Now you just need to place the function in your application, specify where it'll get its inputs, and place its return.

That's it. Now for something a little more complicated.

**NEW TERM**   The following example takes input (*arguments*) from three fields—`Principal`, `Interest`, and `Years`—and calculates the payment to amortize a loan having those factors. Most of the examples you see that accept arguments use only one argument. This is a more complex example, but it won't be too tough to follow. The payoff for not going for the simplest example is that after you catch on to what's to follow, you won't have any trouble creating either simple or complex functions of your own.

17

This example creates a function that will, when fed the user-supplied numbers, calculate the payment amount. As in the hypotenuse function, the first thing you need is a formula. The formula for this example is seen in Figure 17.5.

**FIGURE 17.5.**

*The formula.*

$$Payment = \frac{(Present\ Value\ )(Rate)}{1 - \left[\frac{1}{(1 + Rate)}\right]}$$

Now it's time to declare it to Access. The following task will walk you through the steps. Keep in mind that this function will take three arguments, each of which is of a different data type. Here are the three arguments with their data types:

| Argument | Data Type |
| --- | --- |
| PresentValue | Currency |
| Interest | Double |
| Years | Integer |

In addition, the overall function will return a value that has the data type of Currency. Keep in mind that these data types under discussion are the same as the data types you declared when you created tables.

## Task: Creating the Loan Payment function

1. Since this will be a function that can be called from anywhere in the application, start a new module by clicking the Database window's Modules tab and clicking the New button.

2. To declare this function you first give it a name, and then add in placeholders for each argument it will take along with their data types. Finally, you tell Access the overall data type this function will return. Enter the following lines of code into the code window at the current cursor position:

```
Function LoanPayment(curPresentValue As Currency, dblInterest As
Double, _
intYears As Integer) As Currency
```

Your screen should now resemble Figure 17.6.

**Note**

Look closely at Figure 17.6, which shows the start of this function-making process. The character at the end of the third line is a line-continuation character that allows a long line of code to fit on one screen. The line-continuation character in Visual Basic is a space followed by an underscore.

The argument placeholders are `curPresentValue`, `dblInterest`, and `intYears` for the current value of the loan, the interest rate, and the years of the loan, respectively. Note that the placeholders have data types of `Currency`, `Double`, and `Integer`, respectively, but the function `LoanPayment` has its own data type, `Currency`. What this means is that Access will treat the present value argument as a currency value, interest as a double-precision number, and length of the loan as an integer. The function itself will return a value of the `Currency` type.

> **Note**
>
> Did you notice that after you pressed the space bar following the first occurrence of the word As, Access opened a drop-down list box filled with data types? This is called AutoComplete. You can type the first few characters of the data type and press the comma key as a quick way to enter the data type. Try just typing Cur, and you should get the same results as typing it all out manually. If this doesn't happen, go to the Options dialog (use the Tools|Options menu item), click the Module tab, and check the box labeled Auto List Members. Notice that there are many other Auto options that Access provides to make your time spent coding more efficient.

**17**

2. When you've finished entering the function's declaration line, press Return. When you do so, Access will create a new function and your screen will look like Figure 17.6.

**FIGURE 17.6.**

*The new function underway.*

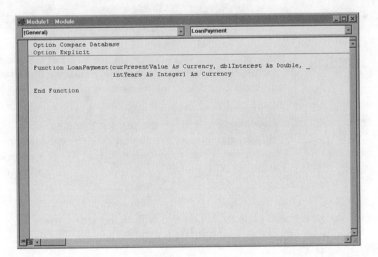

```
Module1 : Module

(General)                                    LoanPayment

    Option Compare Database
    Option Explicit

    Function LoanPayment(curPresentValue As Currency, dblInterest As Double, _
                         intYears As Integer) As Currency

    End Function
```

▼    3. The next task is to duplicate the payment equation in the function. First, you need to declare (or Dim) two variables that will be used to convert the years argument to months and also change the yearly interest rate to a monthly one. This is because the output of the function should be the monthly payment, but both the term of a loan and the interest rate are traditionally given in years. Figure 17.7 shows the statement to declare or Dim these variables.

**INPUT**
```
Dim intNper    As Integer
Dim dblRate    As Double
```

**FIGURE 17.7.**

*The variables to convert yearly numbers to monthly.*

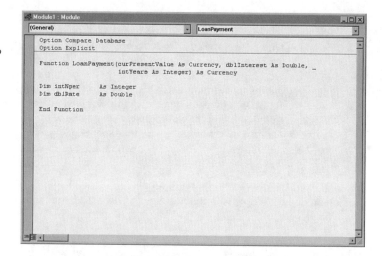

```
Module1 : Module                                                      _ □ ×
(General)                                    ▼   LoanPayment                ▼
Option Compare Database
Option Explicit

Function LoanPayment(curPresentValue As Currency, dblInterest As Double, _
                     intYears As Integer) As Currency

Dim intNper    As Integer
Dim dblRate    As Double

End Function
```

 **Caution**   You can Dim multiple variables on one line, but this example uses two for clarity and also because it's very easy to assume that the variables all have the same data type if they're declared as

```
Dim x, y, z As Long
```

**NEW TERM**   but in fact they do not. In this example, only z is a Long. The others have no defined data type (these are also known as *variant* variables because their data type will vary depending on what values are assigned to them).

4. Next you'll code the action that will do the yearly-to-monthly conversion. In the case of periods, you multiply by 12; for interest, you divide by 12 (see Figure 17.8).

**INPUT**
```
'convert from years to months:
intNper = intYears * 12
dblRate = dblInterest / 12
```
▼

**FIGURE 17.8.**

*Changing from yearly to monthly values in the function.*

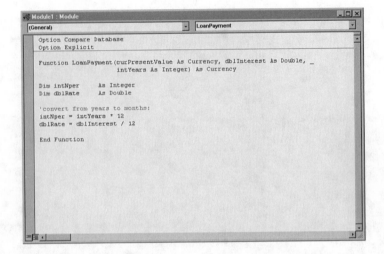

> **Note** You can insert comments into your code by starting them with either a single quotation mark (as in the case of the first line entered in this step) or the keyword REM (although this is a less-used method). Comments allow you to explain what's going on in your code. You'll learn more about them later in this chapter in a section titled "Annotating Code."

In other words, a mortgage with a yearly rate of 12 percent for 30 years will have a monthly rate of 1 percent and 360 payment periods.

5. There's nothing left but to re-create the equation with the existing variables (see Figure 17.9).

**INPUT**
```
'calculate the loan amount:
LoanPayment = (curPresentValue * dblRate) / (1 - (1 / (1 + dblRate))
^ intNper)
```

6. Save the module with the name modFinacials. You'll find this function as part of the sample data for this chapter.

> **Note** As in previous examples, this function lacks error handling for the sake of clarity and simplicity. This isn't a good idea in your real-world applications, though.

**FIGURE 17.9.**

*The actual equation reproduced in Visual Basic.*

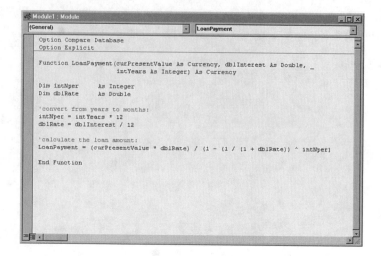

## Using the Function

Now that you have the function, it's time to see how to use it. This example uses a simple unbound form with fields for the three arguments—principal, interest, length—and for the function's return, the payment. The following steps will accomplish that feat:

1. Create a new unbound form by clicking the Database window's Forms tab, clicking the New button, and then clicking OK with the Design View option selected and no query or table in the combo box.

2. Add four unbound text box controls. Name the controls `txtPrincipal`, `txtInterest`, `txtTerm`, and `txtPayment`. Change the control's labels to reflect these changes. Figure 17.10 shows the results of these steps.

3. The point of this new form is to enter numbers into the unbound text boxes for principal, interest, and term in years, and then see the payment show up in the final text box, txtPayment. To accomplish this, add the following as the Control Source for the txtPayment unbound text box.

   ```
   =LoanPayment([txtPrincipal],[txtInterest],[txtTerm])
   ```

   This will take the values in the three text boxes and "feed" them to the function, `LoanPayment`. Your screen should look like Figure 17.11.

**FIGURE 17.10.**

*A form to show off the function.*

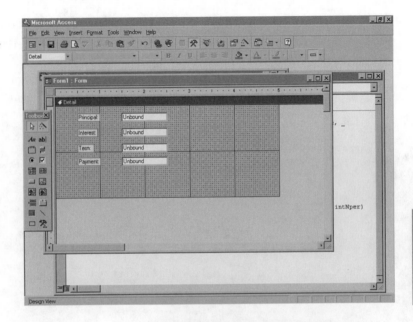

**FIGURE 17.11.**

*Entering the function as a Control Source.*

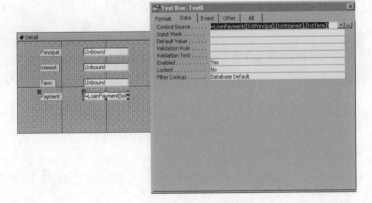

**Note**

The parameter names in this function—`curPresentValue`, `dblInterest`, and `intYears`—aren't the same as the text box names feeding into this function, `txtPrincipal`, `txtInterest`, and `txtTerm` from this form, but they don't have to be (obviously).

The parameter names in the function declaration are placeholders and nothing more. In this function, you must supply all three arguments—one for each placeholder. Access does, however, allow you to declare certain placeholders optional by prefixing them with the keyword `optional`. For more information on this, search Online Help.

4. There's nothing more to do, so switch to Form View. Initially, your Payment text box will be in an error condition because it's confused about being fed null information from the other text fields.

5. Enter appropriate numbers for the principal, interest, and term of the loan. Figure 17.12 shows the form in action after clearing the error condition.

**FIGURE 17.12.**

*The loan calculator in action.*

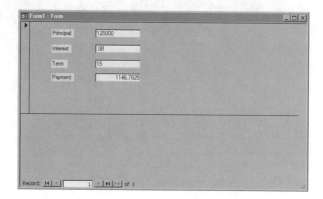

Be sure to enter the interest rate as a decimal when entering numbers for your payment calculator to grind away on.

## Enhancing the Loan Payment Calculator

This function is missing two important elements. The first is a checker to make sure all the "feeding" fields have data in them before the function tries to fire. This is as simple as adding an If...Then...Else statement to the function. If you prefer, you can do the same thing by creating default data for the form.

That's not all, though. If you're in an adventurous mood, enter a zero for the interest rate. Since the function uses this number as a divisor, Access will immediately enter an error condition, as shown in Figure 17.13.

Surely you don't want your users to see such messages, but think—it's conceivable that a user will enter a zero for interest rate, either in error or as an experiment. In this particular case, you can forestall having your users scared by error messages, such as the one in Figure 17.13, either by creating an error-trapping routine of your own or by entering >0 as a Validation Rule for this field, as shown in Figure 17.14. If you don't mind a little extra work and want your applications to run well, do both.

**FIGURE 17.13.**

*A scary error condition.*

**FIGURE 17.14.**

*One way to eliminate the error condition shown in Figure 17.13.*

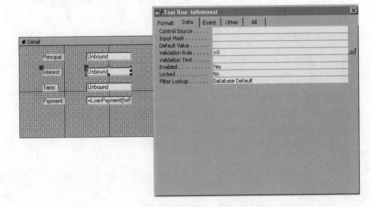

If you want to save your work, do so now. You'll find the form for doing payment calculations as part of the sample data as frmPayment.

## Making a Function Summary

The section immediately preceding this one is the type many find difficult, as it requires a lot of code entry. Most people make seemingly insignificant typos when entering functions that prevent them from running. This is particularly distressing when starting out, because you have no way of knowing if the function's failure is due to a typo or to your programming error. If you got through this section all right, you are unusual.

If you, like most, made some errors, got frustrated, or even resorted to dropping the whole thing and using the sample data, that's all right. This was a complex example to show differing data types at work together. Don't give up! To keep you going, here's some good news for you. Making your own functions is easier than following any book's because you're in charge of your own naming conventions and the direction of the programming.

If you didn't catch all the nuances of this example, but at least followed the general principles outlined in this section, you've gained quite a bit of insight into making your own custom functions, as well as passing arguments back and forth from your applications to modules. The ability to create functions, such as LoanPayment(), is what distinguishes an Access expert from an intermediate user. If you followed the previous example, you've crossed that line—congratulations!

# Error Trapping

When distributing a program, expect the unexpected. Your users will constantly find interesting ways to mess up your fine application—even ways you'd never anticipate. Sometimes you might even know a condition exists, but can't imagine a user will ever encounter it. Trust me, they always do! This is the reason software vendors like Microsoft engage in extensive beta or external testing. Even so, bugs slip by and into shipping products.

**NEW TERM**   Take the last part of the LoanPayment() function as an example. If this were your application, you could have anticipated some error conditions, such as the new form popping up with blank fields, and performed an IsNull test for those fields, but what about those situations you don't anticipate? These are called *runtime errors* and you can address them even if you can't anticipate the specific errors that will occur.

**NEW TERM**   *Error trapping* means anticipating that some errors, or a specific error, will occur and gracefully handling them (or it). The following steps show the generic way to handle errors in Visual Basic.

1. Give Access a hint as to what to do (or where to go to) when it stumbles on an error. Usually this means including an On Error statement in your function with a "jump to" label.

2. Create a routine that comes alive when an error happens. This routine will probably differ, depending on the type of error. Some developers have generic error trap libraries for errors with things in common.

Looks simple, and, in concept, it is. The only complex part is creating custom routines for specific errors; then you must know the return codes for those specific errors.

Take a look at Figure 17.15. This is a subprocedure generated by a wizard with an error handler.

**FIGURE 17.15.**

*A generic error handler.*

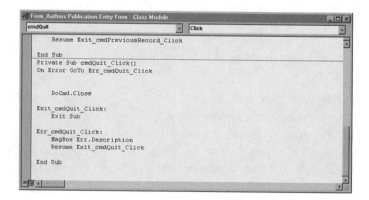

This sub simply closes a form. You can see that in the third line shown in Figure 17.15: DoCmd Close. Here's the sub with comments and line numbers added so you can follow the wizard's logic (remember that comments can start with either a single quote or with the Rem keyword):

```
 1: Sub cmdQuit_Click()
 2: Rem Where to jump to when an error occurs. Err_cmdQuit_Click is a
label
 3: On Error GoTo Err_cmdQuit_Click
 4:
 5: Rem if no error, do it
 6:     DoCmd.Close
 7:
 8: Rem jump to here after error message box or fall through to here if no
error
 9: Exit_cmdQuit_Click:
10: Rem exit the sub
11:     Exit Sub
12:
13: Rem here is the label to jump to in the event of an error
14:
15: Err_cmdQuit_Click:
16:     MsgBox Err.Description
17:     Resume Exit_cmdQuit_Click
18:
19: End Sub
```

**ANALYSIS**  Now for specifics. Say you want to construct an error handler for the function created in the previous section. The first thing you need to do is add an On Error statement and a label to jump to in case an error happens, as in line number 3. Here's an example of such a statement:

```
On Error Goto TroublesVille
```

The next thing is to construct the code for the error handler. You could just create a generic handler for all circumstances, as shown in Figure 17.15, or you can include some custom touches. Since you've seen that users entering zero for an interest rate is a possibility, handle that potential error specially. First add a label to jump to:

```
TroublesVille:
```

Remember to add a colon as a suffix on any identifier you want to make a label.

Now create the error handler itself. Look in Access's Online Help and you'll see the error number for Overflow is 6, and Divide by Zero is 11. So here's a simple If...Then statement to follow the label TroublesVille:

```
If Err.Number = 11 Or Err.Number = 6 Then
    Divide = Null
Else
```

**17**

```
    MsgBox "I've hit an unanticipated error: " & Err.Description
End If
Resume Next
```

Access is internally aware of what error condition it finds itself facing. To take advantage of this, the `If...Then` statement asks whether the errors are either 6 or 11. If so, it nullifies the divide operation. However, other errors can happen; in those cases, the user will see a message box with the message `I've hit an unanticipated error`. In all cases, Access will execute the `Resume Next` statement, which instructs it to move to the statement following the one that caused the problem.

There's only one thing left to do. If this code is to be entered into the `LoanPayment` function, you want to make sure it doesn't fire unless there's an error condition. If you placed the following code at the end of the function (really the only practical place), it would execute every time, error or not:

```
LoanPayment = curPresentValue * dblRate / (1 - (1 / (1 + dblRate)) ^
intnper)
```

Effectively then, you'd be executing your error handler every time the function ran. This would cause great confusion to users and Access—the latter because Access would wonder why it found a `Resume Next` statement when there was no error.

Therefore, you need to exit gracefully after the last working line of your function to prevent the error handler from handling the vaporous error. Doing this is as simple as adding the following statement

```
Exit Function
```

after this one:

```
LoanPayment = curPresentValue * dblRate / (1 - (1 / (1 + dblRate)) ^
intnper)
```

And that's about it.

## Error-Trapping Summary

Like other topics in this chapter, this has been a quick dash through errors and their handling in Visual Basic. You now have the basics down, but there are many "devils" in the details. Keep in mind the following:

- If you're going to bother writing code (or generating it with a wizard) include error-trapping routines.
- You can create generic error trappers to paste into your functions and subs. You don't need to customize each one from the ground up.

- Include custom error-handling routines for specific errors you figure have a reasonable chance of happening.

- As with so much else in Access, don't bother to memorize the error numbers for each error. Instead, use Online Help and save your memory for remembering your wife's birthday, your anniversary, and so forth.

# The Event-Driven Model

In the past, database programming languages—for example, one that comes with the MS-DOS dBASE family of products, such as dBASE III—executed procedurally, from top to bottom. Visual Basic, on the other hand, is event-driven, meaning it responds to events usually caused by users. The examples used in this lesson respond to the event of a pushed button. They could just as easily respond to form events such as On Exit, On Enter, On Open, and so forth.

## What's the Difference?

Programs using traditional procedural programming languages like Pascal or dBASE III execute outside the user's control. Once started, a procedural program just goes, following its own programmed path unless a hard interrupt ends its run, stopping only occasionally to either display a message or get some user-supplied information. The program and programmer are in control.

Windows programs, however, are all independent processes that can be started and stopped by the user at just about any point. As event-driven programs, they respond to the user's needs or actions. Actions such as clicking the mouse, moving a cursor into a field, pressing a button on a form, loading a form, and exiting a field are all events that can trigger any action you care to program into the event.

## You've Already Done One

In Day 16, "Working with Macros," you created a routine that responded to a control's contents. The macro then either posted a message box or didn't. Note that there would never have been a message box if the event of exiting an updated control had happened.

## Identifiers

Visual Basic uses the same identifier syntax that Access macros do. The following line of code checks to see whether the contents of the control Test Field, embedded in the form Test Form, has a value that evaluates to a number less than 10:

```
If Forms![Test Form]![Test Field] < 10 Then...
```

If so, Visual Basic executes the code following the word Then.

## Annotating Code

Unless you create the simplest functions and subroutines, you should annotate your code with comments. Comments don't execute with your code, instead they enable you or others to know what a particular segment of code is supposed to do. Comments can be a nuisance when you create code, but they're invaluable when you need to come back to the code weeks or months (or sometimes hours) later to do maintenance or alter the code to serve a slightly different purpose. Comments also help others to follow your coding logic.

| Do | Don't |
|---|---|
| **DO** use comments well. If you program Access for others, you have an ethical responsibility to use comments extensively in your Visual Basic and macro code. Not doing so might make the code you write inaccessible, and your customer might need to modify or rewrite what you've created. Failing to add comments to your code, thus making it difficult or impossible for someone else to modify it, is similar to a car dealer putting a combination lock on a car's hood so that only dealership personnel can perform maintenance on the engine. | **DON'T** fall into the trap of not adding comments while writing the code with the excuse that you'll come back to it later. That time rarely comes, and if it does, you might have forgotten what remarks need to be made. I've been guilty of this rationalization more times than is healthy! It's not worth the aggravation, trust me. |

You insert comments into your code by starting them with either a single quotation mark or the keyword REM. Look at the following code fragments:

```
Rem This example demonstrates remarks in Visual Basic

If Sales > Expenses THEN '> symbol means greater than
```

The first line uses the REM statement to tell Access, "Don't execute anything on this line." Similarly, line two uses the single quote (') after the If...Then statement. The single quote mark says "Don't execute anything on this line after the quote mark."

# A Question of Style

Its critics say Basic is a difficult-to-maintain programming language, but the problem is caused more by the way people use it than by anything inherent in the language itself.

Three traps people fall into are cramming too many instructions on one line, not adding comments, and using non-descriptive (or too many) labels. Each trap makes the code much more difficult to understand than if separate instructions were each given on separate lines, the code had remarks added liberally, and variables had descriptive labels and were of a reasonable number. Basic doesn't care if each instruction gets its own line, if remarks exist, or if variables have long names. Code Example One and Code Example Two execute identically:

Code Example One:

```
Dim DepartmentNumber As Integer:Dim NumberOfEmployees(0 To 50):GoSub X1
```

Code Example Two:

```
Dim DepartmentNumber As Integer 'Department Number is a whole number or
integer
REM Each Department has no more than 50 people.
Dim NumberOfEmployees(0 To 50)
GoSub Initialize 'Go to initialization routines
```

In Code Example One, the programmer crams all the code on one line and fails to either add remarks to the code or use descriptive labels. Code Example Two uses separate lines, descriptive labels, and plenty of remarks. Which one do you think will be clearer if this programmer or another one needs to return in three months to modify this code snippet?

> **Note**
>
> Don't worry if you can't follow these code snippets. They're here only to illustrate principles. Actual instructions for using Visual Basic's vocabulary follow this conceptual introduction. In the preceding case, the Dim code word is a holdover from early Basic days. It's short for "dimension" and was first used to tell the computer how much storage space to reserve for a particular array.
>
> NEW TERM  *Array* is computer talk for a matrix, so the following line means "computer, reserve enough space for 51 entries in a matrix under the name NumberOfEmployees":
>
> ```
> Dim NumberOfEmployees(0 To 50)
> ```
>
> Visual Basic uses the Dim statement for more than arrays. It also tells Access the type of variable; the following line, for example, tells Access that DepartmentNumber will be a whole number or an integer:
>
> ```
> Dim DepartmentNumber As Integer
> ```
>
> If you're new to computer programming, you might have some trouble understanding some of these concepts. Just plow on until you start working the examples later on, and then many of these abstractions will come into focus.

17

# Functions, Declarations, and Subs

Visual Basic is composed of three building blocks: function procedures, declarations, and subprocedures.

The declarations section of a Visual Basic module globally defines constants, variables, and data types for later use in subs and functions. A global declaration is valid for the entire scope of the Visual Basic module but not valid across different modules. Visual Basic, like many Basics, allows implicit declarations. This is terrible programming practice and is the prime reason for Basic having a bad reputation among professional programmers. You can force Visual Basic to error on implicit declarations by adding the following line in the module's declarations section:

```
Option Explicit
```

Access 97 defaults to include this line.

**NEW TERM**  A *module* is a collection of at least one Visual Basic function, declaration, or sub (although a declaration without a sub or function doesn't make much sense). Modules appear in the Database window, but when calling functions or subs, you use the function or sub name, not the name of the module.

## What's This Implicit/Explicit Business All About?

Unless you're an experienced programmer, the preceding section might seem a little difficult to follow, so this section offers some explanation. When writing programming code, you assign names to variables and constants.

**NEW TERM**  *Variables* are values that can change during the code's execution; *constants* are values that can't change during code execution. A constant could be the value of an interest rate, declared as

```
Const conInterestRate = .08750
```

in the declarations section. Then the following code line would multiply the value `.0875` with the variable `varMyInterest`:

```
varMyInterest = 100 * conInterestRate
```

Variables change depending on program code or user input. In the preceding example, you don't ask your user for a value of `varMyInterest` —you declare it. In the example used in the following section, `varGotUserNumber` is a variable because its value depends on user input.

## Danger in Variable Land

Now see what can happen if you *don't* use Option Explicit. Take a look at the way the following code snippet works: Access displays a message box with the title "Implicit Variable Demo." It then sets zero as the value for the variable varDefvalue, takes input from the user, and triples it in the last line. If you have some difficulty following the logic of this code snippet, look up INPUTBOX in the Online Help system. However, this code will not run correctly because of a typo:

```
1: Prompt = "Enter the number you want to triple" 'sets msg
2: Mtitle = "Implicit Variable Demo" ' Title of msgbox.
3: varDefvalue = 0 ' set a default value to zero
4: varGotUserNumber = InputBox(Prompt, MTitle, varDefvalue)
5: REM Get a number using an input box.
6: varGotUserNnmber = varGotUserNumber * 3 'What's wrong here?
```

If you're a careful reader, you might have spotted the error. The intent of this code is to triple a number specified by a user. The number entered by the user is given the variable label varGotUserNumber by the program in line four. The last line is supposed to change the variable to three times the user-entered amount, but it doesn't. In other words, the intent of this code is for the variable varGotUserNumber to be equal to three times the value entered by the user.

There's a minor typo that throws a giant-sized monkey wrench in this code. The programmer mistyped the variable name varGotUserNumber as varGotUserNnmber in the last line. This means that the variable varGotUserNumber will contain the original amount given by the user, and a new variable, varGotUserNnmber, implicitly declared, will contain the triple value of varGotUserNumber.

**Note**

> This lesson uses a lot of jargon specific to computer programming. Terms like *declarations, variables, constants, code, function, array,* and *subs* are familiar if you've programmed a computer before, but might be vague concepts at this point if you haven't. Rather than worry about memorizing the exact definitions now, continue along and, with use, these terms will become clear. If you forget a definition now, look for it next to a new term icon or use Access's Online Help.

If the programmer later uses the value of varGotUserNumber in a calculation, the calculation will come out wrong. Can you imagine the gravity of this error if this final calculation is critical?

**17**

Had the programmer used the `Option Explicit` instruction in the declarations section of this module and then declared `GotUserNumber` as a type of variable, Visual Basic would have complained when it hit the `GotUserNnmber` word because that variable hadn't been declared previously by using a `Dim` statement.

## Function Procedures

**NEW TERM** You create *functions* for use in Access tables (such as the `Default Value` property for a field), forms, queries, reports, and macros. Other Access objects, such as forms, can call these functions, once they're made. Here's a section of an Access function to determine the commission amount:

```
Function CommissionRate(SalesValue as Long) As Double
If SalesValue > 10000 THEN
CommissionRate = .05
Else
CommissionRate = .025
End If
```

## Subprocedures

**NEW TERM** *Subprocedures* are identical to function procedures except they can be called only by other subs or functions and can't return a value to the caller. In the preceding section, the value `CommissionRate` is returned by the procedure, and the function itself is called by a form event. Subs are used for housekeeping chores within modules. Most of the time, you'll be using function procedures rather than subs.

Use subs for altering values already contained in calling functions or implicit within Access itself. Access uses subs as event procedures when you've used a wizard to create a control.

# Another Simple Code Example

The next code exercise is simplicity itself, but it demonstrates basic programming concepts and how to tie an Visual Basic function to a form object.

### Task: Tie a Visual Basic function to a form control

This exercise links a new function to a form control.

▼ TASK

1. Launch Access. Open the `BookStore` database, if necessary. Click the Modules tab, and then click New. Access moves you to the empty Module screen like the ones you've been using to this point.

▼ Before moving on, take a look at the space just below the toolbar. There are two combo boxes; the one on the left lists Objects and the one on the right lists Procedures. The right combo box has (Declarations) showing, which means you're in the declarations section of this yet-to-be-named module. When you pull down the combo box, you'll see that the only entry is (Declarations) because you've yet to add a function or sub to this module. Later on, when you have several functions or subs in a module, these combo boxes will help you navigate between them. (See Figure 17.16, which will guide you through this task.)

**FIGURE 17.16.**

*Starting a new function is as easy as typing it into a module.*

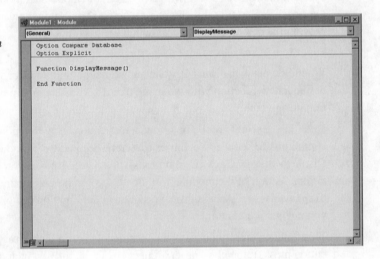

**17**

Note

Access modules can contain many functions or subs, just as macros can; for example, one macro at the database level might contain many named macros. If you have a series of related procedures, contain them within a module rather than have a new module for each procedure. This makes them easier to get to. Also, related procedures might have code in common. Having them in the same place will make copying and pasting easier.

▼ Back to the screen. Run your cursor over the buttons on the toolbar to familiarize yourself with each one's function. Don't worry if many of them seem unfamiliar; also, you'll notice that some are inactive at this point.

**Note**

> The Option Compare Database declaration is an Access-exclusive part of the Visual Basic for Applications language. This declaration tells Visual Basic to use string compares according to the order of database. The default for compares in Visual Basic is Text, which is a case-sensitive compare. This may or may not match the rest of the database containing the module, so Microsoft gave Access the exclusive database option for string comparisons.

2. Position the cursor back to where it was in the module (right under the Option Explicit declaration) by clicking at the cursor's original place. Next, without moving the cursor, enter the following:

```
Function DisplayMessage()
```

When you press the Enter key, Access scans the line, realizes you're trying to define a new function with the name DisplayMessage, and moves you to a function design area.

3. Note that the right combo box now contains your new function. Pull down the combo box to see the two entries that have been added: (Declarations) and DisplayMessage. Click (Declarations), and Access moves you back up to the declarations section of the module. Pull down the combo box again and click DisplayMessage. Access takes you back to the function design area. This is how you navigate in a module.

4. This function simply displays the message I are a computer programmer! at a button press (remember, programmers are social misfits, including their use of the English language). Add the following line right below the Function DisplayMessage() line:

```
MsgBox "I are a computer programmer!"
```

Your screen should now look like Figure 17.17.

5. Choose File|Close from the menu. When Access asks whether you want to save the changes to the module, click Yes and save it under the name modFirstPrograms. That's the name of the module in the sample data. This example used a function that is overkill as it returned nothing. A subprocedure would have served equally well.

**FIGURE 17.17.**

*Entering the executing code within a function.*

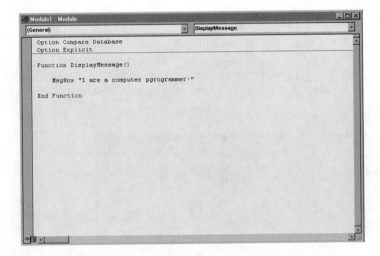

## A Place to Show Off

You need a place to demonstrate the new function. The next task puts it into use and also shows you how to vary it.

### Task: Using the function

1. Click the Forms tab in the Database window and the click the New button. Don't bind the form to any table or query, and choose Design View rather than a wizard. When you get to the Form Design View, make sure that the Toolbox is showing, but that the Control Wizards button isn't selected. Click the Command Button tool and draw a command button in the detail section of the form (see Figure 17.18).

**FIGURE 17.18.**

*A place to attach a function.*

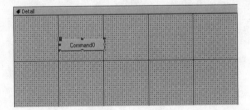

2. Open the Properties window for this control and find the On Click property. Enter =DisplayMessage() on the line next to On Click (see Figure 17.19).

**Note**

If you were assigning a macro called DisplayMessage to the OnClick event of this command button, you'd enter DisplayMessage at the OnClick property line in the Properties window for this button. Since DisplayMessage is a function written in Visual Basic, you have to indicate this to Access. The syntax of starting the property with an = and ending with a () tells Access to look for DisplayMessage as a function in a Visual Basic module.

**FIGURE 17.19.**

*Entering the new function.*

3. Switch to Form View and click the command button. When you do, the form should bring up the message box shown in Figure 17.20.

**FIGURE 17.20.**

*The running function as it responds to the OnClick event of the command button.*

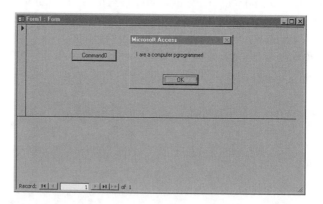

4. Now to modify the function. Click OK to close the message box. Close the form, saving it as TempForm. Return to the module by clicking the Modules tab in the Database window. Highlight the modFirstPrograms module (if necessary) and click the Design button. Pull down the Procedure combo box and select the

▼          `DisplayMessage` function or just click in it—it should be visible on your screen.
Modify the second line to match the following:

```
MsgBox "I am a computer programmer!", vbInformation + vbOKCancel,
➥ "Progress in Access"
```

Your screen should now look like Figure 17.21.

**FIGURE 17.21.**

*The modified code that will change the message box.*

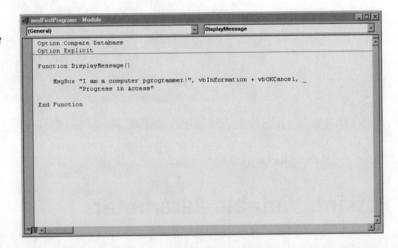

A message box takes three parameters separated by commas: the message, the display type, and the title. The second parameter tells Access to alter the message box to one having an Information Message icon and two buttons: OK and Cancel. Message boxes in Access have three numerically set properties: button count/type, icon type, and default button. Did you notice that Access again helped you complete this line by providing constants to represent the various possible values for this parameter?

Adding the string `"Progress in Access"` as the final property changes the message box's title to one saying `Progress in Access`.

5. Close and save this module. Open the `TempForm` in Form View and click its single
▼          button. Your three-parameter message box is done (see Figure 17.22).

**FIGURE 17.22.**

*The modified message box in operation on a form.*

Congratulate yourself—you've just entered the ranks of Visual Basic programmers! Click OK or Cancel and close this form. The finished form is part of your sample data under the TempForm name.

# Passing Variable Parameters

Remember, one of the reasons you might need to code in Visual Basic is to get more user input than just a parameter query. The following task adapts the message box from the previous one to accept user-defined criteria for use in a message box display.

The chief tool for getting user input in Visual Basic is the Inputbox function, which is similar to the Messagebox function, but with three significant differences:

- You need to choose the right Inputbox function, depending on whether you want a variant or a string returned.

- An Inputbox passes its contents to a variable.

- You can place an Inputbox anywhere on the screen.

## Defining a Global Type

The section "Functions, Declarations, and Subs" in this chapter mentions declaring variables. The message box example used no variables, so no declarations were needed. An input box requires an implicit or explicit variable declaration because Visual Basic uses it to capture user input and move it to the message box.

Since you'll be using only one variable in the following task, it's slight overkill to explicitly declare just one variable; however, it's never too early to learn good programming practice.

## Task: Declaring variables

1. From the database window, click the Modules tab, and then the `modFirstPrograms` module, and finally the Design button.

2. Click the Procedures View button at the lower-left corner of the status bar. This lets you add new lines to the General part of the declarations section. Enter `Option Explicit` on the first empty line, if it's not there already, and `Dim Response As String` on the last line of the declarations section.

**Note**

> The line `Dim Response As String` can, and usually does, appear in a function or sub rather than in the general declarations section. The example declared it in general just to show it can be done.

Remember `Option Explicit` forces you to declare variables before using them. The line `Dim Response As String` declares there will be a variable with the name `Response` and it will be a string. See Table 17.1 for some other types of Visual Basic variables.

**Tip**

> You can have two basic views of the module window, depending on how you like to work. Choose between the two views by clicking the buttons Procedure View or Full Module View in the status bar. The screens in this exercise switch between these views to clarify the process of making the module.

**TABLE 17.1.** VISUAL BASIC VARIABLE TYPES.

| Type | Meaning |
| --- | --- |
| String | Alphanumeric and non-printing characters. Strings represent literally. The string 1234 represents the literal figures 1, 2, 3, and 4. The numeric 1234 represents the value 1,234 in the decimal system. |
| Long | Whole numbers from –2,147,483,648 to 2,147,483,647. |
| Integer | Whole numbers from –32,678 to 32,676. |
| Single | Single-precision floating-point data type. Uses less storage space than Double. |
| Currency | A high-precision data type optimized for monetary transactions. Use this data type for critical calculations, such as accrued interest. |
| Double | A general-purpose high-precision floating point. |
| User Defined | One you dream up. |
| Variant | The default Access data type used for undeclared data types. |

17

Of course, there are other types of Access objects. The subject's very wide in scope, but much of the discussion is an advanced topic beyond the scope of this book. Refer to Sams *Access 97 Unleashed* for complete coverage of this topic.

3. Pull down the Procedure combo box and click `DisplayMessage` to move to the procedure. If you're in Full Module View, you can just click the function. Enter the following on the second line of the procedure, below the `Function DisplayMessage()` line:

```
Response = InputBox$("Enter a Message",
➥"Input Box Demo", "I choose nothing")
```

Next, modify the third line like this:

```
MsgBox Response, vbInformation + vbOKCancel, "Progress in Access"
```

Your screen should now look like Figure 17.23.

**FIGURE 17.23.**

*Input box code added to the function.*

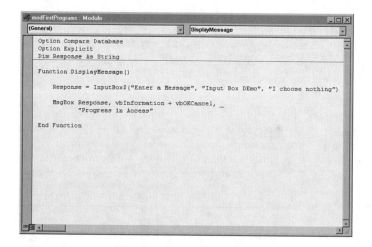

4. Close the module, saving the changes.

Open the `TempForm` form in Run mode, if it's not there already, and click the command button. Access displays the input box shown in Figure 17.24.

**FIGURE 17.24.**

*The input box springing into action at the click of a command button.*

▼ 5. Enter anything that comes to mind on the input line; the example uses
Programming is Easy After All! Click OK. Access runs the message box with
your line included (see Figure 17.25).

**FIGURE 17.25.**

*The message box with the input box's contents.*

▲

## How the **DisplayMessage()** Function Worked

Examine the second line of code in the DisplayMessage() function:

**ANALYSIS** Response = InputBox$("Enter a Message", "Input Box Demo", "I choose nothing")

**17**

The first word is Response, which is the variable you declared as a string type in this module's declarations section. This part of the line tells Access where to store what you enter in the input box. In this case, Access stores the string in a variable called Response.

The rest of the line just defines the input box. The first part, InputBox$, tells Access to use an input box. The $ part of the InputBox$ statement tells Access the input box will return a string type variable. Had this read InputBox, Access would have expected a variant type of variable. Using InputBox$ is another example of good programming practice, rather than dire necessity.

The next part, "Enter a Message", is the prompt for the input box. "Input Box Demo" is the title of the input box, and "I choose nothing" is the default value for the input box. If you didn't enter a string in the input box but just clicked OK, Access would have displayed I choose nothing in the message box. Click Cancel to close the input box.

Additionally, the InputBox$ parameters could have included x and y positions for the input box; these placement parameters are numbers representing how far in twips the coordinate position of the input box should be from the upper-left corner of the Access screen.

**NEW TERM** A *twip* is a real unit of measure in the computer world; it equals 1/1440 of an inch. There are about 575 twips in a centimeter. Another interesting unit of measure in the computer world is a *Mickey*, which measures mouse actions.

Close the form, saving any changes you've made. Return to the module, making it active, and close it, saving the changes.

# Summary

Access has been carefully designed so that no programming is necessary in most cases. However, it also includes both macros and Visual Basic. Most people find programming Access macros much easier than using Visual Basic because Access steps you through the macro process, but there are times you'll need to use Access's supplied Basic programming language.

Programming Access yields to the 80/20 rule, which means that 80 percent of what you need to do resides within 20 percent of the total Access information store. Mostly what you will need to do by using Visual Basic within your Access applications boils down to feeding information from your applications to Visual Basic for some manipulation.

The trick to using Visual Basic from within Access is to keep it small and simple. Make your code as modular as possible. Be sure to test all parts of it, using known data before trying to assemble all the parts into a huge whole. Keep in mind that one minute of testing is worth then minutes of debugging.

The first example showed how you can define a small algebraic calculation (a function) in Visual Basic. Using an Access form you can enter several numbers and then feed them in their proper place to that function and have Access return the results of the calculation on the form.

An important thing to remember when programming in Visual Basic is to use the `Option Explicit` statement in the declarations section of a module. This forces you to declare variables before using them. Using `Option Explicit` prevents you from inadvertently implicitly declaring variables by making the inevitable typo. One of the options in Access is to make `Option Explicit` the default for modules. Figure 17.26 shows the option in the Modules tab of the Options dialog box.

**FIGURE 17.26.**

*The check box to make Option Explicit the default.*

Another thing to remember is to annotate your code with comments. You define a comment by starting a Basic statement with the REM (short for "remark") keyword or the single quote (preferred). The examples in this chapter were too simple to require many comments, but if your procedures or declarations grow to more than ten lines or so, or if you feel your programming logic isn't obvious, make sure to use a liberal number of remarks.

These examples created a new function, DisplayMessage(), for use anywhere in the BookStore database. It's a simple function, but it also demonstrates the fundamentals of Visual Basic programming.

# Q&A

**Q Can I use a Visual Basic function in a macro?**

**A** Yes. Use the RunCode macro action and specify the function you want to run, along with any parameters the function needs.

**Q I've heard Basic is a bad language to use because it's so full of GoTo branches. How true is this? Should I avoid GoTos when I program?**

**A** This is a preposterous charge against Basic. Sure, some people misuse GoTo statements to create spaghetti-like code that's quite difficult to follow, much less maintain, but all programming languages need to have some branching. It's not the use of branching routines, but the misuse of them that's the problem. There are just as many bad practices committed when using other languages, such as Fortran or C, as there are in Basic.

It's true that Basic is a bit freer, though, and will let you go much further astray than "tight" languages, such as Pascal or Modula. As with any kind of freedom, the freedom Basic allows you must be practiced with responsibility.

As soon as you start doing high-power Visual Basic programming, you'll need some branching, and there's no reason to avoid the GoTo statements. The first thing to keep in mind when creating these structures is to annotate in a remark where the jump goes, why it jumps, and where it will jump back to. The second thing is to clearly label where you're jumping to. The following statement, for example, isn't terribly clear:

```
Goto A
```

This one, however, is much better:

```
Goto DoSortRoutine
```

The third thing to remember is to avoid jumping to another jump. The following is just about impossible to understand after it's written:

```
Goto Animate
...
Animate:
Goto SectionEight
....
SectionEight:
Goto DoItNow
DoItNow:
```

The fourth rule is to jump to labels, which are descriptive words followed by a colon, rather than line numbers. Jumping to line numbers is a practice particularly fraught with danger.

Finally, use GoTos only when you can't use more structured statements, like these:

```
If...Then...Else; For...Next; Select Case; or Do...Loop
```

**Q Is there some way to use Visual Basic to put pictures on command buttons?**

**A** You can do this, but you don't need Visual Basic. With the button highlighted in Design View, open the Properties list box for the tool and find the Picture property. Just enter the full path for the bitmap you want to include on the button on this line. For example, if you wanted to place the picture c:\windows\skylight.bmp in the button shown in TempForm, enter c:\windows\skylight.bmp on the line to the right of the Picture property. Make sure to include the entire path for your bitmapped picture when trying this trick. You also can click the ellipsis button and browse for the picture.

**Q What's the button limit for a toolbar?**

**A** You can place as many buttons as you have room for. Don't overdo it, though, because too many buttons make it difficult to find any.

# Workshop

Here's where you can test and apply the lessons you learned today.

## Quiz

1. Say you have the following statement in the declarations section of an Visual Basic module:

   Dim I as String

   You also have this statement in a procedure:

   Dim Interest As Double

   Will Interest be a string or a double-precision floating-point type when used in the procedure?

2. If you want to execute a loop ten times, should you use a macro or a module?

3. How would you use Visual Basic to create a custom menu on a form?

4. When would you use the Currency data type in Visual Basic? What's the disadvantage of using this data type?

5. How do you create a comment in Visual Basic code?

## Exercises

1. Start a new module.

2. Declare two String and one Integer data types. The two strings will be a title and a message in a message box; the integer will be the message box type.

3. Create a new function, Chapter17() with three input box lines to give the user an opportunity to enter a message box title, message box message, and message box type.

4. Add a message box function to the user-defined function that will display a message box, using the criteria from the input boxes.

5. Add placement parameters for each of the input boxes. Search Online Help for the exact syntax to do this. Close the module, saving it as ProgrammingExercise.

6. Open TempForm in Design View.

7. Attach your custom function to the On Click property of the command button.

8. Test the function by switching to Form View and clicking the button.

9. Close the form and module. You can discard the changes, if you like, since neither the module nor the function is part of the sample data.

17

# WEEK 3

# DAY 18

# Advanced Programming with Data Access Objects and ActiveX Controls

Today's lesson covers the following topics:

- Using ActiveX controls
- Registering ActiveX controls
- Using OLE to link or embed Office documents
- Inserting ActiveX controls
- Older controls and performance considerations
- Programming with database objects
- The DAO hierarchy
- Programming with DAO

This chapter also contains a helpful list of methods and properties for your information both for this day's tasks and for future reference.

# Using ActiveX Controls

The two easiest ways to program in Access 97 both avoid programming. No, that statement is neither an oxymoron nor a paradox. It's the plain truth. You've seen one way to program in Access 97 without actual "programming" by using wizards. The trend in all programming environments, from Access 97 to C++, is to have wizards or pre-built objects remove the laborious and repetitive grunt work from coding. Many professional programmers protest that they use neither, but don't believe them. Even if that's true, why should you bother reinventing everything?

Access 2 was the first commercial application capable of using the new OLE custom controls. They were a new specification that, from a user standpoint, were a superset over the original VBX standards.

---

**A COMPUTER LEGEND**

**NEW TERM**   The *VBX control* (now evolved to the *ActiveX control* specification), which lets a user add functions to a program with little or no programming, arrived with Visual Basic—the program. VBX is what made Visual Basic the success it has become. Other similar programs, such as those from Borland, preceded or came at the same time as Visual Basic, but they lacked VBXs. The VBX specification launched a huge industry and assured Visual Basic's market leadership where it remains today.

Legend has it that the programmers at Microsoft didn't intend to include VBX support in Visual Basic, but that it was included at the insistence of Bill Gates himself.

---

**NEW TERM**   ActiveX and the older OLE controls are known collectively as *OCXs*—from their traditional file extension. After the release of Access 2, Microsoft widened the specification for OCXs, which made Access 2 somewhat out of date in this area. Access 97 goes a long way in playing catch-up. Today Microsoft has renamed controls with the OCX extension from OLE controls to ActiveX controls.

The change of label reflects an expansion of purpose. Once OLE controls were only 32-bit extensions of the older VBX controls, aimed at programming ease and the eventual emergence of an object-oriented operating system. The idea of object-orientation is to build component-based applications that allow you to buy OLE or OCX controls to extend the basic core functionality of the applications. Today, with the expansion of the Internet, Microsoft has extended OLE controls to include the capability to plug these controls into Internet objects—usually Web pages.

# Registering ActiveX Controls

Before you use ActiveX controls in Access 97 or any other application, you need to register them in your Windows registry. You can do this several ways:

1. Use a custom REG script.
2. Run the vendor's setup program, which not only copies the ActiveX control to your system, but also registers it, making it ready for use.
3. Manually register the control by editing the registry.
4. Manually register the control by telling Access to do the work.

Of these, only options 2 and 4 are realistic from a standpoint of spending your time profitably. Figure 18.1 shows a complex REG script. Writing this or manually editing the registry to include these values is obviously a tedious task you want to avoid.

**FIGURE 18.1.**

*A complex REG file, a script for updating or adding to a Windows registry.*

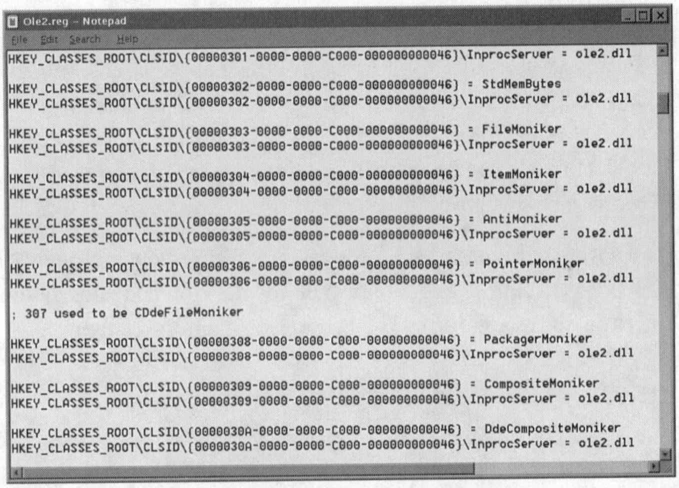

```
Ole2.reg - Notepad
File  Edit  Search  Help

HKEY_CLASSES_ROOT\CLSID\{00000301-0000-0000-C000-000000000046}\InprocServer = ole2.dll

HKEY_CLASSES_ROOT\CLSID\{00000302-0000-0000-C000-000000000046} = StdMemBytes
HKEY_CLASSES_ROOT\CLSID\{00000302-0000-0000-C000-000000000046}\InprocServer = ole2.dll

HKEY_CLASSES_ROOT\CLSID\{00000303-0000-0000-C000-000000000046} = FileMoniker
HKEY_CLASSES_ROOT\CLSID\{00000303-0000-0000-C000-000000000046}\InprocServer = ole2.dll

HKEY_CLASSES_ROOT\CLSID\{00000304-0000-0000-C000-000000000046} = ItemMoniker
HKEY_CLASSES_ROOT\CLSID\{00000304-0000-0000-C000-000000000046}\InprocServer = ole2.dll

HKEY_CLASSES_ROOT\CLSID\{00000305-0000-0000-C000-000000000046} = AntiMoniker
HKEY_CLASSES_ROOT\CLSID\{00000305-0000-0000-C000-000000000046}\InprocServer = ole2.dll

HKEY_CLASSES_ROOT\CLSID\{00000306-0000-0000-C000-000000000046} = PointerMoniker
HKEY_CLASSES_ROOT\CLSID\{00000306-0000-0000-C000-000000000046}\InprocServer = ole2.dll

; 307 used to be CDdeFileMoniker

HKEY_CLASSES_ROOT\CLSID\{00000308-0000-0000-C000-000000000046} = PackagerMoniker
HKEY_CLASSES_ROOT\CLSID\{00000308-0000-0000-C000-000000000046}\InprocServer = ole2.dll

HKEY_CLASSES_ROOT\CLSID\{00000309-0000-0000-C000-000000000046} = CompositeMoniker
HKEY_CLASSES_ROOT\CLSID\{00000309-0000-0000-C000-000000000046}\InprocServer = ole2.dll

HKEY_CLASSES_ROOT\CLSID\{0000030A-0000-0000-C000-000000000046} = DdeCompositeMoniker
HKEY_CLASSES_ROOT\CLSID\{0000030A-0000-0000-C000-000000000046}\InprocServer = ole2.dll
```

18

Any ActiveX controls you buy should come with a setup program. At the very least, there should be a REG file already created. If you see the setup program, just run setup.exe and the setup program will register the controls for you. If you have the REG file, just double-click the REG file from Explorer and let Windows do all the work for you.

From time to time, Windows might lose its registry entries for an ActiveX control. This will surely happen if you reinstall Windows clean, or if you make an error editing the registry. In these cases, you'll have to re-register your ActiveX controls to get them to work again. You can do this by running Setup for the controls, double-clicking the REG files for the controls if they exist, or using Access's built-in registration routine.

To see Access's routine, choose Tools|ActiveX Controls from the menu. Your screen
should look like Figure 18.2. Click the control you want to register, and then click the
Register button.

**FIGURE 18.2.**

*Asking Access to regis-
ter your ActiveX con-
trols.*

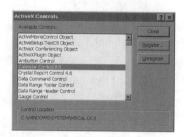

# Using OLE to Link or Embed Office Documents

You can combine different Microsoft Office applications in many ways. How you choose
to do so depends on the results you need and the method you prefer. Day 21, "Integrating
Access with the Web," covers how to publish some Access objects to HTML documents.
Such documents can be opened in Microsoft Office applications or by using a Web
browser, such as Internet Explorer.

Take a look at Figures 18.3 through 18.5. They show a sequence in which a document in
Word 97 gets converted to a scrap on the desktop and subsequently to an embedded
object on an Access form. The captions explain the sequence.

**FIGURE 18.3.**

*To create a scrap,
highlight a file or part
of a file, and then drag
it to the desktop.*

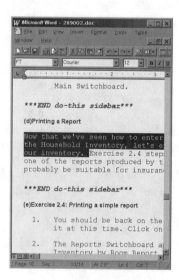

**FIGURE 18.4.**

*Dragging the scrap from the desktop to the Access form embeds it there.*

**FIGURE 18.5.**

*Dropping the scrap on the form places it there.*

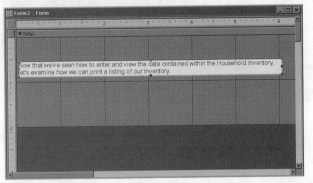

**18**

The finished embedded object shown in Figure 18.5 can be edited in Word by double-clicking the object in Design View.

Office 97 actually makes the entire process even easier than that shown in the preceding sequence. There's a standard menu entry for using other Office applications from within Access 97.

Say you want to do some numeric analysis on a table or query in Access 97 that's beyond the functions built into Access 97. Any business chore you need to do is probably within Excel 97's abilities, so wouldn't it be nice to be able to call on that when you need to? As you're probably guessing, you can.

Figure 18.6 is the `OrderDetails` table from the `NorthWind` sample database. To use Excel's analytic tools, follow Figures 18.6 through 18.8. The captions explain the sequence.

**FIGURE 18.6.**

*A table with a lot of numeric data can present analysis difficulties for Access's built-in functions.*

| Order ID | Product | Unit Price | Quantity | Discount |
|----------|---------|-----------|----------|----------|
| 10248 | Queso Cabrales | $14.00 | 12 | 0% |
| 10248 | Singaporean Hokkien Fried Mee | $9.80 | 10 | 0% |
| 10248 | Mozzarella di Giovanni | $34.80 | 5 | 0% |
| 10249 | Tofu | $18.60 | 9 | 0% |
| 10249 | Manjimup Dried Apples | $42.40 | 40 | 0% |
| 10250 | Jack's New England Clam Chowder | $7.70 | 10 | 0% |
| 10250 | Manjimup Dried Apples | $42.40 | 35 | 15% |
| 10250 | Louisiana Fiery Hot Pepper Sauce | $16.80 | 15 | 15% |
| 10251 | Gustaf's Knäckebröd | $16.80 | 6 | 5% |
| 10251 | Ravioli Angelo | $15.60 | 15 | 5% |
| 10251 | Louisiana Fiery Hot Pepper Sauce | $16.80 | 20 | 5% |
| 10252 | Sir Rodney's Marmalade | $64.80 | 40 | 5% |
| 10252 | Geitost | $2.00 | 25 | 5% |
| 10252 | Camembert Pierrot | $27.20 | 40 | 0% |
| 10253 | Gorgonzola Telino | $10.00 | 20 | 0% |
| 10253 | Chartreuse verte | $14.40 | 42 | 0% |
| 10253 | Maxilaku | $18.00 | 40 | 0% |
| 10254 | Guaraná Fantástica | $3.60 | 15 | 15% |
| 10254 | Pâté chinois | $19.20 | 21 | 15% |
| 10254 | Longlife Tofu | $8.00 | 21 | 0% |
| 10255 | Chang | $15.20 | 20 | 0% |
| 10255 | Pavlova | $13.90 | 35 | 0% |
| 10255 | Inlagd Sill | $15.20 | 25 | 0% |
| 10255 | Raclette Courdavault | $44.00 | 30 | 0% |
| 10256 | Perth Pasties | $26.20 | 15 | 0% |
| 10256 | Original Frankfurter grüne Soße | $10.40 | 12 | 0% |
| 10257 | Schoggi Schokolade | $35.10 | 25 | 0% |
| 10257 | Chartreuse verte | $14.40 | 6 | 0% |
| 10257 | Original Frankfurter grüne Soße | $10.40 | 15 | 0% |
| 10258 | Chang | $15.20 | 50 | 20% |
| 10258 | Chef Anton's Gumbo Mix | $17.00 | 65 | 20% |
| 10258 | Mascarpone Fabioli | $25.60 | 6 | 20% |
| 10259 | Sir Rodney's Scones | $8.00 | 10 | 0% |
| 10259 | Graved lax | $20.80 | 1 | 0% |
| 10260 | Jack's New England Clam Chowder | $7.70 | 16 | 25% |
| 10260 | Ravioli Angelo | $15.60 | 50 | 0% |
| 10260 | Tarte au sucre | $39.40 | 15 | 25% |
| 10260 | Outback Lager | $12.00 | 21 | 25% |

Record: 1 of 2155

**FIGURE 18.7.**

*The Tools | Office Links menu selection brings up a set of choices, depending on which Office components you have installed.*

Duplicating a table or query into Excel, then, is as simple as making a menu choice. In a similar way, Excel lacks Access's management tools, so it can use Access's facilities with similar menu choices. For example, the Data menu in Excel 97 has the View MS Access Form entry that lets you use a previously created Access form to enter data into Excel.

## Live Links

You can also link a live Excel workbook (or any other OLE-enabled application) to an Access 97 object. Figures 18.9 through 18.12 show one of several sequences to create a live OLE link to another application—again, Excel 97. This example could have used any fully OLE-enabled application, however.

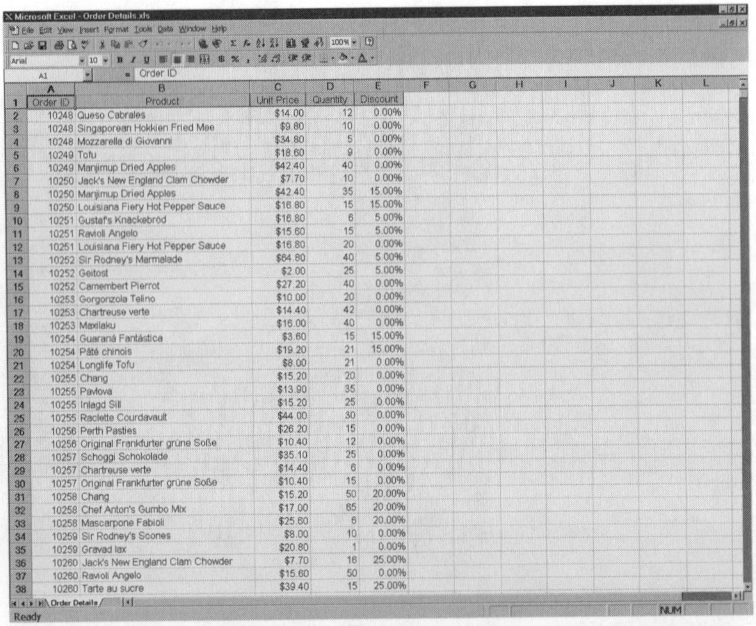

**FIGURE 18.8.**

*Clicking Excel launches Excel and creates a worksheet with the table or query's name; it also creates the file on disk.*

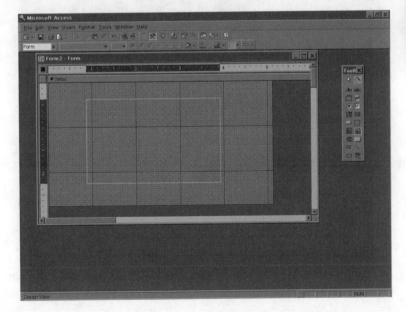

**FIGURE 18.9.**

*Add a Bound Object Frame object to a form for a place to insert the OLE object.*

18

**FIGURE 18.10.**

*Switch to Form View and choose Insert\Object from the menu.*

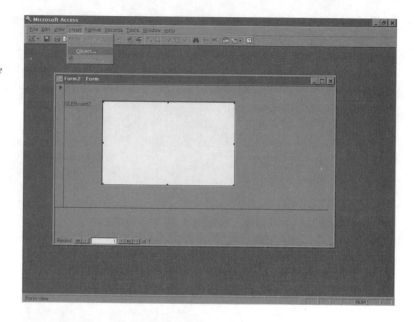

**FIGURE 18.11.**

*The Insert Object dialog.*

This brings up a dialog where you can choose which type of OLE object (from all those registered) to insert and determine whether it exists on file or if you want to create a new one. This demonstration uses an Excel Worksheet and the New option.

You can use this worksheet in a form, just as you would any other worksheet. When this new control has the focus, your menu and toolbars change to reflect that you're working within Excel. Contrast Figure 18.12 with 18.9. Figure 18.12 has a new control inserted in the form to show how the menu and toolbars differ depending on which control, the Access 97 native one or the one linked to Excel, has the focus.

**FIGURE 18.12.**

*Clicking OK returns to Form View with the new worksheet as part of the form.*

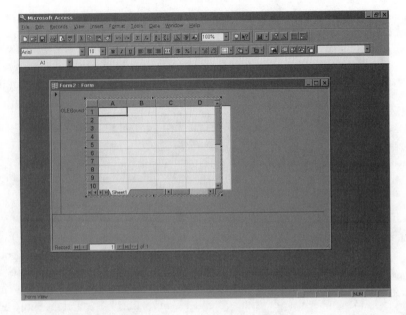

## More You Can Do with OLE Links

18

The few examples in this chapter just barely scratch the surface of the many ways you can use OLE to create compound documents within Microsoft Office or with any other OLE-enabled application.

Consider these options and their related applications

- Create a literary database that can pull lines of poems from Word documents to demonstrate the style of different poets. To do this, you would need to link Word documents containing your collection of poems to your Access 97 database.

- Create a car collectors' database that contains pictures of classic automobiles. To do this, you would need to link a bitmap image from Paintbrush or some other OLE-enabled graphics application to your Access 97 database.

- Create a stock analysis database that contains spreadsheets illustrating the particular stocks' growth or decline. To do this, you should link your stock spreadsheets from Excel to your Access 97 database.

- Create an insurance database that contains photographs of all the valuables that are located in your home. To do this, you should link bitmap images of those valuables to your Access 97 database by using Paintbrush or some other OLE-enabled graphics application to your Access 97 database.

# Inserting ActiveX Controls

ActiveX controls or OCXs are special dynamic linked library (DLL) applications you can include in your Access 97 applications. Take a look at Figure 18.13. How long do you think it took the programmer to include the calendar as part of the form?

FIGURE 18.13.

*Including a calendar in a form by using an ActiveX control.*

The answer, if you haven't guessed it, is about 10 seconds. What you see in Figure 18.13 is an ActiveX control from Microsoft called the Calendar Control 8, part of Access 97. If you don't have this control in your ActiveX list, run Setup again to choose Add-Remove Components. Select the Calendar Control check box and let Setup do the rest.

Not only does this custom control display a calendar, form fields (controls) can respond to the dates on the control. You can, for example, set dates on your form by clicking calendar dates. Obviously, trying to do this by programming Access 97 manually would be a chore.

All ActiveX controls have properties, methods, and events, just like any other control. Naturally, they vary depending on the control's purpose. Because of the specialized nature of ActiveX controls, you'll often find properties very different from those you'd expect to see applying to the standard controls in the Access toolbox.

Figure 18.14 shows the addition of two command buttons that scroll through the months on the form shown in Figure 18.13. Figure 18.15 shows the Visual Basic code behind the `On Click` event for the Next Month> command button.

FIGURE 18.14.

*Adding command buttons that let users scroll through the months.*

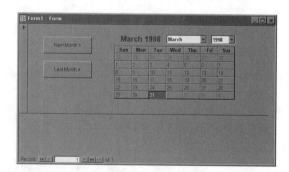

**FIGURE 18.15.**

*One line of code is all it takes to control the calendar in the form.*

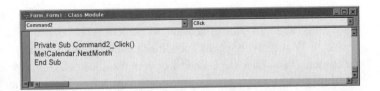

```
Form_Form1 : Class Module
Command2                              Click

    Private Sub Command2_Click()
    Me!Calendar.NextMonth
    End Sub
```

To learn about the methods, events, and properties of ActiveX controls, open their help files.

 **Tip**

Each ActiveX control comes with its own help file. Access 97 itself has no specific information on the methods, properties, or events for a particular ActiveX control. Even though Access uses illustrations of its Calendar control for its generic discussion of ActiveX controls, you won't find specific tips for the control in the general help file. Seek help either from the vendor's manuals or from the supplied online help file. In the case of the Calendar control, the control's name is MSCAL.OCX and the help file is MSCAL.HLP. Double-clicking the help file from Explorer brings up the help file.

You can find several useful ActiveX controls to get you started at the following URLs:

> http://www.microsoft.com/workshop/prog/controls/ctrlref-f.htm
>
> http://www.activeX.com
>
> http://www.activex.partbank.com/
>
> http://www.devx.com/home/devxhome.asp
>
> http://www.activex.org/

18

## ActiveX Properties

Using custom controls is similar to using the controls that come with Access 97 (such as text boxes). You add the controls, set properties either in Design View or during runtime (or both), and optionally program them to handle events.

 **Tip**

If you are interested in the version and copyright information for an ActiveX control you have installed into your application, right-click the control and then click Properties in the pop-up menu. Click the Other tab and select the About Property box. Then click the Build button to access the version and copyright information for the control.

Many custom controls have extra property sheets that add to their flexibility and complexity. Figure 18.16 shows the standard properties list box for the Calendar control, and Figure 18.17 shows the special Properties dialog for this control. Note the similarity of the entries. If you have the Calendar control installed on a form, you can see the dialog in Figure 18.17 by right-clicking the control in Design View, and then choosing Calendar Object|Properties from the menu.

**FIGURE 18.16.**

*The standard properties list box for the Calendar control.*

**FIGURE 18.17.**

*The custom Properties dialog from the right-click menu of the control itself.*

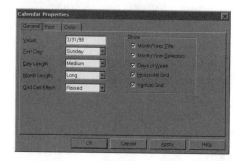

Changing properties in either property box will affect both. You can change these properties, such as the date displayed, by using Visual Basic or, in some cases, macros.

Follow the steps in the following task to add an ActiveX control to a form in your application. For this exercise you will go through the steps of adding the Calendar control to a simple form created especially for this purpose.

### Task: Adding an ActiveX control to a form

**▼ TASK**

1. Create a new form and open it up in Design View.

2. Ensure that the toolbox is visible and click the More Controls tool that appears in the bottom-right corner of the toolbox.

3. Click the Calendar Control version 8.0 that appears on the list and then click and drag to an area on your open form. This will create an instance of the Calendar control on your form.

4. Click the resizing handles and resize the Calendar control to fit your form.

5. Once you have inserted and sized your form, right-click the Calendar control and click Properties in the pop-up box that appears. Set any properties that you need as shown in the previous section. If you need help for any property, select the property in the property sheet and press the F1 key.

6. You have now installed the Calendar control on your form. Close the form and save it when prompted. You can open the form later in design mode to customize the look and functionality of the Calendar form.

▲

# Older Controls and Performance Considerations

**18**

For the past several years, the specification for custom controls has been a moving target. Microsoft itself hasn't fully standardized a universal container for its applications. Vendors have, therefore, had to choose between universality of use and feature sets when making their controls. Often, in the past, they've settled on features, which has left many controls useless or only partly useful under Access.

There are three ways you can determine whether a control works under Access 97:

- Check the properties of the control for the vendor's name and ask the vendor via email or phone if the control works under Access 97, and hope that the vendor will give you an honest reply.
- View the ReadMe file that ships with Access 97.
- Test the controls yourself.

The good news is that most controls made to the OCX or ActiveX specification work at least partly in Access 97. The part that works is usually the most important, and the part that doesn't usually won't adversely affect the whole. More good news is that the controls that work poorly are generally those related to data control, which is inherent in Access 97 so it's redundant in any potential control. Most of the new controls you'll want to use work just fine.

There's a downside to including ActiveX controls in your applications. They slow down your application and increase its overhead. The amount of parasitic drag from an ActiveX control is greater than if you hand-coded stuff like the calendar form in Visual Basic, but the trade-off is slight performance degradation for greater ease in programming.

The key to deciding whether to use an ActiveX control is your target market. If you have a strong user base, one with 16 megabytes of RAM assured in the typical machine, it's safe to use an ActiveX control. If your target market user base is slight, watch out. You might push the performance mark down past what's tolerable—only you can decide.

# Programming with Database Objects

NEW TERM    *Data Access Objects* (DAO) is a programming interface that allows you to use Visual Basic to manipulate the objects and data in your database. You can manipulate tables and queries, the objects that represent the data stored in your database, and the objects that represent the structure of your database; you can even secure your database using DAO.

DAO allows you to set your database environment to enable access to data through the Microsoft Jet Database Engine or by using ODBCDirect. The Microsoft Jet Database Engine can use databases that were created with the Microsoft Jet Database Engine, ODBC databases, or ISAM databases. The file that the Microsoft Jet Database Engine typically creates ends in the .mdb extension. ODBCDirect bypasses the Microsoft Jet Database Engine and uses the Open Database Connectivity (ODBC) protocol to attach to external databases. Using ODBCDirect you can access Microsoft SQL Server among other database servers.

NEW TERM    A database environment is also known as a *workspace* in Access 97. The Microsoft Jet Database Engine is a component that can be used to retrieve and store data in a database. The Microsoft Jet Database Engine can be said to "manage" the data in your database. Access 97 is built on top of the Microsoft Jet Database Engine.

The DAO code that is included with Access 97 is made up of objects, methods, and properties that use the Microsoft DAO 3.5 object library. This code is compatible with previous versions of DAO code, but some of the older objects, methods, and properties might not be supported. If you are going to use an ActiveX control that uses an older version of the DAO library, you need to set a reference to the Microsoft DAO 2.5/3.5 compatibility library. This library is automatically referenced if you convert an Access 1.x, 2.0, or 7.0 application to an Access 97 application. It is a good idea to make sure that your application only uses the Microsoft DAO 3.5 object library. This way you don't have to distribute the additional Microsoft DAO 2.5/3.5 compatibility library when you distribute your Access 97 application.

> **Tip**
>
> One way to ensure that your Access 97 application only uses the Microsoft DAO 3.5 object library is to clear the check box beside the Microsoft DAO 2.5/3.5 compatibility library that is in the References dialog and then recompile your application. If your application compiles without any errors, you can safely assume that you have no need to include the Microsoft DAO 2.5/3.5 compatibility library with your application's distribution.

# Programming with DAO

The Microsoft Jet Database Engine version 3.5 is the heart and soul of Access 97. The Jet Database Engine is the engine that does the database management work of your Access 97 application. The Jet Database Engine handles all elements of your application that relate to database access. This includes such tasks as reading from your database, writing to your database and database security, and transaction management. The Jet Database Engine can even use drivers to access data stored in external databases.

The Data Access Objects (DAO) interface allows you to control the Microsoft Jet Database Engine programmatically through the use of Visual Basic code. DAO manifests itself as a set of objects that represent components of your database and that can be used to work with the data in your database application. These objects are arranged in a hierarchy of objects. This hierarchy and the objects contained within it are described in detail in the next section. You can refer to that listing as you go through the following exercises or at any time you need this information in the future. For now, though, let's get some practice with how you'll use this information.

## Introducing Object-Oriented Programming

Object-oriented programming (OOP) is a very complicated subject that can and does fill several books by itself. This section presents a very brief overview of some OOP concepts that you will use if you use DAO to programmatically control your Access 97 application.

Using OOP, you tackle the tasks in your application by working with objects that represent portions of those tasks. Each object has properties that describe it, and methods you can use with that object. For a simple example, if you were describing a bike in OOP terms, you could say that the material the bike was constructed of was a property of the box and that riding the bike was a method of using the bike to perform work. Translating this concept into your database application, if you are describing the Database object that represents your open database, you could say that the Updatable property is a property of the database that describes whether the database is updatable, and that the Execute method is a way of using your database with a query.

Objects in your Access 97 database can represent either data elements or data types among other things.

## Accessing the Current Database

Follow the steps in the next task to access a database that is currently open in your application.

### Task: Getting a handle on the current database

This task demonstrates how to programmatically access the currently opened database.

1. Open the Northwind sample database that comes with Access.

2. Click the modules tab in the Database Window.

3. Click the New button and enter the following code into module window.

```
Sub CurrDB()
    Dim dbs As Database
    ' Return a variable pointing to the current database.
    Set dbs = CurrentDb
End Sub
```

4. Save the module as CurrDB.

5. You have now written a code sample that will access a database you have currently open.

## Opening a Recordset

The following task will walk you through a recordset's results.

### Task: Iterating through a recordset's results

This exercise will demonstrate how to create a recordset and iterate through that recordset.

1. Open the Northwind sample database that comes with Access.

2. Click the Modules tab in the Database Window.

3. Select the CurrDB module you created in the last task and click the Design button to open it in Design View.

4. Cut and paste the following code into the CurrDB module right before the line that says End Sub.

```
Dim rec As Recordset
    ' Create a recordset
    Set rec = dbs.OpenRecordset("SELECT * FROM Customers")
```

```
' Iterate through the specified Recordset object.
    Do While Not rec.EOF
        Debug.Print , rec.Fields(0), rec.Fields(1)
        rec.MoveNext
    Loop
rec.Close
```

5.  Your module should now look like the module shown in Figure 18.18. You have now created a code sample that will allow you to access a recordset.

**FIGURE 18.18.**

*Using DAO code to iterate through a recordset.*

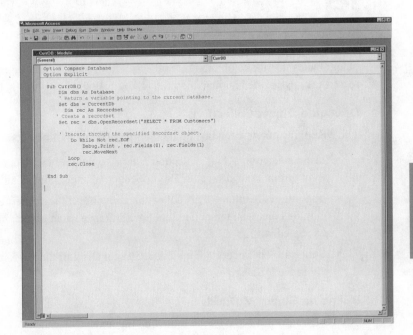

# Objects and Methods Reference

Use the following lists of objects, properties, and methods to increase your knowledge of the possibilities you have for programming with objects in Access. You might find some of these more helpful than others, but, more importantly, you can find here what you might not be able to find in the Access documentation.

## The DAO Hierarchy

DAO objects, along with their collections, form a hierarchical model of your database you can use within your Access 97 applications to control the components of your database programmatically. All DAO objects are derived from the top-level object that is the DBEngine object.

Except for the DBEngine object, all DAO object types also have a collection that includes all the objects that exist of that type. Each of these collections is part of an object on the level immediately above the collection. For example, if you are utilizing three recordsets as part of your Access application, those recordset objects are part of a recordset collection that is part of a database object on next higher level.

## DBEngine

NEW TERM    The *DBEngine object* is the top level object in the DAO hiearchical model of your database. The DBEngine object represents the Microsoft Jet Database Engine on which your Access 97 application is built. You cannot create additional DBEngine objects within your application because the DBEngine object contains all the other objects that make up the DAO objects within your Access 97 application. For this reason the DBEngine is not an element of any collection.

### DBEngine Object Collections

The DBEngine object contains the following collections of objects:

- Errors collection—This collection is used to hold all the data access errors that occur within your database. This collection also contains details about those errors.

- Properties collection—This collection contains all the properties that are associated with the objects in the collection. Each instance of an object has separate properties associated with it.

- Workspaces collection—This collection contains all the workspaces that are active within the DBEngine.

### DBEngine Object Methods

The DBEngine object allows the following methods:

- BeginTrans    This method is used when controlling transactions within the default workspace. Beginning a transaction sets a marker that the DBEngine can use to rollback an uncommitted transaction.

- CommitTrans    This method is also used to control transactions within the default workspace. Committing a transaction allows it to be written to the database.

- CompactDatabase    This method allows you to compact a database and can only be used with the Microsoft Jet Database Engine.

- CreateDatabase    This method can be used to create a new database, this method can only be used with the Microsoft Jet Database Engine.

- CreateWorkspace    This method is used to create a new workspace.

- `Idle` When you use this method, you allow the Microsoft Jet Database Engine to complete running any tasks that are pending. This method can, of course, only be used with the Microsoft Jet Database Engine.

- `OpenConnection` This method is used to open a connection to an ODBC database within the default workspace. This connection can only be used within an ODBCDirect workspace.

- `OpenDatabase` This method is used to open a database within the default workspace.

- `RegisterDatabase` This method is used to provide ODBC information to the database engine.

- `RepairDatabase` This method allows you to repair a database and can only be used with the Microsoft Jet Database Engine.

- `Rollback` This method is used to control transactions within the default workspace. A transaction that is rolled-back is not written to the database.

- `SetOption` This method allows you to manually override Windows Registry settings for the Microsoft Jet Database Engine.

## DBEngine Object Properties

The DBEngine object has the following properties:

- `DefaultPassword` This property is used to set the password that will be used within the default workspace of your database.

- `DefaultType` You can use this property to set the default type of workspace that will be opened in your database. The workspace can be either an ODBCDirect or Microsoft Jet Database Engine workspace. This property will not take effect until the next workspace is opened within your database.

- `DefaultUser` This property is used to set the default user of the default workspace of your application.

- `IniPath` This property can be used to indicate the location of the Windows Registry information for the Microsoft Jet Database Engine.

- `LoginTimeout` This property can be either used to retrieve or set the ODBC login timeout property of the database. The ODBC login timeout is the number of seconds that elapse before a connection attempt to an ODBC database errors out.

- `SystemDB` This property is used to indicate the location of the workgroup information file that is used by the Microsoft Jet Database Engine.

- `Version` This property can be used to retrieve the DAO version number.

18

### DBEngine Object Syntax

If you are going to refer to a collection that resides within the DBEngine object, you should use the following syntax. This syntax is also used to refer to methods or properties that pertain to the current DBEngine object.

```
[DBEngine.][collection ¦ method ¦ property]
```

## Workspace Objects

When your Access 97 application is opened by a user, the way that user is able to interact with the data stored in your application is controlled by the workspace. The workspace defines the session that your user is working in and defines whether your user is accessing data by means of the Microsoft Jet Database Engine or ODBCDirect. Within each workspace your user can open multiple databases or maintain connections to multiple databases. Each workspace is linked to a user ID and password. This user ID and password define the permissions that are granted to the user of your application. Every time that a workspace is used for the first time, a default workspace is created. If security is enabled on your Access 97 application, the workspace is opened under the name of the user who logged on to your application. If security is not enabled, the workspace is opened with the "Admin" user ID.

You use the Workspace object to manage the current session of your application or to start a new session or sessions. A session is defined by the period that a user is logged on to the application. All database operations that occur during that session are checked for the proper permissions with the user ID and password of the logged on user.

### Workspace Object Collections

The Workspace object contains the following collections:

- Connections collection—This collection contains all the active connection objects that are contained within the workspace. This collection applies to ODBCDirect workspaces only.

- Databases collection—This collection contains all the active database objects that are contained within the workspace.

- Groups collection—This collection is used to establish group permissions to objects that are contained within the workspace. This collection is only available when using a Microsoft Jet Database.

- Properties collection—This collection contains all the properties that are associated with the objects in the collection. Each instance of an object has separate properties associated with it.

- Users collection—This collection is used to establish user permissions to objects that are contained within the workspace. This collection is only available when using a Microsoft Jet Database.

## Workspace Object Methods

The Workspace object allows the following methods:

- `BeginTrans`   This method is used when controlling transactions within the default workspace. Beginning a transaction sets a marker that the DBEngine can use to rollback an uncommitted transaction.
- `Close`   This method is used to terminate a session.
- `CommitTrans`   This method is also used to control transactions within the default workspace. Committing a transaction allows it to be written to the database.
- `CreateDatabase`   This method can be used to create a new database, this method can only be used with the Microsoft Jet Database Engine.
- `CreateGroup`   This method can be used to create a new group. This method can only be used within a Microsoft Jet Database Engine workspace.
- `CreateUser`   This method is used to create a new user. This method can also only be used within a Microsoft Jet Database Engine workspace.
- `OpenConnection`   This method is used to open a connection to an ODBC database. This connection can only be used within an ODBCDirect workspace.
- `OpenDatabase`   This method is used to open a database within the workspace.
- `Rollback`   This method is used to control transactions within the default workspace. A transaction that is rolled back is not written to the database.

## Workspace Object Properties

The Workspace object has the following properties:

- `DefaultCursorDriver`   This property is used to set or retrieve the type of cursor driver that is used within the workspace. This property is only used with an ODBCDirect workspace.
- `IsolateODBCTrans`   This property is used to isolate multiple transactions that run against the same ODBC database. This database must be connected using the Microsoft Jet Database Engine.
- `LoginTimeout`   This property can be either used to retrieve or set the ODBC login timeout property of the database. The ODBC login timeout is the number of seconds that elapse before a connection attempt to an ODBC database errors out.

**18**

- Name   This property is used to either retrieve or set a session name.
- Type   This property is used to either retrieve or set a session type.
- UserName   This property is used to either retrieve or set the owner of the workspace.

### Workspace as a Collection under DBEngine

The Workspace objects are the first objects in the DAO hierarchy of objects that reside within a collection. Since the DBEngine object is the parent object of the Workspace object, this collection is contained within the DBEngine object. The Workspaces collection contains all active Workspace objects that are not hidden.

The Workspace collection allows the following methods:

- Append   This method is used to add a new Workspace object to the Workspace collection.
- Delete   This method is used to delete a Workspace object from the Workspace collection.
- Refresh   This method is used to update the Workspace collection to reflect the current Workspace objects that are contained within the collection.

The Workspace collection has the following property:

- Count   This property is used to return the number of Workspace objects that are contained within the Workspace collection.

As with many of the objects that are contained in the DAO hierarchy, you can refer to a Workspace object that is stored in a Workspace collection in one of three ways. Either by its number or its name combined with one of the following syntax forms.

```
DBEngine.Workspaces(0)
DBEngine.Workspaces("workspacename")
DBEngine.Workspaces![workspacename]
```

## Database Objects

The Database object is used to represent an open database within the workspace. You can use the Database object and its methods and properties to accomplish various tasks within an open database. When you close a Database object, any open Recordset objects that are part of that Database object are also closed. Any pending transactions are rolled back and any pending updates to the Database object are lost.

> **Tip**
>
> To make sure that no data edits are lost when closing a Database object or when using a procedure that declares a Database object locally, you should complete all pending transactions and edits and close the open Recordset objects and Database objects. If you are using a Database object locally within a procedure, you should close the open objects before exiting the procedure.

## Database Object Collections

The Database object contains the following collections:

- Containers collection—This collection contains all the Container objects that are defined within the database. This collection may only be used with a Microsoft Jet Database Engine workspace.

- Properties collection—This collection contains all the properties that are associated with the objects in the collection. Each instance of an object has separate properties associated with it.

- QueryDefs collection—When you are using this collection with a Microsoft Jet Database Engine workspace, this collection contains all the QueryDef objects that are associated with a Database object. If you are using this collection with an ODBCDirect workspace, this collection contains all the QueryDef objects that are associated with a Connection object.

- Recordsets collection—This collection contains all the open Recordset objects that are contained within the database.

- Relations collection—This collection is only used with Microsoft Jet Database Engine workspaces and contains all the Relations objects that are saved within the database.

- TableDefs collection—This collection contains all the TableDef objects within a database and can only be used with a Microsoft Jet Database Engine workspace.

## Database Object Methods

The Database object allows the following methods:

- `Close`    This method is used to close an open Database object.

- `CreateProperty`    This method is used to create a new Property object for a database. Or to define properties for a new database. This method can only be used with a Microsoft Jet Database Engine workspace.

- `CreateQueryDef`    This method is used to create a new QueryDef object for a database. The QueryDef object is a query definition.

18

- CreateRelation  This method is used to create a new Relation object for a database. This method can only be used with a Microsoft Jet Database Engine workspace.

- CreateTableDef  This method is used to create a new TableDef object for a database. This method can only be used with a Microsoft Jet Database Engine workspace.

- Execute  This method is used to run an Action query or a SQL statement. An Action query is a query that changes data or copies data.

- MakeReplica  This method is used to make a copy of a database. This method can only be used with a Microsoft Jet Database Engine workspace.

- NewPassword  This method is used to change a password for a database or a user of the database. This method is only used with a Microsoft Jet Database Engine workspace.

- OpenRecordset  This method is used to open a new Recordset object and to execute a Select query against the database.

- PopulatePartial  This method is used to synchronize a partial database replica with a full database replica. This method is only used with a Microsoft Jet Database Engine workspace.

- Synchronize  This method is used to synchronize two database replicas. This method can only be used with a Microsoft Jet Database Engine workspace.

## Database Object Properties

The Database object has the following properties:

- CollatingOrder  This property is used to define the alphabetic sorting order for text fields in the database.

- Connect  This property is used to retrieve or set information about an open connection to a database.

- Connection  This property is used to retrieve the Connection object that is associated with the database. This property is only used with ODBCDirect workspaces.

- DesignMasterID  This property is either used to retrieve or set a unique value that identifies the Design Master in a replica set. This property is only used with Microsoft Jet Database Engine workspaces. The Design Master of a replica set is the first replica in the set. There is only one Design Master at a time in a replica set, but the replicas can take turns being the Design Master. For more information about Replicas and Design Masters, search the Access 97 online help files for Replicas.

- `Name`   If you are using this property from within a Microsoft Jet Database Engine workspace, this property can either be used to retrieve or set a string that contains the path of a database file. If you are using this property from a ODBCDirect workspace, this property can be used to either retrieve or set a name of a Connection object that represents the connection to the ODBC database.

- `QueryTimeout`   This property can be either used to retrieve or set the ODBC query timeout property of the database. The ODBC query timeout is the number of seconds that elapse before a query to an ODBC database errors out.

- `RecordsAffected`   This property can be retrieved to determine the number of records that were affected by an action query run against the database.

- `Replicable`   This property is used to either retrieve or set a value that determines if a database can be replicated or not. This property is only used with a Microsoft Jet Database Engine workspace.

- `ReplicaID`   This property is only used with a Microsoft Jet Database Engine workspace and is used to either set or retrieve an unique value that identifies a database replica.

- `Updatable`   This property is used to indicate whether you can update a database or not.

- `V1xNullBehavior`   This property is used to determine if zero-length strings that are used to fill `Text` or `Memo` fields are converted to `Nulls`.

- `Version`   This property is used to retrieve the version of the database engine that was used to create the database.

**18**

### Database Objects As Workspace Objects

The Database objects reside within a collection that is contained within the Workspace object. The Databases collection contains all open Database objects that were opened or created within the Workspace object. Every time you create a new Database object or open an existing one, it is automatically added to the Databases collection.

The Databases collection allows the following method:

- `Refresh`   This method is used to update the Databases collection to reflect the current Database objects that are contained within the collection.

The Databases collection has the following property:

- `Count`   This property is used to return the number of Database objects that are contained within the Databases collection.

You can refer to a Database object that is part of a Databases collection by using one of the following syntax forms:

```
Databases(0)
Databases("databasename")
Databases![databasename]
```

## TableDef Objects

NEW TERM   The TableDef object is only used with the Microsoft Jet Database Engine workspace. A TableDef object is a representation of a base table or a linked table within the database. A base table is a table stored within your Access 97 database. A *linked table* is a table that resides in another database but is linked to your Access 97 database. Linked tables were known as attached tables in previous versions of Access.

### TableDef Object Collections

The TableDef object contains the following collections:

- Fields collection—This collection contains all the Field objects that are related to a TableDef object.

- Indexes collection—This collection is used only with Microsoft Jet Database Engine workspaces and contains all the Index objects that are associated with a TableDef object.

- Properties collection—This collection contains all the properties that are associated with the objects in the collection. Each instance of an object has separate properties associated with it.

### TableDef Object Methods

The TableDef object allows the following methods:

- CreateField   This method is only for Microsoft Jet Database workspaces and is used to create a new Field object related to a TableDef object.

- CreateIndex   This method is also only for Microsoft Jet Database workspaces and is used to create a new Index object that is related to a TableDef object.

- CreateProperty   Again, this method is only for use with a Microsoft Jet Database workspace. This method is used to create a new property method for a TableDef object.

- OpenRecordset   This method is used to open a new Recordset object and to execute a Select query against the database.

- RefreshLink   This method is only used with Microsoft Jet Database Engine workspaces and is used to refresh the connection information for a linked table.

## TableDef Object Properties

The TableDef object has the following properties:

- `Attributes`   This property is used to retrieve or set a value that defines a characteristic of a TableDef object.

- `ConflictTable`   This property contains the name of the conflict table resulting from the synchronization of two replicas. A conflict table contains the database records that conflicted during the synchronization. This property is only used with a Microsoft Jet Database workspace.

- `Connect`   This property is used to retrieve or set information about an open connection to a database.

- `DateCreated`   This property is only used with Microsoft Jet Database workspaces and is used to retrieve the date the TableDef object was created.

- `KeepLocal`   This property is only used with a Microsoft Jet Database workspace and is used to indicate objects that you do not want to replicate when your database replicates.

- `LastUpdated`   This property is only used with Microsoft Jet Database workspaces and is used to retrieve the time that the TableDef object was last updated.

- `Name`   This property is used to either retrieve or set a name for a TableDef object.

- `RecordCount`   If you are retrieving this property from a base table, this property will contain the number of records in the table. If you are accessing a linked table, this property always has a value of -1.

- `Replicable`   This property is only used with Microsoft Jet Database workspaces and is used to either retrieve or set a value that indicates whether a TableDef object can be replicated.

- `ReplicaFilter`   This property is also only used with Microsoft Jet Database workspaces and is used to either set or retrieve a value for a TableDef object that indicates which subset of records is to be replicated.

- `SourceTableName`   This property is only used with Microsoft Jet Database workspaces and specifies the name of a source table to be used.

- `Updatable`   This property indicates whether you can update the TableDef object.

- `ValidationRule`   This property is used to validate a field in a TableDef object. This property is only used with Microsoft Jet Database workspaces.

- `ValidationText`   This property is used to indicate what text is displayed if a field is not validated within a TableDef object. This property is only used with Microsoft Jet Database workspaces.

**18**

### TableDef Objects with Microsoft Jet Database Engine

The TableDefs collection is used only with a Microsoft Jet Database Engine work-space. The TableDefs collection is used to contain all the TableDef objects within the database. The TableDefs collection allows the following methods:

- Append    This method is used to add a new TableDef object to the TableDefs col-lection.

- Delete    This method is used to delete a TableDef object from the TableDefs col-lection.

- Refresh    This method is used to update the TableDefs collection to reflect the current TableDef objects that are contained within the collection.

The TableDefs collection has the following property:

- Count    This property is used to return the number of TableDef objects that are contained within the TableDefs collection.

## Index Objects

Index objects are only used with Microsoft Jet Database Engine workspaces, and they provide more efficient access to the data that is stored in your database. The Index objects can be used to indicate whether duplicate records are brought back and the order that records are accessed in your database tables.

### Index Object Collections

An Index object contains the following collections:

- Fields collection
- Properties collection

### Index Object Methods

An Index object allows the following methods:

- CreateField
- CreateProperty

### Index Object Properties

An Index object has the following properties:

- Clustered
- DistinctCount
- Foreign

- IgnoreNulls
- Name
- Primary
- Required
- Unique

The Indexes collection is also only used with Microsoft Jet Database Engine workspaces, and the Indexes collection contains all the Index objects that relate to a TableDef object. As with several other DAO collections, the Indexes collection allows the Append, Delete, and Refresh methods and has the Property Count.

## Field Objects

A Field object is used to indicate a column of data. This column has a common set of properties and uses the same data type. The Fields collection is used to store all Field objects that relate to a given object. A Field object can be associated with the following DAO objects:

- Index object
- QueryDef object
- Recordset object
- Relation object
- TableDef object

## Recordsets

A Recordset object contains the results of running a query or the records that are stored in a base table within the database. The Recordsets collection is a grouping of all the open Recordset objects that are associated with a Database object. Recordset objects are created in memory when they are used, so they are not stored in a database.

When you work with the DAO object set, you will mainly use the Recordset object. All Recordset objects use rows and columns to store the data they contain.

## Additional DAO Objects

There are several additional DAO objects that can be used with the DBEngine object. These DAO objects are listed next with a brief explanation.

- Connection object—This object is only used with an ODBCDirect workspace, and it represents a connection to an ODBC database.
- Container object—This object is used to contain similar types of Document objects.

- Document object—This object is only used with Microsoft Jet Database Engine workspaces and contains information about one instance of a database, table, query, or table relationship.

- Error object—This object contains data access errors and details about those errors.

- Group object—This object is only used with Microsoft Jet Database Engine workspaces and contains a group of user accounts that have common permissions. This object is only used when security is turned on for the workspace.

- Parameter object—This object is a value that is used with a query.

- Property object—This object is used with all DAO objects and contains a characteristic of the object that it is associated with.

- QueryDef object—If this object is used with a Microsoft Jet Database Engine workspace, it contains a stored query. If this object is used with an ODBCDirect workspace, it contains a temporary query.

- Relation object—This object is only used with Microsoft Jet Database Engine workspaces and contains the definition of a table or query relationship.

- User object—This object is only used with Microsoft Jet Database Engine workspaces and contains a user account when security is turned on for the workspace.

# Summary

OLE is an industry standard for linking or embedding objects in documents. It also acts as an inter-application protocol for exchanging information, expanding what the older DDE (Dynamic Data Exchange) did.

Windows NT and Windows 95 are OLE-enabled operating systems, and Office 97 is an OLE-enabled suite of applications, so all work together well. Using Office 97 under any appropriate operating system enables you to easily share and exchange information between applications. You can also create compound documents, in which more than one application creates objects in the final document.

ActiveX controls are an extension of the OLE custom control specification that was, in turn, an extension of the VBX control type. Using ActiveX controls in Access 97 can greatly extend the usefulness of your applications with very little or no programming effort.

Tomorrow you will learn the intricacies of Access 97 database security. This will enable you to deploy your Access applications without fear of the data contained in your database falling into the wrong hands.

# Q&A

**Q** How can I tell if I am able to use a certain ActiveX control within my Access 97 application?

**A** One good way to know is to view the ReadMe file that ships with Access 97. This information is also kept updated on the Microsoft Web site at `http://www.microsoft.com`.

**Q** When should I use a Microsoft Jet Database Engine workspace?

**A** You should use the Microsoft Jet Database Engine workspace when you are programmatically working with a database that was built with the Microsoft Jet Database Engine or any ISAM database.

# Workshop

Here's where you can test and apply what you have learned today.

## Quiz

1. What is a quick definition of DAO?

2. What is the only DAO object that does not contain a collection?

3. What is the database environment known as in Access 97?

4. What two types of workspaces can be used within Access 97?

18

# DAY 19

# Maintaining and Securing Your Access Databases

Today's lesson covers the following topics:

- Why maintenance is important
- Repairing corrupted databases
- Compacting your database
- Locking down your database by using an MDE file
- Securing your database
- An introduction to replication

# Why Maintenance is Important

Once you have built a database application in Access 97, you will want to make sure that the application continues to run reliably for your users. Access 97 provides several ways to make sure that your application is reliable and secure. This chapter walks you through the process of repairing a corrupted database, compacting your database for reliability and performance, securing your database, and replicating your database.

After you have distributed an Access 97 database application, there are several things that can go wrong with your database. The following list shows a few of the many reasons why database maintenance is so important:

- Loss of data resulting from database corruption
- Loss of database files because of hardware or software failures
- Corruption of data because of incomplete write operations

These are all reasons to make sure that you perform regular maintenance on your database applications. Your database can become corrupted if the computer it is housed on experiences a hardware problem or is shut down improperly. The next section shows you how to repair a database that has become corrupted.

 **Caution**

Another means by which a database can become corrupted, is, of course, by a virus. As a precaution, you should visit Microsoft's Web site for the latest information on virus reports. A new virus, called AccessIV, which can cause corruption in Access was recently reported, though the risk of transmission is relatively low and no users have reported problems with the virus. Check out `http://www.microsoft.com/access/virusinfo/default.asp` for tips on how to secure your Access database from this and other viruses.

# Repairing Corrupted Databases

There are many reasons that a database can become corrupted. Usually when a database is corrupted, Access 97 will be able to detect the corruption when you attempt to open the database or if you attempt to replicate or backup a corrupted database. If this happens you may see an error message like that shown in Figure 19.1.

**FIGURE 19.1.**

*Attempting a replica-*
*tion with a corrupted*
*database.*

Most of the time Access 97 will give you the option to repair the database when it detects the corruption. There are times however, when the corruption is a more subtle one and Access 97 does not detect the problems. If you have a database that starts behaving oddly, you should attempt to repair the database. If you are attempting to repair a multi-user database, you must inform the other users of the database that they will not be able to access the database during the repair process. If you cannot open the database in exclusive mode, an error will occur.

When a database is repaired by Access 97, all the system tables and indexes associated with that database are validated. Any data that resides in the database that cannot be repaired is deleted.

**Tip**

After you have repaired an Access 97 database, you should compact the database to defrag the database file. The section titled "Compacting Your Database," later in this chapter, will show you how to do this.

The next section shows you how to repair an Access 97 database. There are two examples, the first shows you how to repair a database that is currently open, and the second shows you how to repair a database that is not currently open in Access 97.

**19**

## Task: Repair a corrupted database

To repair a database that you have currently open in Access 97 follow these steps.

1. Open Tools|Database Utilities from the menu bar shown in Figure 19.2 and click the Repair Database option.

To repair a database that is not currently open in Access 97 follow the steps listed below:

1. Close the database that is currently open.

2. Open Tools|Database Utilities from the menu bar and click the Repair Database option.

**FIGURE 19.2.**

*Repairing the current database.*

3. In the dialog that appears, enter the name and location of the database you want to repair and click the Repair button.

## RepairDatabase Method

You can also use Visual Basic code to repair a database that has become corrupted. This method will only work on Microsoft Jet Database Engine workspaces. For more information about workspaces see Day 18, "Advanced Programming with Data Access Objects and ActiveX Controls." The syntax for the RepairDatabase method is

```
DBEngine.RepairDatabase dbname
```

Where dbname is the name of the database you wish to repair. See your Access 97 help documentation for more information about this method and other methods that help maintain your database.

# Compacting Your Database

As you use your Access 97 database application, you will find that over time the application starts to use more space than it really needs. This is especially true if you delete a number of tables. When you compact a database, you are essentially defragmenting the database and arranging the data in a more efficient manner. This will often reduce the disk space your database occupies and will most often result in an increase in speed when operating your database application.

When you compact your database, Access 97 will make a copy of the database while it is compacting and will then prompt you for a name and location to which you want the compacted database saved. If you choose the same name and location as the prior uncompacted database, Access 97 will replace the uncompacted database with your new compacted database.

One side effect of compacting a database is that it usually speeds up the queries that are contained within your database. Compacting the database has this effect because during the compacting operation, the database records are reorganized into a more efficient manner. This will minimize the time needed to retrieve those records after the database has been compacted.

> **Note**
>
> Although compacting a database has several benefits, compaction of a database does not convert databases into Access 97 format. That is, if you compact a prior version of Access in Access 97, it will not result in an Access 97 database.

There are several possible reasons that an Access 97 database will not compact. If you have too many indexes on a table in your database, that database will not compact. This is because an Access 97 table is limited to 32 indexes. When you compact a database several new indexes are created. If you attempt to compact a database that contains a table with 32 indexes, Access 97 cannot add indexes to that table and the compaction will fail. When an Access 97 database is compacted it makes a copy of the database being compacted as part of its process. If you do not have enough disk space for both the compacted and uncompacted versions of your database, the compaction will fail. Another reason that a database compaction will fail is not having the proper permissions on the tables contained in the database. If you do not have Modify Design or Administer permissions on all tables in the database the compaction will fail.

The next section shows you how to compact an Access 97 database. There are two examples, the first shows you how to compact a database that is currently open, and the second shows you how to compact a database that is not currently open in Access 97.

To compact a database that you have currently open in Access 97 follow these steps.

## Task: Compacting Access databases

1. Open Tools|Database Utilities.
2. Click the Compact Database option.

To compact a database that you do not have currently open in Access 97, follow these steps.

1. Close the database you have currently open.
2. Open Tools|Database Utilities.
3. Click the Compact Database option.
4. When the dialog that says Database to Compact From appears, indicate the database you intend to compact and click the Compact button.
5. When Compact Database Into dialog appears, enter a name and location where you want the database to be compacted to and click the Save button.

**19**

**▼ TASK**

▲

# Locking Down Your Database Using an MDE File

Saving your database as an MDE file prevents users from using the Design View mode of Access 97 to view or modify the forms, reports, and modules contained within your Access 97 application. Saving your database as an MDE file also prevents users of your application from creating, importing, or exporting forms, reports, or modules. Once you have saved your database as an MDE file, the users of your database cannot view or change your database's Visual Basic source code.

**Tip**

> If you have used VBA code in your database, saving your database as an MDE file will reduce the size of your database, because saving the database as an MDE file removes the Visual Basic source code that resides in your database application.

If you want to save a replicated database as an MDE file, you must remove all replication system tables and all replication properties from your database.

If you have a series of databases that refer to each other and you want to save one or more of them as MDE files, you must save the databases as MDE files as a chain of references starting from the first database that is referenced in the chain. If, for example, you have a series of three database (titled DB1, DB2, and DB3, respectively) that refer to each other in such a way that DB1 references DB2 which then references DB3, you could save the databases as MDE files by saving DB3 as an MDE file first and then opening DB2 and changing its reference to DB3 to point to the new MDE file that was just created. Once you have done that you can safely change DB2 to an MDE file, open up DB1 and change its reference to DB2 to point to the new MDE file that was just created from DB2. Finally, you can save DB1 as an MDE file.

If you have assigned a database password or have installed user-level security to a database file, and you save that file as an MDE file, those security features will still be in effect with the new MDE file. If you have a file you have installed user-level security, on and you wish to save that database file as an MDE file, you must make sure that you follow these steps.

1. You must join the workgroup file that was used to install user-level security on your database.

2. The user account you are using must have Open Exclusive permissions for the database you want to convert. This user account must have Read Design permissions for all objects contained in the database you want to convert.

3. The user account you are using must be able to modify tables in the database, or must have Administer privileges for the tables in the database file you want to convert.

If you have converted a database file to an MDE that has security features enabled and you wish to disable these features, you must disable the features in the original database file and re-save it as an MDE file.

## Creating an MDE File

The following task will show you how to lock down your database by compiling all the modules into an MDE file.

Once you have saved your database as an MDE file you cannot change the design of any of the forms, reports, or code modules that are contained within your database. Make sure that you save a copy of the original database file so you can make changes to your database if necessary. If you do have to change something in a database you have converted to an MDE file, you must change the original database file and reconvert the original file to an MDE file. You should then discard the first MDE file.

### Task: Creating an MDE file

1. Close the database and make sure that no other users have opened it.
2. Open Tools|Database Utilities and click the Make MDE File option.
3. In the dialog that appears, indicate the database you want to convert to an MDE file and click the Make MDE button.
4. When the next dialog appears, enter a name for the new MDE file and select a location in which to store the new file.

**19**

# Securing Your Database

There are three primary means of supplying database security from within Access 97. The first is by setting a password on your database, the second is by enabling user-level security for your database, and the third method is by saving your database as an MDE file. The last method is covered in the previous section. Methods one and two are covered in detail in this section.

## User-Level Security Wizard

Access 97 includes a Wizard that helps you set up user-level security for your database application. You can reach this Wizard from the Tools menu by clicking the Security sub-menu. The User-Level Security Wizard works by creating a new database and copying all the objects from the original database into it. The User-Level Security Wizard then revokes the users group permissions for all the object types you clicked in the first dialog of the wizard. The new database is then encrypted. Because the User-Level Security Wizard creates a new file before revoking permissions or encrypting the database, the original database is not changed in any way.

**Note**

> Because the User-Level Security Wizard copies all the objects in your data-base, exports them to a new database, and encrypts them, it can take a little while for the Wizard to secure your database.

## Encrypting the Database

Access 97 allows you to encrypt your database to make it unreadable when using any program other than Access 97. You can reverse the process by decrypting an encrypted database. You cannot encrypt or decrypt a database while it is open. If you are attempting to encrypt or decrypt a multi-user database, you must make sure that no other user is using the database. When you encrypt or decrypt your database, Access 97 will prompt you for the name and location where you want to save the newly encrypted or decrypted database. If you choose the same name and location as the original database, Access 97 will replace the original database file with the new encrypted or decrypted database.

**Note**

> Encrypting a database does not secure the database from users that are authorized access to your database objects. If you want to enable object-by-object security, you should enable user-level security as shown later in this section.

Because the encryption/decryption process copies your database while it is performing the encryption/decryption, if you do not have enough disk space on your machine to sup-port the original database plus the new copy, the encryption/decryption process will fail. The process will also fail if you do not have proper permissions to all the tables in the database when you are encrypting/decrypting a database that has user-level security enabled.

## Task: Encrypting the database

Follow these steps to encrypt your database so unwanted eyes cannot read your data.

1. Open Tools|Security and click the Encrypt/Decrypt Database option.

2. In the dialog that appears, indicate the database you want to encrypt or decrypt and then click OK.

3. In the next dialog, enter a name for the newly encrypted or decrypted database and choose a location in which to store the database.

4. Click the OK button.

# Setting a Database Password

The easiest way to secure your database is by setting a password on it. This method will work well if you are using a database on a single computer or with a limited amount of users. This method does not provide any security other than forcing the database users to log in to your database. Access 97 does encrypt the password so it cannot be read by opening the database file outside of Access. If you are going to set a password on your database, it would be wise to make a backup copy of the database and store it in a secure location. This way, you will still be able to access your database, even if you forget your password. Without the backup file, your database will be inaccessible if you forget your password.

You should not set a database password if you are planning to replicate the database. You cannot synchronize a replicated database if a password is set on it. You cannot set a password on a database that has user-level security enabled if you do not have Administer permission for all the objects in that database.

**19**

## Task: Setting passwords

1. Make sure you have the database opened in Exclusive mode.

2. Open Tools|Security and click the Set Database Password option.

3. A dialog like the one shown in Figure 19.3 will appear.

**FIGURE 19.3.**

*Setting a password on a database.*

4. Enter your password in the Password box.

5. Enter the password in the Verify box to confirm your password choice. Remember that passwords are case-sensitive within Access 97.

6. Close your database.

Your database is now password-protected. The next time a user wants to open your database, he or she will be prompted for a password by a dialog like the one shown in Figure

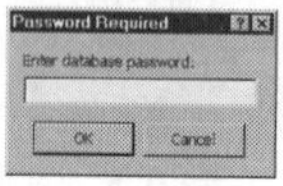

**FIGURE 19.4.**

*Opening a database that is password protected.*

19.4.

You can also remove a password on a database if you decide that it is no longer needed. The following task shown how remove a password from a database.

## Task: Unsetting passwords

1. Open the password-protected database in Exclusive mode.

2. Open Tools|Security and click the Unset Database Password option. You will only see this option if you are using a password-protected database.

3. A dialog will appear like the one shown in Figure 19.5. Type the password for the database into this box and click the OK button.

**FIGURE 19.5.**

*Removing the password from a database.*

4. The password has now been removed from your database.

# Dealing with Workgroup Security

The best way to secure your database is to enable user-level security. This method of securing your database requires users to login as they were required to when you set a password on the database, but this time the user must provide a user name in addition to his or her password. Users of an Access 97 database application that has user-level security enabled are group together in workgroups. Access 97 provides two default workgroups when you enable user-level security. These groups are the Admins group, for administrators of your database, and the Users group, for users of your database. In addition to these default groups, you can build groups of your own and add users to them.

After you have grouped the users of your application, you can grant permissions to the various objects contained within your database. You can either set permissions on a group- or user-level. The information about your users (their account names, passwords, and the groups they belong to) is stored in a file Access 97 reads when it starts up. This file is called the Workgroup Information File. Prior to Access 95, this file was called the System.mda. In Access 95 and Access 97 this file is known as the System.mdw.

## Creating a Workgroup

The users you create are stored in workgroups which are in turn stored in a Microsoft Access Workgroup information file. The default workgroup your users belong to is created in the directory you installed Access 97 into when you ran Access 97 Setup. You can either continue to use this default workgroup file, or you can create a new one. If you really want to ensure that the workgroup you are creating is unique, you should not use the default workgroup. Instead, you should create a new workgroup that includes a workgroup ID (WID) by following the steps listed in the following task.

**▼ TASK**

### Task: Creating a workgroup and some users

Follow these steps to create a unique workgroup.

> **Tip**
>
> If you are using Windows 95, the wrkgadm.exe file is located in the windows/system directory. If you are using Windows NT 4.0, the wrkgadm.exe file is located in the WINNT/System32 directory.

**19**

1. Open the wrkgadm.exe file by double-clicking it in My Computer or Windows Explorer.

2. When you double-click the wrkgadm.exe file, a dialog will appear (see Figure

**FIGURE 19.6.**

*Opening the Workgroup Administrator application.*

19.6) that gives you the choice of creating a new workgroup, joining an existing workgroup, or exiting the Workgroup Administrator application.

▼

3. For this exercise, click the Create button to create a new workgroup. The dialog shown in Figure 19.7 will appear.

4. Enter your name and organization into the appropriate boxes.

5. If you want to add a Workgroup ID to ensure that your workgroup is unique, enter

**FIGURE 19.7.**

*Adding a workgroup ID.*

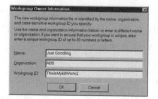

 **Caution**

Make sure you write down all three of these entries and store them in a safe place. If you lose your workgroup information file and have to recreate it, you will need this information, including whether the entries are written in upper- or lowercase.

any combination of four or more (up to twenty) numbers and letters.

 6. Click OK to proceed.

7. In the next dialog, enter a name for the new workgroup information file you just created and click OK.

You have just created a new workgroup information file that you can now populate with users and groups. The next time you start Access 97, this workgroup information file will be used instead of the default workgroup information file.

## Remove User-Level Security

You may have enabled User-Level security on your database and then found out that the users of your application do not want such a tight degree of security applied to the database. Or you may have realized that you do not need to secure your application as closely as you once thought. Whatever the reason, the following task shows how to remove User-Level security from an Access 97 database.

### Task: User-level security

1. Open Access 97 and log in to the application as an administrator of the workgroup of which you are a member.

2. Open the database from which you want to remove User-Level security.

 3. Open Tools|Security and click the User and Group Permissions option.

**FIGURE 19.8.**

*Giving the Users group full permissions to the database.*

4. When the dialog shown in Figure 19.8 appears, give the Users group full permissions to all objects in the database.

5. Exit and restart Access 97.

6. Log on as the Admin user of the workgroup.

7. Create a new blank database in the location where you want to save it, and leave the database open.

8. Import all the objects from the old database into your new one by right-clicking the Database window and selecting the Import option from the pop-up box that appears.

9. You should then clear the Admin password to prevent the Login dialog from appearing. You do this by opening Tools|Security and clicking the User and Group Accounts option.

**19**

**FIGURE 19.9.**

*Using the Admin User to clear a password.*

10. When the dialog shown in Figure 19.9 appears, make sure the Admin user is selected in the pull-down box, and click the Clear Password button.

After completing these steps, you will have restored your database to a completely unsecured one. You can now retain the open security settings on your database or go to a lower level of security, such as that provided by assigning a password to the database.

# An Introduction to Replication

*Database replication* is the process of copying a database, along with the objects that are contained within the database. Replication involves synchronizing these copies of the original database so that changes made in a table in one replicated database are sent to the other replicas, and the table is changed in the same manner in those databases.

## Creating a Replica

A *replica* is a member of a replication set and can be synchronized with other replicas in that set. When you make changes in a replica database that is a member of a replication set, the changes you make are sent and applied to the other replica databases within that replication set.

If you do not want to replicate your whole database, you can create a partial replica of your database. This partial replica is a subset of the records that are stored in your database. There are several advantages to using partial replicas. Using a partial replica takes less time to synchronize with the member replicas in its replication set because you are essentially using a smaller database. Partial replicas can help your security by restricting access to the data stored in your database. If you do not replicate sensitive data, you can be sure that unwanted eyes do not see the sensitive data stored in your database.

## Task: Replicating a database

1. Open the database you want to replicate. If you are using the database as a multi-user database, be sure that no one else has the database open.

2. If your database is password-protected, remove the password by following the

**FIGURE 19.10.**

*Creating a replica.*

steps in the "Setting a Database Password," earlier in this chapter.

3. Open Tools|Replication and click the Create Replica option (see Figure 19.10).

**FIGURE 19.11.**

*Closing the database for replica creation.*

4. You will be prompted to close the database by the dialog shown in Figure 19.11. Click Yes.

5. When you are asked if you want to save a backup of the database first before creating a replica, click Yes.

6. When the location dialog appears, select the location of the directory where you want to store the replica. Click OK.

## Performing a Replication

Access 97 supplies four different tools you can use to replicate a database and manage the database replication. These tools are the following:

- Briefcase Replication
- Replication commands from within Access 97
- DAO methods and properties
- Microsoft Replication Manager

The following task walks you through the steps of performing a database replication by using the Briefcase application installed on your desktop when you installed Windows 95 or Windows NT 4.0. For this method to work, you must be sure the Microsoft Briefcase Replication component is installed on your system. If it is not installed, Access 97 will prompt you to install the component when you attempt the following exercise. If you need to install the Microsoft Briefcase Replication component, you can do so by running

**19**

the setup.exe for your Microsoft Office 97 installation and using the Add/Remove component function of Setup.

## Task: Performing replication using Briefcase Replication

**FIGURE 19.12.**

*Starting replication with the Microsoft Briefcase.*

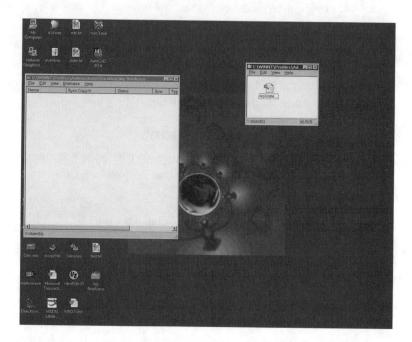

1. Double-click the My Briefcase icon located on your desktop to open the Briefcase.
2. Open Explorer and browse through the directory structure to locate the Access 97 .mdb file you want to replicate. Your desktop should now look like Figure 19.12.
3. Drag the database icon from Explorer to the Briefcase.

**FIGURE 19.13.**

*Replicating your database will make changes to your database.*

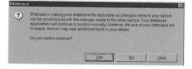

4. You will be prompted by the dialog shown in Figure 19.13. This dialog informs you of the changes that will occur in your database if you proceed with replication and asks if you want to continue. Click Yes.

**FIGURE 19.14.**

*Making a backup of your database before replication.*

5. The replication process will prompt you with the dialog shown in Figure 19.14. You can use this dialog to have the replication process create a backup of your database before making the changes to it that the replication process requires.

6. Click Yes.

7. You will then be prompted by the dialog shown in Figure 19.15. This dialog informs you that your database has been converted to a Design Master and that a

**FIGURE 19.15.**

*Deciding in which copy to allow design changes.*

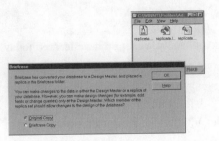

19

replica of your database has been placed in the Briefcase folder on your desktop. This dialog then asks in which copy of the database you want to allow design changes. Choose a copy and click OK.

8. Your database is now replicated and the replicated copy is stored in the My Briefcase folder located on your desktop.

# Summary

Today you learned about the security and database maintenance features of Access 97. You used the tasks in this chapter to walk through the process of repairing a corrupted database. Then you learned how to compact your database and why it is a good idea to perform regular database maintenance.

You also spent a considerable amount of time learning the different ways you can make your Access 97 database applications more secure and reliable. Finally, you learned how to replicate your Access 97 database to other locations.

Tomorrow you will learn how to integrate Access 97 with the rest of the Office 97 suite of applications.

# Q&A

**Q  Can I print information about the users and groups in my application?**

**A**  Yes, you can print this information by opening Tools|Security and clicking the User and Group Accounts option. On the Users tab of the resulting dialog, click the Print Users and Groups button.

**Q  Can I turn off the Logon dialog?**

**A**  Yes, Open Tools|Security and click the User and Group Accounts option. Select the Users tab and make sure that the Admin user is selected in the pull-down box. Click the Clear Password button to turn off the Logon dialog.

# Workshop

Here's where you can test and apply what you have learned today.

## Quiz

1. Name one method to replicate your database.

2. What are the two default member groups of a workgroup information file?

3. What do you need to do to create an unique Workgroup information file?

4. List one benefit of compacting your Access 97 database.

# DAY 20

# Integrating Access with the Rest of Microsoft Office

The journey's almost complete! It's hard to believe it's been 19 days since you started this journey, but it has. Today you learn all about integrating Access with the other applications available in the Microsoft Office suite.

Integration of the Office 97 applications is done almost exclusively through the use of tools called Office Links. An Office Link is a built-in wizard that assists you in using the information or data provided by one Office application in another Office application.

Access 97 includes the following Office Links:

- Merge It with MS Word
- Publish It with MS Word
- Analyze It with MS Excel

**Note**    You must have the appropriate Office 97 applications installed on your computer in order to use the Office Links.

Today you'll also learn about exporting data from Access 97 to other file formats or even
other database systems. It's a shorter day than most in this book, but the concepts you
learn today, though simple to utilize, will greatly improve your productivity.

If you aren't using the full Office 97 suite, you'll probably just want to skim the first
three sections of this chapter to learn what the Office Links can help you accomplish. In
either case, don't miss the final section, "Exporting Data to Other Sources," where you'll
learn an important technique for converting your Access data to some other file format.

# Using Your Data for Microsoft Word Mail Merges

One of the most useful tools available from the applications in the Microsoft Office suite
is Word's mail merge. Performing a mail merge involves creating a Word document that
contains special merge fields and then combining this document with a data source.
Word uses the data source to replace the merge fields with real data. A separate document is created for each record in the data source.

For example, the online bookstore occasionally hosts online chats with the authors of
some of the more popular books for sale at the bookstore. These events are typically
coordinated through the publisher. A month or so before the events are scheduled, the
bookstore sends a letter to each publisher announcing the event and asking for their participation.

A simple query provides the desired data from the various tables. The Merge It with MS
Word Office Link then provides that data to Microsoft Word to merge with the template
letter.

As you'll see in the following task, combining what you've learned about queries with
the Office Link makes this an extremely simple process.

**Note**    The Merge It with MS Word Office Link can be used with data contained in
tables or returned by a query. However, you cannot use this Office Link with
forms and reports.

## Task: Performing a mail merge

1. Launch Access and open the BookStore database. The first step is to create a query containing the data for the merge. Click the Queries tab and click New to start a new query. Leave Design View selected and click OK in the New Query dialog.

2. The Add Table dialog appears. Add the Publishers, Publications, and OrderDetails tables. Click Close to close the dialog.

3. Click the Totals button in the toolbar to turn this query into one capable of using aggregate functions. Your screen should look similar to Figure 20.1.

**FIGURE 20.1.**

*Preparing for the query.*

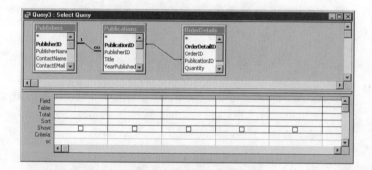

4. Double-click the Quantity field in the OrderDetails field list. In the Total row of its design grid column, drop down the list box and select Sum. Click the Show check box to clear it. Enter >0 in the Criteria row. This will return only those publishers that have actually had books sold through the bookstore.

5. Next, double-click the PublisherName, ContactName, ContactEMail, Address, City, State, ZIP, and Active fields to add them to the query.

6. Find the column for the Active field. Change the value in the Total row to Where. Clear its check box in the Show row. In the Criteria row, enter Yes. This ensures that only publishers marked as active will be included.

7. Run the query. Your results (if you've not added any new data) should be similar to Figure 20.2. Notice that some of the publishers don't have complete addresses and some don't have a contact name. If the lack of addresses bothers you, make up some addresses for the sake of this exercise. However, leave at least one row with an empty ContactName. There's an important feature of Word's Mail Merge that can only be demonstrated if data is missing.

20

**FIGURE 20.2.**

*The Mail Merge query running in Access.*

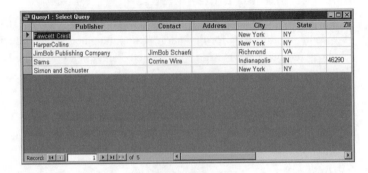

8. Close the query, saving it as `ActivePublisherMailMerge`. On the Database window, select the query. Use the Tools|Office Links|Merge It with MS Word menu item.

9. The initial dialog of the Microsoft Word Mail Merge Wizard, shown in Figure 20.3, appears. Click the Create a New Document and then Link the Data to It radio button. Click OK to continue.

**FIGURE 20.3.**

*The Microsoft Word Mail Merge Wizard's initial dialog.*

**Note**

Unlike most wizards, the Merge It Office Link uses the selected table or query as its only available data source. While most wizards allow you to pick and choose among the tables and queries defined in your database, this Office Link does not.

10. Not much seems to happen, and then Word launches and displays the Mail Merge toolbar. To see that the `ActivePublisherMailMerge` query really was used as the data source for the merge, drop down the merge field list by clicking the Insert Merge Field button in the toolbar. Your screen should appear similar to Figure 20.4.

**FIGURE 20.4.**

*Starting the Word Merge document.*

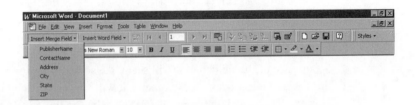

11. You use the Insert Merge Field button to insert placeholders for your data into the document. Simply click the button to drop down the list of available fields (as shown in Figure 20.4) and click the desired field. A merge field is inserted into the document at the current cursor location. You can type text around the merge fields, of course, to include the data within the actual text of the document. Use the Insert Merge Field button to make the document look like Figure 20.5.

**FIGURE 20.5.**

*Creating the text of the merge document.*

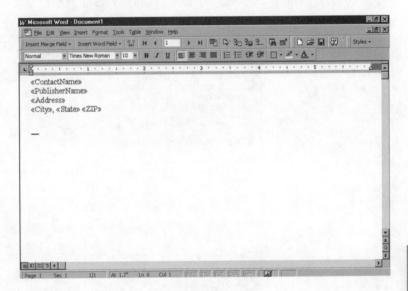

**20**

12. Next, click the Insert Word Field button and select If...Then...Else from the menu that drops down. The Insert Word Field: IF dialog appears. Select ContactName in the Field name drop-down list and Is Not Blank in the Comparison drop-down list. In the Insert this Text box, enter Dear , and in the Otherwise Insert this Text box enter To Whom It May Concern:. Click OK.

▼ 13. When you're back on the document window, right-click over the text that was just inserted and select Toggle Field Codes from the shortcut menu. This will show you what's going on behind the scenes. Click right before the comma following Dear. Click the Insert Merge Field button and select ContactName. Word may change the appearance of the field, and it will seem like something went awry. Even if you use the Toggle Field Codes shortcut menu, it will appear as if nothing is different. However, it is. Click the View Merged Data button (it's just to the right of the Insert Word Field button) and scroll through the records using the now-familiar record selectors to the right of the View Merged Data button. You should find some Dear salutations in the documents.

14. After you've located one, click the View Merged Data button again, select the salutation merge field and use the Toggle Field Codes shortcut menu. Now you'll see the merge field within this Word field.

15. Type the body of the letter, as shown in Figure 20.6.

**FIGURE 20.6.**

*The body of the merge document.*

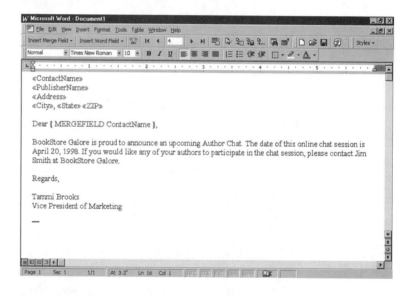

16. Click the View Merged Data toolbar button once again; this time the letter looks ▼ complete. A sample is shown in Figure 20.7.

**FIGURE 20.7.**

*The completed document including the merge data.*

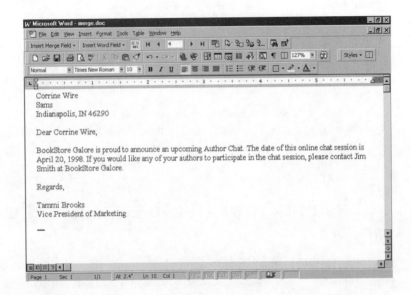

Now that your merge document is complete, you have several options to choose from regarding its output. Word allows you to merge to a new document, the printer, electronic mail, or fax (if installed). To select from these options, click the Mail Merge button in the toolbar. The Merge dialog, shown in Figure 20.8, appears. Here you select the destination, the range of records to print, and what to do if a blank line is present in the merged document.

**FIGURE 20.8.**

*The Merge dialog.*

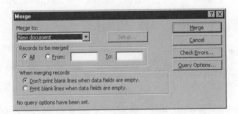

If you choose to email the merged document, select electronic mail and click the Setup button. The Merge To Setup dialog, shown in Figure 20.9, appears. Select ContactEMail in the drop-down list box, enter a subject line, and choose whether or not to include the document as an attachment file to the messages. If you leave the Send Document as an Attachment check box cleared, the text of the merged document will be placed within the email message. Depending on your mail system, you may lose any formatting contained within the document. If you're using Microsoft Outlook or Exchange, and your recipients are also using one of these mail systems, you should leave this box cleared.

**20**

FIGURE 20.9.

*The Merge To Setup dialog.*

The merge document and the query you created, along with the link between them, can be used again the next time you need to send this letter. Word links to the live data, so any changes you make to the data in the database will be reflected next time you execute the mail merge.

# Publishing Your Database with Microsoft Word

The Publish It with MS Word Office Link allows you to quickly create a Word document from the datasheet view of tables, queries, and forms. It can also create a document from a report. This Office Link creates a file in the Rich Text Format (RTF) and immediately launches Word 97 with this document.

For tables, queries, and forms, the Publish It Office Link will produce a document that uses a table to display the data. For a report, the document will closely resemble a printed report, except that charts embedded in the report will not be ported to the Word document.

Using this Office Link is simple, as the following task demonstrates.

### Task: Publishing a table with Word

1. If necessary, open the BookStore database. Move to the Queries tab. Select the Bibliography query to use as the source for the new document.

2. Use the Tools|Office Links|Publish It with MS Word menu item.

3. Access will choose the name for the file based on the name of the query. If the file name already exists, Access will ask you whether or not you want to replace the existing file. If you answer no, a File Save dialog will appear allowing you to choose a different name or folder for the file. If you answer yes, the existing file will be replaced with the new one.

4. The Office Link launches Word (if necessary) and opens the newly created document. Figure 20.10 shows the results of this with the sample data.

▲TASK

▼

**FIGURE 20.10.**

*The results of the Publish It with MS Word Office Link.*

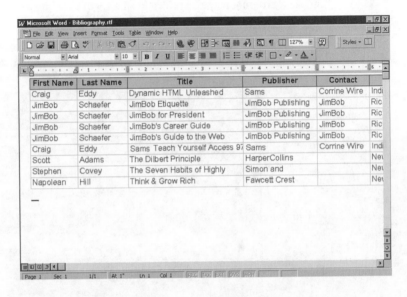

That really was too easy. You can now embed this Word table in another Word document or build a new document around this table. Use this technique whenever you want to export data from a table or query into a report, memo, or other static document that depends on data from your database.

# Analyzing Data with Microsoft Excel

The final Office Link is the Analyze It with MS Excel Office Link. This Office Link allows you to transfer your tables, queries, forms, and reports to an Excel spreadsheet. Most of the formatting in the datasheet views, forms, and reports is preserved in the spreadsheet. Forms are saved using their datasheet views. If you have grouping levels in your reports, they are saved as outline levels in the spreadsheet.

Using this Office Link is just as easy as the Publish It Office link, as the following task demonstrates.

### Task: Analyzing data with Excel

1. If necessary, open the BookStore database. Move to the Reports tab. Select the Title By Publisher report to use as the source for the new spreadsheet.

2. Use the Tools|Office Links|Analyze It with MS Excel menu item.

3. Access will choose the name for the file based on the name of the report. If the file name already exists, Access will ask you whether or not you want to replace the existing file. If you answer no, a File Save dialog will appear allowing you to

▼     choose a different name or folder for the file. If you answer yes, the existing file
      will be replaced with the new one.

4. The Office Link launches Excel (if necessary) and opens the newly created spreadsheet. Figure 20.11 shows the results of this with the sample data.

**FIGURE 20.11.**

*The results of the
Analyze It with MS
Excel Office Link.*

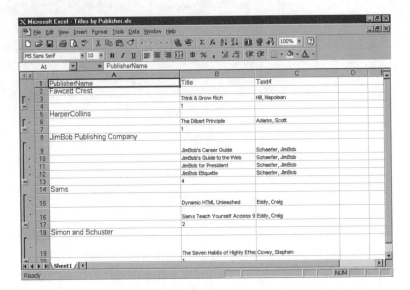

5. Notice that the spreadsheet still needs a little work. The column with the authors'
   names is labeled Text4. This is the name of the control from the report. It just so
   happens that in the report the control displaying the publications' titles was named
   Title and so its column has the proper header. Change Text4 to Author. Also, the
   summation from the report's grouping is also displayed, but there is no label. You'll

▲     probably want to add some sort of label.

## Exporting Data to Other Sources

In addition to the means already discussed, Access 97 provides a way to manually export
data from your database to an external file or database. The available recipients for this
export feature depend on the options you installed when Access 97 was installed.
Likewise, different components have different possible export capabilities. For example,
forms and reports cannot be exported to other database systems but tables and query
results can.

**Note**
If an external file type or database is not available when you follow along in this section, it simply means you haven't installed that option. To do so, head to Appendix B, "Installing Access 97," for instructions on installing Access 97.

To export an object to an external file, follow these steps:

1. Select the object in the Database window.

2. Use the File|Save As/Export menu item or right-click the object's name and select Save As/Export from the shortcut menu. The Save As dialog, shown in Figure 20.12, appears.

**FIGURE 20.12.**

*The Save As dialog.*

3. Since you're saving to an external file or database and not making a copy of the selected entity within the current database, leave the default option button selected and click OK.

4. The Save Query 'Bibliography' In dialog shown in Figure 20.13 opens. On this dialog you specify how and where you want to save the entity.

   If you're exporting a table or query to another database using ODBC, follow steps 1 through 4, and then skip to steps 7 through 9.

**FIGURE 20.13.**

*The Save In dialog.*

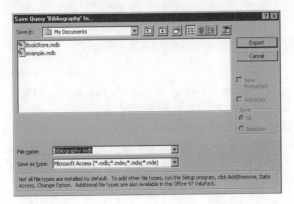

**20**

5. Select the type of file to which to save the entity using the Save as Type drop-down list box at the bottom of the dialog. Open the list box to see which types are available on your system. Select the type desired.

6. Use the top portion of the dialog to specify the location and file name for the file to export to and click Export.

7. Select ODBC Databases() in the Save as Type drop-down list.

8. In the Export dialog that appears next, specify a name to use for the entity in the destination ODBC database. Click OK.

8. The Select Data Source dialog appears. Specify or create an ODBC data source name for the database you're exporting to. The choices of databases and ODBC drivers available varies greatly from system to system.

9. Click OK and the data is exported to the specified data source. If any errors occur during this process, you will receive the appropriate message boxes informing you of the problem.

Access can also export to a variety of Internet formats, including creating Active Server Pages based on your database. Publishing data on the Web is tomorrow's subject in Day 21, which is appropriately entitled "Integrating Access with the Web."

# Summary

Hopefully by now you've discovered a wealth of ways to put the data in your database to good use. Today has shown you how you can create Word and Excel documents from you data and how to export your data to just about any other file or database.

Access 97 really removes the limits as to what you can do with data once it's placed in your database. In other words, the data is not stuck in the database serving little or no purpose. You can always act on and use your data in the way that best matches how you operate.

# Q&A

**Q I have an existing database system I'd like to export data to. Where can I find the ODBC drivers for this system?**

**A** Access 97 ships with quite a few ODBC drivers. If the driver you're looking for isn't currently on your system (use the 32-bit ODBC Control Panel applet to find out which drivers are installed), try running Access 97 Setup again to see if it's available within Access 97. If it isn't, contact the database vendor to see if they have a 32-bit ODBC driver available. Chances are most commercial database systems have such a driver available. You can also check Microsoft's Universal Data Access Web site at `http://www.microsoft.com/data` for additional drivers.

# Workshop

Here's where you can test and apply what you have learned today.

## Quiz

1. When should you use the Publish It with MS Word Office Link?

2. If you need to have a Word document updated with current data whenever it is opened, should you use the Merge It or the Publish It Office Link?

3. Do you have to create the merge document before running the Merge It Office Link?

4. Can reports be exported to other Access databases?

20

# DAY **21**

# Integrating Access with the Web

Today you'll learn about the following topics:

- Converting a table/query to an HTML document
- Static and dynamic Web objects
- Publishing a form/report to an HTML document for Web viewing
- Hyperlinks to other Microsoft Office documents plus other non-Microsoft applications if they're so enabled
- Hyperlinks to Web documents in forms/reports

# The Web: Both Static and Dynamic Data

The World Wide Web (now commonly known as just "the Web") is a part of the Internet. It was initially a way for scientists to publish and view hypertext documents online. Online viewing has two main benefits: First, you don't need to use up your own disk space for these files, and second, the hyperlinks to other documents let you jump to those documents while you're online. In essence, the Web is a huge library of hypertext documents.

You've seen Access's online help system; documents on the Web operate similarly. You can jump from document to document by hyperlink (embedded link to an external reference), and the documents can contain illustrations or graphics.

It wasn't long before the Web grew to include multimedia objects as well as hypertext. Although the early pioneers of the Web probably take a jaundiced view of the animation, sounds, and even real-time audio now available on the Web, there's no doubt that these new developments have caught the public's imagination.

**NEW TERM** With the spread of the Web over the Internet, corporations discovered that this technology could be used for their internal needs. What followed was the growth of *intranets*, which is the Internet Web technology (for the most part) behind a firewall or security screen. Unlike the Internet, which is mostly public, intranets are for internal use by those authorized by the corporation or other publishing entity.

The fundamental protocol of the Web is HTTP—Hypertext Transfer Protocol. To view and interact with Web documents, you need three things:

- An Internet connection capable of HTTP support.
- A way for your computer to connect with the Internet. This is generally a Winsock (or TCP/IP layer) for your network. Windows 95/98, NT, and later versions have a Microsoft-supplied capability to connect to the Internet through either a LAN or dial-up (modem) connection.
- A browser that can interpret HTTP. There are many browsers on the market, but the two dominant ones are Microsoft Internet Explorer and Netscape Navigator. The Microsoft offering is the browser shown for the screens in this chapter.

Microsoft Access 97 is Web-enabled, so you can use it to publish objects to the Web for all to see. Access 97, when used with Windows NT IIS (Internet Information Server) or the Personal Web Server for Windows 95/98, can also create dynamic Web pages that let users view, edit, and do other database chores online through the Web.

The choice of whether to create static or dynamic Web pages is entirely up to you and your requirements. If you simply want to provide a canned output from a fixed set of data, you'd choose a static Web page. If you need to display up-to-date data, you'd use one of the dynamic creation techniques described in this chapter. Remember, though, that these techniques require a Web server that provides a specific set of functionality. This functionality is available in the Microsoft Web servers and may be available in others as well.

# Exporting Data to HTML

Access 97 provides several ways to publish your data to the Web. You can publish either static or dynamic data. Static pages never change; they always display the same data. Dynamic pages, however, generate queries against your Access databases and produce Web pages on-the-fly, using current data from the database. This section discusses creating static Web pages using the export method. The section that follows explains using the Publish to the Web wizard to create either static or dynamic Web pages.

## Creating an HTML Template File

Access 97 can create Web pages from datasheets, forms, and reports without any input from you. However, you can also specify an HTML template file to be used as a starting point when creating these Web pages. This template file allows you to specify your own standards for the Web page to be created. You can add graphics such as company logos and backgrounds, as well as specify text colors, link colors, and background colors.

You can use any text editor or even a specialized HTML editor, such as Microsoft's FrontPage, to create the HTML template file. Store it in a common directory so that you'll have no trouble locating it when you perform an export. If you installed the sample databases when you installed Access 97, a sample template for the Northwind database is installed in the same directory as the MDB file. It's named `NWINDTEM.HTM` and can be opened using Internet Explorer (see Figure 21.1) or Notepad.

In addition to HTML code, template files can also contain tokens that Access replaces with appropriate material, as shown in Table 21.1.

21

**Figure 21.1.**

*The Northwind HTML template sample.*

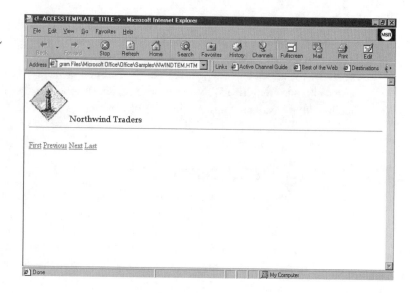

**Table 21.1.** HTML Template file tokens.

| Token | Replacement |
|---|---|
| `<!--AccessTemplate_Title-->` | The object name is placed in the Web browser's title bar. |
| `<!--AccessTemplate_Body-->` | The exported data. |
| `<!--AccessTemplate_FirstPage-->` | A link to the first page. |
| `<!--AccessTemplate_PreviousPage-->` | A link to the previous page. |
| `<!--AccessTemplate_NextPage-->` | A link to the next page. |
| `<!--AccessTemplate_LastPage-->` | A link to the last page. |
| `<!--AccessTemplate_PageNumber-->` | The current page number. |

# Performing the Export

To export to an HTML format, perform the steps in the following task.

## Task: Exporting to HTML

1. In the Database window, click the Queries tab. Select the `Bibliography` query.

2. Use the File|Save As/Export menu item.

3. Select To an External File or Database in the dialog that appears. Click OK.

4. In the Save dialog that appears next, select `HTML Documents` in the Save as Type drop-down list.

5. Select the location where you want the HTML file to be saved and stored. Leave the name of the file as `Bibliography.html` as suggested by Access. If you want to use an HTML template file, check the box labeled Save Formatted. Click Export.

6. If you elected to use an HTML template file in step 5, a dialog will appear where you specify the location of the template file. You can either type the file's name or use the Browse button to locate the template using the Familiar Files dialog.

7. The HTML file is created in the location you specified. You can use Internet Explorer to view its contents. Figure 21.2 shows the query exported without using a template file. Figure 21.3 shows the same query using the `NWINDTEM.HTM` template file (the graphic is missing because the exported file was not saved into the same directory as the template and the graphic it references).

**FIGURE 21.2.**

*The* `Bibliography` *query exported to HTML without a template.*

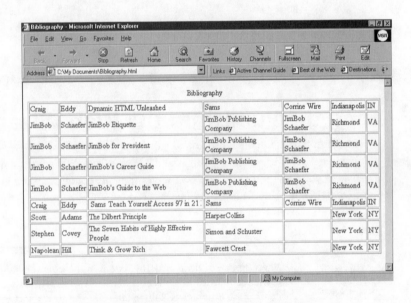

Notice that the template-created file has a better look and feel than the straight export. If you'll be using the Export to HTML feature often, you should probably create a template file or two to provide a consistent look and feel across all of your Web pages.

21

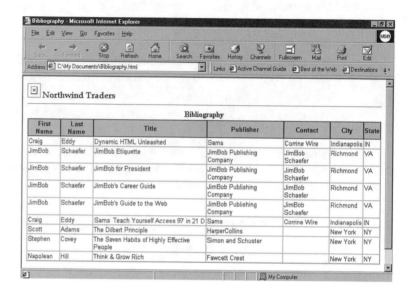

▼

**FIGURE 21.3.**

*The* Bibliography *query exported to HTML using the Northwind sample template.*

▲

# Using the Publish to the Web Wizard

In addition to the manual process of exporting data to HTML, discussed in the previous section, Access 97 sports a Publish to the Web Wizard. This wizard assists you in publishing your data to the Web in a variety of manners: static as seen in the previous section, dynamic using Microsoft's Internet Database Connector, and dynamic using Microsoft's Active Server Pages.

> **Note**
>
> When I speak of dynamic HTML pages in this chapter, I am not speaking of "Dynamic HTML," which is an extension of the HTML specification to make pages more interactive. Rather, I'm referring to the fact that the *data* on the pages is dynamic—it can change each time the page is loaded.

**NEW TERM**   The *Internet Database Connector* (IDC) is a specialized application that can be installed on either the Personal Web Server or the Internet Information Server. You can produce Web pages that display live data by using the IDC. The IDC uses a template file that contains tokens for each database field and a script file that contains the information necessary to retrieve the data from the database. The template files have an extension of `.HTX`, while the script files have an extension of `.IDC`. When you create a link to an IDC page, you should link to the IDC file. The Web server (if IDC has been properly installed) knows to provide the requestor with the database-aware Web page when the requestor attempts to retrieve an IDC file.

**NEW TERM**  *Active Server Pages* run on Internet Information Server as well as the Personal Web Server. These pages contain some scripting language, typically (but not necessarily) VBScript, which executes on the Web server. After the script executes, it returns a Web page to the requestor but doesn't return any of the script code that executed. Active Server Pages can access any ActiveX/COM component installed on the server machine, including database-aware components and ActiveX controls. By using Active Server Pages, you can create an entire Web-based application, and the details can become quite complicated.

## Creating Static HTML Pages

Although Access 97 allows you to quickly create an HTML page using the File | Save As/Export menu item, the Publish to the Web Wizard provides you greater flexibility. You can select multiple tables, queries, forms, and reports to export, and you can automatically launch the Web Publishing Wizard (discussed in the next section) to transfer your HTML pages to a Web server.

The next task describes how to use the wizard to create a static HTML page (again using the Bibliography query) and store them on your hard drive.

### Task: Creating a static HTML page

**▲ TASK**

1. With the BookStore database open, use the File | Save As HTML menu item. One of the wizard's dialogs allows you to specify which items of the database to export, so it doesn't matter what you have selected in the Database window.

2. The first dialog is introductory and explains what's about to happen. It also allows you to select a previously saved profile. If this is the first time you've used this wizard, or you have never saved any profiles, this option will be disabled. The final dialog in the wizard provides you with the capability to save the steps you're about to complete in a profile that can be used again by selecting it in this dialog. Click the Next button to continue.

3. The next dialog, shown in Figure 21.4, is where you'll specify what components to export. You can click the tabs to select which type of component to export, and then select the specific items to export by clicking the check boxes or the Select and Select All buttons. You can remove items by using the Deselect All button or by clearing its check box. For this exercise, select the Bibliography query. Click the Next button to continue.

**▼**

**21**

**FIGURE 21.4.**

*Publish to the Web Wizard's component selection.*

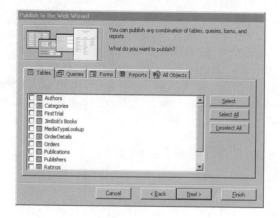

4. In the next dialog you specify the HTML template file to use if you want to use one. You can type the filename or use the Browse button to locate it. If you have selected multiple items on the previous dialog, you can check the I Want to Select Different Templates for Some of the Selected Objects check box. If you choose this route, the next dialog will present you with a list box where you can specify different template files for each of the exported objects. Click the Next button to continue.

**Caution**

> If you use a template file that contains graphics, make sure that the graphics exist in the folder you'll specify as the output folder in step 6. Otherwise, the graphics will not be loaded when you open the pages in a browser.

5. This dialog is where you specify how the export file should be created. Leave the Static HTML option button selected. Again, if you wanted to create different types of export for the different objects you've selected, there is a check box that allows you to do so in the same manner as specifying the HTML template file. Click the Next button to continue.

6. The next dialog (shown in Figure 21.5) is where you to specify the location to which to publish the exported query results. The text box is where you enter the name of the folder into which Access will place the HTML file. You can type the folder name or use the Browse button to locate the folder. If you were going to move the files to a Web server as well, you'd select one of the Web Publishing Wizard option buttons in the middle of the dialog. For now, leave the default selected. It is best to store all of your Web content in a single folder or in subfolders of a specific folder. This will make it easier to manually copy the content to

▼ your Web site or to use the Web Publishing Wizard described later. After you've selected the folder to export to, click the Next button to continue.

**FIGURE 21.5.**

*Publish to the Web Wizard's output dialog.*

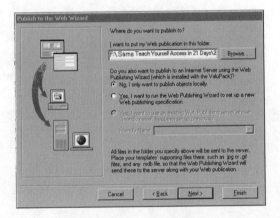

7. This dialog allows you to specify whether a home page is created for your exported data. If you choose to create a home page, you should specify the name for the file in the text box provided. The home page will contain links to the individual pages created for each object you export. Because you're only doing a single object right now, leave the check box unchecked and click Next to continue.

8. In the wizard's final dialog you can instruct the wizard to save the answers to the previous dialogs into a publication profile. You can then use this profile in the future and your current choices will already be selected for you. It's also a great way to figure out what steps you took to create the Web page if you forget. After you've made your choice on this dialog, click Finish to create the HTML files.

9. Launch Internet Explorer and use the File|Open menu to locate the HTML file created. It will be placed in the folder you specified in step 6. The resulting page for the `Bibliography` query is shown in Figure 21.6.

**Note**

Figure 21.6 shows how Microsoft Internet Explorer displays the resulting page. If you're using a different browser, your results may be slightly different.

▼

21

**FIGURE 21.6.**

*The Web page produced for the* Bibliography *query.*

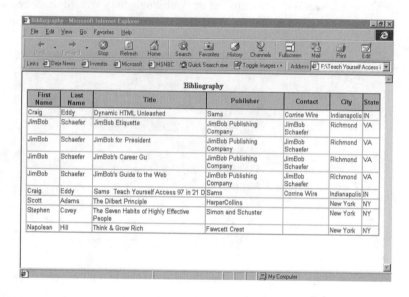

Notice that, even though you didn't use a template file, the Web page looks very similar to the page created with the Northwind template. This is another advantage of using the Publish to the Web Wizard.

## Creating Internet Database Connector and Active Server Pages

Now that you've seen how easy it is to create a static HTML page based on data in your database, it's time to learn about dynamic Web page creation. The process you'll use is nearly identical to the steps for creating static HTML pages, so there won't be an explicit exercise to go along with these steps.

The first difference is that instead of selecting the Static HTML option button in step 5 you'll select either the Dynamic HTX/IDC or the Dynamic ASP option button. When you do so, the dialog that appears when you click Next is where you'll specify an ODBC data source name to use when someone requests the IDC or ASP file. This dialog is shown in Figure 21.7.

Here you'll enter an ODBC data source name. The actual data source specification does not need to exist yet; you can create it later. Unless you have secured your Access database using the techniques discussed in Day 19, "Maintaining and Securing Your Access Databases," you can leave the User Name and Password boxes empty.

**FIGURE 21.7.**

*The dynamic Web page properties dialog.*

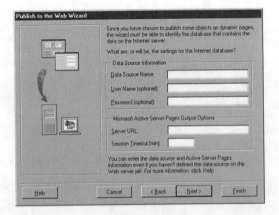

To create a Microsoft Access ODBC data source, follow these steps:

1. Launch Control Panel and double-click the 32-bit ODBC icon.

2. Click the Add button. Select Microsoft Access Driver and click Finish.

3. The ODBC Microsoft Access 97 Setup dialog appears. Here you assign the name for the data source, select the database to be used, set any advanced options, and perform some database utilities. All that is required is a data source name and a database filename. When you've entered the required information, click the OK button to add the data source.

The second difference from creating static HTML pages is that you must store the files in a directory accessible by a Web server. Otherwise, when you open the files using Internet Explorer you'll only see the actual contents of the files, not the data from the database.

Figure 21.8 shows the results of the IDC page created for the Bibliography query. As you can see, it doesn't look any different from the other pages you've created. The difference, though, is that if data in the database changes, the next time this page is loaded it will automatically show the updated data.

21

**FIGURE 21.8.**

*The results of an IDC page created for the* Bibliography *query.*

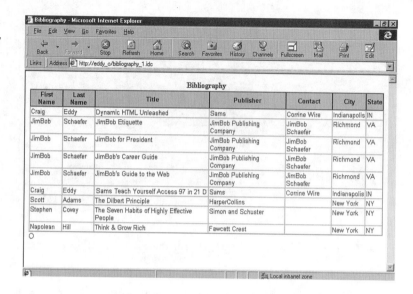

## Using the Web Publishing Wizard

Now that you've created all these wonderful Web pages, you might want to publish them to a Web server so that the rest of the world (or perhaps just others on your company's intranet) can view the data as well. Microsoft Office 97's ValuPack (which is installed if you install Office 97 from a CD-ROM) includes a Web Publishing Wizard that can be used to transfer Web content to a Web server.

You can use the Web Publishing Wizard in one of two ways: launch it automatically while using the Publish to the Web Wizard or launch it from the Start menu. To use it with the Publish to the Web Wizard select one of the Web Publishing options discussed in step 6 of the second task earlier in this chapter.

In next task, you create a new server specification for a Web server installed on your machine. You have many options for Web servers depending on the operating system you use. If you're using Windows 95/98, you should use Microsoft's Personal Web Server. If you're using Windows NT Workstation 4.0, the Peer Web Services included with the NT Option Pack should be used. If you're using Windows NT Server 4.0, use the full-blown IIS. The downloads and instructions for all of these can be found on Microsoft's Web site. Start at `http://www.microsoft.com/windows` and follow the path for your particular operating system.

## Task: Publishing your Web pages

1. From the Database window, use the File|Save as HTML menu item. Click Next on the first dialog.

2. Select the Bibliography query on the Queries tab and click Next. Skip the use of a template file by clicking Next in that dialog.

3. Leave the Static HTML option button selected on the output format dialog. Click Next.

4. Click the Yes, I Want to Run the Web Publishing Wizard to Set Up a new Web Publishing Specification option button. Click the Finish button to accept the defaults for the remaining dialogs and launch the Web Publishing Wizard.

5. The Web Publishing Wizard launches. The first dialog of the Wizard is shown in Figure 21.9. If you've already used the Web Publishing Wizard to publish pages to a Web server, you may have some Web servers in the drop-down list. If you care to publish this new page to one of those servers, select it in the list. Otherwise, Click the New button to start a new specification.

**FIGURE 21.9.**

*The Web Publishing Wizard's server selection dialog.*

6. On the dialog that appears, enter a friendly name to identify the Web server. The default (My Web Site) is fine for our purposes. Depending on your Internet service provider (ISP) or intranet setup, either leave <Other Internet Provider> selected in the list box for selecting Internet service providers or select the appropriate ISP. Click Next.

7. The next dialog is for the Internet address of the Web server. Enter the URL for your Web server and click Next to continue.

8. On this dialog you choose the connection type for the Web server. Choose the appropriate option and click Next to continue.

9. The Web Publishing Wizard verifies the accessibility of the Web server. If all goes well, you'll see a dialog with a Finish button. Click it and your Web pages will be copied to the Web server.

21

This exercise is obviously over-simplified. Your steps will depend a great deal on your Web server and its location. If you're running the Personal Web Server or Peer Web Services on your workstation, you can use the URL `http://localhost` in step 7 above. If you run into complications while publishing your pages and you're using a Web server controlled by a third party, it's best to contact the server's administrator for technical assistance.

# Hyperlinks to Office Documents or to Web Sites

Access 97 has added the capability to create link fields to documents on your local machine, your LAN or WAN, plus the Web. In fact, you can place a link in a table, query, form, or report to any document that you have rights to access or open. You can also embed hyperlinks in Access objects that let you link them to other Office documents. You can link the following, as well as many other objects, to other documents:

- Office 97 documents on your local computer
- Office 97 documents on an intranet
- Office 97 documents on the Internet
- HTML documents on your local machine
- HTML documents on an intranet
- HTML documents on the Internet

Placing a link to any document on a network, the Internet, or your local machine is identical. Because I know that readers of this book have at least a local machine, the following task shows how to link to a local document.

Keep in mind that linking to remote documents is exactly the same as linking to a local document except that you'd alter the UNC or URL to match the remote document's location.

**New Term**     The term *UNC* stands for "Universal Naming Convention." It's the standard way to refer to a document locally or across a local area network. The convention looks like this: `\\server\[path]`. Therefore, a file called `readme.txt` located in the subdirectory `docs` on the server named `development` would look like this in UNC: `\\development\docs\readme.txt`.

Similarly, the UNC for the local file `readme.txt` located in the subdirectory `docs` of drive C: would be `C:\docs\readme.txt`.

**NEW TERM** *URL* stands for Universal Resource Locator and it's the way to locate documents and other resources on the Web. The address `http://www.microsoft.com` is the URL for the Microsoft Corporation's home page. The `http` part tells the browser (or other searcher) that the address uses Hypertext Transfer Protocol. The balance of the address is the specific address for Microsoft's site.

There are three basic ways to include hyperlinks in Access:

- Add a field with the `Hyperlink` datatype in a table. This field will then appear in forms, reports, and queries.
- Add a label to a form or report and set the `Hyperlink` property to a UNC or a URL.
- Add a command button to a form and set the `Hyperlink` property to a UNC or a URL.

Now, you'll add a hyperlink to a command button to a form.

## Task: The command button hyperlink

1. Figure 21.10 shows a table with a `Hyperlink` datatype field. This table, `Publications`, is part of the sample data and one that you should be familiar with by now. To jump to any URL or UNC entered in this field, you just need click the field, and Access jumps to that document. In addition to highlighting the URL or UNC address, Access's cursor changes to the conventional hand when passed over such an address. Figure 21.10 shows the hand cursor over one of the URLs in the `Publications` table.

**FIGURE 21.10.**

*A table with a hyper-link as part of a data field.*

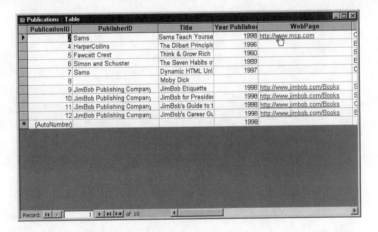

2. The following exercise jumps to a specific place in a Word 97 document. This document, `Linker.doc`, is part of the sample data. (See Figure 21.11.) It's nothing more than a series of paragraphs with the words "Not Here" and one paragraph with the line "Here is the place you should have landed on!" There's a bookmark—LandingZone—at that one different line.

**21**

**FIGURE 21.11.**

*A document to serve as a landing spot for a hyperlink.*

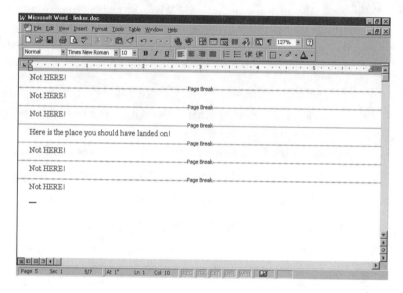

3. Launch Access if necessary and open the BookStore database. Open a form in Design View or start a new form and open it in Design View. This exercise uses the TabbedBibliography form.

4. Add a command button to your form. You could also have added a label or chosen Insert|Hyperlink from the menu. That menu choice puts a label on the form rather than a command button. Set the Caption property for the new button to read Word Document.

   To add the link, edit the Hyperlink property on the Format tab. The Hyperlink property should contain the URL or the UNC. The Hyperlink SubAddress will hold the bookmark to jump to within the opened document. Figure 21.12 shows the hyperlink added that's right for one local machine. If you're following along, you'll need to add the right UNC for your setup. The Hyperlink SubAddress is the bookmark name in the document. In this case, it's LandingZone, to match the sample document's bookmark.

5. Note how Access altered the appearance of the caption as soon as you told it this button is a link to a UNC.

6. Switch to Form View and click the command button you just made. Access will open Word 97, load the document Linker.doc, and jump to the LandingZone bookmark. Figure 21.13 shows the form in Form View. When you click the command button, you should see the same document from Figure 21.11.

▼

**FIGURE 21.12.**

*The* Hyperlink
*address and the*
Hyperlink
SubAddress
*properties.*

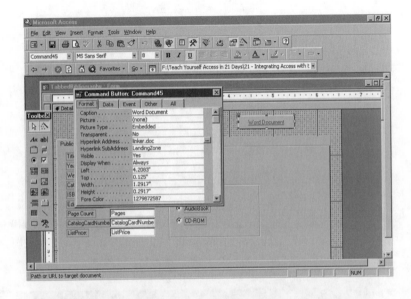

**FIGURE 21.13.**

*The command button
hyperlink ready for
action.*

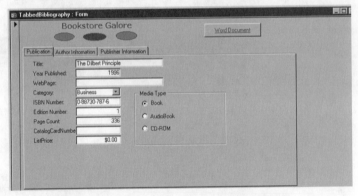

7. To return to your Access form, click the Back button in the Web toolbar in Word 97.

8. You can also browse for a UNC or URL. To do this, click the builder button on the Hyperlink Address property for an object. Figure 21.14 shows the Edit Hyperlink dialog open.

▼

**21**

**FIGURE 21.14.**

*If you prefer, you can use the Edit Hyperlink dialog.*

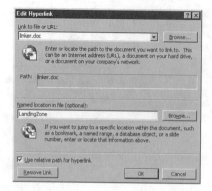

Using URLs is no different from using UNCs. Figure 21.15 shows the TabbedStudentPersonal form with a label added that has a hyperlink to the URL for Microsoft's home page. Notice the hand cursor again.

**FIGURE 21.15.**

*A tab form with a label containing a hyperlink to a Web URL.*

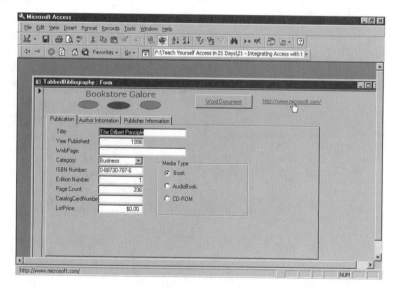

# Summary

The Web started as a protocol for hypertext documents on the Internet. Today, the Web and Web-like institutions exist on domains as small as a single computer, on a LAN to a WAN to an intranet, and even on the Internet itself. The original limits of hypertext documents are being expanded as the Web encompasses multimedia extensions.

You can publish tables, queries, forms, and reports from their native Access format to the HTML format used on the Web. Once converted to HTML, your documents become detached from their underlying data, but become available to anyone with a browser. You don't need Access to view such documents. In fact, you don't even need a computer. You just need a Web appliance to see such documents.

You can also publish dynamic Web pages which present live data to viewers of your Web site. If you want, you can allow the surfer to update, insert, and delete records as well.

Access can include links to documents or other resources in forms, tables, queries, and reports. You can add such links either by specifying a field as having the `Hyperlink` datatype, or by including a label or command button on a form or report with its property set to a UNC or URL.

# Q&A

**Q** **Do I need a TCP/IP protocol to link to documents on my local machine or LAN?**

**A** If your LAN is TCP/IP, you need the layer. Otherwise, you don't need anything more than whatever is your default protocol. This is often NetBEUI for Windows 95/98. You need no protocol whatsoever for local links.

**Q** **How do I install the TCP/IP layer so I can use Dial Up networking in my hyperlinks?**

**A** Open the Add-Remove Programs applet from the Control Panel. Click the Windows Setup tab, and then find the Communications check box. Click the Details button and then the Dial Up Networking check box. You will need your Windows 95/98 CD-ROM to perform the task.

**Q** **Can I jump to a place in an Excel 97 workbook?**

**A** Yes. Say you want to jump to a range named Sales for a worksheet named Colorado in a file called `Finance.xls`. Enter the path to the file as the `Hyperlink` property and enter `Colorado!Sales` for a `Hyperlink SubAddress` property.

**Q** **I am getting complaints that my HTML documents look oddly formatted when viewed by some of my users. What's up?**

**A** Browsers vary as to how they display the data they format. The best way to ensure that your pages look like you hope they will is to make sure all your target viewers use one browser, such as Internet Explorer. Failing that, you can modify your HTML pages to be as simple as possible, or you can view them with all the possible browsers your target market will use. The latter method is tedious, but it's the path chosen by many Web page developers. This problem will naturally go away as the world migrates to one or two browsers from the dozens now in use.

21

# Workshop

Here's where you can test and apply what you have learned today.

## Quiz

1. What does ASP format mean when publishing to the Web?
2. What format is an HTML file?
3. Is HTML a page description language like PostScript?
4. Why does Access output HTML files with the extension HTM rather than HTML?
5. What's the main difference between a UNC and a URL?

## Exercise

For a good introduction to what Access is capable of regarding HTML output, try creating static HTML pages for each type of object (table, form, query, and report) using the Publish to the Web Wizard. Notice how Access handles different situations, particularly for forms and reports. For example, the TabbedBibliography form is shown in HTML format in Figure 21.16. Notice that it doesn't look anything like the original form.

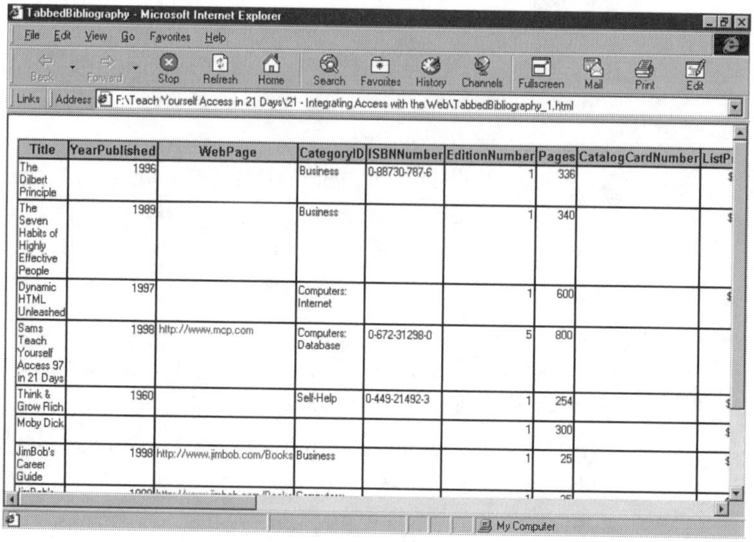

**FIGURE 21.16.**

*The TabbedBibliography form saved as a static HTML page.*

# WEEK 3

## In Review

In just a short time you've come a long way, from learning to navigate a complex application to learning all the pieces to develop your own end-user application in Access 97.

Whether you're a small business owner who's chosen Access to track your income and outgo, or you're a budding developer who wants to begin a career in developing Access applications for other end users, you should now have the tools you need to create a useful Access database. You should also be able to program a front-end application to enable you or your users to manipulate the data in your database and print out polished reports.

"What's next?" you might ask. Now that you have a solid understanding and some practical experience, you might consider moving to more advanced topics and levels of development. If you're looking for more advanced material, try either *Access 97 Unleashed* or *Access 97 Programming Unleashed*, both from Sams Publishing.

# APPENDIX A

# Quiz Answers

## Day 1: "A Short Tour, Including a Stop at Northwind Traders"

1. What shape does the cursor assume when it's capable of reshaping a toolbar?

2. How do you launch Access from the Start menu in the Windows interface?

3. What are the two clues (aside from the picture) hinting at or telling you what a button on a toolbar does?

4. Can you move or resize the menu bar?

**Answers:**

1. A double-pointed arrow.

2. Locate its menu choice and click it.

3. The status bar and ScreenTips.

4. Yes. This is a new feature in Access 97 that is not available in previous versions of Microsoft Access.

# Day 2: "Creating Your First Database"

1. Can I remove any of the suggested fields from the Database Wizard's list of fields?
2. What is the term used for the navigational form in the Database Wizard generated databases?
3. What are the two types of filters you can apply on a form?
4. Can you view the output of a report even if you do not have a printer attached to your computer?

**Answers:**

1. Yes and no. You decide whether or not to include the fields which the Wizard displays in italics. The fields which are not displayed in italics are required by the wizard.
2. Switchboard.
3. Filter by Selection and Filter by Form.
4. Yes. All reports in Access 97 can be viewed in Print Preview mode whether or not a printer is attached to your computer.

# Day 4: "Creating a New Database from Scratch"

1. What's the first step in creating a new Access table?
2. Why use a wizard when making a table?
3. What's the maximum size of a field with the data type set to Text?
4. What is the maximum number of characters (including spaces) for a field name in an Access table?
5. Say you're going to export a table called A List of My Friends to an old database system that can't handle white space in table names. What do you suppose will happen when you try to use this table in the older database system?

**Answers:**

1. Click the Tables tab, and then click the New button.
2. It saves time and effort.
3. 255.
4. 64 characters and spaces.
5. Its name will be shortened (truncated).

# Day 5: "Linking Tables with Relationships"

1. Do the Table Wizard-created relationships specify to Enforce Referential Integrity?

2. What are the fields that match two tables in a relationship called? (You may have to review Day 3 to answer this one.)

3. How do you prevent unmatched records between two unrelated tables?

**Answers:**

1. No. You must set this relationship property manually using the Relationships window.

2. Foreign key and Primary key fields.

3. Select the Enforce Referential Integrity check box in the Relationships dialog.

# Day 6: "Working with Fields"

1. You're in Datasheet View. How can you tell when your cursor is located in the correct position to change a field's apparent width? Apparent height?

2. Will moving a field in Datasheet View change that field's position in the table design grid?

3. Will the validation rule `"A#"` accept the value `A1`?

4. If you set a `Default` property for a field, can you override it during normal data entry? If not, what must you do to override the default value?

5. Will the validation rule `"Between #1/2/90# and #2/1/90#"` accept the value `1/5/91`?

6. Why bother making input masks?

**Answers:**

1. In both cases, it changes into a bar with two opposite-pointing arrows.

2. No.

3. Yes.

4. Yes, you can override default properties without special considerations.

5. No.

6. To help users enter and read field data. It also is a form of data validation. "Exercise Answer: >L<??????????"

# Day 7: "Creating Simple Queries"

1. What are the three sort orders available for a field?
2. Can you OR multiple values for the same field?
3. Do you have to learn SQL (Structured Query Language) to design Access queries?
4. Can a query be based upon other queries?

**Answers:**

1. Ascending, Descending, and None.
2. Yes. Simply enter the expressions on additional lines below the initial Criteria line of the field's column in the query design view.
3. No. The query design view screen can do most of the work for you. However, it's always a good idea to have at least a working knowledge of SQL basics in case you need to fine-tune a query.
4. Yes. You can return results from, and even use criteria on, the results of existing queries. Simply select the Queries tab in the Show Table dialog of the query designer.

# Day 8: "Designing Forms for Data Manipulation"

1. How do you know when a form control has the highlight?
2. What visual indication does Access give you so you know when you can move a form control?
3. What does the mouse cursor look like when it's over a hotspot and able to size a field or control on a form?
4. If you delete a field from a form in Form Design View, can you see that field when you switch to Form Datasheet View?
5. How can you select (or give the highlight to) two non-contiguous controls on a form?
6. How can you select (or give the highlight to) four contiguous controls on a form?

**Answers:**

1. The field changes its color scheme to the opposite of normal. For example, if normal is black on white, highlighted fields will be white on black.
2. The hand cursor.

3. A thin, double-faced arrow.

4. No.

5. Click one, then press shift and click the other.

6. Use a marquee selection; that is, click and drag to surround the fields. You can also use the Shift+click method for contiguous controls.

# Day 9: "Creating Functional Reports"

1. What is concatenation?

2. Will the expression =Ltrim(Rtrim([FirstName])) yield the same output as =Trim([FirstName])?

3. How often will a label in the report Header Band appear?

4. If you want a footer on each page, where should you put the label when in Design View?

5. Can a mailing label report be based in a query if that query has expressions included in it? What will be the adverse consequences of doing this?

6. What properties control the grid spacing in the report design grid? (The same properties control the grid spacing in the form design grid.)

7. Why bother with brackets ([]) for field names?

8. What built-in function does Access have that totals number fields in a group or a report? Hint: Look at the Class Cards report in Design View.

9. Can you bind a report to another report? To a table? To a query?

**Answers:**

1. The linking together of more than one. In Access the link usually refers to field contents.

2. Yes.

3. Once.

4. In the Page Footer band.

5. Yes. Other than some minor slowdown (usually unnoticeable), there are no adverse consequences.

6. Grid X and Grid Y properties.

7. To positively indicate to Access that you mean a field. Also, to be able to include white spaces in a field name when it's used in an expression.

8. Sum().

9. You can bind reports only to tables or queries.

# Day 10: "Designing Queries for Dates and Parameters"

1. If you have a field in a query with the Data Type set to Date/Time, will a criterion of "January" select for those records in the month of January?

2. What does >#1/31/97# mean as a criterion?

3. What function(s) will tell you the year a particular date falls within?

4. Can you use wildcards in a parameter query?

5. Will the parameter Like [Enter a Name:] accept U* as a wildcard criterion?

**Answers:**

1. No. Access will view the criterion January as being a Text data type, not a Date/Time one, so it won't make any match.

2. After January 31, 1997.

3. Year(*date*) and DatePart("yyyy", *date*)

4. Yes.

5. Yes.

# Day 11: "Working with Form Controls"

1. What character tells Access an entry in the Control Source property list box is an expression?

2. What two controls make up a combo box?

3. If you place an Image control image on page 3 of a tabbed form, will you be able to see that image on page 1?

4. What property binds an option group to a table field?

5. You have a form MyForm bound to the table MyTable. You want to enter a combo box, MyCombo, on this form that will look up values in a table called MyLookup. Do you enter MyLookup as the control source or row source for MyCombo?

6. What property must be set to Yes to limit the possible entries to those already entered as a row source for the combo box?

**Answers:**

1. The equals ( = ) sign.

2. A list box and a text box.

3. No.

4. Control Source.

5. Row Source.

6. Limit to List.

# Day 12: "Creating Action and Union Queries"

1. Can you undo (Ctrl+Z) the action of a delete action query? An append action query?

2. If you have a query selecting the top 25 percent of a field, how can you change it to show the bottom 25 percent?

3. Can you use criteria in top queries?

4. Can you make a crosstab that finds average values?

5. Can the update query act on individual fields in a table, or must it work on entire rows, like the delete query?

6. What are the two requirements for the SELECT field list in a UNION query?

**Answers:**

1. No, no. These changes are permanent unless you have a backup of the database to restore from.

2. Changing the sort order from descending to ascending will alter whether Access selects the bottom or top of any percentage in a query.

3. Yes.

4. Yes.

5. Individual fields.

6. Each SELECT must select the same number of fields and corresponding fields must have compatible data types across all SELECT statements involved in the UNION.

# Day 13: "Using Form Control Properties and Subforms"

1. Which property should be set to True if you want to allow users of your form to copy data from a Text Box control but not modify its contents?

2. How do you display only Data properties from the Properties list box?

3. You have a main and subform with a link field SSN. How do you tell Access to synchronize the main and subform using the SSN field?

**Answers:**

1. The `Locked` property.
2. Click the Data tab of the Properties window.
3. The `Link Child Field` and `Link Master Field` properties need to be set to the linked fields, in this case `SSN`.

# Day 14: "Putting the Finishing Touches on Forms"

1. Are the types of control properties the same no matter what type the control?
2. If you want to repeat a small picture throughout your form, which property must be set to `Yes` in the form's properties list box?
3. How would the code line `Sub cmdNextRecord_Click()` change if the event you wanted the sub for was named Clack?
4. Will the filter `Like "Ka"` let the name Kaplan through? What about Kramer? Will the filter `Like "Ka*"` let the name Kaplan through? What about Kramer?

**Answers:**

1. No. Many vary, depending on control types.
2. `Picture Tiling` property.
3. `Sub cmdNextRecord_Clack()`.
4. `Like "Ka"` won't let either Kaplan or Kramer through. `Like "Ka*"` will allow Kaplan but not Kramer.

# Day 15: "Using Expressions and Creating Advanced Reports"

1. What's the significance of the colon in the query column label `Net Cost:`?
2. How often will a label in the Report Header band print in a report?
3. Refer to the `SalesReport` query. If the expression `Author:[FirstName]&" "&[LastName]` were entered in a column's `Field` row, would it be valid?
4. Does the `PublicationID` field need to appear on a report for the report to group on it?
5. Name two ways to change the width of a line or box in reports or forms.

6. Refer to Figure 15.12. What icon does Access use to distinguish the grouping field from a sort within the group field?

**Answers:**

1. The phrase to the left of the colon will be the column's title or label.

2. Yes.

3. Yes.

4. No.

5. Change the width through the Properties window or by selecting the line width choices from within the Formatting toolbar when the line or rectangle has the focus.

6. Group fields have the same icon in the Sorting and Grouping list box as the Sorting and Grouping toolbar button.

# Day 16: "Working with Macros"

1. Look at the way the second task in this chapter, "The switchboard or menu form," had you enter the `Caption` property for the cmdExit button—`E&xit`—in step 5. Now look at the way the button appears in Design or Form View. What do you suppose the ampersand (&) does?

2. If the View option for the `macSwitchboard.OpenBiblioReport` macro was changed to Print, what do you suppose would happen if you ran the macro?

3. What does the period do in a macro name?

4. The word *Not* works as a criteria in queries, but won't work in mathematical expressions. How can you specify a Not or Not Equal To operator in an Access expression? Hint: *Not* is the same as "not equal to."

**Answers:**

1. The & in a caption tells Access that the character that follows, in this case the x, is the hotkey for this control. Pressing Alt+hotkey when the form is active gives this control the focus; in this case, it's the same as a click and you'll exit the form.

2. The `Biblio` Report would print to the printer rather than show on the screen.

3. Separate the macro name from the macro itself.

4. Use the greater than and less than symbols in combination (<>).

# Day 17: "Introduction to Programming in Access"

1. Say you have the following statement in the declarations section of an Visual Basic module:

   `Dim I as String`

   You also have this statement in a procedure:

   `Dim Interest As Double`

   Will `Interest` be a string or a double-precision floating-point type when used in the procedure?

2. If you want to execute a loop ten times, should you use a macro or a module?

3. How would you use Visual Basic to create a custom menu on a form?

4. When would you use the `Currency` data type in Visual Basic? What's the disadvantage of using this data type?

5. How do you create a comment in Visual Basic code?

**Answers:**

1. Double. Access will view `I` and `Interest` as separate variables.

2. Use a module or code behind forms (some say code within forms) to do looping. Macros won't loop.

3. No. You can use the Customize facility to make custom bars—menu bars or toolbars. In addition, Access 97 supports making custom menus through macros, so they will be backward-compatible with previous versions of Access and older programming habits.

4. When calculating monetary fields that require a great deal of precision, such as recursive interest calculations. The disadvantage of this data type is the amount of overhead it adds to your application. Use when you need to, but not otherwise.

5. Preface the remark with a single quote ( ' ) or the `REM` keyword.

# Day 18: "Advanced Programming with Data Access Objects and ActiveX Controls"

1. What is a quick definition of DAO?

2. What is the only DAO object that does not contain a collection?

3. What is the database environment known as in Access 97?

4. What two types of workspaces can be used within Access 97?

A

**Answers:**

1. Data Access Objects (DAO) is a programming interface that allows you to use Visual Basic to manipulate the objects and data in your database.

2. The DBEngine object.

3. The Workspace.

4. ODBCDirect and Microsoft Jet Database Engine workspaces.

# Day 19: "Maintaining and Securing Your Access Databases"

1. Name one method to replicate your database.

2. What are the two default members groups of a workgroup information file?

3. What do you need to do to create an unique Workgroup information file?

4. List one benefit of compacting your Access 97 database.

**Answers:**

1. You can use the briefcase replication method to replicate your database.

2. Users and Admins.

3. Create a new workgroup and give it a Workgroup ID (WID).

4. Compacting your database will defragment your database file.

# Day 20: "Integrating Access with the Rest of Microsoft Office"

1. When should you use the Publish It with MS Word Office Link?

2. If you need to have a Word document updated with current data whenever it is opened, should you use the Merge It or the Publish It Office Link?

3. Do you have to create the merge document before running the Merge It Office Link?

4. Can reports be exported to other Access databases?

**Answers:**

1. Whenever you want to include data from a table or query within a report, memo, or other document.

2. The Merge It Office Link. The Publish It Office Link produces a static, one-time Word table containing the contents of the table or the results of the query at the time the Office Link was executed. The Merge It Office Link creates a link between the Word document and the data source (your database) that is a "live" link.

3. No. The opening dialog of the Merge It Office Link allows you to specify whether to use an existing document or to create a new one.

4. Yes. They cannot, however, be exported to database management systems such as FoxPro or dBase.

# Day 21: "Integrating Access with the Web"

1. What does ASP format mean when publishing to the Web?

2. What format is an HTML file?

3. Is HTML a page description language like PostScript?

4. Why does Access output HTML files with the extension HTM rather than HTML?

5. What's the main difference between a UNC and a URL?

**Answers:**

1. ASP is an acronym for Active Server Page, a server-side script file used with IIS or Microsoft's Personal Web Server.

2. Plain ASCII—that is, straight text.

3. No. HTML is text with tags. The tags themselves are also nothing but text. The browser does the page formatting based on the tags and the bracketed text.

4. DOS and Windows 3.1 aren't long filename (LFN)-enabled and will be out-foxed by any extension longer than three characters.

5. A UNC is used to locate a document on a local area network. A URL is primarily used to locate a document on the Web.

# APPENDIX B

# Installing Access 97

This appendix explains not only how to install Access 97, but also gives you some points to consider as you do so. You'll learn about upgrading your current databases if you've been using a previous version of Access as well as which optional components you need to complete the exercises presented in this book.

 **Note**
> If you are part of a company and on a company network, you might need to consult with your network administrator before installing any software. Your company might also have a special licensing agreement with Microsoft you need to know about before using Office 97.

## What Gets Installed

This section consists of a table, Table B.1, that shows you what gets installed with the Typical Setup (you'll see what that means in a minute), which setup dialog contains various components, and which option to install for use with this book (the Required? Column). The items marked Yes in the Required? column should be installed in order to get the maximum benefit from this book.

**TABLE B.1.** INSTALLATION OPTIONS.

| Component | Typical? | Dialog | Required? |
| --- | --- | --- | --- |
| Access Program Files | Yes | Access 97 | Yes |
| Product Help | Yes | Help Topics | Yes |
| Programming Help | No | Help Topics | Yes |
| Wizards | Yes | Access 97 | Yes |
| Advanced Wizards | No | Access 97 | Yes |
| Northwind Database | No | Sample Databases | Yes |
| Orders Database | No | Sample Databases | No |
| Developer Solutions dB | No | Sample Databases | No |
| Data Access | Yes | Office 97 | No |
| MS Info | Yes | Office Tools | No |
| Spelling Checker | Yes | Office Tools | No |
| Microsoft Graph | Yes | Office Tools | No |
| Microsoft Graph | Yes | Office Tools | No |
| Microsoft Graph VB Help | No | Office Tools | No |
| Briefcase Replication | No | Access 97 | No |
| Calendar Control | No | Access 97 | No |

# System Requirements

The Typical install option of Setup installs those parts of Access 97 that Microsoft believes meet most people's needs. This choice will take up approximately 120MB of space. Setup can't be perfectly specific about the space needed because you might already have some shared components installed, reducing your marginal space needs for Office 97.

If you need to conserve space on your hard drive, you can either choose Microsoft's Compact option or use the Custom option to create your own disk. Setup even enables you to run Office applications from the CD-ROM, which is the most hard disk conservative of all. It's also a bit pokey in response time since it's dependent on CD-ROM throughput instead of hard disk throughput. The Run from CD-ROM option will still use up about 60MB of disk space. If you go all out and choose Custom to install all of Office 97, figure for it to eat up roughly 200MB of disk real estate.

Hardware-wise, you'll need a mouse and at least a VGA video card and monitor. A super VGA card and monitor is recommended, however, to get the most visually from Access. If you want to print anything, you'll need access to a printer either locally or across your network.

# Upgrading from a Prior Version

B

If you already have either Access 2.0 or Access 95 installed on your computer, you can purchase an upgrade version of Access 97. Otherwise, you'll have to buy the full-blown copy.

If you are upgrading, you should consider the following fact: in order to fully utilize the capabilities of Access 97 (including the capability to modify the design of tables, queries, and so on) your databases must be in Access 97 format. If you have any databases that are in Access 95 or Access 2.0 format, Access 97 will prompt you to convert these databases when you attempt to open them with Access 97.

If you choose to convert these databases, users of Access 2.0 and Access 95 will no longer be able to open them. You can choose not to convert the database, but all you'll be able to do is view or modify data and view the design of Access objects (but not change the design).

If you must work with databases in both Access 97 and older versions of Access, I recommend leaving your older version of Access intact and installing Access 97 into a different directory. This way you'll be able to use both versions of Access. However, this will require more disk space and there could be unpredictable results if both Access 95 and Access 97 are installed with optional Office components. Most people in this situation will be running with Access 2.0 and Access 97, though.

# Installing Access

Now that all of the preliminary details are out of the way, let's get on with actually installing Access 97.

**Note**  You'll probably need to re-boot your computer when the installation process has completed. Make sure you're in a position to do so before you start the installation process.

To start the process, grab your Access 97 or Office 97 CD-ROM and insert it into your CD-ROM drive. If your computer is set to auto-start CD-ROMs (most are) the Setup application will start automatically. If it's not, or if the Setup application doesn't start for some reason, click the Windows Start button and click the Run menu item. Enter `g:\setup.exe`, replacing `g:` with the drive letter for your CD-ROM drive.

The installation program will start and might prompt you to close down any running applications that might interfere with the installation process. If it does so, either close the applications noted and click Continue or click Exit Setup, close the applications, and restart the installation process.

If you're installing Access 97 and have never installed any other Office 97 applications, the setup program will ask you for information such as your name, your company's name, and a CD key. You'll find the CD key on a sticker on the jewel case in which the CD-ROM was shipped. After you answer these questions, Setup will present you with your product ID number. This will be needed should you require technical support from Microsoft or if you want to use the Office Update site at `http://www.microsoft.com/Office`.

Next, Setup will ask you where to install the application. The default location is usually `C:\ACCESS` or, if you're installing from the Office 97 CD-ROM, `C:\Program Files\Microsoft Office\Office`. If the location is acceptable, click OK to continue. You can also change the directory to an existing directory or to a new one, which Setup will create for you.

After you continue, Setup will ask you to choose from the three installation options: Typical, Compact, or Custom. Choose Custom to set up the application as described in Table C.1.

If you already have some Office 97 applications installed, the previous three paragraphs won't apply to you. Instead, you'll see an Office 97—Maintenance dialog, as shown in Figure B.1. To change the options installed for Access 97, make sure Microsoft Access is checked and click the Change Option button.

**FIGURE B.1.**

*The Office 97 Setup Maintenance dialog.*

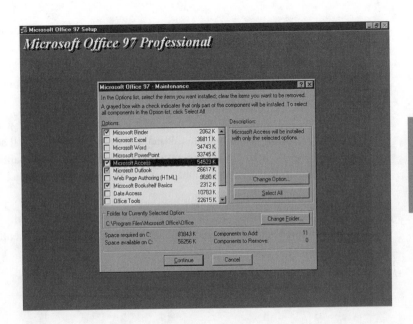

At this point you should be looking at a dialog similar to Figure B.2. In this dialog you select the options you want installed. If you need to go to a subordinate dialog, select the option in question and click the Change Option button.

**FIGURE B.2.**

*The Access 97 Setup dialog.*

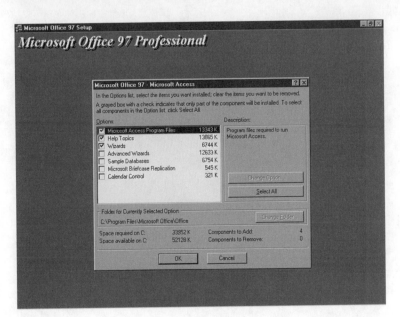

To install as suggested in Table B.1, check Advanced Wizards. Then click Help Topics, click the Change Option button, and check Programming Help in addition to the pre-selected Product Help option. Then click OK to return to the Access 97 dialog. As with Help Topics, check Sample Databases, click the Change Option button, and check the Northwind Database option. Click OK.

Click Continue until Setup starts copying files. Then sit back and wait. The program will install the options you've selected. When it's about finished, you'll see the progress screen change to read Updating your system. Finally, you'll probably be prompted to restart Windows. Close other applications you have running, and click the Restart Windows button.

After Windows restarts, you're ready to run Access 97. You'll find a shortcut to it on your Program Files menu, which you get to by clicking the Start button.

# APPENDIX C

# The Toolbox Illustrated

Microsoft Access lets you choose the controls used to design forms and reports from a specialized toolbar called the Toolbox. This appendix provides an explanation of each tool and an illustration of the Toolbox for easy reference.

**FIGURE C.1.**

*The Access Toolbox.*

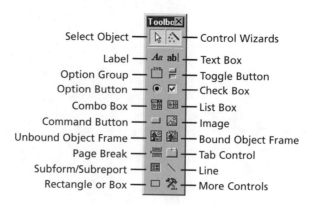

**Select Object**   Click this to return to the pointer cursor. The pointer cursor is used to make selections either on the design grid or from menus, the toolbox, or a toolbar.

**Control Wizards**   With Control Wizards turned on, whenever you place any control that has an associated wizard onto the form or report the wizard will launch. With Control Wizards off, you create the control without the help of a wizard. There are wizards for the Option Group, Combo Box, List Box, and Subform/Subreport controls. These wizards must be installed to activate (see Appendix B, "Installing Access 97" for details).

**Label**   Use this tool to create a label. Use labels for field identification, instructions, or decoration.

**Text Box**   The Text Box control holds text. This is one of the most flexible controls in Access. Text boxes can be used for data entry or display or to hold calculated fields.

**Option Group**   An option group holds other controls—such as option buttons, check boxes, or toggle buttons—in a group. Only one control within an option group can be selected at a time.

**Toggle Button**   A toggle button toggles between being selected and unselected at the click of a mouse button. It's a good control for Yes/No fields.

**Option Button**   Also called radio buttons, option buttons are similar in function to check boxes and toggle buttons. An option button is selected and deselected at the click of the mouse button. Typically, option buttons are grouped together within an option group.

**Check Box**   Another toggle-type tool that's changed from selected to deselected with a mouse click.

**Combo Box**   A combo box is a text box grafted to the top of a list box and tied to the list. Using a combo box, you can choose from a list as you can with a list box, or enter a value not on the list as you can in a text box (as long as the control's Limit To List property is set to No).

**List Box**   A list box presents a list of entries from a field in a table or query, or from a programmatically entered list of values.

**Command Button**   A command button carries out a set of programmed instructions when clicked. In Access, the most common use for command buttons is to execute macros.

**Image**   A control to display a static graphic; that is, one that won't change during run-time.

**Unbound Object Frame**   Displays an OLE object that's not stored in an Access database.

**Bound Object Frame**   Displays an OLE object stored in an Access database.

**Page Break**   This tool inserts a page break.

**Tab Control**   This tool is used to create tabbed forms that conform to the Windows 95 user-interface guidelines.

**Subform/Subreport**   Use this tool to add a subform or subreport to a form or report, respectively.

**Line**   This tool is used to draw lines on a form or report.

**Rectangle or Box**   Used this tool to create squares or rectangles on a form or report.

**More Controls**   Click this button to bring up a selection list of ActiveX controls which are installed on your system. For more information on ActiveX controls, see Day 18, "Advanced Programming with Data Access Objects and ActiveX Controls."

# APPENDIX D

# Access Toolbars

Because you've probably been working with other Microsoft applications and the Windows environment, you're likely to be familiar with many of the icons on the toolbars in this appendix. However, for the first toolbar, you can find any of these more familiar icons. On the remainder of the toolbars, only the Access-specific icons are marked.

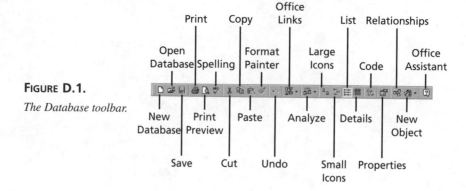

**FIGURE D.1.**

*The Database toolbar.*

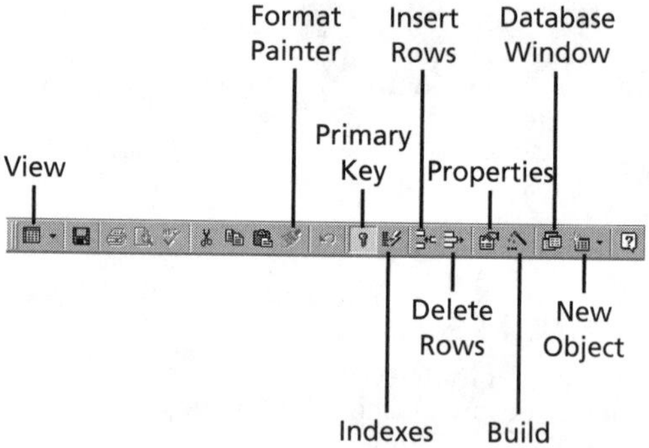

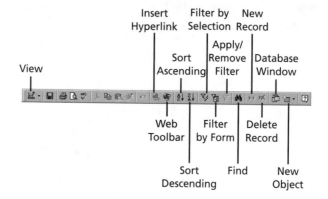

**FIGURE D.2.**

*The Table Design toolbar.*

**FIGURE D.3.**

*The Table Datasheet toolbar.*

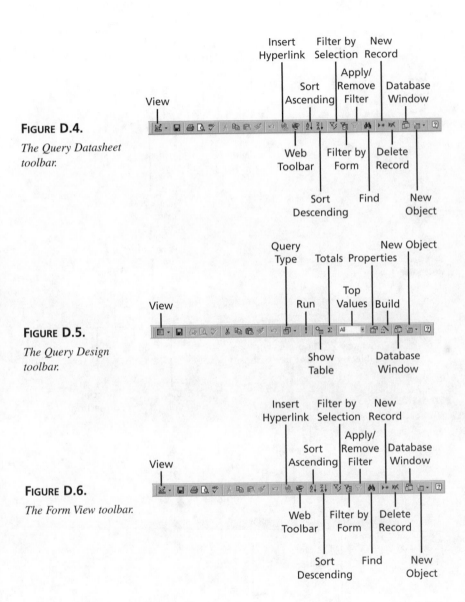

**FIGURE D.4.**

*The Query Datasheet toolbar.*

**FIGURE D.5.**

*The Query Design toolbar.*

**FIGURE D.6.**

*The Form View toolbar.*

D

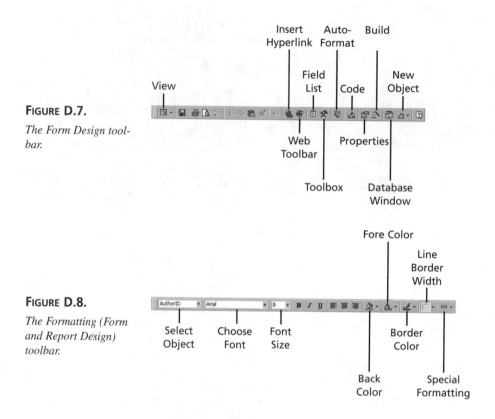

**FIGURE D.7.**

*The Form Design tool-bar.*

**FIGURE D.8.**

*The Formatting (Form and Report Design) toolbar.*

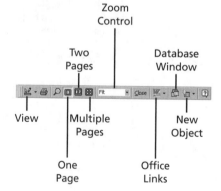

**FIGURE D.9.**

*The Print Preview toolbar.*

**FIGURE D.10.**

*The Report Design toolbar.*

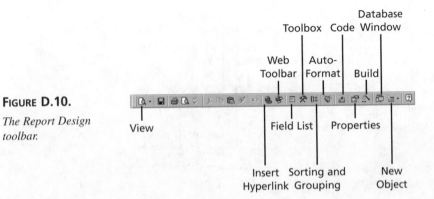

**FIGURE D.11.**

*The Macro toolbar.*

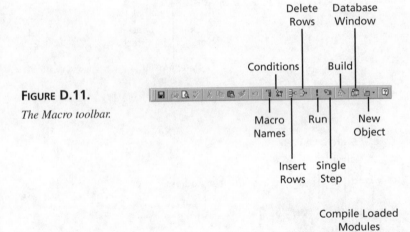

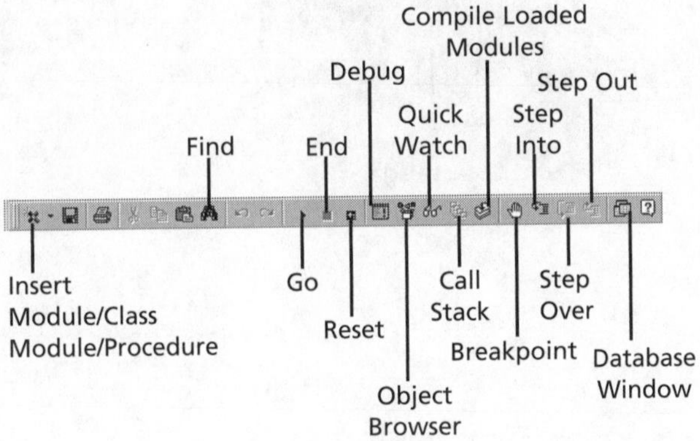

**FIGURE D.12.**

*The Visual Basic toolbar.*

D

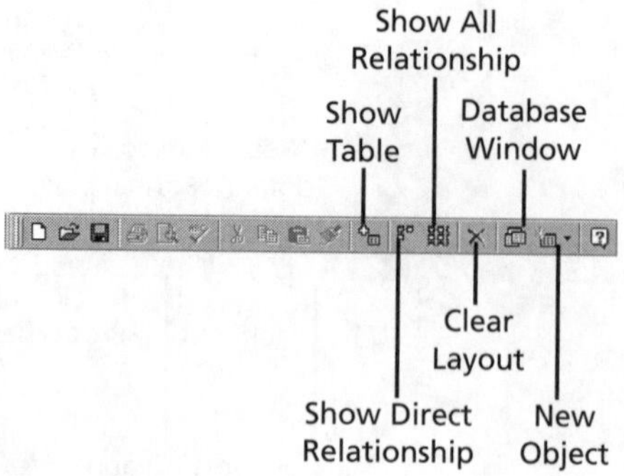

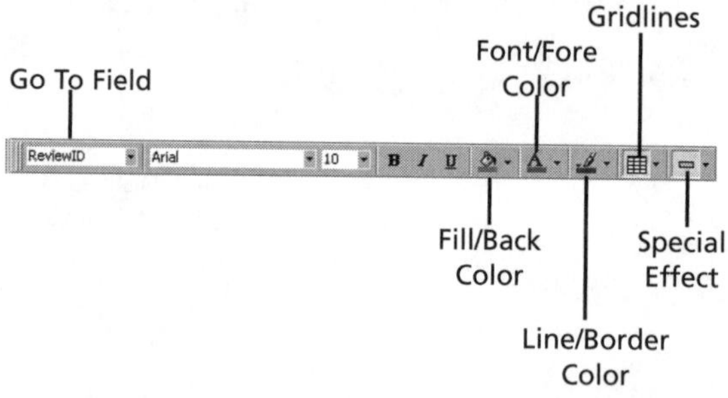

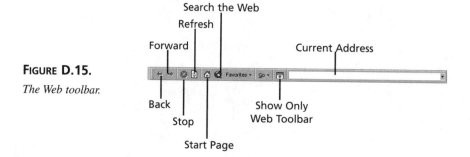

Show All Relationship
Show Table
Database Window
Clear Layout
Show Direct Relationship
New Object

**FIGURE D.13.**

*The Relationships toolbar.*

Gridlines
Font/Fore Color
Go To Field
ReviewID
Arial
10
Fill/Back Color
Special Effect
Line/Border Color

**FIGURE D.14.**

*The Formatting (Datasheet) toolbar.*

Search the Web
Refresh
Forward
Current Address
Favorites
Go
Back
Stop
Show Only Web Toolbar
Start Page

**FIGURE D.15.**

*The Web toolbar.*

# INDEX

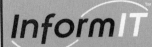 
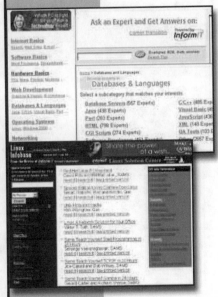

**No Liability for Consequential Damages**    In no event shall Tracscan or its third-party distributors and/or suppliers be liable for any special, consequential, incidental, or indirect damages of any kind arising out of the delivery, performance, or use of this SOFTWARE, even if Tracscan has been advised of the possibility of such damages. In no event will Tracscan's liability for any claim, whether in contract, tort, or any other theory of liability exceed the license fee paid by the user.

**Governing Law**    This Agreement will be governed by the laws of the State of New Jersey as they are applied to agreements to be entered into and to be performed entirely within New Jersey. The United Nations Convention on Contracts for the International Sale of Goods is specifically disclaimed.

# dbQuickPage 1.1.8

## Software End User License Agreement and Disclaimer

**Terminology**   Term USER identifies any individual person, commercial institution, non-commercial institution, and any other group or organization, or an individual person acting on behalf of a single entity installing and/or using a copy of this software product (THE SOFTWARE) on a computer system accessed by the USER. THE SOFTWARE is identified by all binary and non-binary computer files and may include associated media, printed materials, and online or electronic documentation.

**Notice to Users**   Carefully read the following legal agreement. The use of this software is conditioned upon compliance by users with the terms of this agreement. By installing, copying, or otherwise using the software you are agreeing to be bound by the terms of this End User License Agreement (EULA). If you do not wish to be bound by the terms of this agreement or do not agree with the terms of this EULA, do not install or use the software product.

THE SOFTWARE may be evaluated for a period of forty-five (45) days on a royalty free basis. After expiration of the evaluation period the USER is obliged to purchase a copy of the software or remove evaluation copy from the user's computer system.

**Copyright**   THE SOFTWARE is protected by United States copyright laws and international treaty provisions. USER acknowledges that no title to the intellectual property of THE SOFTWARE is transferred to USER. USER further acknowledges that full ownership rights to THE SOFTWARE will remain the exclusive property of Tracscan, and the USER will not acquire any rights to THE SOFTWARE except as expressly set forth in this license. USER agrees that any copies of THE SOFTWARE made by USER will contain the same proprietary notices, which appear on and in THE SOFTWARE.

**Reverse Engineering**   USER agrees that he or she will not attempt, and will use its best efforts to prevent its employees from attempting, to reverse compile, modify, translate, or disassemble this SOFTWARE in whole or in part.

**Limited Warranty**   It is hereby warranted that this software will perform substantially in accordance with the accompanying documentation for a period of ninety (90) days from the date payment is received.

**No Other Warranties**   Tracscan does not warrant that THE SOFTWARE is error free, except for the expressed limited warranty above. Tracscan disclaims all other warranties with respect to this SOFTWARE, either expressed or implied, including but not limited to implied warranties of merchantability, fitness for a particular purpose, and noninfringement of third party rights.

## Getpass '98

**Warranty**   This software is provided as is, without warranty of any kind. To the maximum extent permitted by applicable law, Ashish Computer Systems and its suppliers disclaim all warranties, either expressed or implied, including but not limited to, implied warranties of merchantability and fitness for a particular purpose and any warranty against infringement with regard to the software product.

Ashish Computer Systems will not be liable for any special, incidental, consequential, indirect, or similar damages due to loss of data or any other reason, even if Ashish Computer Systems or an agent of Ashish Computer Systems has been advised of the possibility of such damages. In no event shall Ashish Computer Systems' liability for any damages ever exceed the price paid for the license to use the software, regardless of the form of the claim. The person using the software bears all risk as to the quality and performance of the software.

**Distribution**   You may freely distribute the Evaluation Version of Getpass '98, provided you do not charge in any manner for such distributions. You may also review or publish your comments about Getpass '98 in books, magazines, Internet pages, newsgroups, and emails.

**Terms and Conditions for Use**   Unsetting of database file passwords of database files may be considered a serious crime by the owner(s) of the database. Only database administrator(s) and creator(s) or others should use Getpass '98 with valid ownership/ permission to the concerned database. Ashish Computer Systems in no way is liable for unauthorized usage of this program in this regard or any losses out of this use.

Getpass '98 is not in the public domain—the publisher Ashish, retains ownership and copyright and exclusively reserves all rights to the software.

Modification of the program or its resources without the publisher's explicit written permission is strictly forbidden.

# End User License Agreements and Disclaimers

## Ashish Software

### Compare '98

**Warranty**   This software is provided as is, without warranty of any kind. To the maximum extent permitted by applicable law, Ashish Computer Systems and its suppliers disclaim all warranties, either expressed or implied, including but not limited to, implied warranties of merchantability and fitness for a particular purpose and any warranty against infringement with regard to the software product.

Ashish Computer Systems will not be liable for any special, incidental, consequential, indirect, or similar damages due to loss of data or any other reason, even if Ashish Computer Systems or an agent of Ashish Computer Systems has been advised of the possibility of such damages. In no event shall Ashish Computer Systems' liability for any damages ever exceed the price paid for the license to use the software, regardless of the form of the claim. The person using the software bears all risk as to the quality and performance of the software.

**Distribution**   You may freely distribute the Evaluation Version of Compare '98, provided you do not charge in any manner for such distributions. You may also review or publish your comments about Compare '98 in books, magazines, Internet pages, newsgroups, and emails.

**Terms and Conditions for Use**   Ashish Computer Systems in no way is liable for unauthorized usage of this program, in this regard or any losses out of this use.

Compare '98 is not in the public domain—the publisher, Ashish, retains ownership and copyright, and exclusively reserves all rights to the software.

Modification of the program or its resources without the publisher's explicit written permission is strictly forbidden.

# What's On the CD-ROM?

> **Note**
>
> This CD-ROM uses long and mixed-case filenames requiring the use of a protected-mode CD-ROM driver.

The CD-ROM contains the following:

1. The author's sample database files from the book
2. The MCP Access Knowledgebase
3. Over 25 evaluation software products that relate to the topics discussed in the book

# Installation Instructions

## Windows 95/ NT 4

1. Insert the CD-ROM into your CD-ROM drive.
2. From the Windows desktop, double-click the My Computer icon.
3. Double-click the icon representing your CD-ROM drive.
4. Double-click the SETUP folder.
5. Double-click the icon titled setup.exe to run the installation program. The interactive menu program will open. Simply follow the Navigation menu and online screen instructions.

> **Note**
>
> If Windows 95/NT 4.0 in installed on your computer and you have the AutoPlay feature enabled, the setup.exe program starts automatically whenever you insert the disc into your CD-ROM drive.

# Licensing Agreement